INDUSTRIAL
LIGHT & MAGIC

INDUSTRIAL
LIGHT & MAGIC

INTO THE DIGITAL REALM

by Mark Cotta Vaz

and Patricia Rose Duignan

A Del Rey® Book

BALLANTINE BOOKS • NEW YORK

A Del Rey® Book
Published by Ballantine Books

Library of Congress Cataloging-in-Publication Data
Vaz, Mark Cotta.
  Industrial Light & Magic : into the digital realm / by Mark Cotta Vaz and Patricia Rose Duignan.
     p.   cm.
  "A Del Rey book."
  Includes index.
  ISBN 0-345-38152-1
  1. Cinematography—Special effects. 2. Industrial Light and Magic (Studio) I. Duignan, Patricia Rose. II. Title.
TR858.V39   1996
791.43'024—dc20   95-34797

Printed and bound in Hong Kong

First Edition: November 1996

10 9 8 7 6 5 4 3 2 1

To George Lucas and the creative Force—past, present, and future—of Industrial Light & Magic

. . . and to Don Shay, an exemplary chronicler of the magic, art, and joy of moviemaking
—M.C.V.

CONTENTS

FOREWORD

During Industrial Light & Magic's first decade, three films I directed (*Raiders of the Lost Ark, E.T. The Extra-Terrestrial, Indiana Jones and the Temple of Doom*) featured the company's effects work. All won Academy Awards in the visual effects category, and in working with ILM on those and on all the other films I produced during that ten-year period (*Back to the Future, Young Sherlock Holmes, The Money Pit, Poltergeist*), I saw firsthand how the creative spirit thrived there. It has continued to flourish during ILM's second decade. Six more films I directed (*Empire of the Sun, Always, Indiana Jones and the Last Crusade, Hook, Jurassic Park, Schindler's List*) and nine more produced by Amblin (*Harry and the Hendersons, Innerspace, Batteries Not Included, Who Framed Roger Rabbit?, Back to the Future II* and *III, Joe Versus the Volcano, The Flintstones, Casper*) were also collaborations with ILM. Although ILM's contributions ranged from main characters like the T-rex in *Jurassic Park* to subtle moments like the color inside the flickering candles of *Schindler's List*, all of its shots helped me tell these stories. I am honored to have the distinction as the film-maker who has brought more projects to ILM than any other and extremely proud that the visual effects challenges in my stories have been met by ILM's artists. By exceeding my expectations time and again, they have continued to be the pioneers in their field. The creative team spirit not only thrived from 1986 to 1996, it spurs ILM continually to achieve new heights and change the way a filmmaker can tell a story. It is this spirit that has allowed my vision to fly freely, knowing that if I can imagine it, the brilliantly creative minds at ILM will get it on the screen. The stories in this book illustrate why ILM remains the driving force in its field.

Steve Spielberg

ACKNOWLEDGMENTS

Special thanks to Lucy Autrey Wilson at Lucasfilm, who helped set this project in motion, and to Continuity Editor Allan Kausch, who saw it safely home, and ILM President Jim Morris, for his special help and enthusiasm (and a round of applause for Executive Secretary Cris Welisch into the bargain). Appreciation extends as well to ILM Director of Public Relations Ellen Pasternack, whose office assisted the journalistic aims of this work. Publicist Nagisa Yamamoto was particularly helpful in arranging interviews and providing research materials (even helping this writer hitch a ride from Skywalker Ranch). I'm grateful to all who made special contributions to this book, especially George Lucas, John Dykstra, Bruce Nicholson, Dennis Muren, Doug Kay, Mike Bolles, Mike MacKenzie, Ralph McQuarrie, and John Knoll. A tip of the hat to Lucasfilm's Rick McCallum, ILM's Tom Kennedy, and Tom Gagliano at Fox for *New Hope* help.(A prayer as well to the memory of Andi Merrim.) My special appreciation to Patricia Rose Duignan, my predecessor on the project, who provided interview material that was very helpful in my preparation of the final manuscript.

David Owen of ILM's still-photography department was invaluable in delivering the hundreds of photographs used in this book (thanks as well to Sean Casey and Kerry Nordquist in this regard), while the hard work of Janet Talamantes and Sue Rostoni of Lucasfilm Licensing secured the requisite photo rights and permissions.

Special thanks to Ballantine Books for its superb editorial and artistic sensibilities, in particular Editor in Chief Joëlle Delbourgo, Editor Elizabeth Zack, Editorial Assistant Beth Bortz, Managing Editor Nora Reichard, Assistant Production Editor Alexandra Krijgsman, and Director of Production Frederic Dodnick—without them this book would not have been possible. I'd also like to offer my heartfelt thanks to Sylvain Michaelis, who created the beautiful graphic design of this book.

Thanks go to Risa Kessler, consultant for this book and editor for *Industrial Light & Magic: The Art of Special Effects.* And a tip of the hat to Thomas G. Smith, author of that first ILM book.

My special appreciation to Bruce and Ginny Walters (and XO Digital Arts) for their manifold acts of support. On a personal note, here's a kiss to Olga and a hug for Liza. Thanks to Trish, Kelli, and Tana at the Funny Papers in San Francisco for friendship. Love and blessings to my parents, August and Elizabeth, my brothers and sisters—Katherine, Maria, Patrick, Peter, and Teresa—and the kids: Dano, Johnny, Matt, Michael, Kate, and Joey. And to my sister Katherine: *"Muito obrigado pelos seus bons pensamentos do clube dos fados em Lisbõa!"*   —Mark Cotta Vaz

Through all the many changes in technology, tools, and personnel during my tenure at ILM, there's one thing that's never changed: the commitment to quality by every person, at every level, on every shot.

I'm very grateful to all of the people who generously shared their knowledge and perspective during interview sessions for this book. I'd also like to acknowledge the editorial contributions made by Peter Duignan and Jon Rant. Special thanks to the photographers (Kerry Nordquist, Sean Casey, David Owen, Terry Chostner, Roberto McGrath, and Howie Stein), whose work in documenting the history of ILM made this publication possible.
        —Patricia Rose Duignan

INDUSTRIAL
LIGHT & MAGIC

THE MAGIC SEAL

I n dark space a luminous lightbulb floats, suspended in the air with the wave of a wand held by a white-gloved hand. The illumination reveals a magician dressed in top hat and tux, with a red posy in his satiny lapel, working the magic while rising through the center of a finely machined gear wheel embossed with the initials ILM.

This vision of a magician is the seal of Industrial Light & Magic, the motion picture effects house George Lucas created in 1975 to provide the visual effects for one movie: *Star Wars*. The company name didn't come to Lucas in one revelatory flash but after a process of mulling over the components of a visual effects enterprise: "Industrial," for the hardware of cameras and optical printers that would record and composite film elements; "Light," the very stuff movies are made of; "Magic," an effects artist's stock in trade.

Some ILMers, battle-hardened from the challenges of their work, chafe a bit at glowing press accounts picturing them as wizards who, if not waving wands and chanting magical incantations, are pressing buttons and pulling levers to create marvelous movie imagery. The notion of ILMers as a modern cult of magicians is irresistible, though. And if we pull back the curtain and witness the energetic reality of an effects shop—the plotting of a concept, the design stage of blueprints and sketches and models, the skilled artists building a final effect with the right tools for the job—it does not at all diminish the magical nature of the resulting motion picture image.

The top-hatted illusionist rising out of an old industrial gear wheel is a quaint vision, but things are not always what they seem. Whatever the technology—whether traditional optical printers or high-tech digital scanners—ILM makes magic.

Stage magicians have been attracted to motion picture making from the beginning of the medium. A pair of magicians, James Stuart Blackton and Albert Smith (who would later cofound Vitagraph, a successful early movie studio), produced such seminal movie magic as *The Battle of Santiago Bay*, a two-minute 1899 movie purporting to be an exclusive newsreel of a Spanish-American War naval skirmish. The duo utilized photographic cutouts for ships, a miniature set with an inch of water, and pinches of lit gunpowder and tobacco smoke for the fire and smoke of battle. Awed New York audiences took the film as gospel truth. (All copies of this early effects movie are believed to have been destroyed by a 1910 fire.)

Meanwhile, across the Atlantic, magician Georges Méliès, owner of the Théâtre Robert-

This vision of C-3PO and R2-D2 on the planet Tatooine was the first *Star Wars* concept painting artist Ralph McQuarrie produced for George Lucas. This image was among a few McQuarrie *Star Wars* paintings Lucas used to convince Fox executives to do *Star Wars*. (Note C-3PO's Art Deco styling, influenced by the robot in the 1927 classic *Metropolis*.)

Houdin in Paris, was producing such films as *The Conjuror* (1899), featuring a magician and his female assistant changing shape and vanishing, and the famous *A Trip to the Moon* (1902), in which the first astronauts, perfectly tailored in Edwardian fashion, brought earthly greetings to the moon people. Master illusionist and escape artist Harry Houdini was so inspired by the magic of Méliès's movies—and savvy enough to see the new medium replacing his vaudeville venues— that he produced and starred in his own series of silent film thrillers.

The particular magic required for the movies is, of course, different from the acts of illusion performed by a stage magician. Movie magicians have to conjure up fantastic landscapes, transport their audiences through time and space, and bring to life creatures of imagination. *Star Wars*, for many critics and fans alike, would be hailed as ushering in the age of the effects movie. But *Star Wars* was a breakthrough, not a beginning, as the films of Méliès and his contemporaries attest. Film had always been a sleeping magic, awaiting technology geared to creating the illusions of the senses we experience at the movies.

The human receptivity for moving pictures is based on a phenomenon of the eye and brain first observed by the ancients and later labeled "persistence of vision" by nineteenth-century European thinkers. An English doctor named Peter Mark Roget (1779–1869), who created the *Thesaurus*, helped explore the persistence-of-vision notion after watching from his study window the clattering passage of a cart. It struck him that the actual movement was a series of stationary moments blended together by the watching eye and perceived as continuous motion. Without this capacity of retaining each image in succession we would be unable to perceive light-projected film frames as continuous moving images.

The first invention that harnessed light to project images was the magic lantern of the sixteenth century, a device consisting of a candle or lamp within a box that projected the light through a glass slide-painted image and a lens; the light, when shone on a surface, magnified the still picture. In the centuries to come, the magic-lantern show became a popular art form experienced in "shadow theaters" and salons or spontaneously staged by traveling magic-lantern showmen.

Not content with a motionless image, the magic-lantern inventors and exhibitors of long ago struggled with the next big trick, endowing these light-projected pictures with the illusion of motion. Painted glass disks were made to revolve in opposite directions, images were dissolved into each other with the aid of two lanterns fitted with shutters that alternately dimmed or brightened in unison, mobile magic lanterns (equipped with focusing devices to maintain a sharp image) were wheeled back and forth to shrink and enlarge images, and special effects were achieved by projecting onto glass or sheets of gauze.

When the fusion of light, image, and motion finally occurred, the subject matter was not dreamlike fantasy but reflections of the everyday world: a man and woman sharing a kiss, a train chugging into a station. But these scenes of the ordinary were a short-lived thrill, and the movies evolved into a storytelling medium. The evolving techniques of

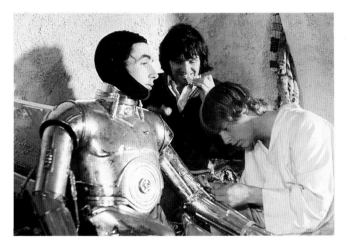

visual narration—establishing shots, cuts, close-ups, pans, pull-backs, dissolves, and more—often required special effects and engineering ingenuity to accomplish.

The act of viewing a moving picture itself developed from a parlor amusement to the communal viewing experience of the *cinématographe* theaters, arcades, and vaudeville programs. The success of showman Thomas Tally's popular "Electric Theater," which opened on Spring Street in Los Angeles in 1896 (and is considered America's first movie house), convinced thousands of hustlers, ex-carnie barkers, and the odd legit businessman to set up their own movie arcades, ushering in the nickelodeon era (so called for the price of admission). This was a time when motion pictures were advertised as "Moral and pleasing to Ladies" and the movie theaters championed for being "Fumigated hourly."

By the end of the twentieth century's first decade, the film industry had begun to take form: Movie moguls began to get into the act, new studios formed, a star system was created (it was a revelation to studio heads that audiences would respond to specific *performers*, not merely a picture's theme), and the nickelodeon arcades were transformed into grand palaces that eventually formed theater chains under the control of studio empires.

An emerging new entertainment industry

Top: Luke Skywalker (Mark Hamill, right) helps C-3PO (Anthony Daniels) suit up for the next shot.

Left: Director George Lucas lines up some Imperial stormtroopers, on location in Tunisia.

of studios, and stars, and multireel motion pictures soon after set up shop in the Los Angeles basin. The first dream merchants of the silent film era were drawn to the year-round sunshine and the open countryside. Those days were prior to the development of indoor lighting technology, and natural light had to illuminate production filming, either at an outdoor location or in glass-enclosed stages.

By the mid to late twenties sound technology completely recast the world of movie-making. The revolution of the talkies swept away the glass-enclosed stages of the silent era, replacing them with soundstages upon which filmmakers could create and control any environment imaginable. This was a time when each studio carved out a personality: MGM became storied for its lavish historical and musical spectacles, Warner Bros. for its hard-boiled gangster epics, Universal for

its eerie pantheon of monsters and ghouls. Behind their walls each studio developed like a medieval manor, a self-contained little city with dozens of acres of back lots and soundstages.

But whether building the towering temples of Babylon on a back lot or the wonderful land of Oz on a soundstage, picture making required not only the theatrical trappings of set design and construction, costume, and makeup but also special effects departments[1] responsible for producing images too difficult or impossible to obtain by theatrical means. The art of special and visual effects encompassed a range of crafts, including matte painters whose oil-painted "glass-shot" images could be incorporated with live action; stop-motion masters who crafted puppets, complete with machined skeletons, that when manipulated and photographed one frame at a time achieved the illusion of motion on film; model makers who designed and constructed props and miniature sets; and post-production experts who manipulated film imagery to achieve dissolves, transparencies, and other optical effects.

But the film industry, which had been in its ascendancy for half a century, began to resemble, by the close of the 1960s, "a company town where the mine has closed," according to a *Life* magazine article of the time. A whole Pandora's box of troubles that had been plaguing Hollywood for years were now doing so with a vengeance: A 1950 Supreme Court decision had broken up the studios' theater-chain monopolies, television was keeping folks at home and out of the theaters, debt and bad business moves were draining many a studio coffer, and the demographics indicated a younger moviegoing audience hungering for the gritty realism of an *Easy Rider*, not the effects-laden spectacles of old, like *The Ten Commandments*. It had also

Right: That adventuring archaeologist Indiana Jones, dreamed up by George Lucas and brought to life by director Steven Spielberg, exults as a team of workers dig out the buried Well of Souls, the once lost repository for the Ark of the Covenant.

Below: All hell breaks loose as evil Nazis open the ancient Ark and Indy (Harrison Ford) and Marion (Karen Allen) hang on for dear life. *Raiders*, and the ensuing sequels, would join Lucasfilm's *Star Wars* epics as being among the greatest box-office hits of all time.

1. ILM senior visual effects supervisor Dennis Muren notes that although there were FX departments, many FX artists—such as stop-motion animators and model makers and mechanical effects technicians—were usually freelancers hired by the studio as needed.

Far left: "A long time ago in a galaxy far, far away . . ." 1978 rerelease poster; art by Charlie White III and Drew Struzan.

Left: A new face of adventure, 1984 poster; art by Richard Amsel.

become more economical to shoot on location, or merely to market the work of independent producers, than to maintain the hierarchical structure of old. To stay aloft, studios began dismantling and discarding the trappings of the studio system, selling off back lots, auctioning off props and equipment, and closing departments.

The aforementioned *Life* article[2] featured the particular travails at Gulf & Western Industries' Paramount Studios. Studio power Adolph Zukor, at age ninety-seven, still had the run of the place, but the hum and bustle of a fabled dream factory were gone. The article described old, neglected prop houses filled with models of pirate ships and steamboats, Civil War cannons, plaster horses, statuary of figures of history and gods of antiquity.

"Bogus reality in fantastic abundance—but who needs it?" the article asked. "Today's movie makers and audiences want their reality absolute. This can be achieved most easily and cheaply by shooting on location instead

of in a studio. 'These kids,' says Martin S. Davis, senior vice-president of Gulf & Western, 'aren't going to the movies to take home dreams.'"

Effects departments were a casualty of this corporate downsizing. Artists scattered to the four winds or retired; cameras and optical printers and other finely built instruments were consigned to scrap heaps, put in storage, or sold off cheap. Without a creative structure in which retiring craftsmen could pass on their specialized knowledge to students of the magical arts, it was hard to imagine how special effects, and the sense of wonder they had brought to the movies, could survive.

Certain individual films recalled past glories, most importantly the work of Douglas Trumbull, Con Pederson, and the other effects artists of *2001: A Space Odyssey*

2. "The Day the Dream Factory Woke Up," *Life*, February 27, 1970, p. 40.

(1968). The production, however, staged under Stanley Kubrick's direction in England, did not usher in a new effects renaissance back in the U.S. "Kubrick's *2001* was the big special effects movie, but it was so big and expensive and awesome that it really didn't open up a lot of other possibilities [for effects], other than be an inspiration that effects could be done in a quality way," George Lucas recalled. "Almost from the moment film was invented there was this idea that you could play tricks, make an audience believe they were seeing things that really weren't there, stretch the imagination. But this was completely lost by the 1960s." What Lucas envisioned for *Star Wars* would be light-years beyond the production values of previous science fiction movies with their often crude models and painted backdrops.

Lucas labored for two years on his *Star Wars* script. The film's goal was to create a universe, one that would serve as a staging ground for a new kind of mythology. "I was struck [at the time of *Star Wars*] by the fact that the Western was the last American myth and there'd been no mythology created since the mid-fifties," Lucas recalled. "I thought space was the next environment where you could begin to develop that mythology."

Star Wars began with words on paper, drafts of screenplays in which Lucas envisioned a celestial staging ground of starry beauty, strange worlds, and pitched battles in space duplicating the lethal realism he had studied in old camera footage of World War I and II aerial dogfights.

But the tale of Rebel forces in war against the evil Empire set "a long time ago in a galaxy far, far away"—with those now legendary characters Luke Skywalker, Princess Leia, Han Solo, and Darth Vader—was originally perceived as an impossible dream by most in Hollywood. The doubters, convinced the magic didn't exist to create a universe on deadline and with a shoestring budget (Lucas recalls the entire effects budget for hundreds of shots was a mere $2.5 million), were only

being realistic. Visual effects was, at the time, a dying art. Even the convincing effects of *2001*, with its individual space stations and shuttles drifting dreamlike in the void, was hardly the model for the hyperspace speeds and multiship aerial battles Lucas wanted for *Star Wars*.

A number of studios passed on the script (including United Artists and Universal) before Twentieth Century-Fox picked up the project. *Star Wars* was a certified risk that, in order to be convincingly brought to the screen, required both the universal playbook of traditional effects and a breakthrough in both filming and compositing visual elements.

Lucas emulated the studio effects departments of old by forming Industrial Light & Magic. The original ILMers themselves were perceived by many as an insurgent group, young (the average age was late twenties) and eager but unschooled in Hollywood ways—certainly not cast from the mold of the old pros who had once created motion picture effects in the days of the studio film factories. Undaunted, the *Star Wars* effects team, which made up in enthusiasm and ingenuity what it lacked in calendar years and filmmaking experience, went to work in a thirty-thousand-square-foot industrial warehouse in Van Nuys, sixteen miles northwest of Los Angeles. When the production wrapped, many members of that first ILM group (identified in the credits as "miniature and optical effects unit") were confident in the film's potential and happy with their work—but few expected the phenomenon of global proportions that would come with the film's release.

With the resourcefulness of film *noir* gumshoes, those first ILMers searched Hollywoodland for the tools—notably abandoned VistaVision format cameras and printers—with which to create a revolution in visual effects.

The group would also develop motion control, a new form of movie magic-making that evolved from an electronic to a computerized system of programming and repeating specific motions for cameras and models. Motion control had been pioneered by Douglas Trumbull in 1971 on *Silent Running* as an outgrowth of the slit-scan technology he had developed for *2001*. John Dykstra, who would create the breakthrough motion-control system for *Star Wars*, had worked with this technology as a member of the *Silent Running* team.

"Motion control is the ability to control the movement of the camera, the photographic subject, and its lighting in synchronization to the movement of the film through the camera," said John Dykstra, special photographic effects supervisor for *Star Wars*. "In normal movies, one second of action on the screen is broken into twenty-four frames presented sequentially. If we make a camera move that lasts two seconds on the screen, we can also say the camera moves forty-eight frames. Motion control records electronically the positions of the motors [which control the movement of everything—cameras and models] in the system on frame one through frame forty-eight. Now that we have a positional map for each frame, we can run the camera as often as we'd like, knowing that the camera and subject positions would track the map exactly based on frame count.

"ILM enormously accelerated the integration of electronics and filmmaking," Dykstra added. "We took archaic cameras, built before we were even born, and we created hybrids of them by bolting different parts together. Nobody else was inventing cameras to make films in 1975. We were there when a genre was being born and reborn."

During his *Star Wars* writing phase Lucas had developed a story of such epic length that he realized it would potentially require nine movies to tell the tale. When the film achieved its unanticipated global box-office success, Lucasfilm decided to gear up for more *Star Wars* campaigns—but far away from the soundstages, back lots, and boardrooms of Hollywood. Lucas relocated ILM (and his larger Lucasfilm enterprises) just north of

Early Ralph McQuarrie concept painting for the main *Star Wars* characters.

San Francisco's Golden Gate Bridge, in Marin County. The ILM shop itself was established in a busy commercial and warehouse district of San Rafael, not far from the old downtown business strip where Lucas filmed some of *American Graffiti* in 1973, and the effects group immediately plunged into *The Empire Strikes Back*, which was released in 1980. Old-time employees who worked production on the ground level recall the dust and debris constantly shaken down on them from the ongoing second-floor construction, the lack of heat and air-conditioning in the building, and the round-the-clock work schedules needed to meet the requisite shrinking deadline for their *Empire* effects work.

The dust has long since settled at ILM. The company, entering its third decade, has worked on 110 films (including six of the top ten box-office hits of all time), from such Lucasfilm productions as the *Star Wars* and Indiana Jones trilogies to *Who Framed Roger Rabbit?*, the *Back to the Future* films, *Jurassic Park*, and *Forrest Gump*. It has also worked on theme park attractions, videos, and commercials. In 1989 *Star Wars* was honored as one of the first twenty-five films

With the Empire vanquished and the Jedi triumphant, it's time for a group photo in the Forest of Endor.

placed in the National Film Registry in accordance with an act of Congress designed to preserve American movies of historic significance. The *Star Wars* trilogy remains a global phenomenon of mythic proportions (as does the success of another Lucas creation, a certain two-fisted, whip-cracking university professor and adventuring archaeologist).

ILM remains at its original San Rafael location, although the complex of buildings, stages, and offices has been rebuilt and added on to through the years. Yet no neon lights flash the company name, no bronzed statuary of *Star Wars* heroes graces the entrance; it's a nondescript address with some street-facing buildings unmarked and others decorated with the fading logos of long-vacated tenants.

But once through the front door of the main address a visitor will see iconic trophies of past magic acts. In a small reception area Captain Hook's hook gleams in its display case, while on the walls are matte paintings of Neverland, one an aerial view of the fantasy island, the other a nocturnal harbor scene where pirate ships are anchored (all featured in director Steven Spielberg's 1991 *Hook*). In another case are five nearly twelve-inch-tall sculpted models of the metamorphic stages of the deadly liquid metal Terminator—a shape-changing liquid metal blob, a featureless chrome figure, a completely chrome-skinned humanoid, a transitional chrome man, and a final human-looking figure—that nailed down the look that would be developed by the computer graphics department for the breakthrough *Terminator 2: Judgment Day* (1991).

Around a corner is a wall-size painting of commercial aircraft crowding a snowy runway, a work that was photographed and scanned into a computer for more groundbreaking digital manipulations in *Die Hard 2* (1990). Opposite the painting stands a nearly seven-foot foam Godzilla, Japan's popular radioactive monster, re-created for a Nike shoe campaign. As for ILM's "full-motion" dinosaurs that astounded the world in *Jurassic Park* (1993), there are only framed photographs on the

wall; those amazing creations inhabit the digital realm as the sum of numbers in a computer and images on a view screen (as do the filmed image of the T-1000 and other computer graphics creations).

In their first decade George Lucas and the artists of Industrial Light & Magic rescued visual effects that have become an indispensable part of the craft of moviemaking. This book is a time-traveling journey through ILM's second decade (1986 through the mid-nineties), an era in which the company redefined visual effects and blazed a trail into the digital realm. But, as we shall see, many of the traditional, hands-on effects crafts still starred in some of the major ILM productions of this period. At other times ILM would create hybrid techniques that utilized both traditional effects and the emerging digital technologies.

ILM's second decade may be more digital than industrial, but to the men and women who weave the visions technology has always been just a tool, a way to harness the imagination and make magic a play of light.

CHAPTER ONE

OPTICAL DOGS AND
HOT ROD CAMERAS

In ILM's Building C entranceway stands an Egyptian sarcophagus, its masklike face set with an inscrutable smile, the trunk riddled with hieroglyphics. A prop from *Raiders of the Lost Ark*, it watches over a machine known as the Anderson optical aerial printer.

The Anderson, equipped with two projectors facing a mounted camera for optically compositing separately filmed elements onto negative film stock, was one of the legendary discards of industrial magic picked up by the first ILMers in 1975 and used for *Star Wars* production. By the time it was decommissioned in 1993 and relegated to museum-piece status, the Anderson had processed millions of feet of film (from the *Star Wars* and Indiana Jones trilogies to 1992's *Death Becomes Her*) and was still in perfect working order.

Prior to its ILM service, the Anderson,

built in the fifties by Howard Anderson for Paramount Studios, had produced the images of God's wrath upon Egypt and Moses parting the Red Sea for the 1956 production of *The Ten Commandments*, and helped director Alfred Hitchcock put Gary Grant through his paces in *North by Northwest* in 1959. By the time ILM was scouting around for equipment, the Anderson had been in disuse for years and was purchased by the *Star Wars* visual effects unit from Paramount for $11,000. (Estimated market value at the time of its decommission: $300,000.)

VISTAVISION: THE FORMAT OF CHOICE FOR SPECIAL EFFECTS

But the Anderson optical printer was more than a piece of compositing equipment to that first *Star Wars* team. It was a special kind of printer, which, along with companion

Above left: Visual effects editor Art Repola busy with an editing task.

Above: "The Greatest Event In Motion Picture History!" Its wonders—the plagues on Egypt, Moses parting the Red Sea—were helped by the VistaVision negative, with its double-the-normal image area, and the special printers that composited elements. This poster hung for years in ILM's optical department and is now alongside the decommissioned Anderson printer.

Bottom left: In the fifties, Paramount created the widescreen VistaVision process, a format soon abandoned but later revived by ILM for *Star Wars*. One of ILM's old VistaVision tools, the Anderson optical printer, was still in perfect working order when decommissioned in 1993. Today the Anderson is on display at the ILM facility.

cameras and film, constituted a lost moving picture production process: VistaVision, one of several fifties film formats designed to produce more spectacular big-screen images and lure back audiences lost to the phosphorescent glow of the home television set.

Developed by Paramount Studios (and advertised as "motion picture high-fidelity"), the process took standard 35 millimeter film, which normally ran vertically through the gate of a camera or projection system, and ran it horizontally, doubling the frame's exposure area for filming and producing a sharper final image when projected. The format was also known as "eight perf" for the number of perforations, or sprocket holes, on each side

of the frame, by which the film was advanced (standard 35mm film has four perforations).

Unfortunately, the promise of VistaVision technology was soon abandoned because of economics. Few studio executives and theater owners were interested in the expensive retooling required to install the requisite horizontal format cameras, optical printers, and projection systems. (At its peak of popularity, fewer than twenty theaters in the U.S. are estimated to have been equipped with the projectors necessary for exhibiting the eight-perf format to full advantage.) But Lucas and ILMers schooled in film history would remember VistaVision during *Star Wars* preproduction.

One of the keys to creating the ambitious visuals of *Star Wars* was the selection of a film process that could maintain image quality through the arduous photochemical optical compositing process. The optical composites on the *Star Wars* drawing board were of a complexity never before attempted, with as many as forty separate elements in a single shot. Each generation would distance the image from its original pristine quality, inevitably increasing film grain (the microscopic silver halide particles in a film's emulsion that become visible when projected) and ultimately degrading the final image, a fate the production team wanted to avoid.

ILM only had a choice between the 35mm and 65mm formats, the global film standards for production and exhibition since the early 1900s. Both were problematic: 35mm had too

Above right: The work area for optical supervisor Bruce Nicholson (with an optical work exposure meter in the upper right-hand corner).

Right and below: A full-scale Imperial Probe Droid is prepared in freezing weather at Finse, Norway, that served as the ice planet Hoth in *The Empire Strikes Back.* When temperatures dip to freezing, and a crew has to contend with blizzards and whiteouts, moviemaking becomes a gritty survival test.

small an exposure area to hide the inevitable grain of repeated generations, while 65mm, with its desirable image exposure area, was still unsuitable because of the limited availability and expense of cameras, film stocks, and laboratory processing for the format.

But the old VistaVision live-action cameras and optical printers were available—and for bargain prices. With VistaVision, ILM could produce complex composites of higher quality before optically printing the finals back onto standard four-perf 35mm film for cutting into a movie. So ILM not only adopted VistaVision for *Star Wars* but for all of its subsequent effects work.

MOTION CONTROL AND COMPOSITING ELEMENTS

The breakthrough for *Star Wars* was the Dykstraflex system, which replaced the old method of flying a model on wires past a camera, with blue-screen photography and programmable, repeatable motion-control track camera systems. "The Dykstraflex system was built before the advent of personal computers," said Dykstra, who headed up the team that created the system for *Star Wars*. "Its electronics were custom-designed and hardwired. The interaction between the motion-control system and the camera operator was critical. Not only did the system have to provide mechanical flexibility, accuracy, and speed, it needed to be user-friendly. Its control interface used camera terminology and acted like expert system software. The ability to operate intuitively and the inclusion of the occasional artful flaw gives a sense of live operation to these scenes. Perhaps the most important attribute of the system was its ability to reliably record moves that could be duplicated whenever needed."

The Dykstraflex system would enjoy years of dependable service at ILM. "The only real improvement we needed to make during its fifteen years of life was new software for position entering [allowing for programming any desired frame] and curve editing [to plot the

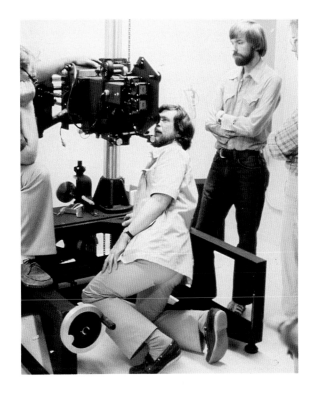

geometry of a computer move and change it at any specific point]," adds Dennis Muren.

That motion-control system of the first *Star Wars* film allowed a camera unit, consisting of a boom arm at the end of which was a mechanized camera, to be programmed to move itself down a steel track, with the camera executing the desired pan, tilt, or roll motion. Motion control allowed numerous separate elements for a composite shot to be

Left: Richard Edlund (middle) eyeballs an *Empire* camera while Pete Kuran (right) looks on.

Below: Wade Childress checks out a motion-control camera setup of a miniature bridge set for *Indiana Jones and the Last Crusade*. The resulting background plate would later be combined with blue-screen photography of Harrison Ford and other elements.

Above: Craig Hosoda operates a motion-control system, complete with track camera and computer programming capabilities.

Below left: Motion-control track camera readied for blue-screen photography of the Imperial Star Destroyer model.

Below right: Dennis Muren takes a blue-screen motion-control shot of the Imperial Star Destroyer model.

made possible because the base material of motion picture color film stock is either cellulose acetate or polyester-coated with three layers of photosensitive silver halides, each sensitive to one of photography's three primary colors of light: red, green, or blue. When any subject is photographed in front of an illuminated red, green, or blue screen, that object can be easily isolated from its background by generating color separations and "mattes" (opaque images that prevent the exposure of an area of film) on an optical printer. (Blue has been the preferred primary color because it is the color least present in flesh tones.) The background plate itself is optically composited into a shot from an intermediate positive, or "IP," which is a positive image made from the original negative.

Until the computer revolution hit with full force in the 1990s, the compositing process was in the hands of ILM's optical department, a crew that adopted (or had thrust upon them) the title "optical dogs." The term implied galley slaves toiling to death—hardly the appropriate moniker for a department in which skilled technicians handled strips of film with white-gloved hands in a dust-free environment. But optical artists were, indeed, a beleaguered lot. Waiting at the end of the effects process pipeline, they had to handle an incoming rush of film elements while ignoring

programmed, leaving it to the optical department to fit the jigsaw pieces together into one final image.

The process of creating and optically compositing various elements into one image has typically involved combining an element shot in front of a blue screen with live-action footage. (Both blue-screen and background photographic elements are referred to as "plates," a term from the early era of filmmaking when backgrounds were filmed as still photographs on glass plates.)

Blue screen as a production technique is

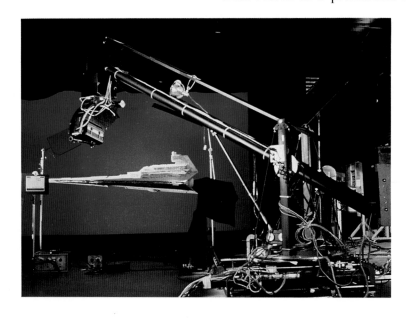

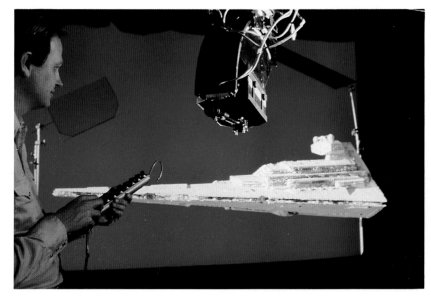

Left: In *Back to the Future, Part III*, time traveler Marty McFly takes a ride on a flying skateboard, an effect that begins with blue screen and ends with a close brush with a locomotive. The final composite was created as a digital, not an optical, composite.

Below: Locomotive model ready for blue-screen photography (note the blue-covered pylon model mount).

the heat of deadline pressures. But in their domain a certain esprit de corps prevailed. In particular, the optical dogs were on speaking terms with their equipment, usually christening the VistaVision optical printers with an appropriate name—"Quad," "Work Horse," "L.S." (for inventor and longtime ILM optical ace John Ellis). The Anderson, named for its inventor, was also celebrated by the old *Ten Commandments* poster that for years hung above the printer in the optical department (and was moved to hang alongside the Anderson's retirement post in Building C).

OPTICAL PRINTERS: THE TOOL OF COMPOSITING

With an optical printer an unlimited number of strips of photographic elements could be rephotographed on a new (or "duplicate") film negative. Constructed with one or more projectors and lamphouses facing a taking camera loaded with negative film, a printer evokes the magic lanterns of old: Projected strips of exposed film elements are shined into the eye of the facing camera lens, which photographs it, and any subsequent elements, on the same strip of negative film.

With an aerial image printer (like the Anderson), a strip of film placed between several projectors and a taking camera can have

projected and recorded several images simultaneously on the same strip of film: One image can be projected into thin air (invisible to the casual observer, the aerial element is picked up through the eyes of a camera lens) and lined up with the unexposed frame area and combined with an already exposed area of that strip of film.

"In understanding optical compositing

Above: Mike Bolles works on lens design for one of the optical printers.

Right: Parts to the VistaFlex camera.

Far right top: VistaVision Moviola, the portable unit used by editors to view film.

Far right bottom: Optical printer, detail.

and matting techniques, one needs to consider that an optical is broken down from background to foreground," explained Bruce Nicholson, who began his ILM career as an optical camera assistant on *Star Wars*. "For example, a composite shot in *Star Wars* of a Rebel X-wing fighter flying through space would consist of a starfield background and an X-wing foreground, each photographed separately onstage. When it's time to composite these two separate pieces of film, a matte, which is an opaque silhouette of the X-wing, would need to be utilized so that the starfield background would not bleed, or print, through the spaceship. With the opportunity to use photographic mattes during optical photography, we are able to create a composite that looks as if everything was photographed at one time. What's more, it is possible to combine any number of foreground pieces with a background as long as photographic mattes are available for each one. In the *Star*

Wars films it was not uncommon to have thirty to forty separate foreground pieces combined with a background onto one piece of duplicate negative film. I used to refer to this as 'ripping the envelope.'"

When *Star Wars* achieved its historic global box-office success, ILM became the permanent special effects unit of Lucasfilm Ltd. A renaissance of VistaVision technology flourished at the San Rafael facility during the production of the second installment in the saga, *The Empire Strikes Back*. Cameraman and effects supervisor Richard Edlund (who would eventually relocate back to Southern California and start the Boss Films effects house) directed adaptations for the Anderson, the design and construction of two new VistaVision cameras (dubbed

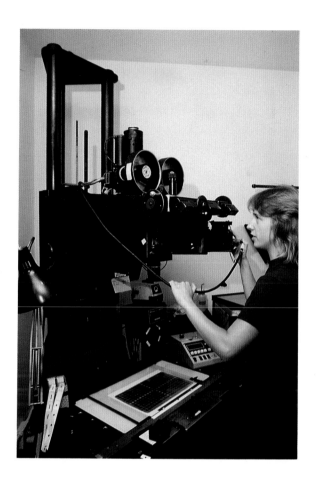

Far left: Sandy Ford Karpman works an animation stand, a setup in which a special camera, designed to shoot single frame, is mounted to a vertical column above a flat piece of artwork.

Left: Optical ace John Ellis tends the Quad printer during the glory days of the optical department.

Above: During the making of *Who Framed Roger Rabbit?* more than 70 percent of the total film went through ILM's optical printers. With the "optical dogs" under the gun, John Ellis received this Ken Ralston cartoon.

"Empire cameras"), and an optical printer (dubbed the "Quad").

The Quad, which won an Academy Award for technical achievement, was characterized by its four projector heads instead of the standard two (although two projectors would later be removed to create a new printer prior to *Return of the Jedi*), a distortion-free optic lens system designed by David Grafton that was a breakthrough in the clarity of its composited images, and a cubic beam splitter (a mirror device allowing light from the projectors to be directed into two separate camera lenses).

HOT ROD EQUIPMENT AND CAMERA MOVEMENTS

The two Empire cameras built by Edlund and his crew were the first live-action VistaVision cameras built since the days of *The Ten Commandments*. But unlike the heavier models of the 1950s, the Empires were designed as light, compact, motion-control units with shutter speeds ranging

from one-frame-per-second to ninety-six FPS. "We had no choice but to build our own kind of hot rod photographic equipment from scratch," said Edlund. "There were no VistaVision cameras anywhere in the world that would run at the kind of high speeds we needed, and the standard optical printers weren't geared for the intricacies of this level of composite photography."

The building of such specialized equipment as optical printers and cameras has always had its hot rod aspect. The Anderson, for example, was constructed with parts from older equipment when it was built during the 1950s. (John Ellis observes that the date "1927" is scratched onto one of the Anderson's cannibalized parts, denoting an old machinist's custom to mark the completion date of an original piece of equipment.)

The most vital aspect of this industrial tradition has been the creation of specialized parts so delicate they have to be machined by hand. For ILM's VistaVision cameras, the key

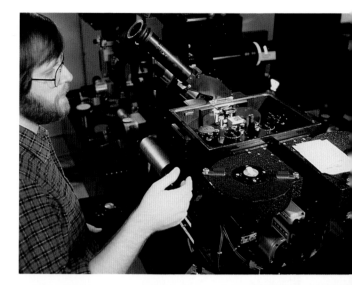

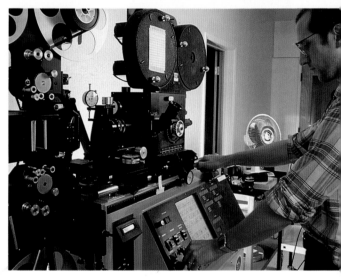

Above: Jon Alexander operates an aerial-image motion-control optical printer, which allows an image to be projected in midair between the projector and camera lens and rephotographed along with other projected images on one strip of film.

Above right: Ken Smith checks the film threading through the camera of the Quad printer.

Right: Donald Clark surveys the Anderson optical printer.

Far right: David Berry works the "L.S." (for John Ellis), a bench printer.

part, known as the "camera movement," had to physically move and position perfectly the film frame by frame during each exposure or the various elements produced would not match in the final compositing phase. Originally two registration pins held and advanced film until the breakthrough of the three-pin movements created for the Vista-Flex, an incarnation of the VistaVision camera, built by ILM for *Who Framed Roger Rabbit?*

"We custom-build three-pin film movements where the registration pins have to insert into the eight perforations of each frame and hold it perfectly still in the aperture for exposure—a process repeated twenty-four times a second," explained ILM engineer Mike Bolles, who joined the effects house in 1978. "It's analogous to the working of a still camera, except you're making successive exposures onto successive frames twenty-four times a second, so you have to take the first frame of film and then close the shutter, move the film, and take another frame a twenty-fourth of a second later. The film has to be held steady for one ten-thousandth of an inch for every single frame or you'll be able to see movement when it's composited later. Building a movement is almost an Old World craft. We have to build it by hand in our machine shop. It's very tedious to get it correct, a trial and error process where we have to build it, then shoot film and test it."

The industrial part of the ILM equation changed dramatically during the period 1990–1993. The company's trek into the digital realm had shifted into high gear with the computer graphics and image-processing successes of *Terminator 2: Judgment Day* and *Jurassic Park*. By the spring of 1994, the old photochemical optical process was completely replaced by the electronics of digital, in which separate elements of VistaVision film

Above and far left: To make the rocket-pack-powered Rocketeer fly, ILM utilized this puppet (with internal armature by Tom St. Amand, figure sculpture by Richard Miller, and costume by Jean Bolte) for stop-motion animation and optical compositing work.

Left: Here animator Tom St. Amand is deep into the concentration it takes to move, and then film, a puppet frame by frame.

Top left: To rescue an unconscious buddy from a falling biplane, the Rocketeer zooms to the rescue. The layering of elements required for our hero to save the day begins with separations of blue-screen elements of the stop-motion puppet . . .

Top right: . . . an intermediate matte of that element preparatory to the final composite . . .

Middle left: . . . the background plate of an actor in a rickety, circa 1916 Standard biplane that, to avoid a process-shot look, was staged as a mockup mounted on a gimbal at a cliff edge, with plenty of sky and distant mountain views . . .

Middle right: . . . a holdout matte, used to create a silhouette (or "black hole") in the background plate into which the Rocketeer image will be printed . . .

Bottom left: . . . the Rocketeer blue-screen elements combined with the plate . . .

Bottom right: . . . and the finishing touch: a flame element, drawn frame by frame in black and white by animation supervisor Wes Takahashi, with coloring provided by John Ellis in opticals.

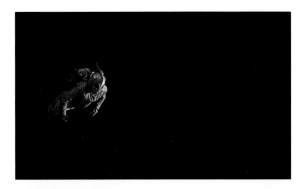

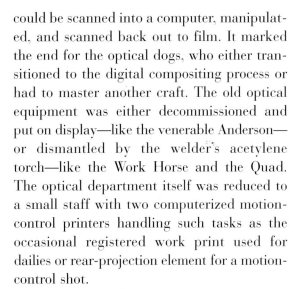

could be scanned into a computer, manipulated, and scanned back out to film. It marked the end for the optical dogs, who either transitioned to the digital compositing process or had to master another craft. The old optical equipment was either decommissioned and put on display—like the venerable Anderson—or dismantled by the welder's acetylene torch—like the Work Horse and the Quad. The optical department itself was reduced to a small staff with two computerized motion-control printers handling such tasks as the occasional registered work print used for dailies or rear-projection element for a motion-control shot.

At the time of the Anderson's decommis-

sion, talk had begun that film itself was on the verge of extinction. In the anticipated future, digital cameras would be used in production to record live-action or composite elements, computer graphics would generate three-dimensional characters and sets, and compositing and editing would be accomplished in the digital realm. The final movie would be beamed directly to home viewers by satellite or through computer modem or electronically projected in the quaint confines of a movie theater.

Mike Bolles was philosophical about the overnight demise of the photochemical compositing process and the technological revolution, although he now had a special affinity for the phrase "Future Shock."

"I've never seen such a rapid change in my life anywhere, in anything," he said with a slight smile. "It's just stunning. But digital-image processing is more powerful and versatile than optical printing was. In optical printing you changed your image by masking, or blanking out, certain areas and replacing them with areas of film from another piece of film, and you can only do that with sections. With the digital-image manipulation you can go in and change any point of an image in any manner you want. It's a very powerful tool."

But while optical printers had seemingly gone back to the anonymity from which ILM had first rescued them, the machinist's Old World tools of mills and lathes were still needed to service VistaVision cameras and build digital printers. Bolles noted that in addition to cameras and digital printers, special projects included a camera setup for filming video images to create temporary work prints of computer graphics works in progress. In the machine-shop tradition, one of the cameras used for the video work print setup had been built in the 1920s.

"The equipment gets recycled," Bolles explained. "The work print camera is a Bell and Howell 2709, the first movie camera to have a standardized pull-down mechanism [the portion of a camera movement that advances film through the film gate]. They did such a good job of building and designing them that they're still in use for effects work. How long can a machine like this last? It's lasted seventy years already and it'll keep going. And it's still got the original movement. Who knows if a computer can last that long?"

PICTURE PUZZLES: TERMS OF OPTICAL COMPOSITING

The Great Train Robbery (1903) ran a full 740 feet of film (slightly more than twelve minutes) with a simple plot pretty well summed up by the title. This seminal effort at movie narrative by Edwin S. Porter also had one of the first optical compositing shots used to create a realistic scene: Two robbers hold a telegraph operator at gun-point while a train is seen outside the telegraph office window, the train composited into the scene by in-camera matte technique.

Traditional compositing, in which separately filmed elements are combined into one image, can be accomplished through either a variety of in-camera techniques (which keeps the final image at first-generation quality) or on an optical printer. Creating that final image is like putting together a jigsaw puzzle—except the separate elements have to blend together perfectly. If elements are improperly matted into a scene, telltale "matte lines" will be visible along an element's edge.

BLUE-SCREEN PROCESS

Optical compositing has traditionally involved shooting at least some of an image's elements with the use of blue screen, a limbo background in which a subject can be either front or back lit. Through a series of steps on an optical printer the blue is extracted and used to generate both "male" and "female" mattes. A male matte (also known as the "holdout matte" or "black center matte") is a black silhouette of the blue-screen element against a clear field, while the female matte is a clear silhouette of the same element against a field of black. The male matte then serves as a

"black hole" over the background, blocking exposure in the area in which the original photography will be printed. The photography is then exposed into the black hole with the female matte, which prevents any blue-screen contamination of the background.

There are a variety of in-camera techniques for compositing separate elements, particularly matte paintings and live action:

• **Rear projection**, a compositing method popularized in the early 1930s, involves placing a subject in front of a large, translucent screen onto which a background image is projected from behind while a camera placed in front of the foreground and background subjects records the composited scene.

• **Front projection** has been used primarily for creating live-action in-camera

composites. Unlike rear projection, the background image is projected from the *front* of the screen, with a semireflective and semitransparent mirror (also known as a "fifty-fifty mirror") both reflecting and transmitting 50 percent of the projected light while the taking camera records both the background and foreground elements as one image.

• **Latent image** is another way of compositing a matte painting and a live-action scene. In the process a live-action element is shot, but a specific part of the camera lens is blacked out. The film is not processed but rewound to the beginning and used to film the matte painting, which will then be exposed over the previously blackened portion of the film. The final shot blends both real and painted material onto the original negative, providing the highest-quality, first-generation image.

For the epic fantasy *Willow* (1988), ILM utilized some classic in-camera compositing tricks, as with the use of this canyon maze set (modeled by Paul Huston) through which heroes Willow and Madmartigan will ride on horseback. Chris Evans adds final touches to a Caroleen Green matte painting of distant mountaintops and a cloud-filled sky, while the foreground black hole in the miniature canyon will later be fit with a screen for rear-projecting images of the horseback riders.

CHAPTER TWO

ART DIRECTION

In the Hong Kong action movie *Full Contact* (1992), a shoot-out in a crowded nightclub features a camera zoom that isolates and follows the deadly trajectory of a bullet. It's the kind of shot ILM art department manager Mark Moore calls "highlight material," and it goes on his personal video highlight reel. Moore has collected some twenty-two hours of moving images, from shots of Captain Nemo's ship and the giant octopus from Disney's *20,000 Leagues Under the Sea* to such esoterica as the live-performance video of Survival Research Labs,

a heavy-metal destructothon in which machinery and robots tear into each other.

"The highlight reel is all inspirational; a lot of it boils down to just the feeling of something," said Moore. "For example, in *Memoirs of an Invisible Man* (1992) I art-directed a sequence where an entire building disappears, which was inspired by an episode of *The Invaders*, the sixties television show starring Roy Thinnes, in which an alien caused a building to disappear in stages. The building in *Invisible Man* didn't look anything like the one in the TV show, but that was the source

The main work area for the old art department, prior to its expansion into more spacious quarters at the ILM facility. (Art director Doug Chiang is in the foreground.)

Right: *The Invaders*, an old sixties sci-fi TV show, inspired the design concept for this disappearing building from *Memoirs of an Invisible Man*.

Below: Effects magic begins with a screenplay, in which a few printed words can mean months of work and a lot of dollars, such as this scene from *Ghostbusters II*.

of my inspiration, to design the building fading out. The inspirational reel also involves thinking about what people at the time did to achieve a certain shot."

In addition to the highlight reel, further visual inspiration can be found on department shelves lined with art books and bound storyboards from all of ILM's major projects. The department overflows with visual images: Polaroid snapshots pinned to bulletin boards, concept art for the latest projects on drawing boards, storyboard drawings laid out on a conference table for discussion. The art department is the first port of call for all projects flowing into ILM, the place where the visual look of things is worked out to the most precise camera angle. Here image is everything, from the look of a creature and the lay of a landscape to the composition and fine details of each effects shot.

Patty Blau, ILM's executive in charge of production, explains the preproduction process of considering an idea, assembling a production team, and beginning the all-important concept and design work: "We'll be sent a script and either I or one of my bidding producers will read through it and do a breakdown of what we perceive to be the potential visual effects. During that process we also start a dialogue with the client, asking if our estimation of the effects is realistic and if the client saw a way of staging a shot without requiring effects. Then we need to open up a preliminary conversation with the director and the producer of the project. If it's further along, and they've got to start production in a few months, [ILM president] Jim Morris and I will talk about the type of effects that might be involved and who amongst our roster of talent seems well suited to the project and to the team on the client's end and to the team we can put together on our end.

"The most critical thing about film is that the creative communications have to be right on. The director and the visual effects supervisor need to be able to have the same vision. Once we set up the team that will work on the

SHOT:		5272 SENT/APP'D		STATUS:	
RR 11		DESCRIPTION: Fireballs/bolts stream from Vigo's ey into Janosz'.			
STAGE:	PLATE:	PRECOMP:	ANM:	CG:	OPTICAL:

Above and left: Storyboards are visual blueprints for creating a shot. Effects boards usually include notes on the technical game plan. In this scene for *Ghostbusters II*, the evil Vigo the Carpathian is trapped in an old painting until he hypnotizes an unlucky art restorer to do his bidding.

project throughout, we have them read the script and do the breakdown together. They also bring in at this point an art director, and again, you're looking for chemistry and suitability of talent between that ILM team, the client, and the project."

To meet the challenge of giving form to the scripted word, the department has on staff six full-time art directors and hires concept and storyboard artists as needed. ILM's emphasis on keeping the art department fully staffed at all times allows an art director to

follow each assigned project from start to finish.

The design of a character and the composition of a shot have always been important to the entire filmmaking process, but they are particularly vital for planning and executing the complexities of effects work. Even back at the dawn of filmmaking, effects pioneer Georges Méliès worked out his fantastic sets and mechanical effects with production paintings and detailed schematics before a shot went before the camera.

Above: Production paintings work out the atmosphere of a scene. In this Kathy Swain painting for *Indiana Jones and the Last Crusade*, the evil Nazi hireling Walter Donovan, speedily aging into oblivion after drinking from a false Grail, lunges for his double-crossing partner in the "Donovan's Destruction" effects sequence.

Right: The "Donovan's Destruction" production painting is elaborated on, with story-boards working out the camera composition for the terrifying action.

When Twentieth Century-Fox showed an interest in his *Star Wars* script, Lucas wanted to expound his vision beyond mere typescript, so he hired artists such as illustrator Ralph McQuarrie, whose initial designs helped earn vital money for the production. The dynamic visuals of the film itself, from Lucas's concept of the opening shot of the Star Destroyer passing overhead to the aerial battles of the Death Star finale, were accomplished with the help of effects designer and illustrator Joe Johnston's storyboards, which served to communicate visually the director's inner vision during production. "The art director helps define and visually interpret the script," said ILM art director Doug Chiang. "The best part is to push the boundary to find the visual limits. The key is to create storyboards that eliminate most of the questions and serve as the literal blueprints for our visuals."

STORYBOARDS: VISUAL BLUEPRINTS

Movie storyboards graphically plot out the shot-by-shot look of a scene. Alfred Hitchcock was legendary for his meticulous

Above: A starting point for the fantasy epic *Willow* were production-concept illustrations that helped conjure up the look of a fairy-tale land. Painting by Richard Vander Wende.

Left: *Willow*, production painting by Richard Vander Wende.

Right: The green, gluttonous Slimer returns from the first *Ghostbusters* for a few sequel scenes. These character sketches helped capture the personality of the spectral character.

Below: In *Ghostbusters II*, freakish phantoms return from the dead to wreak havoc in Manhattan, particularly the criminal Scoleri brothers. Production illustrations kicked off the creation of Nunzio (bottom left) and Tony (bottom right). Art by Henry Mayo.

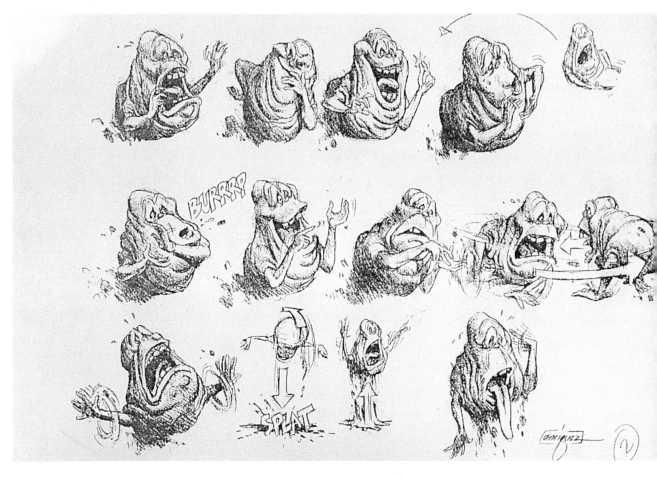

preproduction periods in which every shot and angle was designed and drawn out on storyboards. (For Hitch, the actual shooting of the film was anticlimactic.) The boards for the famous knife-slashing shower scene in *Psycho* (created by Saul Bass), for example, were detailed down to the bloodstained hands of the victim. Storyboards have been compared to comic books, but although both mediums have a sequential graphics dynamic, the comic-book illustrator can design or disregard panel structure as necessary, while storyboarders must work within the strict perimeters of the film frame.

"Storyboard artists are so hard to come by because you have to have such a background knowledge," said Moore. "You're locked into the format of the frame and its aspect ratio [the ratio of an image's width to its height], which you have to take advantage of. For example, if it's a 2.35:1 anamorphic [the Panavision wide-screen process], you

have a very narrow image. Then you have to consider what the director wants, what kind of lens is being used, and the camera motion. Is the shot going to be motion-control or hand-held? A pan, a zoom, or a tilt? Then, the object you're rendering, whether it's a person or vehicle or an environment, can you get tight on it or not? You have to keep all these things in mind when you're doing

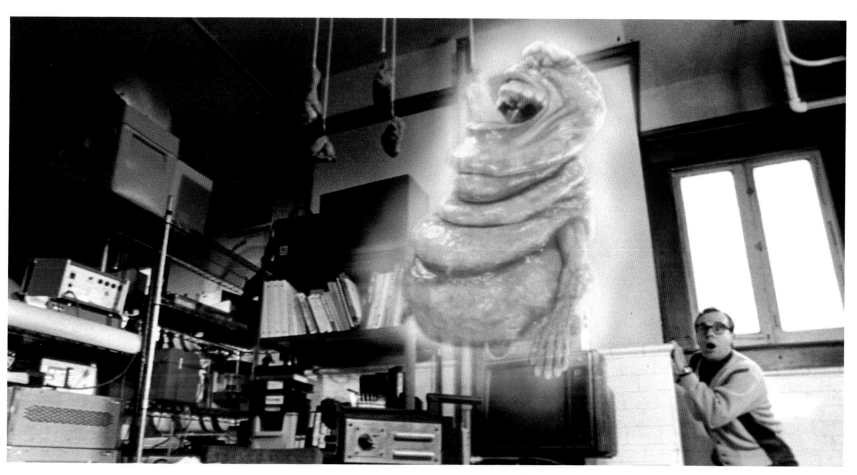

Above: The Slimer was ultimately created as a suit (worn by actress Robin Navlyt) shot blue-screen and optically composited into a background plate of a cowering Louis Tully (Rick Moranis). This scene did not make the cut for the final film.

Far left and left: Since the Scoleri brothers would be brought to life with performers wearing creature suits, it was important to consider how the two-dimensional character designs would work as fully dimensional forms. For such purposes, effects artists would produce 3-D prototypes, such as these maquettes of Nunzio and Tony.

Top left: A final production design by Richard Vander Wende for the two-headed Eborsisk of *Willow*.

Top right: *Willow*, early Eborsisk production painting by Richard Vander Wende.

Bottom: For *Ghostbusters II*, this Benton Jew illustration concept of ill-fated *Hindenburg* passengers was discarded in favor of water-logged spirits disembarking a materialized *Titanic*.

boards. It's the same thing with a computer graphics shot; you design characters based on what resolution they're generated at. And if you get too tight, the resolution breaks up, so the storyboard artist has to keep that in mind and get as tight as possible."

Even when a project, like *Jurassic Park*, comes to ILM with storyboards (with many of those *Jurassic* boards drawn by ex-ILMers Dave Lowery and John Bell), the design stage is a collaborative process in which the shots

are worked out to the smallest detail. In *Jurassic Park* those extra touches of realism included making the wheel of an overturned, computer-generated vehicle move slightly as a Tyrannosaurus rex attacked it and providing a rampaging velociraptor with a nictitating membrane.

THE ART OF DESIGN

The journey to the final image is also predicated on the wants of the director and the appropriate approach to a subject. "For *Jurassic*, TyRuben Ellingson [visual effects art director] was obsessed with reality," Moore observed. "We wanted the audience to be able to smell the dinosaurs, to feel the moisture and texture of their skin. So Ty was very glued into reality on that one. With a *Star Trek* film we don't have to be as real. The *Star Trek* series in general has this theme of the future being very upbeat—everything's going to be nailed down, everything's going to work. So for that kind of film, you get away from the grittiness of some of the other, darker future pictures."

In the post–*Jurassic Park* era, computer technology has provided filmmakers with the

Sean Joyce concept painting of
the fearsome General Kael, one of
the villains of *Willow*.

KING KAEL

© MŒBIUS 86

Above: Internationally acclaimed French cartoonist Jean Giraud (who has also worked under the nom de plume "Moebius") produced a series of production illustrations for *Willow*. This shows concept art for the character of King Kael.

Far right: Another fantastic *Willow* character/costume design by visionary artist Jean "Moebius" Giraud. Here's the design for the warrior hero Madmartigan.

ability to create wholly unique characters or digitally manipulate composite elements with a freedom not possible with the old photochemical means. As such, the new digital tools provide a corollary freedom for art directors, who are dreaming up the dynamics and visual look of a shot.

"This [art design] is such a great job from a design aspect," Moore added. "Before coming to ILM I was in toy product design, which had such strict perimeters. Some people liked designing with those strict perimeters, but I hated it. 'We have to make this toy safe, not too small that it could be swallowed; it can't have sharp corners; it can't pinch'—and we're talking about a red ball here! Coming into the effects field it's like, 'We need a futuristic, quasi-military base that's fifty years in the future; come up with something'—Yes!"

Moore, who joined ILM in 1989 during production of *Back to the Future, Part II*, has witnessed the tremendous changes within the company, as it went from being an optical effects house to a digital house, dismantled such unique equipment as the cloud tank [a square glass container of water, some four feet long, used to film cloud effects using paint in water], and decommissioned optical printers like the Anderson. Even the group ritual screening of film dailies (the photochemically

Above: John Bell concept art for the professor's lab in *Back to the Future, Part II*.

Left: Illustration concept for throne room set of the evil Queen Bavmorda, for *Willow*. Art by Jean "Moebius" Giraud.

Far right, top to bottom: *Star Trek VII: Generations* storyboard showing primary warp engine unit separating from *Enterprise* dish; art by Mark Moore.

Right, top to bottom, and below left: Armed with the new digital technologies, concept artists can dream up and deliver ever more fantastic imagery. For a sequence of an exploding sun scripted for *Star Trek VII: Generations*, classic Robert Edgerton atomic bomb explosion photos (below) were scanned and manipulated by Mark Moore with Photoshop software to design the film's cosmic conflagration . . .

Bottom right: . . . with additional Mark Moore Photoshop art visualizing the look of a nearby planet being torn apart by star explosion shock waves.

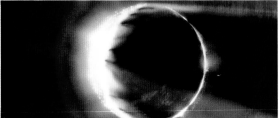

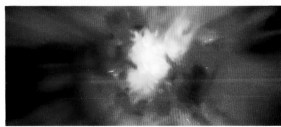
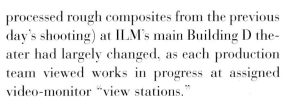

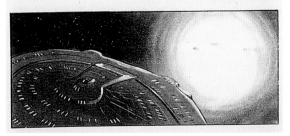

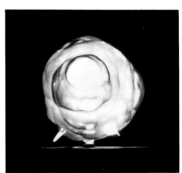
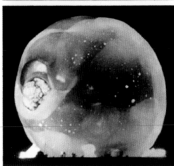

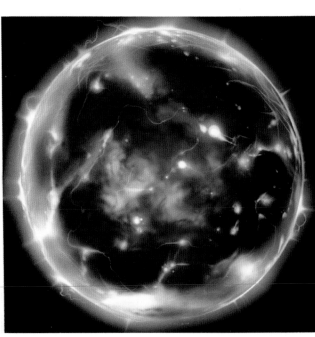

processed rough composites from the previous day's shooting) at ILM's main Building D theater had largely changed, as each production team viewed works in progress at assigned video-monitor "view stations."

But digital was not the answer for every project. Often models and creatures, or a combination of computer and practical effects, were still the best techniques. As always, technology was a *tool*, and sometimes it was possible to deliver shots without space-age wizardry. And, of course, there was always the chance for a little inspiration from the old, and sometimes forgotten, effects artists whose work had been captured on the highlight reel.

"I really love B movies because a lot of those [effects artists] got so creative under pressure," Moore noted. "Sometimes a lot of

Left: *Willow*, creature study by John Bell.

Below left: *Back to the Future, Part II* character and costume concept designs by John Bell.

Below: *Future II* kids, concept designs by John Bell.

the things we do with all our new resources is no better than what they did the first time around. On my highlight reel there are clips from *The Monolith Monsters* [a 1957 Universal-International release advertised as "Living Skyscrapers of Stone Thundering Across the Earth!"]. It's this really cool story about a meteor that hits Earth and shatters into all these rocks that, when exposed to water, grow into these monoliths that can wipe out towns. The way they did the effects was they shot prestressed obsidian falling on models. We were looking at that footage for some scale reference—just looking at how well some of these rocks broke apart on these models. I'm sure they did it for a fairly low budget, and it looked great."

Moore smiled as he recalled the many times a production has come to ILM with the request "We want something that's never been done before." Often, a review of the highlight reel could show that an imagined idea had already been dreamed up and real-

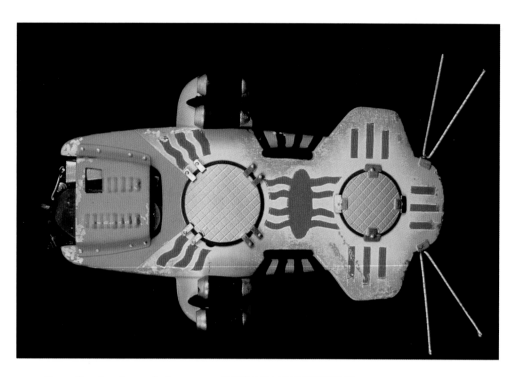

Above: Hoverboard prop; design by John Bell.

Right: John Bell character/costume designs for the well-dressed skateboard jockeys of the future in *Back to the Future, Part II.*

Far right, top to bottom:

Tucker automobile design for *Tucker.*

Back to the Future, Part II production illustration by John Bell for a sleek taxicab, model year 2015.

Production illustration of the ghost-busting "Ectomobile," by John Bell. (Painted on the side of the live-action vehicle are the words "Call Us: We Believe You.")

Griff's Hoverboard; concept illustration for *Back to the Future, Part II* by John Bell.

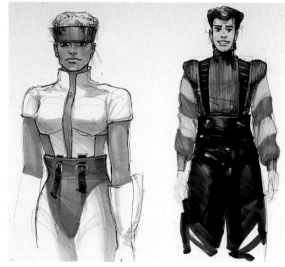

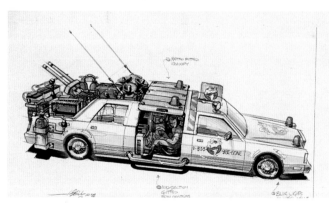

ized. But with the possibilities being opened up by the new digital technologies and the hybrid of traditional effects and computers, it seemed the frontier of imagination was being pushed out a little further.

"You know what I think the next big design challenge is going to be?" Moore rhetorically asked. "For someone to do cyberspace—what the world inside a computer would look like if you were to travel inside the network of a computer brain. That's something that's completely open to interpretation. It's total blue sky."

THE ARTIST'S DREAM

In artist Ralph McQuarrie's studio, a little nook in his rustic Berkeley, California, home, are collected many of the paintings and drawings from which he conjured up the *Star Wars* universe. In addition to depictions of George Lucas's famous characters and alien landscapes, McQuarrie's work portrayed *Star Wars* visions that never appeared on the big screen: floating ghost towns lost in the clouds of Bespin, vantage points of Jabba the Hutt's palace in sight of caravans passing across the hot sands of Tatooine, the Imperial City of Coruscant with its pyramidal buildings, and the Plaza of Ancient Monuments rising above that stronghold capital of the Empire.

McQuarrie had first been introduced to Lucas when the filmmaker's swashbuckling saga was still a dream without a title, before even the completion of *THX 1138*

(1971), Lucas's first feature film. As McQuarrie recalls, Lucas particularly liked one of his paintings, American astronauts greeting a group of fur-covered aliens on a grassy planet. Soon after that fateful meeting, McQuarrie was tapped for production-design duties on Lucas's space opera (making him arguably the first ILMer, according to Thomas Smith in *Industrial Light & Magic: The Art of Special Effects*). When Lucas's *Star Wars* script stalled at Twentieth Century-Fox, it was McQuarrie's concept paintings, including renderings of the droids and Darth Vader, that helped shake out some vital seed money from the studio.

McQuarrie concept art from *Cocoon*, a tale of terrestrial and alien contact.

Ralph McQuarrie adds a finishing brushstroke to an early *Star Wars* Darth Vader concept painting.

Besides his *Star Wars* work, McQuarrie's career highlights include designing the spaceship in *E.T. The Extra-Terrestrial* (1982), contributing production designs for *Cocoon* (1985), and doing visual consulting work for *Star Trek IV* (1986), a body of work characterized by a fascination with outerworldly wonders. In addition to being a superb artist, McQuarrie has always been a dreamer—a perfect combination for conjuring up creatures, alien worlds, and fantastic spacecraft. Most of McQuarrie's film work has reflected a fascination

Alien beings dally in this entrancing McQuarrie *Cocoon* concept painting.

his soft-spoken voice. "It was really surrealistic, but frightening and sickening when it was over—remembering, like, when you see a bullet hit and pass right through somebody, and the guy drops and squirms around and screams and hollers, and hours later he's still there moaning and you wonder when the guy is going to die. And when you go down to lunch every day, there's the smell of corpses. There are trucks that dig up these corpses that are in the mud and you see the blood on [their] hands. It's terrible. What kind of business is this for humans to be doing? After all these centuries! What's going on here? I thought to myself, 'You know, this is absurd, and these are guys who are not going to live their lives.' When I got back from the war I was so shocked from having seen people dying in such a dramatic manner."

It was understandable that after combat McQuarrie's artistic expression drifted to off-world visions, as he took up painting images of spaceships and lunar surfaces for CBS News Special Events during the era of the Apollo space programs. "I was a technical illustrator before any flights to the moon were even considered," he noted. "Back then we [the other technical artists] would joke around, saying 'So and so has been here a long time, he'll be here after illustrating the first rocket to the moon,' never thinking it would actually happen."

Some of McQuarrie's grandest designs bubbled up to his consciousness in dreams. The most significant was the great mother

with alien contact. "The spaceship comes down and you see and have to relate to the first aliens on Earth, which is certainly a dream of mine," McQuarrie observed.

McQuarrie had always looked at the world through the prism of a true artist, even during one long night in a machine gunner's trench during the Korean War. As a gunnery assistant he was hunkered down in a fixed position gouged out of a hillside, the first line of defense against waves of Chinese soldiers that periodically descended from the mountaintop. McQuarrie's battalion, sent in to replace an earlier group during a lull in the fighting, had presumed the enemy would wait out the night. But instead of an uneventful watch, the enemy launched waves of attack, each beaten back at great cost to both sides.

In one sublime moment—with proximity fuses, flares, and flashes from shell bursts lighting up the sky and silhouetting the enemy soldiers, and the screams of fighting men and the thunder of explosions filling the air—the young McQuarrie found himself enraptured by the scene's surreal beauty and thinking, "I've never seen such good war shots; these are the best I've ever seen." But the fantasy of living the ultimate war movie was, of course, a passing wisp of thought during that night of terror. McQuarrie himself was hit in the head by a burp-gun blast as he prepared to toss a grenade. As his combat buddies were bandaging him they found that he was still alive only because the liner on his helmet had stopped the bullet.

With the coming of dawn, a hellish tableau was revealed, a wasteland blasted clear of any vegetation and littered with the dead. "When the barrage lifted, there was sudden silence," McQuarrie recalled in

Much of the artistic brainstorming of the preproduction phase does not end up on the screen. For the icy planet Hoth of *The Empire Strikes Back*, George Lucas opted for a wasteland populated only by such animals as the tauntauns and the wampa ice creature. McQuarrie's production art also envisioned a desolate place, yet one full of evidences of some ancient, perfectly preserved Hothian civilization. In this McQuarrie painting, Rebel explorers discover the spires of a mysteriously deserted city that extends below the icy surface of the planet.

ship he created, at Steven Spielberg's request, for 1977's *Close Encounters of the Third Kind*. That inspirational dream had taken place years before, not long after he had returned from the war to his parents' home in Seattle.

As McQuarrie recalled, in his dream he found himself in his parents' living room when he was overcome with a strange feeling that he should go outside. The deserted neighborhood was a suburban pastoral of flowering apple trees, hedges, and quiet houses with fenced-in lawns. "I looked up—it was one of those flat, gray, overcast days—and coming out of the clouds was this huge structure," McQuarrie recalled. "There were all these towerlike cylindrical forms with platforms and detailed metalwork just hanging there, and I thought it had to be a spaceship from outer space. I was about to jump through the hedge and knock on my neighbor's door, to get some confirmation on what I was seeing, when this godlike voice comes on in my head—a voice that you couldn't ignore, couldn't discount, and you absolutely had to obey— saying: 'Stop! Don't tell anybody about what you've seen! Go back in your house and forget about this.'" Nearly twenty-five years later, when McQuarrie sat in a screening room with Spielberg and other *Close Encounters* production principals to watch the mother ship shots that had evolved from his designs, his strange dream came back to him in a flash.

McQuarrie production sketches for *The Empire Strikes Back* work out the particulars of another world, from the tauntauns that prowl Hothian ice caves to the "cathedral" of the deserted city.

"I hadn't thought of the dream when I was doing the sketches, but when I watched the screening the dream came back to me," McQuarrie marveled, musing about the mysteries of the unconscious mind. "When somebody asks me to invent something, I think what happens is that in my brain I've got a conscious little guy, who's me, who sits there watching this screen, and up on this screen come these things from the subconscious. It's like a library in the subconscious where things are brought as needed to my consciousness. In my estimation, this consciousness is totally miraculous."

Through the years, his muse had often come unbidden in dreams, and to this day he still lets his unconscious mind guide his artist's hand, often sitting down with pen and paper to watch random doodles take form. In McQuarrie's mind, you don't get in the way of dreams. An artist, after all, has to let the subconscious surface. In 1995 McQuarrie was asked by Lucasfilm's Rick McCallum, producer of the upcoming feature-film episodes in the *Star Wars* saga, to be part of the project's conceptual design team. For McQuarrie, whose artistic renown grew from his seminal work on the original trilogy, the assignment was a chance to

explore once again the limitless possibilities of an entire universe.

McQuarrie had a pre–*Star Wars* dream take him on a flight to the ends of the universe where, while passing over alien worlds, he could project his mind to observe strange life-forms and environments. "I woke up the next morning and thought, 'That was a hell of a trip, but I'm back in the world,' " he recalled. "I'd gotten the message that life is a constant show, and the ending of the show you don't know. The next scene you don't know either, which makes it very interesting. And it doesn't matter what it is—you could be getting shot at in a war, having a hell of a good time with somebody you just adore, or seeing a good movie. It doesn't matter what it is, and you don't know the outcome of it. We're all fixed in the moment that keeps passing and never gets there. Everything is in motion, and it works, it's life. And it's perfect the way it is."

McQuarrie rough painting of the manta ray–like sky creatures that fly among the floating cities (and floating ghost cities) of the planet Bespin, another image that did not make the final for *The Empire Strikes Back*.

CHAPTER THREE

MODELS IN ACTION

The model ships of *Star Wars* not only featured realistic craftsmanship and detailing but told a story: Han Solo's *Millennium Falcon* was a souped-up hot rod in space; the Rebels' X-wing starfighters had worn and scarred hulls from many a deep space dogfight; and the Empire's Death Star was a forbidding, planet-shaped citadel of evil orbiting in space.

ILM models have ranged from miniatures measured in inches and ounces to large-scale productions many feet in length and weighing hundreds of pounds. Most models require intricate internal riggings, from electronic systems powering propellers and lights to special compartments in which pyrotechnics can be rigged for explosives work. The internal workings of major models also require heat-extracting, compressed air cooling systems to prevent model meltdown from the heat of the inner electronic works and the glare of stage lights.

The typical motion-control setup that brought the *Star Wars* ships to life mounted the models in front of blue screen on pylons that allowed for programmed positions of roll,

Left: ILM's model shop crowded with the scale planes used for *Always*, a saga of aerial firefighters who protect the forests of Montana.

Below: Tony Sommers prepares a model plane for *Always* (with Charlie Bailey in the background).

Right: For *Always*, rather than shooting the model planes blue-screen, ILM's effects crew opted for staging the action in-camera, with a miniature forest created on an old airstrip in Tracy, California. Here a fifth-scale model flown from a trucking crane rig passes over the forest set.

Below: A special ILM "MASH" tent serves for tending those model planes (and providing some respite from the burning sun of the San Joaquin Valley).

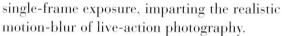

pitch, and yaw. The movement of the motion-control track camera on the models provided the illusion of the ships in motion. Motion control added to the authenticity of flight by keeping the camera shutter open during each single-frame exposure, imparting the realistic motion-blur of live-action photography.

Motion control could also program multiple exposures (or "passes") of a subject, which provided a realistic layering of detail in a shot. Multiple exposures might require a beauty pass to record the significant detail along with a shot of the model's interior lighting. The camera would do its programmed beauty pass, and then, with the set darkened except for the model's lighting element, the camera would repeat the same move, exposing the light pass with the beauty-pass exposure. The layers of passes would finally be composited in the optical compositing phase.

In the decade following the *Star Wars* trilogy the model department underwent a creative transformation. As Jeff Mann, the model creature department supervisor from 1986 to 1992, observed: "After *Return of the Jedi*, the floodgates opened. We got out of our niche of miniature and blue-screen photography and started to get into realistic landscapes. Still later we got into second-unit live-action and practical large-scale effects for pictures like *Always* [1989], *The Hunt for Red October* [1990], *Die Harder* [1990], *Backdraft* [1991], and *The Rocketeer* [1991]."

Two dramatic examples of models working in realistic environments are *Always* and *The Hunt for Red October*. In *Always* ILM would have to simulate firefighting aircraft battling blazes in timber country while *The Hunt for Red October* required ILM to create an underwater world and fill it with submarine models that had to look like multi-ton ships on-screen. The two productions not only accounted for some memorable effects scenes but some true adventures in production.

ALWAYS
1989 (Amblin/Universal)
Flying Through Fire

Always, directed by Steven Spielberg, was a remake of *A Guy Named Joe* (1943), which starred Spencer Tracy as a World War II bomber pilot who sacrifices himself during a mission only to return as the angelic guide of a rookie pilot. In Spielberg's version the setting became present-day Montana and the flying aces were replaced by aerial forest-fire fighters. Two key aerial sequences too dangerous to attempt with real pilots and planes—one a daylight scene featuring clouds of smoke, the second a full-blown burning forest set at night—were tagged as ILM effects shots. Joe Johnston, an ILM veteran since *Star Wars*, who had just directed his first feature (Disney's 1989 *Honey, I Shrunk the Kids*), was called on to direct ILM's aerial effects sequences.

The daylight sequence had Pete (Richard Dreyfuss) and Al (John Goodman) fighting a forest fire in their planes. Al's plane catches fire and Pete flies by to drop a load of fire retardant on his buddy's burning aircraft, ultimately sacrificing himself as his own plane catches fire and explodes in midair. The climactic sequence featured Dorinda (Holly Hunter), a pilot and Pete's girlfriend in life,

Left: Falling debris was dropped from this hovering balloon onto a fire below.

Below: ILM shot some background plates of a burning forest to be optically used with live actors in cockpit mockups. Here a camera car films plates of the miniforest going up in flames.

making a daring night flight to help open up an escape route for firefighters trapped in the forest.

Johnston and his team had two different strategies for staging and filming the sequences: The daylight scenes featuring

Top: Tending ILM's Christmas tree forest.

Right: To duplicate a forest in Montana for *Always*, ILM selected an abandoned airstrip in California's agricultural bread-basket, bulldozed gorges at the location, and transplanted hundreds of six-to-ten-foot Christmas trees.

Bottom: Pyro work on an A-26 miniature.

smoke effects would be filmed using radio-controlled (RC) planes at an outdoor location, while the night scenes would feature a miniature forest fire and wire-rigged model planes staged in an abandoned steel plant.

FLYING BY RADIO CONTROL

ILM model supervisor Mike Fulmer contracted with Custom R/C Aircraft to build the two key planes, an A-26 Invader flown by Pete and a PBY Super Catalina flying boat for Al. ILM built some half-dozen A-26s, some for pyrotechnics and others for flying effects. With fuselages constructed mainly of foam core and Fiberglas, and the wings and spars made of wood, the Invader weighed 75 pounds and the flying boat weighed almost 150 pounds and had a wingspan of 21 feet—impressive scale for both, yet relatively lightweight. The aircraft were designed and engineered to serve as either free-flying, radio-controlled models or wire-rigged flyers. ILM's model shop prepped the planes for filming by constructing retractable landing gear for the A-26 and completing the fine detailing and painting of all the models.

An old World War II navy runway in the town of Tracy, in the middle of California's agricultural San Joaquin Valley, was secured

Far left: For *Always* night shots, ILM set up another forest environment inside an abandoned steel plant in San Francisco. The back side of the hillside set was made of steel pipe, lumber, and wire mesh and was covered with foil, paint, and dirt. Robert Finley III is shown here.

Left: Keith London (left) and Jack Haye (right) used a network of pipes to insert the Christmas trees in the hillside set.

Below: Christmas trees were lifted into place on the hillside set.

for the radio-control work. "The Tracy location was selected because the wind would blow from eight to fifteen miles per hour every afternoon," said Johnston. "For the smoke we were using the same type of smokers they use on naval destroyers to create a smoke screen on the ocean. When we put all that smoke in the air, it blew horizontally down the runway. We had people from [as far as] five miles downwind who thought they were experiencing some kind of nuclear winter!"

Alongside the old airstrip a five-hundred-foot-long, three-hundred-foot-wide set was constructed, with hundreds of six-to-ten-foot Christmas trees representing thick stands of Montana timberland. Bulldozers were utilized to dig some ravines in the set, and a network of propane gas tubes that could simultaneously ignite the miniature forest was laid down. The location work was made more grueling by temperatures in excess of one hundred degrees, but the hot weather would turn out to be the least of the problems Johnston's crew faced.

From the beginning there were problems controlling the models with radio waves. The models would take off smoothly on the runway, but instead of an anticipated forty mph clip, the planes were streaking through the sky at eighty-five mph, outracing the camera

Right: ILM veteran and features director Joe Johnston (middle) directed the aerial effects sequences for *Always*. Here Johnston confers with Patrick McArdle (left) and Bruce Nicholson (right).

Far right: Johnston aligns an Empire Flex Camera to catch the mirror image of the model plane. The model crashing through the mirror simulates a head-on impact into the lens.

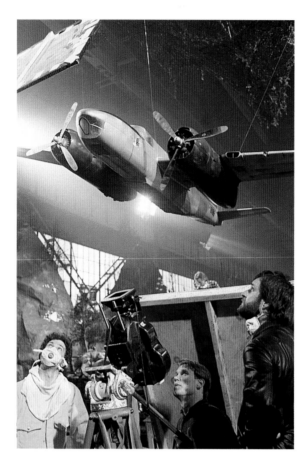

cars that were trying to follow and film the models from ground level. "We were trying to keep pace, to track these planes from our camera car, but when you're barreling down the runway at eighty-five mph, you run out of room real fast," Johnston said. "Remote control was starting to seem very dangerous. We had guys riding in the camera car using boards and sticks as baseball bats, to fight off the plane if it went out of control so that it wouldn't crash into us."

A planned tactic was using a piloted ultralight plane outfitted with a camera mount replacing the backseat for air-to-air shots. But the camera plane fared no better than the grounded camera cars in keeping pace with the speeding RC planes. The danger of the airborne models spinning out of control and crashing into the camera plane led the crew to abandon the air-camera option.

The final deathblow for the use of remote control came during tests for flying the mod-

els through smoke. A straightforward shot was arranged in which a plane would burst through a cloud of smoke and head straight down the runway toward the camera. The plane was positioned at the end of the runway, the area smoked up, and Johnston called for "Action."

"The plane flew into the cloud of smoke," recalled assistant director Ed Hirsh. "We waited and waited for what seemed like an hour, though it was probably only five or six seconds. When the plane finally came out, it was going straight up in the air, corkscrewing inside a tunnel of smoke. It went up, up, up, until it stalled and fell to the ground. That's when Jim Morris and Johnston pulled the plug on RC."

When the RC approach was abandoned, the crew turned to wires and cranes. Flying model airplanes from wire rigs was an art that had been developed by the Republic Pictures team of brothers Howard and Theodore Lydecker for the war pictures of the forties.

Spielberg himself had utilized the Lydecker system for the model airplane flying in his comedy *1941* (1979).

For the *Always* outdoor shoot, the main shooting setup featured a '58 Ford flatbed truck with a cantilevered crane arm mounted to the bed. The mount, developed by key grip Dick Dova, required a variable counterweight system to balance the huge boom, which had a one-hundred-foot reach from which either the VistaVision camera or the airplanes could be suspended. The wire rig itself was classic Lydecker, with balanced wire mounting points on both wings, the fuselage, and tail.

FIRE AND FLYING EFFECTS

The fire effects for ILM's scenes of planes fighting fire from above were cut with live-action scenes of firefighters at ground level. The full-scale, live-action fire work, engineered by physical effects supervisor Mike Wood and his crew, required construction of forty-one artificial, nonflammable trees more than thirty feet tall. The fake trees were

Left, top to bottom: A marionette rig flies the wire-suspended model plane into the fiery heart of the propane-stoked inferno.

Above left: The aftermath of the steel plant forest fire.

Above right: Joe Johnston gets the plane in his sights.

Right: Letting it rip, after a hard day of creating and putting out forest fires, are, left to right: Tony Sommers, Jack Haye, Bill George, and Keith London.

trucked to an already burned forest clearing in Montana, erected, and rigged with propane pipes to ignite the full-scale fire effect. With the help of the U.S. Forestry Service the fires, which required 15,000 gallons of propane gas, were set and stuntmen in the guise of firefighters interacted with the blaze.

Although the ILM blazes were staged in miniature, the crew was still dealing with fire—a powerful, sometimes uncontrollable element. The valley winds at the outdoor location often fanned the flames, or the smoke clouds created visibility problems for the production team. As a safety precaution for the Tracy shoot, a crew dressed in flame-resistant suits and equipped with fire-retardant materials patrolled the perimeters during each fire take.

ILM staged Dorinda's heroic night run at an old Bethlehem Steel manufacturing plant in San Francisco, a place that could withstand the heat of a miniature forest fire and, at five hundred feet long with a ceiling of seventy feet, was big enough to stage the action. The miniature landscape used in this shoot, built at ILM and transported to the location, measured 250 feet long by 30 feet wide and was constructed from a base of two-inch steel

pipe over which were wired fire-resistant one-by-fours covered by a thick foil that could then be painted and dressed with dirt and vermiculite. Once again, Christmas trees would create the forest, and they were inserted into a framework of steel tubes and wired to a steel support bar. As with the full-scale and outdoor fires, propane pipes were used to set the steel plant blaze.

Once the miniature forest was ignited and the planes were flying, the operators following the action in camera cars had only thirty seconds to capture the full visual power of a forest inferno before the trees were reduced to

In-camera formation shot of fire-fighting planes (a still from the film).

blackened stumps and steel support bars.

To fly the model aircraft, a team led by Dave Heron built an overhead track-mounted system from which was hung a marionette-style gantry rig capable of flying planes at thirty mph with a full range of yaw, pitch, and boom motions. "We had to get speed out of the plane," explained Heron. "But getting it to move fast was one thing; getting it to stop was another. We had a little problem the first day we tried flying the plane at thirty mph; [we had] this huge, empty warehouse with nothing inside but one forklift sitting all alone against the back wall—which we managed to crash our plane right into."

Given the potential dangers of a vast, enclosed space erupting with fire and smoke, trained pyrotechnicians were assigned to start the fires and another team was assigned to put out the blazes. But unlike the outdoor shoot in Tracy, the ILM crew did not have to battle unpredictable winds, so they could exert more control in the enclosed set environment. The building did have a few surprises—a few pigeons roosting in the high ceiling overcome by smoke and dropping to the floor, the heat causing sprinkler heads from a defunct sprinkler system installed in 1941 to pop out with such force that the crew momentarily thought the roof was collapsing—but there were no major setbacks or mishaps, and the night sequences were completed on schedule.

"This picture was a real highlight in my career, the most fun I've ever had making movies," said Johnston. "I was storyboarding what I wanted to see in the movie; I wasn't thinking about technique. And I got to fly my ultralight plane at dawn every day on location, see glorious sunrises, and get to the set by seven A.M. What more could I ask for in a summer job?"

THE HUNT FOR RED OCTOBER
1990 (Paramount)
Deep-sea Submarines

In 1984 Tom Clancy's novel *The Hunt for Red October* was a hot-button bestseller, a cold war thriller about a renegade Soviet

Above: Before ILM could create the underwater world and submarine action for *Hunt*, the model subs (created by outside contractor Greg Jein) had to be prepared for production, such as this twenty-one-foot *Red October* being detailed by Kim Smith.

Top left: Model makers Keith London (left) and Tony Sommers (right) add more of the detailing that give a model realistic scale.

Top right: Tony Sommers airbrushes a model.

naval captain who commandeers a doomsday nuclear submarine. A mere six years later the $35 million movie version of the book would be released into a world transformed by the policies of glasnost, perestroika, and the fading of tribal cold war hatreds.

But for director John McTiernan, *The Hunt for Red October* had the makings of a classic sea story, not a political propaganda piece. The hero, CIA bureaucrat Jack Ryan (Alec Baldwin), represented the archetypal youth who joins a ship and sails across a watery world of wonders and boundless adventure. Of course, unlike the old sea ships, the *Hunt* submarines had to voyage deep down into the proverbial darkness of Davy Jones's locker.

"My goal was total realism, except that would mean blackness—or would it?" McTiernan recalled of the early concerns of placing submarines—which have no external lights or portholes and travel blind by sonar—into the darkness at the bottom of the sea. "I was struggling with this conflict between realistic darkness and the need for an apparently sourceless light that could clearly show all the submarine action. And then I learned that in the great, dark depths of the ocean there are phosphorescent glowing microorganisms reflecting light onto particulate matter. I felt that could be the realistic justification for the subtle lighting on the submarines."

MODEL SUBMARINES: SCALE AND ENVIRONMENT

The models themselves would have to capture the spectacular dimensions of real submarines. The Soviet *Red October*, for example, was described in the novel as a modified Typhoon class ballistic missile sub 650 feet in length and weighing thirty thousand tons—nearly equal in size to a World War II aircraft carrier. Chasing the *Red*

October would be submarines half its size, the U.S.S. *Dallas*, a Los Angeles class ship, and the Soviet Alfa class *Konovalov*.

Although ILM had bid on the project, the work was initially awarded to Boss Films. Although Boss spent nearly a year on model making and effects preproduction, early Boss test footage did not meet with studio approval (although Boss would maintain it had delivered work according to its client's specifications) and ILM was brought on board in mid-October of 1989.

In the mercurial business of big-budget moviemaking, changing contractors was not unusual. Unfortunately for ILM, neither was it unusual for an effects house to be expected to provide miracles on short notice. The film's scheduled March 1990 opening was locked in: A month before release, the promotional campaign was scheduled to kick off with a Super Bowl halftime spot and full-page newspaper and magazine ads proclaiming "The Hunt Is On. 3–2–90." ILM had less than four months to produce fifty shots—about a third of the time the company had estimated for

completion during the original bidding process. For ILM effects supervisor Scott Squires and his key crew members, including cameraman Pat Sweeney and key grip chief Pat Fitzsimmons, the looming deadline obliterated the luxury of preproduction planning and required the *Hunt* team to produce an average of a finished shot every two days,

Above: Patrick Sweeney, visual effects director of photography, sees things through the camera eye.

Left: Although the largest *Red October* model was mounted on a pylon, most of the other models could be lifted up by motion-control crane arms and suspended from wires.

Above left: The stage is smoked as Bill Barr sits amid the underwater geologic spires of the deepsea canyon (created from wooden frames with sculpted latex skins).

Above right: Sweeney is illuminated from the glow of the overhead grid of lights in the "Fruit Bay" shooting stage.

Right: Setting up to send the *Red October* on a perilous route through an underwater canyon.

immediately ruling out time-consuming bluescreen photography and opticals.

ILM did receive all the Boss submarine models, stock footage, storyboards, and film tests. The submarines (built by model maker Greg Jein, a veteran of such films as *Close Encounters of the Third Kind*) had required nearly five months to design. Jein, an independent contractor hired by Boss, had worked from reference photographs and

input from active and retired navy submariners. National security concerns prevented complete accuracy—the antiecho tiles of the Los Angeles class subs could not be shown, for example—but the models were, nonetheless, faithful representations. The models also reflected an early decision that the submarines not be shot underwater but be designed to fit on motion-control pylons and motorized for rotatable propellers, sliding

hull doors, and other moving parts. Although those considerations dictated that the final models not exceed three hundred pounds each, they were still of impressive scale: two *Red October* submarines (one twenty-one-foot styrene model weighing 250 pounds, the other four feet long), a nine-foot *Konovalov*, two ten-foot *Dallas* attack subs, and a two-foot model of a rescue submersible. ILM model makers would contribute additional work, including a twelve-foot Fiberglas *Red October* finished off with a styrene tail and conning tower.

ILM decided to hang the submarine models on wires thin enough to be virtually invisible to the camera eye and fill a shooting stage with cracker smoke (a nontoxic mineral oil base) to create the murky look of the under-

water world. "The concept was to shoot real time with cameras on cranes, kind of a typical live-action situation," Squires said. "The idea was that the submarine footage generated on the stages, including the ships' wakes, the particulate matter, and the torpedo trails, would be given to computer graphics for enhancements. The hope was that computer graphics could add texture to the smoke and character to the subs that would make the sequence both unique and realistic."

The shooting stage had to be airtight to handle the smoke-fill effect, big enough to move the large models in scale to each other, and high enough for a lighting setup in the ceiling. The crew found its stage across San Francisco Bay, in an empty warehouse used to house fruit for summer storage. Located in an

The combination of a flying sub, smoky set, and the overhead "curtain of light" combines to simulate an underwater world.

industrial zone in the town of Richmond, the warehouse (dubbed "Fruit Bay" by the *Hunt* team) would be divided into two stage areas, with the main shooting stage comprising 15,000 square feet of floor space and twenty-nine feet from the floor to the rafters.

The crew's original plan to shoot live

Below: To fly the flying saucers of *Batteries Not Included*, Tad Krzanowski (pictured here) came up with a special wire rig able to pitch and roll a model but keep it in balance—which also proved perfect for the needs of the sub models in *Hunt*.

Right: The Krzanowski marionette rig in action on *Batteries*.

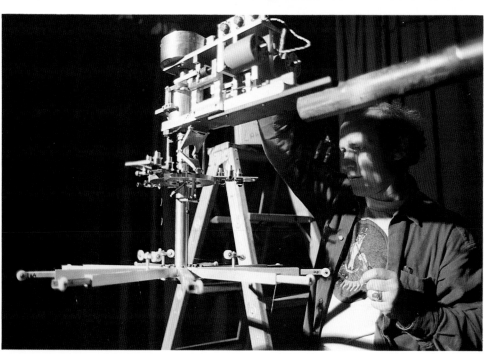

action gave way to motion-control photography when it became apparent that more control of the cameras and cranes was needed to capture the gargantuan scope and scale of the subs. "We changed from real-time live-action to motion control because there was no way to control the camera and crane to within an inch," recalled Pat Sweeney. "We had multiple ships that had to fly past one another and close to camera to create the drama and tension McTiernan was after. After a few nicks and bumps between camera and model, we realized motion control was the way to go. Plus, motion control had the added advantage of allowing us to get so close to the models that they would fill the screen and give the subs tremendous scale."

STONE AGE MOTION CONTROL AND FLYING RIGS

The changeover to motion-control photography involved a major reoutfitting of the Fruit Bay storage. In three weeks stage technician Joe Fulmer and his crew had to build twelve motion-control rigs to fly the models, accomplishing setups on the spot utilizing tape, clamps, and vise grips in the manner of a stagehand on location doing quick setups—"Stone Age motion control" Fulmer proudly called it.

The main flying rig, which could move one submarine model at a time, was a masterwork of motion-control technology and Stone Age grip work. A twelve-foot-high bank of scaffolding was anchored to the warehouse floor and a fifty-foot-long motion-control track was laid on top and secured. The actual device to move models along the track required a multi-ton Chapman crane arm to provide twenty-five feet of linear movement along the track. To mount it, the crane arm was taken off its normal Chapman base and secured to a motion-control base, an engineering feat that was safely executed in two days.

The Stone Age motion-control setup next required a flying wire rig that could be attached to the end of the crane arm. The device for suspending sub models required not only a separate motion-control mechanism allowing for pitch and roll but the means to keep a model in balance (since the slightest wobble of a suspended model would betray the illusion of a large underwater craft). Called in as consultant for the wire rigging design was Tad Krzanowski, who had designed a unique flying rig for *Batteries Not Included*. But while the *Batteries* setup had flown round spaceship models weighing only ten pounds, the *Hunt* rig had to control weighty and unwieldy conical submarine models.

Krzanowski's final design required four hanging wire points for the subs, with each point requiring three wires in a triangulate pattern to keep steady the suspended models. The wires were attached inside the models through thin holes in a threaded pin in the mounting bracket, allowing them to hook in and come out. After threading the hole the mounting bracket could be screwed down flush to the model's surface. To conduct the

programmed moves through the wires, a motion-control rotator affixed to the end of the crane arm transferred the moves through a gimbel—which Krzanowski likened to a helicopter swash blade—down through a four-foot square aluminum frame unit the crew dubbed "the star." The star, hanging halfway between the gimbel and the suspended model, spread the wires out and provided stability as the various tilt-and-roll moves were accomplished.

Since the main rig could only handle one sub at a time, a "floating scaffold" on wheels was built to handle additional models. At twelve feet tall and sixteen feet square, with a sixteen-foot motion-control track and crane arm on top, the scaffold was so large it required five crew members to push the rig in place and an additional person riding on top with the crane arm.

THE CURTAIN OF LIGHT

As complex as the flying rigs in *Hunt* was the lighting setup. Since the underwater environment precluded showing shafts of light

A model of the Soviet Alfa class *Konovalov* flies through a smoky set.

The *Red October* deep in the labyrinthine canyon passage.

and other direct illumination, Fitzsimmons and his crew opted for a diffused look, with hundreds of lights arranged along a grid network in the rafters. What Fitzsimmons called a "curtain of light" established a background lighting source, with clustered arrangements of middle and foreground lights providing different densities. The curtain was powered through 172 circuits, each circuit handling one or two lights that ran down through a multicable back to a theatrical-style dimmer board where the light intensity was manually controlled. Fitzsimmons marveled how dimmer operator R. A. Johnson "had to be kind of a Zen master to slide the lights smoothly and avoid a pop during the motion-control photography of the moving subs."

The lights, combined with the nontoxic cracker oil smoke filling the stage, provided the illusion of murky depths in which to fly the submarines. Although the effect allowed the team to accomplish shots in-camera, the downside was the time-consuming process of programming model moves in perfect synchronization with the smoke and lights. The smoke effect alone required forty minutes before two drums of cracker oil smoke could sufficiently cloud up the stage.

THE SHOOTING STAGE

Programming each shot was complicated given the task of providing the illusion of scale necessary for vessels McTiernan characterized as "cities underwater." According to Sweeney, half the shots had two subs in frame, requiring a fluid choreography of hanging subs in concert with moving camera dollies. Adding to the difficulty of setting up a shot was that the VistaVision cameras were too bulky to get closer than several inches to a model—translating, in Scott Squires's estimation, to the visual equivalent of being twenty-five feet above the deck of a real sub. To close those inches, and retain the sense of scale, mirrors were arranged at forty-five-degree angles above or below the camera lens, allowing the camera to read the image as the mirrors literally scraped model surfaces.

The sense of scale treaded the edge between the speed McTiernan desired for dramatic effect and ILM's concerns that six-hundred-foot ships could not appear to start, stop, and turn abruptly. "We usually shot three speeds—one slow, one medium, and one fast version," said Sweeney. "Once we were set up and lit, it was easy enough to give the director and editors a choice of speeds. Ultimately, we knew that McTiernan knew his movie a lot better than we did. Because of the way he built the tension in the live-action scenes, there was a real need to get these subs moving through that water. When I watched the movie, I really understood why he kept pushing us to move those subs faster. It wasn't realistic, but it was definitely dramatic."

A typical day at the Fruit Bay set would begin with morning setup and rigging for the models, and the lighting scheme and motion-control programming were completed in the

afternoon. Throughout the day fax or phone communications with the director would finalize specific shots. By 8:00 P.M. the crew was able to smoke the stage, start the camera, and sit back and watch the action. Shooting at a frame per second, the motion-control camera took an average of fifteen minutes to half an hour to record the programmed move, bringing to an end the long workday.

Some crew members devised ingenious methods for passing the seemingly interminable wait between setups. "We spent a lot of our dead time hitting golf balls from the parking lot onto abandoned train tracks," remembered Fitzsimmons. "We'd ride out on our bicycles to shag the golf balls, bring 'em back, and hit 'em again until we got the call to change the lighting."

An unexpected delay came in the form of the 7.1-magnitude earthquake that shook the Bay Area on October 17 shortly after 5:00 P.M. A hanging *Dallas* sub test model came off its wires and neatly cracked along the seams from nose to tail, and the twelve-foot *Red October* hit the ground and lost its styrene tail

Above left: *Hunt* model propellers, made by Marc Thorpe and Tony Sommers.

Left: Homing torpedoes are added to the action via blue-screen photography optically composited with ILM's "underwater" Fruit Bay footage. Here camera assistant Kate O'Neil programs a motion-control torpedo pass.

and conning tower. Despite several days lost to Fruit Bay safety inspections, there were no injuries, the model damage was easily repairable, and building inspectors allowed the production to proceed.

When the Fruit Bay shots were completed, computer graphics and the optical department added the final level of detailing. The computer graphics department scanned in plates and added undersea particulate matter created from particle-generating software, while opticals matted blue-screen shots of torpedo miniatures in front of computer-generated wakes.

By the end of ILM's work, the fifty-shot schedule had grown to seventy-two completed shots. But neither shot count, deadline, nor earthquake could stop the *Hunt*. Prerelease press conjectures that without real-life "evil empire" tensions the film would sink at the box office were proven wrong, as the movie was a critical success and brought in more than $70 million in gross domestic receipts in its first month.

Fruit Bay ultimately was razed by its owners, who decided that the earthshaken warehouse was no longer safe to store fruit.

FLIGHT OF THE *ENTERPRISE*

The crew of the Starship U.S.S. *Enterprise* began boldly going in search of new worlds and new civilizations as a 1966 television series. The original show *Star Trek* envisioned a "warp-powered" ship riding the cosmic seas, a starship with its components (a saucer-shaped primary hull for the bridge and main phasers, a secondary cylindrical hull, and twin propulsion units) built at the Star Fleet Division in San Francisco and assembled in space as a 947-foot, 190,000-ton vessel.

For the *Star Trek* movie series, which began in 1979, the U.S.S. *Enterprise* was realized as an eight-foot-long model (with an off-the-shelf model kit *Enterprise* repainted and used for long shots) built by a non-ILM vendor. For ILM's visual effects work on the series (which included sequels *II, III, IV, VI, VII*), the company had to work with all the models built for the first film, which included not only the *Enterprise* but a Klingon battle cruiser, a Regula space station, and the Vulcan shuttle—what model maker John Goodson laughingly called "the same models that have been handed down through the ages." ILM's model shop also produced significant models for each episode in the series: a Klingon warship and the *Reliant* for *Star Trek II*; the *Excelsior*, the Grissom research ship, and the Spacedock for *III*; and the Probe that opened *Star Trek IV*.

In *Star Trek III*, the *Enterprise* was destroyed, so even though the original model was being used for *IV*, it would be a "new" starship for story purposes. For the new installment an "A" was added to the Federation identification to characterize the new starship. Here model makers Eben Stromquist (left) and Larry Tan detail a blasted area of a large-scale model of the starship's dish.

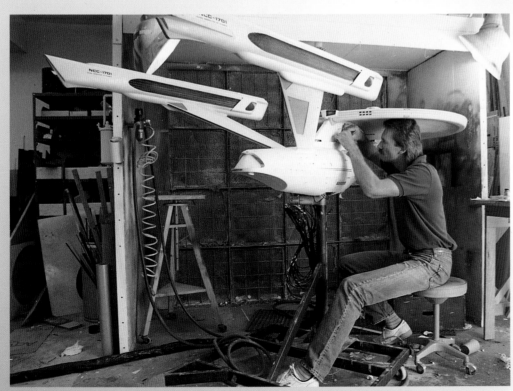

In *Star Trek IV*, ILM utilized the original *Enterprise* model for the production, which required special restorations and rewiring by Eric Christensen.

In terms of the models created for the first film, particularly the original *Enterprise*, the model crew was responsible for making the models ready so they could fulfill current requirements. "A lot of times you'll inherit a model that doesn't come with a power supply, so somebody has to go through all the wiring and figure out what the voltages are and how everything works," Goodson explained. "Every model has a bunch of wires that come out of it off-camera and which basically make the model work—running all the neon running lights and cooling fans. When we got the *Enterprise* back for *VI* [a New York company had taken on visual effects duty for sequel *V*], for some reason all the power cables had been hacked off! So we had this model that was more than a decade old and everything was sealed inside [without the access panels ILM usually builds into its own models]. So Jon Foreman, our electronics guy, had to sit down with the end of the umbilical, with stubs of like fifty wires that go to things in the ship, and figure out what every one of those lights was and rewire the whole thing."

In *Star Trek III: The Search for Spock* (1984), the *Enterprise* was destroyed. For the effect, ILM was not about to touch the venerable starship model, creating instead a separate saucer-shaped dish and a six-foot wooden model for the pyro work. For *Star Trek IV: The Voyage Home* (1986), an ostensibly new *Enterprise* was put into service, but for purposes of production, it was actually the original model. Refurbishments to the *Enterprise* included changing the famed NCC-1701 dish identifying lettering to NCC-1701-A, and giving it a new paint job to cover over laser hit effects from the previous installment (which had been simulated with a coating of rubber cement and airbrushed black patches).

The U.S.S. *Enterprise* had its last flight in the sixth *Star Trek* movie, *Star Trek VI: The Undiscovered Country*. For the next chapter, *Star Trek VII*, the Federation ship and crew of *Star Trek: The Next Generation* TV series would make the leap from television to the silver screen. ILM had built the *Next Generation Enterprise* (Federation ship NCC-1701-D) for its TV debut eight years before, a six-foot model that had been used until the fourth season, when it was replaced by a new, four-foot *Enterprise*.

The *Star Trek VII* movie debut would feature the original six-foot TV model. After four years of use in a weekly TV series and four years more in storage, however, the ship was in serious need of renovation. "Anytime you're using a model onstage it's real rough for them because they're being exposed to a lot of heat from the lights or they might get hit by the camera," said John Goodson. "The original

Next Generation ship was pretty well hammered. So we just went through it, rebuilt whatever was broken, cleaned up the windows, changed a little bit of the detailing, put a lot of new neon in it, and gave it a new paint job. It's like getting an old, wrinkled car and going through it and bringing it back up to museum quality."

In *Star Trek VII*, the *Enterprise* had to crash-land on a jungle planet, an effect that required the use of the old six-foot TV model, a specially built twelve-foot model of the *Enterprise* dish for the actual crash into a jungle planet set, and a digital matte painting effect for the crash aftermath. "There are still happy combinations between traditional and CG [computer graphics] effects," observed Jeff Olson, model and creature shop manager. "For

the crash of the *Enterprise* you have so many things in the landscape and vista. Anytime you have to move and give some specific three-dimensional geometry and see a perspective shift, a computer-generated, 3-D model requires layers and layers of very complex geometry. Although *Star Trek VII* has a lot of combinations of both CG and practical, we can dress a set and add a level of detailing that would take an incredible amount of time and expense to accomplish with a computer."

The alien jungle world was produced by the model department as an approximately forty-by-one-hundred-foot outdoor set on ILM's back lot. Over a plywood foundation rose Styrofoam mountains (ten feet at the lowest point) covered by approximately seven thousand square feet of used office

Orbiting space station and *Enterprise*.

The *Enterprise* and the *Excelsior* sail into the eternity of space in this ILM scene for *Star Trek VI.*

carpeting to provide a soft, rolling terrain. The whole set was then sprayed with foam, painted, and dressed out with ten thousand ten-to-fourteen-inch-tall dried plants, and processed dirt, powders, and moss laid to a depth of six to eight inches in the crash area.

A complex rigging was required to crash the twelve-foot *Enterprise* dish (originally discussed as an outsized twenty-four-foot model, which Goodson noted would

have been like bringing down a Cessna plane). What Goodson called a "ship-on-a-stick" rig was designed to allow two operators above the set to send the model down a pipe that went straight through the jungle set. Hidden within the set itself were a track and a cart for two additional operators that moved on a cable that extended from the set and was affixed to a pulling pickup truck. The interior set operators were each equipped with cable levers that

could manipulate the model through various controlled motions as it was dragged through the jungle set.

The traditional strength of matte paintings—the ability to realize expansive environments impossible to create as a set or difficult to produce as a location shoot—was used to reveal the grounded *Enterprise* and a miles-long path of fresh ground cleared of jungle by the skidding starship. The composite effect utilized

A convoy of Federation starships evacuate the *Enterprise* crew from the crashed saucer section in the final shot of *Star Trek VII*.

scanned-in footage of a motion-control stage element of the six-foot *Star Trek VII* model and a painting of the alien landscape. And because the matte department had been recast as a digital unit, the shot could be produced with a complex camera boom, tilt, and pan move, a freedom-of-camera movement impossible in the old days of brush, oils, and glass surfaces.

"We did a test to convince visual effects supervisor John Knoll that the painting would perfectly match the camera move and distortion change," matte artist Yusei Uesugi said. "Something like changing perspective was impossible to do in the

old optical process. For the shot we basically did a two-dimensional distortion to make it look three-dimensional. The biggest thing was the camera did an elevation change, which I represented by squeezing the vertical of the painting above the horizon line."

The old U.S.S. *Enterprise* model, retired after *Star Trek VI*, did make a triumphant tour of the Smithsonian Institution in Washington, D.C., before finally docking at Paramount Studios storage. With the *Star Trek VII Enterprise* presumably shipshape for future adventures, John Goodson made a sly addition to the model prior to crating

it up to send back to Paramount at the conclusion of *VII*, changing the ship's identification marking to NCC-1701-E.

"For me, *Star Trek* is real personal," Goodson revealed. "When I was five years old I used to watch the TV show and I was intrigued with the hardware—the spaceships, props, and sets. And from that time of watching *Star Trek* I always knew I wanted to work in film special effects. And *Star Trek* has been going on for thirty years and I've had the opportunity to actually work on it. I can't believe it. That just amazes me no end!"

CHAPTER FOUR

RETURN TO THE
CREATURE SHOP

There has always been a magic about making puppets, in taking inanimate materials and crafting a creature that will be given the illusion of life. The ILM creature shop, the setting for a modern incarnation of this age-old craft, was the place where the otherworldly rancor monster from *Jedi*, the dragon from *Dragonslayer*, and even the miniature but lifelike figures of Indiana Jones and friends in the mine-car chase in *Indiana Jones and the Temple of Doom* were created.

But in the digital age the creature shop would not be immune from the revolutionary wave of computer graphics technology upsetting the traditional effects crafts. For one, the computer-generated dinosaurs of *Jurassic Park* seemed to usurp the creature shop's traditional province as the place where monsters were made. The expansion of ILM's computer graphics (CG) division had also forced the creature and model departments to merge in 1991 and consolidate into one building on the

There goes Tokyo! Godzilla returns to his old haunt, ready for a basketball face-off with hoops superstar Charles Barkley, courtesy of ILM (with the creature a good old-fashioned man-in-a-suit).

Right: The creature known as Sardo is revealed in hellish flames in a scene from *The Golden Child*.

Below left: A traditional method of creating creatures has been with puppets, which necessitate machined, skeletonlike armatures to allow for realistic movements (such as the winged demon Sardo pictured here).

Below right: Sardo puppet, sculpted by Randal Dutra, awaiting its devilish wings.

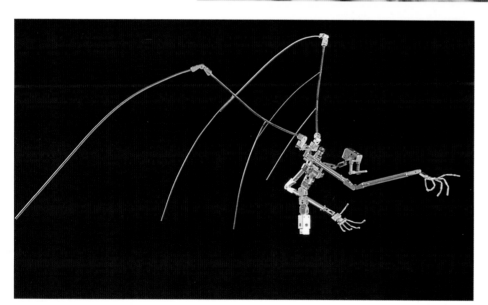

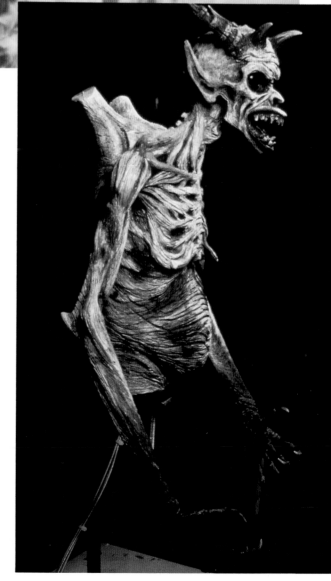

ILM lot. Model and creature shop department head Jeff Olson estimated the CG expansion cost them about seven thousand square feet, bringing the new department space to ten thousand square feet.

But, as Olson noted, the space still afforded plenty of room to handle the project-driven needs of the department, where work crews fluctuated from fifteen to forty people. ILM's growing commercial workload had proven a godsend to the new model and creature shop, according to Olson. With the short lead times and quick turnarounds required for advertising productions (many between three to six weeks), Olson's department was often the logical place to handle most assignments. And no matter the digital advances, Olson was not singing the blues; digital was just another gadget in the toolbox.

"A lot of times it's better to do a large creature, like a dinosaur, as a synthetic computer character," Olson observed. "However, there are many effects done more cheaply and effectively with traditional creature and model work. Actually, when you hear the word 'traditional,' it seems to imply old-fashioned, which we're not. For example, a lot of our architectural model buildings we used to cut out, mill, and machine, but now they're designed on a computer and then cut out on a laser cutter."

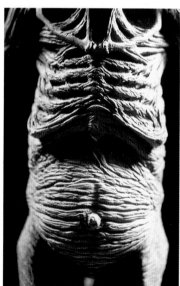

Top: Puppets can be animated with hand-held stop-motion techniques or as animatronic creations. Sculptor Randy Dutra tests the animatronic Sardo before its blue-screen debut.

Left: Terry Chostner (left) takes a light reading, while Bob Hill (right) adjusts the light level.

Above: Sardo puppet torso (detail).

Right: In *The Witches of Eastwick* Jack Nicholson plays the Devil, who answers the occult wish of some suburban witches. The ribald dalliances turn ugly, leading to his monstrous transformation. The sequence required several large-scale mechanical puppets designed by Rob Bottin's shop and a twenty-person puppeteering crew. Here director George Miller (left) discusses some animation details with ILM visual effects supervisor Michael Owens (far right), while a monster puppet looms over all.

Bottom right: One of the monstrous incarnations of Jack Nicholson designed by Rob Bottin's shop.

PUPPETS IN MOTION:
ANIMATRONICS TO STOP MOTION

Many of the modern methods for animating creatures employ a hybrid of tradition and cutting-edge technology. In the 1989 ghost-fest *Ghostbusters II*, the ghoulish Nunzio Scoleri was created as a ghost-suit, and lip synch was provided by a series of pneumatic cylinders in the lower jaw that were linked to the repeatable program of a computer. The Slimer, which had appeared in the first *Ghostbusters* (1984) as a cable-mechanized and directly puppeteered ghost creature, was rigged in the sequel with more complex remote-operated servo motors and pneumatics.

For a 1992 Nike shoe ad featuring a basketball duel between Godzilla and Phoenix Suns star Charles Barkley, the radioactive monster was realized as a near-seven-foot costume worn by an actor. The action was played out on the streets of a mythical Tokyo, a model department set where the twelve to fifteen 124th-scale buildings (filling a thirty-by-forty-foot space on ILM's main stage)

allowed Barkley and Godzilla to appear as tall as the skyscrapers. Godzilla, created out of lightweight latex and urethane foam, had three built-in levels of animation: radio-controlled eyes, cable-actuated lips and mouth, and the main movements provided by an actor wearing a suit.

One classic creature shop animation technique, dating back to such early work as Willis O'Brien's prehistoric monsters in *The Lost World* (First National Pictures, 1925) and his classic King Kong animation, had always been to create a puppet with armature and shoot it stop-motion. Building the creature would involve sculpting oil-based clay and laying it over the machined, skeletal armature to form the basic shape. A mold could then be made, the clay pulled out, the armature positioned back into the mold's hollow impression of the creature, and foam injected into the mold. The mold could then be baked in an oven, then dressed and made ready for camera.

The actual hands-on animation, in which a puppet is moved and filmed by each frame,

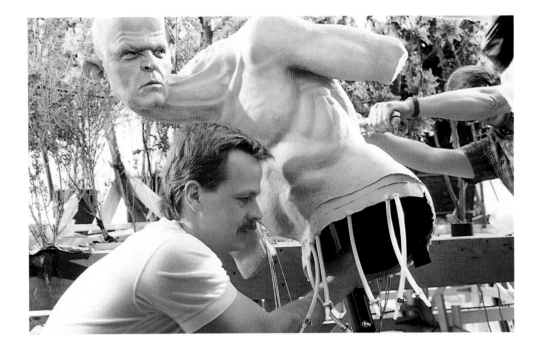

requires a superb sense of animation and an ability to go into a zone of ultimate patience. For Randal Dutra, who worked on *Willow* (1988), the sculpting and animation process was akin to the ancient, shamanistic practice of becoming an animal.

Dutra, a painter and sculptor of wildlife,

Above: ILM's Erik Jensen adjusts one of the mechanical puppets in preparation for a terrifying shot of the monster peering into a kitchen window.

Left: Puppeteers ready Monster Jack, while director George Miller checks out the interior set. To make the monster appear bigger, some of the puppets were used with miniature-scaled sets.

Above left: The final stage in the Jack Monster metamorphosis is this strange image of a childlike creature form filmed blue-screen, composited, and cut into the final sequence. Here Michael Owens checks the creature during the blue-screen work.

Above right: The final touch for the blue-screen child-creature is continuous footage of Nicholson's face projected onto the sculpted face, combining for a countenance both weirdly alien and strangely human. The effect was inspired by Disneyland's Haunted Mansion attraction, in which a real face was projected onto a puppet figure for a ghostly effect.

had developed his eye for creatures by tracking down and sketching prowling, grazing—and occasionally charging—animals in wilderness preserves in Canada. To him nature was the primary font of inspiration, providing insights that could be applied to even such fantastic monsters as the two-headed Eborsisk monster in *Willow*.

"After I read a script and see what a creature is called upon to do, I'll go into my mental isolation tank and think of the different types of creatures on that theme that could be designed," Dutra explained. "Some may be nightmarish, others more character-oriented; it depends on what physical actions it's called upon to do. Then, beyond that, there are considerations of whether it's supposed to be active or lethargic. Structure follows function or vice versa. Then you go about basing it on different types of animals—it could be mammals, reptiles, birds, or all three thrown together. On something like the two-headed Eborsisk, when you're going from a two-dimensional painting or drawing to the actual sculpting, you have to do things that will structurally accommodate the extra head."

ROCKET MAN AND SPACE ALIENS

A lifelike figure of the rocket-pack-charged character Cliff Secord (alias The Rocketeer) was created and stop-motion-animated for many of the flying sequences in *The Rocketeer*. The film, based on a comic-book character created by artist Dave Stevens in 1982, was a loving evocation of 1930s Los Angeles and the golden age of daredevil pilots.

The first unit had explored a number of practical methods for the flying scenes, including flying a stunt actor by wires from a helicopter, as well as blue-screen wire work. But none of those techniques seemed to capture the sound-breaking speed director Joe Johnston was after. Stop-motion animation of a Rocketeer puppet was opted for as the best method, with ILM motion-control camera operator Peter Daulton working with puppet

"EBORSISK"

Top left: The Eborsisk was created as a stop-motion puppet under the supervision of creature shop veteran Phil Tippett, pictured here. Tippett shared overall effects supervisory duties with Dennis Muren and Micheal McAlister. Adding to the realism on major moves was ILM's own go-motion technique, in which a puppet can be programmed to move during each frame exposure for realistic motion-blur.

Top right: In this Chris Evans production painting, the two-headed Eborsisk is pictured fighting for the evil Queen Bavmorda.

Middle: Creating a creature starts with a script and is first conjured up in the art department. In this early Dave Carson production illustration the two-headed Eborsisk went solo.

Left: Film of the fire-breathing creation in action (still from film).

Top: Concept studies for Vigo's transformation sequence in *Ghostbusters II.*

Middle: For his *Ghostbusters* return, the Slimer creature suit (here being worked by Camilla Henneman-Adan) would be provided with remote-operated servos and pneumatics to provide a wide range of facial expressions. (Despite the elaborate preparations, Slimer's appearances were limited to a few quick shots.)

Below: Slimer (with Robin Navlyt in the suit) takes the stage with Barbara Hartman-Jenichen (left) and Michael Owens (right) as creature project supervisor Tim Lawrence looks on.

animator Tom St. Amand to photograph an eighteen-inch Rocketeer puppet manipulated by hand and go-motion to provide motion-blur.

"The law of physics is a terrible thing in our business," observed *Rocketeer* visual effects supervisor Ken Ralston. "Actors get so uncomfortable when they're hung from wires. The puppet will do whatever you want it to and never complain, and you can get ultra-realism with motion control and stop motion. It's an advantage because you can plan the shot out like a dance number instead of just praying you get something by hanging the actor and using ten guys to try and turn him

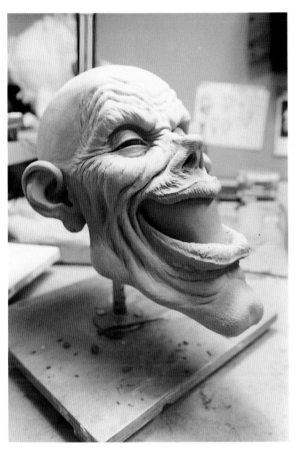

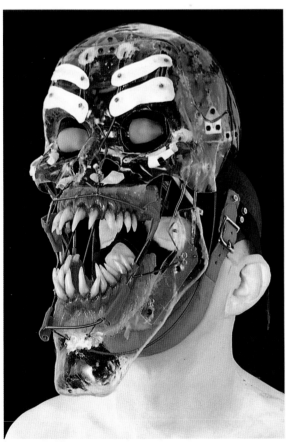

around. Good effects work is based on control. The more control you have on the shot, the better it turns out."

Even with the services of a stop-motion puppet Johnston demanded more speed in *Rocketeer*. "Joe kept saying, 'Faster, faster, faster.' He'd speed up the Moviola to make it bullet-fast," said ILM visual effects producer Patty Blau. "He really wanted to impart fear—to show a pilot who's totally out of control, with a bomb strapped to his back, going a hundred miles an hour."

Two thirds of the stop-motion workload— some twenty-one shots—would be featured in a loving re-creation of an old-time daredevil pilot show. The Bigelow's Air Circus sequence featured Cliff's friend Malcolm dressed in a clown suit and flying a rickety 1916 Standard biplane that begins to sputter out of control, necessitating a Rocketeer rescue. The sequence required a complex intercutting of live action and effects work. An actual air circus, complete with daredevil pilots flying vintage planes and extras crowding grandstands at a Santa Maria, California, location, was filmed and cut with stop-motion puppet work, practical flying work with Rocketeer stuntmen, and matte paintings and models to help create the environment.

Far left: The costume headpiece of the ghostly Tony Scoleri, ready for paint and detailing.

Above: Buzz Neidig provides detailing for final character head to be worn by actor Jim Fye.

Below left: Armature for Tony Scoleri headpiece. As with the character head for brother ghost Nunzio, much of Tony's head action was actuated with servos and pneumatic cylinders linked to a computer setup that allowed for convincing lip synch.

Near right: Howie Weed of the creature shop airbrushes an application of foam latex to the Nunzio Scoleri character head.

Far right: "I'm ready for my close-up, Mr. DeMille!"

Below left: Classic, hand-drawn animation techniques have been a traditional resource for adding everything from laser blasts and fairy dust to lightning bolts and electrical sparks. The Scoleris, originally fried via electric chair, reappear all charged up, with effects animator Kevin Kutchaver painstakingly drawing each spark on an enlarged frame from the blue-screen filming.

Below right: Nunzio (pictured here, with creature shop supervisor Tim Lawrence in the suit) and Tony Scoleri are hoisted into blue-screen position for flying scenes to be composited later.

The ghostly Scoleris, with animated electrical sparks and bolts (a still from the film).

In the 1993 film *Fire in the Sky*, the model and creature departments showed that even in the digital age, puppets and practical sets still had a place. Based on an actual 1975 incident in which an Arizona man named Travis Walton claimed he had been abducted by aliens and subjected to horrifying medical experiments in the alien spaceship, the movie had actor D. B. Sweeney in a practical spacecraft set realistically floating in the zero gravity environment, an effect achieved by flying the actor with wires and later digitally removing the flying rigs. The alien creatures themselves were designed and created by an ILM team that included visual effects supervisor Michael Owens, art director Harley Jessup, model and creature supervisor Jeff Mann, animatronics expert Guy Hudson, and sculptor Richard Miller.

A variety of puppet techniques produced the alien creatures, from rod puppets constructed from foam latex and vacu-formed pieces built over a light framework to articulated body parts moved by trigger controls for specific shots. An elderly alien character was realized as a fully articulated puppet whose face was sculpted to convey immense reservoirs of emotion with a minimum of movement.

Fire in the Sky was a rare in-camera experience for ILM, but the film's small budget prohibited extensive computer graphics and image processing technology. ILM's inventive practical effects, enhanced with digital wire removal, showed that film effects didn't have to be an exclusive product of the digital realm.

Jeff Olson mused that although the computer revolution would result in an attrition of models and creatures, they wouldn't disappear. "I think we'll see more of a marriage between models, creatures, and computer graphics, instead of a total domination," Olson observed. "There will continue to be

STATUE OF LIBERTY ON RAMPAGE - TWILIGHT

Above: In *Ghostbusters II* our heroes battle evil spirit forces by engaging the Statue of Liberty, brought to life after a dousing of positive slime. This production illustration imagines a possible visual composition.

Above right: For close-up shots of Liberty, which required special detail, a larger sculpted head and upper body were utilized.

Right: Sculptor Richard Miller works every fold of the Statue of Liberty suit.

Far right: To have the Goddess of Liberty lumbering through Manhattan required a number of different effects. For shots of the full-length statue a detailed suit was prepared to use for both blue-screen and practical photography of Liberty walking through a miniature Manhattan set. Here, performer Jim Fye (who also donned the Tony Scoleri suit) is transformed with the aid of Buzz Neidig.

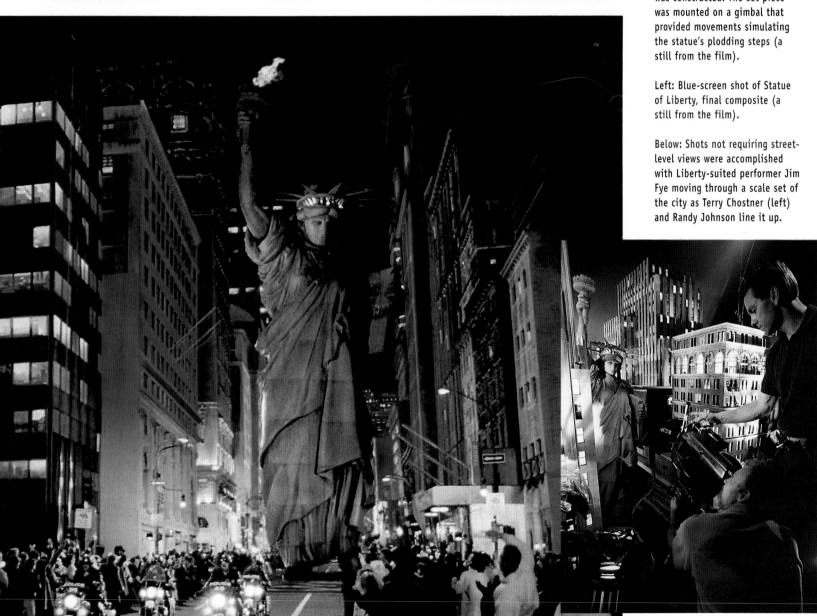

Above: To provide the illusion of the Ghostbusters commandeering the Statue of Liberty, a crown set—larger than normal scale to accommodate the performers—was constructed. The set piece was mounted on a gimbal that provided movements simulating the statue's plodding steps (a still from the film).

Left: Blue-screen shot of Statue of Liberty, final composite (a still from the film).

Below: Shots not requiring street-level views were accomplished with Liberty-suited performer Jim Fye moving through a scale set of the city as Terry Chostner (left) and Randy Johnson line it up.

many cases where it's quicker to build something and shoot it onstage, or to digitize the information from a physical sculpture or model. Ultimately, it's still the model makers' experience and skills that will count in the future, not just knowing the language of the computer. But at the same time, we're encouraging our people to get trained on computers. Obsolescence is not considered a viable option for this department."

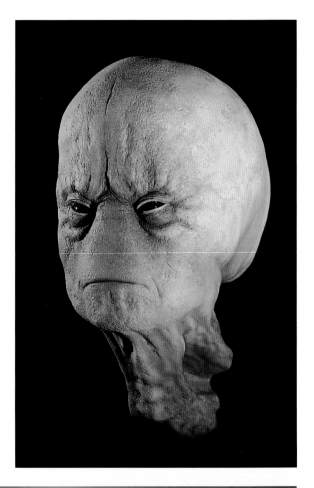

Top, left and right: In *Fire in the Sky*, based on a true report of an alien abduction, ILM not only produced a variety of extraterrestrial creature effects but designed the foreboding interior of the alien ship. Here, the stage crew prepares a chamber full of alien spacesuits.

Right: Jean Bolte (left) and Guy Hudson (right) set up a puppeteered extraterrestrial effect for *Fire in the Sky*.

This page: ILM's Nike "Barkley vs. Godzilla" shoe ad (directed by Michael Owens), featuring a face-off between Toho's famed Godzilla ("King of the Monsters") and pro and "Dream Team" Olympic Gold superstar Charles Barkley, was hyped with theatrical teaser ads prior to the TV campaign. ILM magic included the scale set and Godzilla suit.

Left: Barkley consoles a vanquished foe. (It *had* to be the shoes.)

Below: The two giants face off while ILM's Giovanni Donovan looks on.

DIRECT INPUT DEVICE: EVOLUTION IN STOP MOTION

When *The 7th Voyage of Sinbad* was released in 1958, the visual effects work of Ray Harryhausen was billed as the "Newest Movie-Making Miracle: Dynamation." This was the era when the movies were pulling out all the technical stops—with wide-screen formats like VistaVision, Cinerama, and CinemaScope, and such esoterica as 3-D—trying to create big-screen images impossible to realize on the black-and-white home TV set. "Dynamation," which produced the four-armed serpent woman, horned cyclops, fire-breathing dragon, and battling skeletons of *Sinbad*, was actually the venerable art of stop motion, the same technique used by animator Willis O'Brien in the RKO Radio Pictures classic *King Kong* (1933).

Stop motion had always been a hands-on art form, with animators performing precise manipulations of puppets to be filmed one or more frames at a time, producing the illusion of motion when filmed out. With the 1981 film *Dragonslayer*, ILM introduced the first real stop-motion innovation—"go-motion," which allowed puppets to be

Craig Hayes, Tippett Studio designer, poses with a DID raptor.

moved into position manually with computer-controlled rods attached to the puppets providing realistic motion-blur during the actual exposure. For *Jurassic Park*, ILM, in collaboration with Phil Tippett Studio, developed the "Direct Input Device" (DID), a motion-capture system linking traditional stop-motion talent with computer graphics technology.

The DIDs were created as individual dinosaur skeletal armatures equipped with a system of encoders at individual pivot points that could work with Silicon Graphics workstations (thanks to software developed by Brian Knep). When manipulated in stop-motion style, the encoders would translate the manipulations to the three-dimensional wire-frame models that were visible on the computer monitors.

Although the DID had the same look and feel as traditional armature, the device represented stop motion stripped to the basics; there was no need for perishable foam latex skins, sets, lights, or even cameras. The animator could manipulate the armature (without having to search for joint and pivot points as with traditional, skin-covered puppets) and record each pose as desired. The work of CG artists could then provide the physical layers of bone and muscle, skin and texture.

The DID was composed of three basic components: the physical armature, a controller box, and the computer software that enabled the manipulations to interface with the

The "Dinosaur Input Device" (later dubbed "Direct Input Device") created by ILM and the Phil Tippett Studio for *Jurassic Park* helped the creative team fuse the art of stop motion with the animation freedom possible in the digital realm.

digital realm. The special armature sensors, developed to monitor all possible rotations of movement around a joint, send digital signals to the controller box, which records the raw sensor data and translates it for the computer software. The controller box is composed of a series of plug-in boards capable of accommodating sixteen boards, each of which is able to monitor sixteen sensors; this allows the system to scale up to 256 sensors. The software then allows an exact match between the armature model and a computer model.

Unlike other systems for capturing motion—usually used for capturing the gross movements of an actor with computer-generated models—the DID was specifically designed for stop-motion artists. With the DID, animators were able to get instant feedback, from posed movement to screen display.

The DID would later be remarked upon as an essential technology in the creation of *Jurassic Park*. Four armatures were built—two for the Tyrannosaurus rex and two for the velociraptors. Of the fifty-two CG shots on *Jurassic Park*, fifteen would be animated with the DID.

BREAKTHROUGHS:
THEME PARK THRILLS

A few hours' drive south from San Francisco is the oceanfront town of Santa Cruz. On the beach is the Boardwalk, the oldest and only remaining seaside amusement park in California. There the Giant Dipper roller coaster, the main attraction since the park's opening in 1924, still thrills visitors who ride its five thousand feet of twisting, turning track. At its opening, local advertisements called the roller coaster "a wonderful kick from start to finish" and enthused about the hundreds of thousands of feet of board lumber, the thousands of gallons of paint, even the 21,680 screws used in the ride's construction.

Light-years beyond the dizzy diversions of the past are the modern movie-and-motion simulator rides. Whether sitting in a darkened theater or enclosed in a vehicular mock-up, these rides synch up actual mechanical motion with film images, creating the illusion of a direct experience of the fantastic. The simulator ride is a phenomenon that has remade Las Vegas into a theme park city and has revolutionized attractions from Walt Disney World to Universal Studios. Industrial Light & Magic helped usher in the simulator ride experience in 1987, when Lucasfilm and the Walt Disney Company joined forces to create a *Star Wars*–themed thrill-ride experience.

ILM's early theme park work would include a Disney partnership to produce a different kind of thrill-ride attraction: *Captain EO*, a 3-D outer-space fantasy movie starring pop star Michael Jackson as the savior of the universe. The attraction had been a major corporate and technological production, involving the cooperation of Walt Disney, Kodak, and George Lucas to produce a $20 million, seventeen-minute, 70mm 3-D movie.

Captain EO opened at Disneyland in 1986 with a parade of celebrities down Main Street arriving at the specially built seven-hundred-seat 3-D theater for a ribbon-cutting ceremony presided over by *EO* producer George Lucas, director Francis Ford Coppola, costar Anjelica Huston, and a frenzied crush of 1,400 guests jostling to be the first in the

Pop star Michael Jackson starred as Captain EO in the popular and long-running Disney 3-D film theme park attraction.

Far right: ILM provided *EO*'s spaceships and much of the blue-screen composite work for the *EO* experience.

Near right: Model shop supervisor Steve Gawley details the shuttle station that would be filmed by ILM as an audience point of view for the Disneyland simulator ride *Star Tours*. The attraction was not only a follow-up on the Lucasfilm/Disney *EO* team-up (although based this time on George Lucas's beloved *Star Wars* characters) but a breakthrough fusion of film and theme park ride.

Below: Effects cameraman Scott Farrar tends to a motion-control camera pass of a miniature Death Star set for *Star Tours*.

universe to have the experience. It was a true celebrity event with the only missing guest being Michael Jackson himself, although there were unfounded rumors that Jackson had come to the event disguised as an old woman. Disneyland further celebrated *Captain EO* by keeping the park open around the clock for sixty straight hours.

On Friday, February 26, 1994, a Disney spokesman announced that *Captain EO*, which had become one of the most popular attractions at Disneyland and Walt Disney

World, would be pulled by autumn of that year and replaced with a new show entitled *Honey, I Shrunk the Theater*. But in its day *EO* marked the beginning of a thematic and technological evolution of the amusement park experience that would usher in the new medium of simulator rides.

STAR TOURS
1987 (Disney/Lucasfilm Ltd.)
Disneyland Simulator Ride

When Rediffusion Motion Platform in England began manufacturing hydraulically powered motion-base simulators, the company had no idea it would be producing equipment for American amusement park rides. Its simulators were first produced exclusively for training military and commercial pilots.

The idea of fusing film and motion plat-

forms had been pioneered by *2001* effects wizard Douglas Trumbull, who produced some prototypical "dark rides" (in which customers in mechanical or other conveyances rode through an enclosed attraction) that utilized simulators and his own Showscan process, a big-screen format in which 70mm film could be projected at sixty frames per second to produce a realistic, wide-screen effect.

The Disney organization was entranced by the possibilities of simulator-ride attractions and entered into negotiations with George Lucas about ride films based on his *Star Wars* and Indiana Jones properties. The resulting *Star Tours*, based on the outer-space adventures of the *Star Wars* films, was a partnership between the effects wizards at Lucasfilm's Industrial Light & Magic, which would produce the ride film, and Disney's Walt Disney Imagineering (WDI), which would program the Rediffusion Motion Platform. ILM and WDI agreed they wanted a roller-coaster approach that featured big-thrill moments connected with pauses that allowed riders to catch their collective breaths and anticipate the next big jolt of action.

For ILM the *Star Tours* ride film was a new experience, completely different from producing multi-second effects shots to cut into a movie. This was a new medium, in essence 3.5 minutes of pure visual effects that would have to tell a story. But the first item on the preproduction agenda was trying to *find* the story.

"We were going everywhere in the *Star Wars* universe in those first story outlines," said Dave Carson, who would share simulator co-supervisor credit with Dennis Muren, who directed the overall effort. "There seems to be a common mistake in ride films to attempt a preposterous amount of action in four or five minutes. Finally, George [Lucas] got everybody together in one room and he picked ideas from all the different outlines. He felt that most people have a great deal of curiosity about what goes on behind the scenes. That led to the concept of a rookie pilot taking a

wrong turn and going behind the scenes to embark on a crazy adventure."

The film was divided into ten separate visual effects scenes, which were disguised with the photographic trickery of blinding laser blasts and explosions. Some cuts borrowed the moviemaking technique of a wipe, a transition between scenes in which one image completely replaces another, filling the frame in the process.

Top: Richard Vander Wende paints a wide horizon shot of the Death Star, one of several effects used to depict the Imperial stronghold.

Bottom: *Star Tours* Death Star set painting (detail).

A *Star Tours* audience point of view: a dizzying dive through the Death Star. "As the pioneer of simulator rides, we had to devise clever techniques to hide the cut points, such as an X-wing obscuring the lens for a frame or a white flash frame from an explosion," explained Dennis Muren. "We'd used many of these tricks in the *Star Wars* series to get through a four-second shot—this time, it was a four-minute shot!"

Once Carson storyboarded the ride, Muren determined that an animatic (or videomatic, a sketchy simulation of a scene in which storyboards, drawings, or other visual cues are photographed) was necessary for the production. While optional on most of ILM's projects, animatics (produced as computer-generated wire-frame storyboard images) were crucial in enabling the Imagineering crew to program the motion base to match ILM's visuals.

According to ILM producer Ned Gorman, the *Star Tours* ride film represented an opportunity for ILMers to revisit the *Star Wars* universe, and in fact utilize some of the same models and effects tricks developed during what Gorman calls "the full-blossom of the photochemical age" of the original space trilogy. In the process the *Star Tours* team pushed for a visual experience that would not rely on motion platforms to provide the sole sensation of movement.

The attraction was realized as separate forty-passenger simulator platforms linked to 70mm film projection. The result was a sensation. For many fans it was the difference between viewing and actually experiencing a movie. "The whole popularity of 'ride-the-movies' theme park attractions came out of *Star Tours*," Gorman observed.

The success of *Star Tours* would lead to another production partnership between ILM and Disney: the journey into the human bloodstream called *Body Wars*.

BODY WARS
1989 (Disney)
Walt Disney World Epcot Center Simulator Ride

Innerspace won ILM a 1987 Academy Award for Best Visual Effects for creating the look of a submersible pod and pilot miniaturized and injected into a human bloodstream. A similar voyage into a human bloodstream, with cold war overtones, had been done for the 1966 movie *Fantastic Voyage*.

The idea from *Innerspace* was staged as a simulator-ride experience in *Body Wars*. The ride story featured a female doctor who has left the inner-body craft in scuba gear to investigate a splinter punctured through the host's skin and is suddenly swept away in the bloodstream, with the resulting thrill-ride rescue attempt.

The practical effects for *Body Wars* had been previously developed for the Oscar-winning effects of *Innerspace*, in which some

forty-one scenes were achieved in-camera with more than eighty pod models (ranging from four inches to two feet in length) used in translucent water tank sets.

The bloodstream for *Innerspace* was accomplished with a forty-foot-long-by-one-foot-round translucent tube submerged in circulating water with thousands of molded plastic blood cells floating through the set. For *Body Wars* it was decided to create the bloodstream as hundreds of computer-generated disks flowing through the veins. Once rendered, the CG blood-cell elements were then recorded out to film and delivered to optical for final compositing.

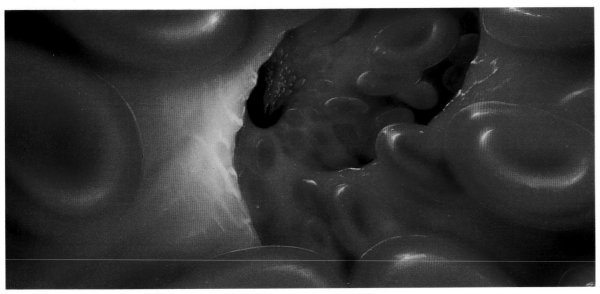

Body Wars would utilize the same simulator ride and film technique as *Star Tours*—only this new Disney attraction would be a miniaturized voyage through the human bloodstream. These early ILM production drawings by Kathy Swain envisioned a scuba-gear-clad explorer and blood cell formations.

Near right: Final set depicting the heart ventricles.

Far right: Blue-screen elements of nerve cells for the brain.

Below left: Pat Sweeney sets up motion-control camera view of heart chambers.

Below right: Model maker Cameron Noble works a large skin section that will be filmed and composited with a blue-screened scuba diver.

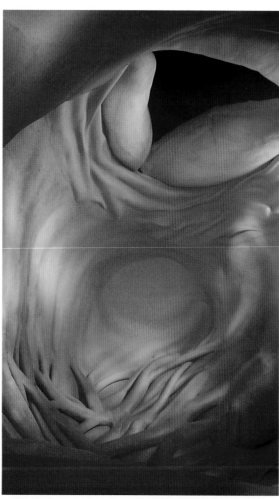

"The *Body Wars* CG blood cells looked good for their day, but not as good as we'd do them now," observed Ned Gorman, *Innerspace* visual effects manager. "Doing the bloodstream practically for *Innerspace* had a realism and immediacy to it, as if a miniature guy was shooting it. At the time pulling mattes would have been problematic, and Dennis [Muren, visual effects supervisor] wanted to do it in-camera. But for both the movie and ride film you have to take liberties, without sacrificing the mystery. For example, obviously there's no light source inside the human body; every light source was unjustifiable, so in reality you wouldn't be able to film. So you have to design anatomy and come up with a lighting scheme that doesn't take the audience out of the movie."

Body Wars, envisioned as an awe-inspiring celebration of the mysteries of the human body, marked the first show in which ILM integrated multiple computer-generated

elements into optical composites. The production also required the biggest motion-control stage setups then conducted at ILM. Some of the set construction representing the circula-

In the "ride film" approach for *Body Wars*, the audience enters a closed shuttle craft. Once seated and "miniaturized" the participants watch a view screen purporting to show the bloodstream the ship is traveling through (with the visuals working in concert with the movements of the simulators). At ILM, the footage was created with huge sets . . .

. . . that combined, in this scene, blue-screen shots of a scuba-suited woman who has left the craft to investigate a splinter that has punctured the host's skin.

Above: Dennis Quaid in the process of becoming microscopic in *Innerspace*, which won the 1987 Academy Award for Best Visual Effects.

Above far right: Erik Jensen (left) and Brad Jerrell prepare the bloodstream pod for a blue-screen shot on *Innerspace*.

Right: Although the bloodstream for *Body Wars* would utilize CG blood cells, *Innerspace* produced its blood flow with a forty-foot-long translucent tube that circulated water and blood cells.

tory system, heart, lungs, and brain was built with two-by-fours and chicken wire. "Sometimes it's industrial," Dave Carson would slyly recall of the construction, "and sometimes it's magic."

SPACE RACE
1991 (Showscan)
Simulator Ride

Effects pioneer Douglas Trumbull had always felt the normal flat-motion picture image suffered from the strobe, flicker, blur, and film grain inherent in the standard format of 35mm film projected at twenty-four frames per second. Trumbull developed his Showscan system—70mm film projected at 60 FPS—in the early eighties as the optimum way of producing an almost three-dimensional big-screen image.

Showscan Corporation, which patented Trumbull's process, provided the next simulator ride film opportunity by inviting ILM to develop *Space Race*, a ride that would eventually play at Showscan venues in some seven countries. The team assigned to the Showscan ride film included ILM producer Ned Gorman, director Scott Squires, art director TyRuben Ellingson, model supervisor Larry Tan, and motion-control photographer Peter Daulton.

Left: The miniature pod of *Innerspace*, created as a blue-screen element for its travels in the human bloodstream, moves through one of many practical re-creations (such as Jell-O casts in water for fat cells). According to supervisor Dennis Muren, the approach was to create a documentary look, as if a tiny camera-man were filming a truly fantastic voyage.

Below: Models and miniature sets usually require precise blue-prints, such as these plans (designed by Bill George and drawn by Jim Poole) for the enemy pod that is miniaturized in *Innerspace*.

"I wrote the original story for *Space Race*, which was inspired by an alluring disco I had visited one night in a remote village in Spain while scouting locations for *Empire of the Sun*—it was the idea of this place in the middle of nowhere where everybody gathers on a Saturday night—and a fifties L.A. TV show called *Jalopy Derby*, updated of course," Dennis Muren noted. "It [the *Space Race* project] was extremely low-budget, and the story was written to work with that in mind."

One of the unusual aspects of *Space Race* was that despite digital graphics and imaging being in ascendance at ILM, not a single frame of ride film would be touched by any manner of digital manipulation. Gorman, for one, refers to this ride film as the last totally optical and photochemical show to pass through ILM. The show was a grand celebration of traditional know-how, with all the motion-control stages booked, the model department working full-tilt, and the optical department handling all the compositing. As if to underline its status as the last of the completely industrial effects at ILM, the design of *Space Race* featured a collection of hot rod,

heavy-metal spaceships racing each other through an outer-space obstacle course.

"*Space Race* is a big old jalopy that didn't try to be sophisticated," Ellingson explained. "Our goal was to give it an MTV-type of youthful spirit. It has a bad-boy attitude with a heavy-metal scorching guitar sound track

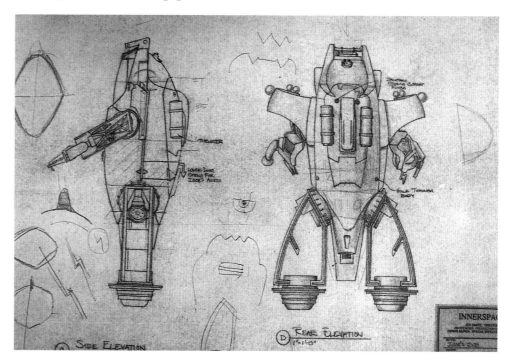

Larry Tan prepares the enemy pod from *Innerspace* for blue-screen duty.

that's boisterous and aggressive. At one point we needed additional set pieces to fill out a pit-stop scene. In desperation, I went behind our pyro bay and pulled pipes out of a ditch and used those to dress the set. We borrowed and scavenged all kinds of props; anything we found that wasn't nailed down became part of our ride. Sometimes strict limitations can actually increase creativity. Knowing that our time and resources were restricted caused all of us to formulate a kind of guerrilla production mentality that forced us to look for new and innovative solutions."

As with *Star Tours* a few years before, *Space Race* would emphasize the movie, not merely the mechanics of motion, in creating the illusion of frenzied spaceflight. "I usually can't ride motion bases because I have lower-back problems, so I'd tell the guys in dailies to make me dizzy with the actual film alone," Gorman laughed. "So the film alone should give you the sense of vertiginous heights and

thrills. The ride shouldn't *rely* on the motion base; the motion base should *enhance* the experience."

The featured set was an eighty-foot, candy-cane-shaped motion-control track that could be struck in a variety of configurations for moving the models while an adjacent track camera filmed the action. The *Space Race* crew did utilize a little high tech in creating wire-frame animatics of the entire race to work out the exact choreography, but the effects were all from the bag of tricks ILM had been developing in the decade following the first *Star Wars*.

"From 1979 through 1986 our arsenal of in-camera gags got very sophisticated," observed Ned Gorman. "For example, there was a shot in *Space Race* where the ship carrying the audience's point of view goes through an explosion. We achieved that as a separate pass by rear projecting a stock explosion frame by frame, like a slide show, on a white card positioned on the model. We just turned off the lights and double-exposed the white-card projection. It's a little stage gag we used on a shot in *Jedi* where a Star Destroyer crashes into the Death Star."

Gorman wistfully reflected on the old industrial age of effects from a vantage point in the post–*Jurassic Park* era: "There's quite a bag of tricks that don't translate to digital technology—tricks like the white-card projection to add explosions. My office is in one of the old optical lineup rooms. Opticals used to be the hub of everything, but with the coming of digital it's become like a ghost town. It's a little like when talkies came in and ended the silent movie era; people then felt there was so much more that could have been explored in a silent medium."

CHAPTER FIVE

PAINTED FILM

When Wilfred Buckland, considered Hollywood's first great art director, left New York for Hollywood in 1913 he was preceded by the renown he had gained as an accomplished Broadway art director (and by the invitation of his old friend Beatrice DeMille, mother of Cecil B.). Early on, when he had begun work for director DeMille, he was asked why he had left the New York stage for Hollywood. He gestured across open fields to the mountains and said, "You see, this is the first time in my life I ever had a stage big enough to work on."

Buckland recognized that unlike theater, the movies could be created without regard to time and space. Seeking the medium's full advantage, he introduced such innovations as klieg lights, allowing action to be staged indoors rather than limited to outdoor locations or sunshine-lit stages. Buckland, interested in any effect that could allow an inner vision to be registered on film, was also, in his words, "seeking an opportunity to picturize in a more 'painter-like' manner, supplying to motion pictures the same rules which govern the higher art of painting."[1]

Buckland and other artistic pioneers literally painted with film, integrating two-dimensional glass-shot matte paintings with live-action elements. Matte painting has been used by directors from Cecil B. DeMille and Alfred Hitchcock to George Lucas and Steven Spielberg, becoming a valuable resource for not only "effects" films but classic dramas

1. Thames Television, *The Art of Hollywood: Fifty Years of Art Direction* (Thames Television Ltd., 1979), p. 15.

With strokes and dabs of brush and oils, matte painters conjure up entire environments. *Willow*, with its fantasy story line and mythic landscapes, is one of the showcase examples of this unsung art form. The creation of the village of Nelwyn, with its surrounding mountains inspired by the limestone formations of Kweilin, a region in southern China, began with this preproduction concept by Chris Evans.

Below left: The final painting of the Nelwyn village, produced by Chris Evans.

Below right: Detail of Nelwyn village (black areas to be composited with live-action footage).

Bottom: Final Nelwyn village composite. The shot began tight on the village and pulled back to reveal the entire valley.

such as *Citizen Kane*, *Gone With the Wind*, and *North by Northwest*—to name but three out of hundreds of examples.

Matte painting has always given filmmakers creative control. Instead of traveling to a distant location, waiting for nature to provide the desired atmospheric visuals, building expensive sets, or constructing miniature models, the filmmaker simply can turn to the unsung matte painter, who can provide the desired image with a few brushstrokes. Matte painting has had all the trappings of traditional painting—brush and oils on glass, canvas, or another flat surface—but it has always been a unique art form in which the projected film frame is the ultimate canvas and the big screen of a movie theater the exhibition venue.

PAINTING ILLUSIONS OF REALITY

Chris Evans, an early member of ILM's matte painting department, compared the secret of a successful matte painting to a magician's sleight of hand: "The magician moves his wand to divert attention while the other hand does the trick. With the matte artist, the live-action plate is the diverting, moving wand, and the painting is the trick hand. A matte artist doesn't just push paint around. He or she is essentially the director of photography and the production designer on the shot. Composition and lighting are the keys to a good matte shot."

"The matte artist is always imitating natural phenomena," added artist Mark Sullivan. "Virtually every matte painting I've ever done has required me to go on location to take photographs of the colors and textures of real life. You learn so much from nature. Artists need to learn it from the inside out—kind of like an actor who becomes a character. Creating these illusions is like counterfeiting—and a good counterfeiter has to spend a lot of time looking at the real thing."

The matte painter must strive for realism, an obvious requirement when the assignment is to paint the background buildings of a city panorama or a pastoral landscape. But a painting of a fantastic environment must have the same illusion of realism. If the primeval jungle of, say, *King Kong* is not rendered realistically, the illusion stands revealed and audiences, who are supposed to leave disbelief at the door and settle into the world of the filmmaker's imagining, snap out of the reverie. This quality of realism is not achieved through a photorealistic but an impressionistic painting approach, ignoring the busy details and sharply defined look for the over-

Above: Willow's adventure begins as he and a small band leave the valley of Nelwyn to return a baby girl (actually an endangered princess) to the outside world. This Chris Evans preproduction painting worked out a farewell look for Willow's band.

Below: Artist Chris Evans, who supervised the film's matte paintings, checks out a series of test exposures designed to match the live-action footage. The final painting would be accomplished as a "latent-image" composite, in which live-action film photographed with the desired portion of the lens blacked out by painted glass, would be rewound and the black part of the frame filled with a matte painting exposure. This in-camera technique traditionally bypassed opticals for a first-generation quality image.

Directly above: Live-action plate exposure; masked area reserved for a matte painting of Nelwyn valley.

Top: Final latent-image composite.

Top right: Lining up placement of a matte line on a VistaVision camera lens for a latent-image *Willow* shot are Chris Evans (left), Wade Childress (center), and Craig Barron.

all impression, one that the moving picture audience can quickly read as real.

To add to their realism, most matte paintings have been realized as composite effects combining live-action elements. This integration of live-action elements is a time-honored way of convincing audiences they are looking at a real environment, not a painted illusion. The fusion of painted and live film into one image

has traditionally been accomplished with a variety of techniques: in-camera glass shots (in which the dimensions of a background set are extended by a glass painting placed between set and camera and perceived by the camera eye as one image when perfectly lined up), rear and front projection (in which previously filmed images are projected onto an area of a glass painting and filmed), and latent image (in which live action is shot with part of the picture blacked out, the film rewound and then used to shoot a painting, blending the two elements in a high-quality first-generation effect).

Another level of illusion is integrating live-action elements within the painting itself. In a film such as *Hook*, in which traditional oil and acrylic matte paintings were featured throughout, the matte department precomposited an establishing shot of Neverland island with live plates of waterfalls and real ocean breakers hitting the painted shore.

Although the matte department would completely transform from brush and oils to the cursor and software of a digital setup by 1992, the department had always been inventing new techniques to expand the traditional craft. Michael Angelo Pangrazio (on staff from 1978 to 1985) was the first painter at ILM to use a slide projector to project pictures onto his easel as a reference. Pangrazio also utilized the "cut-and-paste" technique pioneered by earlier matte artists, a shortcut in which actual photographs, blown up to the appropriate size, could be attached to a painting's surface to save time and add to the overall realism.

The long-lost art of incorporating models and miniatures with paintings was revived by

ILM in the early *Star Wars* era and refined in the ensuing years. "The thing about matte painting is that you have to make decisions on every little detail," noted Paul Huston, a model maker who joined the matte painting department during the making of *Return of the Jedi*. "Every stroke influences the value, color, edges, lighting—and every decision has to be right or the painting will look wrong. If you photograph a model, then all those decisions are made for you. The strength of using a miniature is that it can be lit, the lighting can be changed, and we can do camera moves on it because perspectives will change when you move on a three-dimensional object. The strength of painting is that there's no better way to capture the atmospheric lighting of distant scenes. By combining the two disciplines, we frequently create our best shots."

Left: For *The Golden Child*, Chris Evans (right) adds the final detailing to a Tibetan monastery model to be shot with a painted background, while Craig Barron checks the lighting designed to highlight the monastery. Evans, Barron, Michael Pangrazio, and others in the ILM matte department continued the old tradition of integrating models and paintings for a 3-D effect.

Below: Final scene with the model, painted background, and live-action foreground. To add further realism, a background moving cloud element was provided with paint and cotton on glass placed on motion-control movers.

The Automatte Camera

A motion-control, multiplane camera built in 1980 called the Automatte helped integrate *Jedi* models and matte paintings and allowed for more complex camera moves than were previously possible. "The rule in matte painting photography for a hundred years had been to never move the camera, to actually bolt it down," said Bruce Walters, a trained animation and effects cameraman who helped rebuild the Automatte. "My expe-

Top: Rough layout for the interior of *The Golden Child* monastery.

Middle left and right: Matte painter Caroleen Green begins painting with a reference photo of the live-action plate shot by Craig Barron on set at Paramount.

Bottom: The live-action plate of the monks was flopped to make a second line of monks, a forerunner of the digital crowd-replication techniques to come.

A car approaches a fatal car accident in this pivotal ILM shot from *The Doors*. The elements included live-action shot with a hand-held camera from the backseat of a bouncing car through the windshield to the foreground road, with a Mark Sullivan painting of the background hills and sky. Department supervisor Bruce Walters had the multiplane Automatte camera upgraded to allow camera operator Charlie Clavadetscher to track the subtle perspective shift from the moving car and the two-dimensional paintings, making this ILM's first match-move motion-control matte shot.

rience had always been with motion-control cameras, so we began experimenting with fairly radical moves on matte painting shots."

The multiplane facet of the Automatte had an industrial lineage that went back a half a century to the multiplane setup perfected by Walt Disney Studios for the Oscar–winning cartoon short *The Old Mill* (1937), an atmospheric piece set in the ruins of an old windmill: As a dreamy twilight turns into night, a sudden thunderstorm shakes the windmill and the birds and animals living therein, until the storm passes with the dawn and all becomes right with the world. The achievement of the film was that the animators—handicapped as matte painters were by trying to give dimensionality to two-dimensional art—achieved an illusion of depth, thanks to the multiplane setup in which layers of glass-sheet artwork could be horizontally placed and photographed by a vertically mounted, downward-shooting camera. The use of the invention was limited due

to its expense (few animation houses other than Disney could afford the setup) and unwieldy size (Disney's camera was some fifteen feet tall).

The ILM Automatte worked much like the old Disney multiplane in concept, except the device was a fifty-foot-long, horizontal multiplane setup along the camera track. The multiplane did have the advantage of repeatable and programmable motions from its sixteen-channel computerized motion-control system. Foreground miniatures and sets could also be placed in front of the paintings, allowing the camera to register perspective shifts on three-dimensional foreground objects, adding to the illusion of depth for the overall image. Walters, engineer Mike Bolles, and electronics technician Mike MacKenzie updated the motion-control functions prior to *Hook* in 1991 so the device could work with animation and effects camera systems as well as allow for sophisticated moving-camera matte shots.

Right: For *The Rocketeer*, matte artist Mark Sullivan begins to paint a sprawling aerial view of thirties-era Los Angeles. Sullivan first created and photographed a street mock-up using some three hundred wooden blocks for buildings, projected the image on a drawing surface, and drew it out. The resulting drawing was projected onto a painting surface for the rendering phase.

Below: The final, matte-painted effects scene from the film, with the Rocketeer blasting up into the sky. (The rocket-pack flame is visible at right center.) This is only a section of what was a nineteen-foot-long, six-foot-tall painting rendering two planned cuts—the L.A. cityscape and the Hollywood hills—as one continuous painting.

PAINTING IN THE DIGITAL REALM

In 1990 Ed Jones, ILM director of post-production, initiated a merger of the matte department and the effects-camera department. Bruce Walters, who headed up the new department, was aware that the technologies

being developed by the computer graphics department would soon impact traditional effects and began to move his new department in a digital direction.

"I convinced management to buy the first color Apple Macintosh [a Mac II introduced for *Die Hard 2*] at ILM," Walters recalled. "We didn't even know how we were going to use it, but we knew that the heart of ILM is compositing images and that digital was going to revolutionize that aspect of the company. Once we had the Mac and began experimenting with Photoshop [an image-processing software developed by ILMer John Knoll and his brother Thomas], we realized that we could do matte paintings and compositing on this simple little box. I just gave a push in that direction, but as things got rolling it took on a life of its own."

The department had actually gotten its first taste of life in the digital realm during the making of *Young Sherlock Holmes* (1985), in which Chris Evans became the first ILM matte artist to experiment with digital painting tools.

Left: Mark Sullivan matte painting of a gothic-looking New York apartment building for *Ghostbusters II*. The glass painting, nearly four feet tall and six feet wide, had hung on the ILM walls for years until the day it was taken to a shop to be put into a frame—and the glass warped slightly and shattered. No one was hurt, but thereafter ILM phased away from glass as a medium for doing matte paintings. (Within five years, brush and oils would give way to the digital medium.)

Below: Final composite with city traffic and a sinister "ghost nanny" (created as a blue-screen puppet).

Top: A painting is the medium through which the evil Vigo the Carpathian (played by Wilhelm von Homburg) enters the world in *Ghostbusters II*.

Bottom: An ILM team lines up Vigo's grand entrance.

The scene, itself one of the first computer graphics breakthroughs ever produced for a feature-film release, had a computer-generated stained-glass figure of a knight in a church window come to life and stalk a frightened priest (see p. 109). Evans produced a painting of the background wall of the church and another of the window encasing the knight. The paintings were photographed and the film was scanned into the computer, where Evans used a proprietary program on ILM's Pixar Image Computer to modify the paintings and blend the elements together. The process was slow, but Evans saw the possibilities of the digital tools. "Matching colors between a painting and the live-action plate and hiding the matte lines are always the greatest challenges in a matte painting, but in digital you can pick the exact color you want from the plate and transfer it into the painting. The blending of the matte line between painting and plate is made easy because you can control the edge characteristics and completely merge and dissolve

the pixels [the individual points that together form a computer image] from one side to the other."

The digital advances would add techniques unknown to the artists of the glass-shot era. In *Hook*, a key image was a flyover by Peter Pan (Robin Williams) of Neverland island, an effect that would require digital compositing and matte painting manipulation. "I couldn't use traditional back-lit blue screen to do the kind of crane pull-back on Robin that I needed, so I knew we'd be doing a digital composite, at the very least," visual effects supervisor Eric Brevig observed. "I wanted to try and avoid using a model island, and I wanted to get some perspective change on the island as Peter Pan flies toward it, so we decided to try and wrap a matte painting on a computer-generated shape."

To give dimensionality to the Neverland painting required the digital-image processing technique of "texture mapping," in which the surface texture of one object could be digitally placed over another object. The technique itself was made possible with the use of "Make

Sticky," a software program developed for the 1991 hit *Terminator 2: Judgment Day*. ILM artist Yusei Uesugi's painting of Neverland island and the surrounding ocean were scanned into a computer and applied to the surface of a 3-D computer-generated wire-frame geometry of the island and ocean built by CG artist Stefen Fangmeier. With the painting digitally re-created as a three-dimensional model, the camera move of the final composite, as Peter Pan flew over and dove toward the island from above, gave a realistic perspective shift to the island.

THE ART OF ROTOSCOPING

The animation department would experience some of the same bursts of technological evolution as the matte painting department. The department had its own roots in the industrial era of moviemaking with the rotoscope camera, the key piece of equipment in animation, which was developed as a 1917 patent application by animation pioneer Max Fleischer.

The Fleischer rotoscope allowed animators to project film images one frame at a time

In *Indiana Jones and the Last Crusade*, Indy drives a motorcycle sidecar into a Nazi airport, accomplished as a latent-image live action (shot at Treasure Island in San Francisco Bay, site of the 1939 World's Fair) and a Yusei Uesugi matte painting. Can you find the dividing line between painted image and live action?

Top: Tom Bertino concentrates on rotoscoping part of a blue-screen brownie, one of the magical characters in *Willow*. The film image is projected down onto his animation stand from the locked-off camera above, which is programmable from the nearby computer for "project-down" capacities, frame advances, and other functions. "The work is so exacting," Bertino said. "If there's any wavering of line or camera shake it'll be blown up huge on the screen."

Above right: The finished articulate matte, with the character's outline traced by Bertino from the projected-down image, is traditionally done in pencil before being inked separately.

Right: The finished cel ready to be shot onto negative film for delivery to opticals. (Note the black masking tape that has been used to block out the image before being filled in with black ink.)

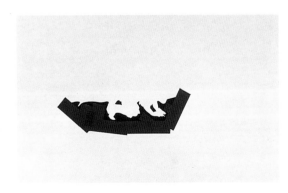

allowed for the creation of hand-drawn traveling mattes, a laborious, time-consuming method in which the frame-by-frame drawn silhouettes punched out "matte windows" in background plates that could later be filled in with film images conforming perfectly to the exact shape of the window—a process utilized by director Stanley Kubrick to composite the spaceships into the star fields of *2001: A Space Odyssey*. (The hand-drawn mattes and in-camera multiple exposures on *2001*, although time-consuming, saved generation loss that would have occurred in the optical-compositing phase.)

"The rotoscope process has been essentially unchanged for more than seventy-five years," observed Tom Bertino, head of the rotoscope department from 1987 to 1992. "Rotoscoping in the twenties and thirties was a very sophisticated concept for the times. If you were to use a rotoscope camera in 1918 or in the 1990s, you would use it in virtually the same way, except that ours are driven by a computer. The rotoscope camera can both shoot or project vertically down onto a horizontal drawing board. It's the same physical structure of frame-by-frame alignment patented by Fleischer. The rotoscope camera is like a delicate elephant, a huge, clunky piece of equipment that has this tender little heart in it. The alignment from one element to another and the project-down relative to the shoot-down relationship has to be perfectly aligned, to within a fraction of a hair, or it's useless."

In the pre-digital era, the rotoscope camera animators could create "garbage mattes," an animated matte used to isolate and remove unwanted imagery from original photography, and "articulate mattes," a hand-drawn traveling matte that conforms frame by frame to a moving image.

"For garbage mattes we cut out swathes of black paper and tape them onto the cel [a clear acetate sheet] as masters," Bertino explained. "If you are lucky you can create one matte that will cover the garbage for as

onto a surface where the outline of the desired image could be traced by hand. By tracing live-action footage, realistic movements could be created, as Fleischer Studios did on its own work, including silent-era Koko the Clown cartoons, the giant Gulliver in *Gulliver's Travels* (1939), and many of the realistic characters in their popular *Superman* animated series of the 1940s. Rotoscoping also

many as ten frames. This got to be a challenge for our department, to see how many frames we could stretch out of one cel.

"Articulate mattes tend to require a lot more precision. It's easier to do an articulate matte around an object that's doing a lot of wild motion; the faster the movement, the

more the rotoscoper gets away with. For example, if foreground and background objects are in a plate, and the effect is going to take place in between these characters, then you have to do a frame-by-frame tracing of the contours of the foreground character which will allow the effect to go in behind.

Top left: For a magical flyover of London for *Hook*, two paintings were overlapped. The shot went from a ten-foot-wide house painting to an extreme pull-back, tilt-up, and pan to an eight-foot-wide London painting physically suspended in front of the house and closer to the camera. Paintings produced by Rocco Gioffre, Eric Chauvin, and Yusei Uesugi.

Above: With the illusory power of perspective, two separate paintings seem as one. The London rooftop painting utilized a blowup photo of the city, allowing artists Gioffre, Chauvin, and Uesugi to paint over quickly.

Left: If you want to meet the Flintstones you have to head for Bedrock (where they're "First with Fire"). The establishing shot was accomplished as a foreground miniature set with a painted backing by TyRuben Ellingson.

Effects animation, drawn and inked on registration paper to line up with a separately photographed image and then colored and composited in opticals, is a rare art. *Howard the Duck,* with its explosive blasts, bursts, and zaps was a showcase of the form, as these images attest. Art by Gordon Baker and John Armstrong.

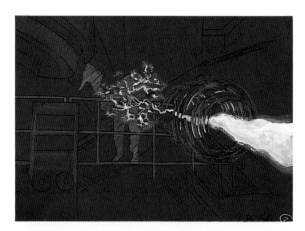

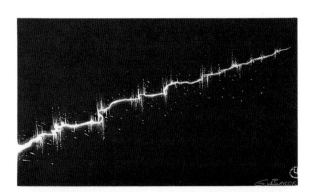

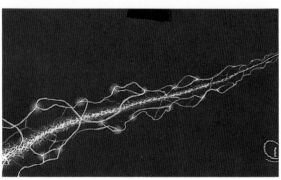

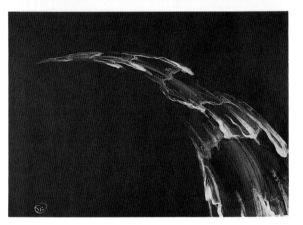

For the really tough articulates we do everything on paper with pencil first, tracing an outline with pencil on paper, usually only every third frame. We never go straight to ink and paint; we go to a light table and stack four or five drawings and ripple them to see if the lines are following through in a straight way. Then we go back and line them up on the roto camera to check tracings against projection. For very nitpicky stuff, we'd even shoot a pencil test. Then, the cel is laid over every paper drawing and retraced during the inking process, an extremely laborious and frequently painful process."

EFFECTS ANIMATION

In the effects-animation process the rotoscope camera was vital in allowing artists to draw art that could perfectly integrate with live-action film. "Whatever sequence we'd work on would require using the rotoscope camera to project down and trace every frame, using that as a guide to putting in our animation," explained animator Gordon Baker. "We'd then put the registered paper on

a light table, put a fresh piece of registration paper over it, and draw our animation, which we've already developed with the effects supervisor in the animation test phase. Our ink and black pencil final animation could then be shot on high-contrast film, which would give us a negative image that we'd send to optical where they'd add color, diffusion, and composite it in with the background plate."

Effects animation is a unique craft in which elemental forces, as opposed to animated characters, are produced with the power of a pencil. In fantasy films from *Howard the Duck* to *Ghostbusters II* bolts of supernatural energy are hand-drawn effects animation. In *Willow* and *Hook* brownie and fairy creatures could be created as separate elements and realistically integrated with animated shadows.

In *The Rocketeer* the rocket pack's propulsion flame elements were provided by a "Flame Crew" in the animation department. Supervisor Wes Takahashi designed artwork that showed a texture inside the flame enve-

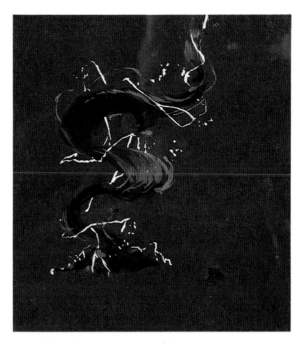

lope that was then photographed onto high-contrast black-and-white film stock. Optical then shot the black-and-white flame element through an orange filter, providing rich gradations of color and a three-dimensional quality to the flames.

Takahashi, who joined ILM in 1983 and was promoted to effects animation department supervisor in 1987, noted the versatility of a department where techniques ranged from traditional hand-drawn animation to 3-D effects (such as the flapping wing rig in *Willow* and the tennis balls photographed and optically added to the supernatural tennis match in *The Witches of Eastwick*). In the department's glory days, when the workforce might swell to thirty artists, there was also a sense of camaraderie on shared creative adventures (such as *The Rocketeer* effects animation unit nicknaming itself the "Flame Crew").

"We were doing things like the warp drive we did for the *Star Trek: The Next Generation* TV show," Takahashi recalled, "where the spaceship gets stretched and shoots off into the distance. On one *Next Generation* episode the director wanted to see people walking on the *Enterprise* bridge. I drew them all and John Knoll took my animated characters and match-moved them each frame to fit into the starship windows. They were almost silhouettes they were so small, but it saved the production costs of having to get extras and shoot the scene all over."

The animation medium had always been a great resource for imaginative directors contemplating unusual effects shots. Such image

Far left: Willow and the evil Queen Bavmorda in a final face-off. Dave Carson production illustration.

Left: A deadly brew intended for the baby princess proves the undoing of Bavmorda. The killer smoke is worked out in this Dave Carson design.

Below: Effects camera supervisor Bruce Walters and head animator John Armstrong created the smoke with a complex slit-scan approach, filming light streaks through rippled glass and adding glows and animated electrical bursts.

Bottom: Close-up of Bavmorda (actress Jean Marsh) going up in smoke.

This page, below: Of the more than twenty *Hook* matte paintings, the centerpiece was "the Neverland reveal," in which Peter Pan, and the audience, catch the first glimpse of the enchanted wonderland. Preproduction art by Mark Sullivan.

Opposite page, top right: Neverland reveal concept painting by Mark Sullivan, with two-foot tall rock-formation models in the foreground.

Opposite page, middle: Bluescreen element of Peter Pan at the base of the Nevertree, gazing out for his first view of Neverland.

Opposite page, bottom: As Peter scrambled to his feet, the camera did a boom-up to reveal Neverland. To integrate the separate photography, the blue-screen motion-control move was fed into the camera that shot the middistance rock models and the painting. The painting included rear-projected footage of shorelines and waterfalls. The inspirations for the fantasy island's varied environments included Himalayan mountains, New Guinea forests, and Yosemite Falls.

creation was often hard to explain, much less create. Takahashi recalled an effects animation brainstorming session for the original *Back to the Future*, in which director Robert Zemeckis wanted an animated effect of an electrical storm and a time portal opening for the speeding DeLorean. According to Takahashi, the shot the director desired fell under the FX adage, "I want something that nobody has ever seen before."

"As the car, driving at 88 miles per hour, hits the time opening, Bob Zemeckis wanted [to portray] something visually violent, with a lot of electricity," Takahashi recalled of the project he worked on with ILM art director Phil Norwood. "Bob said he wanted something like 'a Neanderthal with an ice pick sitting on a DeLorean chipping away at the fabric of time.' The design I came up with had the electrical currents hitting and bouncing off an invisible barrier in front of the car to create areas of light. As the car got closer, these lights then tore open what I called 'a time slice,' with a final explosion and implosion of the car. The thing about effects animation is there are no physical limits, so you

have to get it in the first design because you can't do it all over again."

Traditional effects animation has always been one of the most difficult film illusions, with the most realistic work requiring 24 frames per second to match live action. "I look at a normal effects shot that's five seconds to a stage person and see 120 frames of painstaking animation and rendering," Takahashi observed. "A good animator can see and break down the mathematics of time, just knowing how many frames it takes to do certain motions. Just like in comedy, the secret of the craft is timing. The problem with effects animation using the new digital technologies is it's hard for computers to take high-resolution pictures in real time."

Beginning with *The Rocketeer* in 1991, Takahashi not only provided traditional hand-drawn art to be photographed and processed in opticals, but began using Macintosh computers for some of the animation shots. By 1993, the animation department would be recast by computer graphics, with Takahashi effectively becoming a department of one. "Now animation stands are

Previously, a two-dimensional painting generally allowed for only locked-off camerawork. But this view of Neverland, painted by Yusei Uesugi, would be a breakthrough. To composite a blue-screen image of a Peter Pan flyover (and have the image reveal a natural perspective shift on the island below), the painting was scanned into a computer and texture-mapped to a 3-D computer model.

being sold off or are in mothballs," Takahashi lamented. "But while some computer people are under the impression the new technology has replaced traditional animation, a computer can't generate all the in-betweens—the drawings between main points of action— particularly if it's something erratic, like bolts

Above: *Hook* preproduction concept painting by Mark Sullivan, with Peter Pan and one of the Lost Boys gazing from atop Nevertree to the harbor where Captain Hook and his pirate lackeys await.

Left: Nevertree reverie; still from film.

of electricity. So, a lot of 2-D animation still has to be done, but instead of doing animation on a drawing board, shooting with a camera, and optically printing it, we're drawing on top of backgrounds in SGI computers. We still have problems working on each frame of live-action film because computers still aren't fast enough to take high-resolution, live-action pictures in real time and play them back, which is what an animator needs to get a sense of how something needs to move. So, it's like trying to animate with boxing gloves."

Of the traditional art forms, matte painting seemed to be making the best transition to digital tools. With the new technology, matte painters could single-handedly produce images that once required many effects departments: instead of integrating physical models, the new-age matte artist could create 3-D objects in the digital realm; rather than an effects camera, the artist could employ the virtual camera; instead of an optical depart-ment, the artist could seamlessly composite his or her own work prior to scanning out a final to film.

By 1992 and *The Young Indiana Jones Chronicles* TV series, ILM matte painters and animators would be working exclusively with computers, with special software programs accomplishing the traditional roto duties. As with most traditional effects, the artists who painted with film had to adjust spiritually and technically to the new technologies. "I really miss the enjoyable time I spent painting in the real world," matte painter Yusei Uesugi lamented. "I'd like for the digital toolmakers to develop a kind of virtual reality system to fake the sense of touch and the sound of the brush against the material surface. I really miss that."

CHAPTER SIX

VIRTUAL SPACE
EXPLORATIONS

Deep in space, aboard the Starship *Enterprise*, Captain James T. Kirk was receiving the visual and audio transmission that would reveal the secret of "Project Genesis." The Genesis device, the transmission explained, had the ability to reorganize the molecular structure of dead matter "with life-generating results." As Kirk watched, a simulation showed the device rocketing into a lifeless moon and igniting like a pillar of fire. The resulting firestorm spread over the crater-blasted surface and left in its wake a paradise planet of mountains, seas, atmosphere, and clouds moving across a new-blue sky.

All of the realistic, three-dimensional images of the so-called Genesis sequence, a

highlight of *Star Trek II: The Wrath of Khan* (1982), were generated by the Lucasfilm Computer Division, a department Lucas had organized in the late 1970s. Yet this three-dimensional computer graphics sequence and the computerized motion-control systems developed for the *Star Wars* movies were only the beginning: Lucas envisioned replacing the photochemical optical printing process with electronic input/output scanners that could convert film images into two-dimensional (2-D) digital information for image processing and compositing in computers. But despite his ambitious plans, Lucas was no starry-eyed disciple of the state of technology often referred to as the "digital realm."

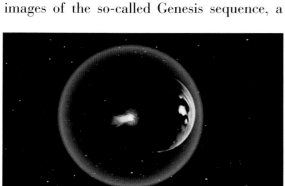

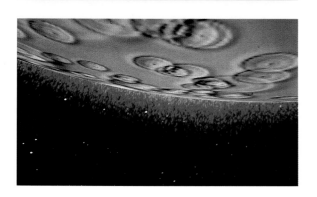

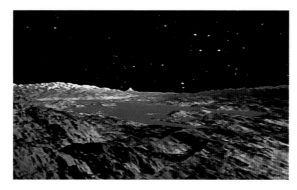

The "Genesis" sequence transforms a dead planet into a verdant world in *Star Trek II*. The effect, accomplished totally with computer graphics, was the first CG sequence ever put into a feature film and a breakthrough for Lucasfilm's Computer Division.

Above: Another early feature-film CG effect was this hologram image for a Rebel strategy meeting in *Return of the Jedi*.

Below: Early laser scanner used for *Young Sherlock Holmes*.

"I've never been that interested in computers," Lucas laughed. "I'm interested in making movies and creating images and in doing it the easiest way possible. When you start out making movies you're trying to get the largest vision with what amounts to a limited amount of resources. So it's a constant struggle to add more colors to the palette, and the way you get more colors is to spend huge

amounts of money. But at some level there are colors you can't get because no amount of money will get you there. With *Star Wars* we were basically off the color palette. The technology did not exist to pan and move with miniatures, but that's what the story was. I wanted to tell this story, but the color only existed in theory. The only way you'll get there is to create technology that will bring those colors into the realm of what's achievable, and that's basically what ILM was. So I had to get involved in computers and the high-tech area, which was very new to special effects at that point. And for a long time at ILM the state of the art was using computers to manipulate hardware—the old-fashioned nineteenth-century celluloid—through sprockets technology. Then, in 1978–79, I put together a computer division because I wanted to get a digital printer. At that point I wasn't as interested in three-dimensional animation as I was at getting to the core issue, which was, 'How do you get in and out of the computer?' That was the big problem."

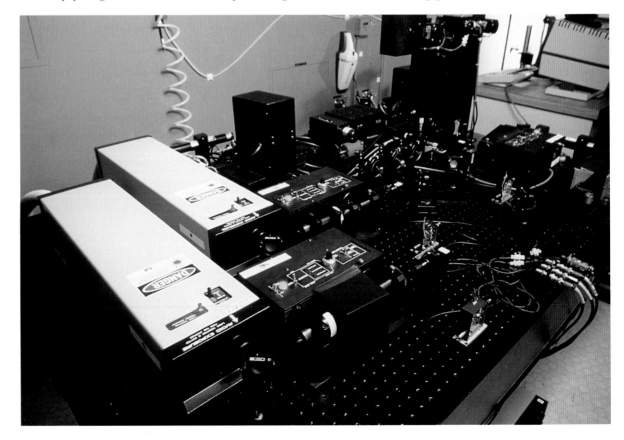

Digital-image processing was the promised land for a filmmaker obsessed with original negative quality: Not only would film scanned-in and manipulated in the computer be free from any generational loss but mistakes in the original photography (such as lighting on a blue-screen element that was inconsistent with its background plate) could be corrected without the costs and time delays of reshooting.

COMPUTER DIVISION R AND D

The new computer division, charged by Lucas to develop a range of digital-image processing capabilities, was largely composed of a computer graphics research group from the New York Institute of Technology. Headed up by Ed Catmull, the group, with their interest in applying computer technology to the world of film and entertainment, was an

anomaly in an era of big mainframe systems serving the exclusive interests of science, engineering, and business.

The 1982 Genesis sequence was a breakthrough in the creation of 3-D computer graphics. Unlike 2-D image manipulation, in which flat film or artwork (images with only height and width, not depth) could be scanned into the computer and manipulated, three-dimensional computer graphics was about constructing three-dimensional subjects within the digital realm itself. The group had successfully detonated the Genesis device in the digital environment, but the excitement surrounding the dimensional images of a barren moon transformed into a verdant world were tempered by the reality that 3-D computer graphics was still in its infancy, too slow and expensive a process to be completely dependable for feature-film work.

"We knew that in order for computer animation to be successful in feature films, some fundamental things needed to be solved," recalled Ed Catmull. "Motion-blur, depth of field, and the capacity to create exceptionally complex environments were the essential building blocks; nothing looks real without these basic capabilities. Also, the artists had

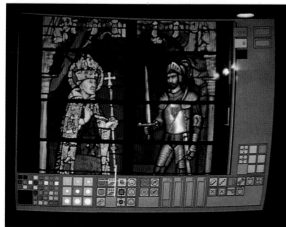

Left: A stunning sequence in *Young Sherlock Holmes*, in which a painted image of a crusading knight comes to life from a church's stained-glass window, was the first use of digital scanning (utilizing an early Pixar laser-based scanner). Here Chris Evans paints the stained-glass window images that will be scanned into a computer.

Bottom left: The stained-glass window, featuring a miter-topped cleric blessing the knight, as viewed on a computer monitor.

Below: Chris Evans manipulates the stained-glass painted elements, the first matte painting to be digitally manipulated for film.

Above: After skewering the cleric, the knight leaps out of the stained-glass window in this digital composite.

Right, top to bottom: Digital image of the knight . . .

. . . and as composited with live action of church interior and priest.

to have much more control over the appearance of the objects. All previous systems, including our own, required a programmer to modify the frames for the final image. So we decided to start all over and restructure the entire problem. We wanted high resolution, great depth, image complexity, and motion-blur. Essentially we had an ongoing competition, trying to outdo each other at our weekly meetings, and one by one we solved the problems. The program we developed eventually became Renderman, the 3-D rendering tool that represents our greatest contribution to computer graphics software to date."

But while Catmull and his team were entranced by the possibilities of the third dimension, Lucas remained focused on his original digital priorities of developing a film input/output scanner, a digital printer, and 2-D software applications. The 1984 Lucasfilm computer graphics production *The Adventures of André and Wally B.*, an animation short that marked the first time realistic motion-blur was accomplished on a 3-D computer film, would be the last major Lucasfilm project of the original computer division. Catmull and his group left to form a separate company that would concentrate on 3-D films and software—Pixar, named after the image-processing system they had developed during their tenure with Lucas. (The group would eventually sign a features animation deal with Disney, resulting in 1995's *Toy Story*, the first completely computer-generated feature.) Meanwhile, Lucas reorganized computer graphics as a production department within Industrial Light & Magic.

ILM COMPUTER GRAPHICS: CREATING THE TOOLS

The Lucas company retained proprietary rights to the technology developed by the first computer graphics group: the Pixar laser scanner, the Renderman 3-D software, and a digital editing system known as the Editdroid. These assets of the new computer graphics department still represented only the prototypical results of Lucasfilm's digital R and D phase. The next challenge was to evaluate the tools and determine the hardware and software the company would need to make digital a dependable tool for motion picture production.

ILM's new CG department was initially staffed by Doug Kay and George Joblove, graduates of the Cornell University Program of Computer Graphics. Their university researches had been conducted at the dawn of computer graphics, a time when the slightest

The ILM/Kodak film scanner. In 1994 this scanner was recognized with a Scientific and Engineering Technical Achievement Award from the Academy of Motion Picture Arts and Sciences.

permutation was fraught with complexity. Kay's own area of study—"simulation of realistic glass and transparent objects"—had culminated in a computer-generated champagne glass placed into a still-life table and fruit arrangement. The leap of CG technology, from a champagne glass image to the Genesis effect, was impressive, but many mysteries still needed to be solved.

INTO THE DIGITAL REALM

Computers have fascinated and perplexed the modern world ever since the earliest mainframe prototypes. Joseph Campbell, the late professor of mythology, once said the inner workings of the computer represented a "hierarchy of angels." In the novel *Neuromancer*, William Gibson described a future in which hackers could project their "disembodied consciousness" into the very circuitry of the computer world. His hero, a hacker cowboy named Case, "lived for the bodiless exultation of cyberspace."[1]

There is a public awe of computers, a Promethean glow surrounding digital matters. At first glance it might seem prosaic for movie fans to hear CG programmers refer to

1. William Gibson, *Neuromancer* (New York: Ace Books, 1984), pp. 5–6.

In the futuristic Hill Valley Town Square, the marquee's hologram image of *Jaws 10* at the multiplex is rather . . . involving. CG effect for *Back to the Future, Part II.*

that this technology is, in fact, creating movie magic.

The computer can be understood as having two main parts that make the whole. There is the "hardware," that is the actual computer, monitor, processor, memory, and disk drives that provide the power, along with the keyboard, a hand-held mouse for positioning the cursor anywhere on the screen, and other devices by which one can interact with the computer. In partnership with hardware power is "software," the programs that actually give the computer specific instructions.

The internal workings of the digital realm itself is a mathematical world in which all functions are carried out in numeral language and images are stored as strings of numbers. While the computer looks at things mathematically, the on-screen computer images that a CG artist sees and manipulates are the sum of individual dot picture elements, or "pixels." (Photographs and art reproductions are composed of similar dots, while the picture element in a big-screen movie is composed of film grain.) The building blocks of a 3-D image are the geometric constructs of interconnecting planar surfaces known as "polygons." The image can be further crafted using four-sided shaped "patches."

In the digital realm, the computer assigns each pixel both a primary color (red, blue, green) and a specific brightness value, the number and degree of value determining the resolution quality of the image. Defining the computer image ultimately becomes a case of making one dot red, the other blue, the next one a brighter red, and so on, with billions of such computations, powered by electrons, racing through the silicon chip circuits.

To achieve a high-resolution film image using digital means was, at the time of the Genesis sequence, a particularly daunting challenge. A film image has some four thousand horizontal pixels, while the cathode-ray pictures transmitted to a television screen are a

the technology as a tool, to learn that the CG artists who created the prehistoric creatures of *Jurassic Park* did not press a "Dinosaur" button but had to spend months laboriously crafting the three-dimensional images with the building blocks of software systems. The fact that computers are tools, however, does not detract from the wonderment of both the accomplishments and possibilities of advances into the digital realm—and the fact

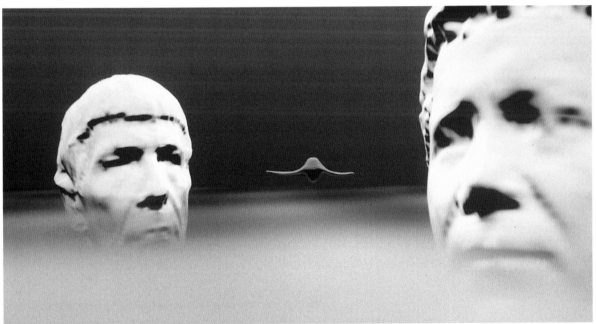

Top left: To help the Starship *Enterprise* crew time-travel to modern-day San Francisco in *Star Trek IV*, ILM computer artists engaged the services of Cyberware Laboratory to help create digital data for a dreamlike sequence. Here Spock (Leonard Nimoy, who also served as the film's director) drops in to get scanned.

Top right: When *Star Trek IV* was filmed, computer graphics was still in its infancy. To create a 3-D image in the computer, early CG artists sometimes had to digitize objects. The laser scans of the *Enterprise* crew, capturing all head and facial data, were used to create three-dimensional Styrofoam sculptures (such as this Spock head).

Middle: After digitizing the model heads produced by the laser scans, ILM animators produced this dreamlike effect (with a floating-whale image to complement the story line). Unlike the real-time CG and image-processing capabilities of a decade later, this sequence—some thirty seconds on film—would require weeks to render.

U.S. standard 525 lines (although ILM makes many TV commercials at 720 resolution). To create computer graphics elements and scan out even one frame of 35mm frame film then required more than seven million pixels.

At the time of the Genesis effect, great unknowns awaited computer graphics artists who were interested in creating realistic images, not cartoon animation. The first scene-simulation experiments, such as the atmospheric effects and color gradations of *Moonscape* (produced by Digital productions) or Lucasfilm's own *Point Reyes*, a digital drive down the Marin County peninsula, raised the question: Could natural phenomenon such as sunlight, and the physical laws governing it, not just be digitally simulated but reproduced over the course of many frames of film?

The views of the time ranged from Ed Catmull's belief that existing technology could only afford artistic interpretations, not realistic simulations, of reality to the ideas

ILM's CG department produced this Praxis moon blast and shockwave in *Star Trek VI.*

of CG researcher John Whitney, Jr., who observed, "It will be possible to create the likeness of a human being . . . to generate speech electronically, and the result will evoke an emotional response. We may be able to re-create stars of the past . . . cast them in new roles, bring them forward into new settings . . . if stills and old films can be used to make the likeness . . . the database. You only have to encode once. Then you've got John Wayne, say, on file. You can put him into any role you can simulate."[2]

MORPHING

The new ILM CG department had to push the envelope of possibilities without losing sight of its charge of becoming a full production unit. Effects supervisor Dennis Muren helped provide the department's first challenge, inviting CG to help create a shape-changing metamorphosis sequence for Lucasfilm's mythic fantasy *Willow.*

"It was a conscious decision to give the computer department a chance to produce actual elements," Muren recalled. "Lucasfilm had put so much money into developing this technology and I knew it wasn't going to happen by itself, so I jumped in and pushed them to create actual elements. I felt it was time to transition from the R and D mode and dive into production, ready or not."

Willow introduced the technique of morphing to the transformation effects shot, a digital image-processing breakthrough in which one image could be progressively altered to transform into another image. "The film scanning and recording process we used on *Willow* was significant in that we were able to scan in live-action film of a woman, tiger, puppets, and other elements, do alterations, and scan them back out to film with basically no artifacts [visible defects in CG images caused by limitations in hardware or software]," Doug Kay noted. "It was a threshold to get over, to be able to output elements to film and not have

them look like they had been digitized. That opened up the whole world of computer graphics and digital manipulation."

SCANNING

Image-processing breakthroughs would be facilitated by new digital scanning technology. The earliest Pixar scanners, used for

2. Christopher Finch, *Special Effects: Creating Movie Magic* (New York: Abbeville Press, 1984), p. 240.

such mid-to-late-eighties features as *Young Sherlock Holmes, Willow*, and *Indiana Jones and the Last Crusade*, utilized a laser-based scanner and film recorder. During the late 1980s, Eastman Kodak and ILM launched a joint R and D effort to build an input scanner for motion picture work that would improve on the existing in-house laser scanning system. After two years of development, the Trilinear Multispectral High Resolution CCD (Charge Coupled Device) Digital Input Scanner came on-line in time to contribute to another breakthrough: the digitally manipulated matte painting end sequence of 1990's *Die Hard 2* (see pages 140–143). The power of the new scanner would allow a frame of film to be scanned in roughly every twenty to thirty seconds—a tenfold increase in previous scanning speed.

WIRE REMOVAL AND PARTICLE GENERATION

An early software breakthrough was a wire-removal program developed for *Howard the Duck* (1986) and *Back to the Future, Part II* (1989). Traditional flying effects required models or actors to be flown from wires shot against blue screen and matted into a background plate. Although flying wires were often thin enough to be nearly invisible, or disguised by lighting, any visible wires, riggings, or props would traditionally have to be removed with rotoscoped mattes before the element could be optically composited.

In *Back to the Future, Part II*, time traveler Marty McFly (Michael J. Fox) finds himself transported to his hometown of Hill Valley in the year 2015, a fantastic future of magical holographic displays, flying cars, flying skateboard and hoverboards. Scenes of McFly and others riding hoverboards, which were able to rise a few feet above ground and fly, were achieved practically by filming the actors on boards attached by pipe to a camera car, suspended from a crane by a marionette rig, and by other setups. The scenes were then scanned into a computer and the pixels on either side of the rig manipulated to meld the surrounding colors and effectively erase the rig. (This process also requires a separate program to add film grain to the pristine digital image, which helps match the original photography.) This kind of wire removal made it possible to shoot a fantastic effect practically, allowing an actor seemingly to interact with objects in real time and space,

In the old days, when props or wires were visible, it would take time-consuming, hand-drawn rotoscoped mattes to remove the offending elements from a scene. An ILM wire-removal program developed for *Howard the Duck* and used extensively on *Back to the Future II* hurdled another creative limitation. These flying skateboarders from *Future II*, who once might have been accomplished as blue-screen elements and optically composited, could now be shot live-action, with rigs, props, and wires digitally removed.

creating a more intricate final illusion than what could be achieved by compositing a myriad of separately produced elements.

The ability to use wire removal to erase digitally extraneous objects captured in the original photography was also a godsend for *Die Hard 2*. In a dozen scenes, cranes, wires,

and cables were visible in the DC-8 model pyro scenes. Instead of extensive rotoscoping or reshooting, computer graphics artist Doug Smythe worked the pixel elements to color out the offending props and added the requisite film grain to match the original image. In 1994, Smythe received a Technical Achievement Award for his development of the digital image retouching system.

Another software breakthrough was a particle-generating system that could imitate natural, random movements such as those of stars, fire, or dust particles. CG had been developing the program since the mid-eighties and first extensively applied it on *The Hunt for Red October* in 1990. The CG *Hunt* work required scanning the submarine footage into the computer and digitally adding such particle-generated effects as floating plankton, submarine wakes, and torpedo trails. In *Hunt*, the particle-generating system, with each particle separately programmed to achieve a random, organic look, required forty thousand particles to be tracked from one frame to the next, with the life span of each particle lasting from twenty-seven frames to more than one hundred.

Above: TV commercial work was a boon to CG artists who could produce 3-D images quicker in the low-resolution video medium than in the high-resolution world of film. Here one of the CG ants that raids a Heinz ketchup picnic lends a hand(s).

Right: Toyota commercial's CG "Lips" sequence.

PHOTOSHOP

A major breakthrough software (which would be published by Adobe and go on the commercial market in 1990) was Photoshop, a program developed by ILMer John Knoll and his older brother Thomas during the late eighties. Designed to manipulate pictures, Photoshop received its first extensive ILM use for *The Abyss* (1989), helping to manipulate digitized photographic data of background plate sets and creating a digital model in which to integrate a computer-generated water creature. Photoshop would become a major digital tool, used in developing art department concepts, in digitally creating matte paintings, and in painting shots to completion.

Photoshop edits digitized pictures, allow-

ing computer artists to perform such image-processing functions as rotating, resizing, and color-correcting images and painting out scratches, dust, or other flaws. The software is versatile enough to be used for texture-map editing in computer graphics, creating matte paintings, and designing concepts in the art department.

In 1991 a comparison test of digital versus photochemical optical compositing was conducted utilizing several blue-screen shots from *Willow* and *Indiana Jones and the Last Crusade*. For the CG side, elements were scanned into the Macintosh, the images manipulated with Photoshop, and the final composites scanned out to film. Reels of the CG and optical composite work were then projected in a screen-

CG hummingbirds sip the nectar from CG flowers in this British Petroleum spot.

This page: In *Star Trek VI*, the illusion of a "Chameloid shape-changer" transforming from a beautiful woman (played by Iman) into Captain Kirk was accomplished with the digital morphing technique ILM pioneered on *Willow*.

ing room. The result: Optical comps had telltale matte lines while the digital comps had significantly eliminated matte lines and improved edge characteristics. While optical techniques were constrained by the quality of the film elements, in the digital realm images could be manipulated down to the individual pixel.

"The thing about the digital compositing process is that it's always a positive step forward," observed ILM executive in charge of production Patty Blau. "When you do something to a file, you can save it and then come back the next day without having sunk back to square one. In optical, you take your best stab at it, and if you still have a matte line, you take another stab at it. Each take in optical is like always starting at ground zero."

DIGITAL AND OPTICAL:
COOPERATION AND COMPETITION

A number of early nineties films required cooperation—some would say competition—between the CG and optical departments. *The Rocketeer*, for example, required effects scenes of the rocket-pack-equipped hero shooting through the sky; this presented the classic challenge of matting a blurred object against the light background of a sky plate. Although some 90 percent of the shots could be completed in optical, there were particular difficulties in shots in which blur would be lost because of the hard-edged matte line in traditional opticals. In such cases digital-image processing could extract the matte and retain the blur for every flying element. Digital also helped save shots contaminated with "blue spill," the result of blue light from blue screen spilling onto the subject being photographed. For blue-spill problems in *The Rocketeer*, digital artist Sandra Ford Karpman used a computer tablet and pen to paint the original

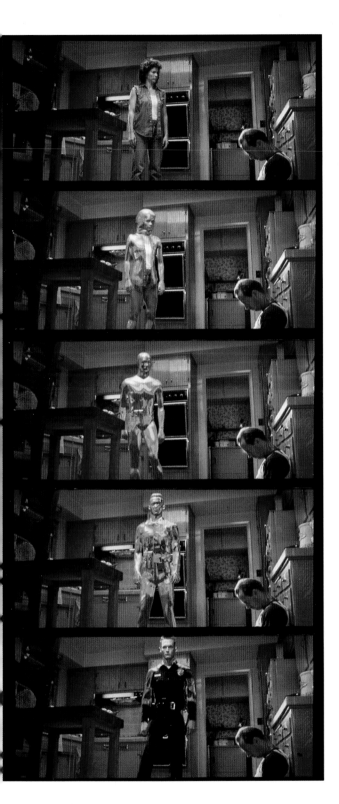

colors back into the character frame by frame.

Although digital supplied the break-throughs required to believably place the speeding Rocketeer in some of the most diffi-cult background plates, effects supervisor Ken Ralston did not accept digital as a panacea. "When CG creates an artificial sharpness, it's actually destroying some of the real detail on the film. In CG there's a danger of getting tunnel vision. It's important to keep the big picture in mind or you can get lost in a maze of pixels."

But computer graphics was coming on like an unstoppable tidal wave. By 1993 ILM had entered into a strategic business alliance with Silicon Graphics (SGI) that allowed for ongoing cooperation in developing and installing high-powered workstations. In 1989 Dennis Muren spearheaded an effort dubbed "The Mac Squad," which was orga-nized as an adjunct to the optical department headed by Ed Jones. The Mac Squad utilized Macintosh computers and Photoshop soft-ware to introduce the digital world to such traditional departments as optical, animation, and rotoscope. While big projects requiring breakthrough computer graphic imaging, such as *Terminator 2*, were attended to by the high-powered SGI systems, the Mac Squad utilized Apple Macintosh units to contribute image-processing work to such films as *The Rocketeer*, *Hook*, and *Memoirs of an Invisible Man*.

"More extensively than ever before, we alternated digital and optical compositing, and we had to write the software that allowed us to do it," recalled Eric Brevig, *Hook* visual effects supervisor. "*Hook* got so big that we had to devise ways for all of the departments to work together. Animation, matte, camera, optical, stage, digital, and computer graph-ics—each department did what it does best. Together, they were better than the sum of their parts. I think synergy is the term that best describes it."

Hook, in particular, was a breakthrough film for the internal demands it put on the company; with an incredible 200,000 accu-mulated work hours, it was second only to *Return of the Jedi* for the most time-intensive production up to that point. For example, ILM's blue-screen plate crew that worked alongside the production's first unit on Sony

In *T2*, a shape-changing, liquid-metal cyborg from the future is after Sarah Connor and her son John (the future savior of the human race). The cyborg, who has killed John's foster parents, transforms from the stepmother to another guise as an L.A. police officer. This sequence was a quantum leap over past trans-formation sequences.

Studios' soundstages in Los Angeles numbered thirty-eight (the largest crew then assembled by ILM for location or studio plate work), the shot total during the production increased from 40 to more than 240, and 85 shots, 461 elements, and 55,330 frames were handled in the digital realm. Only *Death Becomes Her*, in 1992, would require the handling of more digitized frames. The requirements of *Hook* spurred ILM into breaking down the artificial boundaries between departments so that equipment and personnel could communicate and work together interchangeably—a mind-set that would serve ILM well organizationally as the company prepared for the blockbuster projects on its horizon.

The early computer problems of time and expense, which had required a judicious use of digital resources, still led many to believe that it would be years—perhaps decades—before CG could be depended upon for extensive image processing and 3-D animation. But the processing power, speed, and memory of computers was effectively doubling from year to year, affording effects breakthroughs at monthly intervals. By 1993 computer graphics would unleash upon the world the seemingly flesh-and-blood dinosaurs of *Jurassic Park* and digital would almost completely replace photochemical optical compositing.

But traditional opticals still carried the day for many landmark projects during ILM's second decade. One of the greatest image manipulation masterpieces of all time was achieved with traditional opticals: the fusion of cartoon animation and live action of *Who Framed Roger Rabbit?*

FX SUPERVISOR

No matter what style of effects magic ILM has brought to a show, from foam latex creatures to three-dimensional computer graphics creations, the effort has usually been coordinated by a visual effects supervisor. In the early days at ILM the title was often in flux (such as Dennis Muren's title of "supervisor of miniature and optical effects" on 1981's *Dragonslayer*), but the responsibilities through the years have remained constant: to serve as maestros of ILM's creative work for a client. "Our role as supervisors is to be in a creative partnership with the director, to envision in our minds where he or she wants to go, and to then take the necessary steps to translate that in our world," said Scott Squires, a supervisor for such films as *The Hunt for Red October*, *The Mask*, and *Dragonheart*.

"There are hundreds of decisions to be made daily, and most of them have to be the right ones," noted Dennis Muren, an ILM veteran since *Star Wars*. "After many

months, some of these decisions come together into one 'shot.' Then, many shots turn into a sequence. And then into the final film. At that time you can tell if you did your job to the max. We are constantly juggling the budget, the technology, and the artists to achieve a seemingly clear and effortless vision. The job can look transparent to an outsider, but inside our heads it is a continuous chess game."

According to Muren, supervisors are "the primary movers of the technology," able to fund research and development from within a film's budget. The success of such efforts, in Muren's view, comes from the particular energy and vision of the individual supervisor. "Most breakthroughs don't just happen by evolution," Muren said. "They are driven either by an individual or the demands of a project. In *Jurassic Park*, for example, the camera freedom was the result of my pushing our software people to give us the tools to make precise match-moves—tools which were begun on *T2*. Most people

thought this was too risky and foolish. If somebody else had supervised the show, the plates might have been shot more conservatively. We supervisors are so different from one another, and that's why our work is so different."

Supervisors can spend a year or more on a project, particularly for films with dozens, or hundreds, of effects shots. During production an organic process takes over, often necessitating supervisors to scrap planned effects or come up with a slate of new ones.

Supervisors are often involved right from the preproduction stage of the production itself (particularly for films like *Jurassic Park* and *The Mask*, in which not only the execution but the design of the effects are integral to the film's success), shooting background plates alongside the director, actors, and first-unit crew during the principal photography period and then completing the effects work in postproduction (when nerve-racking deadlines for cutting effects footage into the final film are perilously close to nationwide theatrical release dates).

Although FX supervisors each have their own special talents and career interests, all are familiar with the rigors of helming multimillion-dollar effects efforts, coordinating dozens (sometimes hundreds) of skilled artists, and balancing both creative and technical demands. "It takes a lot out of me, and it's really hard to get rejuvenated for the next project," said supervisor Ken Ralston, who, along with Muren, had worked at ILM since the first *Star Wars* installment. "*Roger Rabbit* went on for two years, and the last six months I was working seven days a week, and, like everyone else who worked on it, I was a totally burned-out shell. Because you put so much into it.

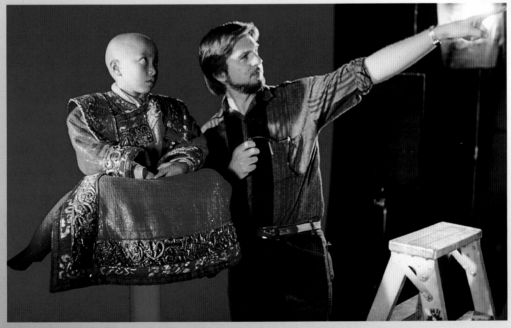

Ken Ralston makes a point on *The Golden Child*.

You have so much personally invested because it's your art and not just your job. Plus, you're always working under horrible deadlines. And people don't come to ILM to see the same old stuff; it's always got to be something you've never seen before—state of the art, pushing the envelope. You can't rest on your laurels. I've never done a show, and nobody at ILM has ever done a show, where you can relax. It's always another step forward."

Most of ILM's supervisors (and many effects artists in general) got their first taste of the magic of effects watching films featuring the work of such stop-motion wizards as Willis O'Brien and Ray Harryhausen. Along the way, there were other historic but unsung effects artists, people like optical printing master Linwood Dunn, who headed up the old RKO effects department work on such films as *King Kong* and *Citizen Kane*, and the Lydecker brothers, Howard and Theodore, whose ingenious flying-rig setups flew everything from movie serial superheroes to model fighter planes for war pictures.

The anonymity that was generally the effects artist's lot ended with the wondrous universe conjured up for *Star Wars*. Movie audiences who had never given effects a thought (or who for years had been watching them unaware) were now eager to be dazzled. Ever since, hundreds of millions of dollars in production budgets and technological R and D has flowed into the effects industry and advanced the field—a far cry from the days

Dennis Muren sizes up Vigo the Carpathian in *Ghostbusters II*. In addition to Ralston, Squires, and Muren, the roster of visual effects supervisors during ILM's second decade includes Bruce Nicholson, Micheal McAlister, Michael Owens, John Knoll, Dave Carson, Eric Brevig, Scott Farrar, Mark Dippé, Steve Price, and Stefen Fangmeier.

of Ray Harryhausen, when the work was created in spite of skimpy budgets, limited resources, and studio indifference. But the likes of Harryhausen, and even that first rough-and-ready band of ILMers, overcame the barriers by sheer ingenuity and the force of artistic vision—qualities that define a successful effects artist in any era.

Although some ILM veterans lament the passing of looser days of more bonhomie (and perhaps look over their shoulders at leaner, hungrier houses), the company is still the Cadillac of the industry, driving full-speed ahead, keeping its edge.

"I think ILM's strength is the people who work here," Ralston said. "I don't know all of the reasons why we're able to create an atmosphere where everyone is inspired to greater and greater heights. I always stress the *artists* involved; I never call them technicians. It takes real artistic skill and expertise to make these films, no matter what tool we're using. The [technology] doesn't mean anything. It's the people behind it that mean everything."

Scott Squires (left) confers with director of visual effects photography Patrick Sweeney on another exacting model shot for *The Hunt for Red October*.

BREAKTHROUGHS:

MAGIC FILM: MANIPULATING MOVIE IMAGES

Moviemaking has always been an act of illusion. There have been productions from the realist school of natural lighting and hand-held cameras, but movie storytellers have generally desired to engineer their imaginations with sets, lighting, complex camera moves, visual effects, and editing.

A high level of movie magic is the optical manipulation of film, such as the glowing orb in *The Wizard of Oz* (1939) that drifts out of the sky to touch the earth and reveal Glinda the Good Witch (Billie Burke). To create the grand entrance the MGM special effects department photographed a silver ball some eight inches in diameter and optically combined it with stationary, tied-down camera shots of the Munchkinland set.

"Now we had two pieces of film: the original set and the shot of the silver ball," MGM effects whiz "Buddy" Gillespie once explained. "Instead of matte-printing that into the original set, which would have made it seem a solid ball, we double-printed it—put one piece of film over the other—so that it was transparent. Then, still with the same tied-down camera, we put Billie Burke in the proper spot and filmed her. Then we lap-dissolved the ball out and Billie Burke was there—a very simple little optical effect."[1]

The commandment of locking down cameras for effects photography was particularly strict in filming and compositing live-action and animated elements. *Who Framed Roger Rabbit?* would not only break the mold and have a lively camera tracking both live actors and animated cartoon characters, it would be up to ILM to see that the twain would meet—to create through optical alchemy a world where humans and cartoons could live together.

The ILM magician pulls a Roger out of his hat. For *Roger Rabbit*, ILM's optical department would have a workload of some 1,040 shots and 10,000 separate elements . . . and you were wondering how they got that nickname "optical dogs."

1. Aljean Harmetz, *The Making of* The Wizard of Oz (New York: Delta, 1977), p. 255.

1988 (Touchstone Pictures/Amblin)
Compositing Cel Animation and Live-action Film

In the world of animated cartoons reality is a joke: Explosions merely leave characters with blackened faces and world-weary expressions, falling anvils only momentarily flatten their victims before they pop up like rubbery accordions, and gravity becomes irrelevant as figures suspend themselves in the space above yawning chasms.

For *Who Framed Roger Rabbit?*, a historic union of Disney's Touchstone Pictures division, Steven Spielberg's Amblin production company, director Robert Zemeckis, and ILM effects artists, the goal would be to create a film in which the surreal dimension of cartoons (or "toons," as the production referred to them) coexisted with human beings in three-dimensional space.

The concept was not new, dating back to the Fleischer Studios "Out of the Inkwell" series of the 1920s (which inspired such animated movies as the 1927 *The Lunch Hound*, in which cartoonist Walter Lantz inserted his live-action self into the cartoon world of Pete the Pup), Porky Pig and real-life producer Leon Schlesinger closing a handshake deal in *You Oughta Be in Pictures* (1940), the cartoon cat-and-mouse team of Tom and Jerry dancing with Gene Kelly in *Anchors Aweigh* (1945), James Baskett playing the gentle Uncle Remus who walks a cartoon path in Disney's *Song of the South* (1946), and Dick Van Dyke and Julie Andrews strolling through an animated landscape in *Mary Poppins* (1964). George Lucas had even suggested to the producers of the 1986 film *Howard the Duck* that the title character, ultimately realized as an actor in a duck suit, could be an animated creation.

Hard-boiled detective Eddie Valiant (Bob Hoskins) watches in amazement as a certain blue-eyed Toon sings a tune.

BRINGING TOONS TO LIFE:
EARLY TESTS AND CHALLENGES

The marriage of live actors and cel-drawn toons, usually accomplished by overlaying cel-drawn animation over large prints made of the live-action footage, had its fanciful moments, but in the main the human actors and cartoon characters just seemed to be going through the motions, occupying the same stage on-screen but not interacting with each other. The technical limits to achieving real interaction included locked-off photography of the live action (which ultimately made for a contrived and static final composite) and cel animation, which seemed flat and pasted on (or vice versa if it was a live-action element composited into a cartoon environment). For *Roger Rabbit* it was not enough to have live action and cartoons merely occupy the same space; for the first time humans and toons would have to reach out and grab each other.

But before matters could receive a green light, Spielberg and Disney needed some assurances that the concept was technically achievable. ILM produced a test in which the cartoon figure of Roger Rabbit bounded down a real staircase and tripped, crashing into and scattering a stack of real boxes. Not only was the animated character physically engaged in a real-world environment, the shot marked the first time a live-action camera had executed a drop move on an animated character. An astonished Spielberg would tell Zemeckis that the test was the second time he had seen film history (the first being *Star Wars*). Disney executives were also impressed, and the work proceeded in earnest.

ILM's task was to composite optically three-dimensional live action with hand-drawn, two-dimensional cel-animated cartoons, in the process giving the toons a believable dimensionality. The scale and complexity of *Roger Rabbit* posed the same challenge ILM would face a few years later when hired to create a liquid-metal cyborg for *Terminator 2*: the success of the movie

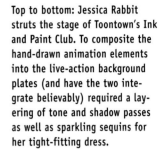

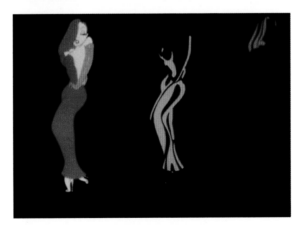

Top to bottom: Jessica Rabbit struts the stage of Toontown's Ink and Paint Club. To composite the hand-drawn animation elements into the live-action background plates (and have the two integrate believably) required a layering of tone and shadow passes as well as sparkling sequins for her tight-fitting dress.

Top right: To drop Bob Hoskins through Toontown airspace, the actor was flown blue-screen. Markers helped the actor line up his eye contact with Mickey Mouse and Bugs Bunny, who would be dropping along with him. To help orient actors who had to interact with invisible toons, dummy figures and props were used as stand-ins throughout the production, although it still required an actor's imagination to conjure up mentally and interact with the unseen.

Right and below: Animation plate with holdout matte for Hoskins . . .

. . . and final composite.

depended on extending effects art and technology to create images never seen before.

In describing the ambitions of the film, *American Cinematographer* noted: "To convince an audience that a talking cartoon rabbit and his animated colleagues really co-exist in the same world with [human beings] . . . demands some high-grade movie making, fine writing and direction, brilliant design and photography, sharp editing, sympathetic

Up angle look at Hoskins's fall, final composite of blue screen and animated background.

scoring, realistic sound, and the dedicated contributions of a lot of craftsmen and technicians. Yet, all these elements would be useless but for the remarkable visual effects artists of Industrial Light & Magic."[2]

Ken Ralston, ILM's effects supervisor on the film, would later characterize the two-year production as the equivalent of creating three *Star Wars* movies. More than 70 percent of the total film would travel through ILM's optical printers—an estimated 1,040 shots incorporating some ten thousand separate elements. Because of the unprecedented use of opticals, nearly all the live action would be shot using the high-quality VistaVision format; *Roger Rabbit* marked the first major feature since the fifties to employ the system. Mike Bolles, Greg Beaumonte, and others in ILM's camera department built specially designed horizontal film format cameras for the main unit and named them VistaFlex cameras.

At the time, ILM was also gearing up for the Lucasfilm production of *Willow*, a mythic

fantasy film with more than 350 scenes of complex visual effects. *Willow* and *Roger Rabbit* alone would require ILM to produce more than 1,500 shots for the year, an unprecedented number given the facility's average annual output of 300 shots. To meet the onslaught of effects shots, Ed Jones, an optical supervisor and cosupervisor for visual effects on *Roger Rabbit*, developed a plan to expand optical department personnel from twenty to thirty-two people and organized both day and late-night shifts.

The principal photography alone would have its own mind-numbing challenges, particularly the creation of special props and rigs as stand-ins for the cartoon elements that would have to be produced later. And although many movie actors were familiar with the peculiar demands of effects acting, which typically involved a few shots in front of a blue screen feigning fear, delight, or awe at some invisible scene that would be optically added later, *Roger Rabbit* would require the entire human cast to interact throughout the *entire movie* with invisible toons. (Bob Hoskins, the film's live-action star, would

2. George Turner, "Cartoons Come to Life in *Roger*," *American Cinematographer* (July 1988), p. 54.

Welcome to Toontown; please watch for falling anvils.

recall how, months after the film wrapped, he was still haunted by the phantom toons he had been conjuring up throughout the production.)

The animation effort, which would provide ILM with the cartoon elements it would have to composite with live action, required a team of some three hundred animators, who were based in England and led by Richard Williams. Additional work was provided in Los Angeles by animation director Dale Baer and a seventy-five-person crew. In the animation process the photostats of each approved live-action frame would be printed onto animation registered photostat paper. With the photostats as a reference guide placed over

clear acetate cels, artists could then hand draw and paint their frame-by-frame animation.

THE ANIMATION PHASE

The animators' work would be exacting in matching hand-drawn toon performances to lively camera movements and real-world actors and environments. Zemeckis coached the animators in the emotions and expressions he wanted from his cartoon actors in each frame. To help spur things along, Ralston gave a special pep talk to the animation troops early in the game.

"There came a day when associate producer Steve Starkey and I had to become the bad cops," Ralston admitted. "We got all of

Williams's people together, and I told them that I'd done a lot of really huge effects pictures like *Star Wars* and *Return of the Jedi* and that I noticed there was something missing in this group: FEAR! I told them that I sensed a real lack of terror. I had to make them understand how big this thing really was and that we couldn't wait until the last second to start working twenty-four hours a day. I laid it on real thick and explained that all these people at ILM were sitting at the end of the line waiting for their elements."

Before the flood of animation elements to be composited reached ILM, Ralston and Jones had begun experimenting with ways to integrate the characters into their real-life environments. There were test-phase concerns that the shadows animated by Williams's unit had a tendency to "chatter" frame by frame—there was an unsteadiness between the matte and its foreground element. These painted shadows also didn't allow ILM to diffuse and soften their edges in

a way that mimicked real shadows impacting real objects.

It was finally decided that the animators would produce three separate layers of animation—the principal character animation, tone effects for highlighting toons, and shadows—which ILM would combine during the final optical compositing phase. Quarter-tone mattes were used to give depth to the images, avoiding the flat look of some cel animation. To save time, quarter tones were used for toon close-ups, while halftones, with their less refined values, were applied to background toons.

TOON TONES AND SHADOWS

The tone and shadow elements were particularly important in giving toons the three-dimensional quality they'd need to inhabit the human world. Prior to *Roger Rabbit*, tone and shadow passes were shot on black-and-white, high-contrast film stocks, which provided grayish-colored highlights when

The Big Kiss.

Right: Shots from the digital morphing effect for *Willow*.

Below: The breakthrough digital-transformation sequence in *Willow*, in which the title character's handling of a magic wand sets off a metamorphic sequence, began with an old-fashioned storyboard by artist David Lowery.

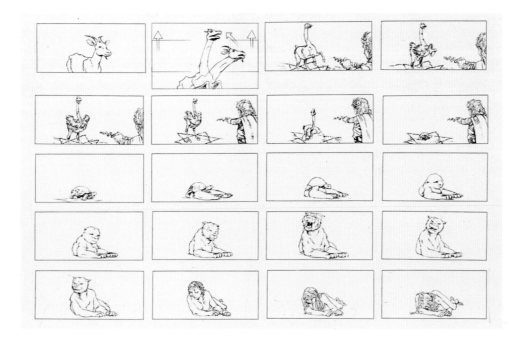

composited. The ILM team, after viewing tone and shadow pass elements during the test phase, felt that this traditional approach muddied the animation, making it stand apart from the live action.

"Peg Hunter, one of our optical team members, came up with the idea of rephotographing the tone elements onto a clear-based color stock instead of the traditional black-and-white stock," said Jones. "We experimented and discovered that it was a tremendous solution in terms of creating realistic shadows and enhancements to the shots. No more muddy tones! It was a real breakthrough. In a way, we created a new dimension on *Roger Rabbit*. The animation didn't look two-dimensional, [although] it didn't look entirely 3-D, either; we called it 2 and ¾-D."

"It's like having a paintbrush and a palette of pastel colors," Hunter added. "We were able to apply a delicate brushstroke and add subtle color to enhance the character's main animation pass. By manipulating the film through filtration, we added layer upon layer of color to the tones to enrich each character. It made the animation blend into the background much more than the old technique of using black-and-white film stock."

BLUE SCREEN IN TOONTOWN

The toons, who for most of the film had to suffer through the logic of the human world, got a little turnabout when Hoskins's character, an L.A. gumshoe named Eddie Valiant, had to enter the cartoon wonderland of Toontown. There Hoskins's flesh and blood character suffered some of the indignities that pass for normalcy in a cartoon world: getting literally flattened to the floor and ceiling of a speeding elevator and experiencing interminable falls through space.

Integrating Hoskins into his surreal cartoon environment required elaborate ILM blue-screen setups. Special wire rigs flew the actor, while the blue-screen photography was designed with all the live-action freedom that marked the entire film's camerawork. An important tool in achieving the shots, and helping to establish the correct scale and perspective needed to place Hoskins in the Toontown animation, was a video compositing system. Toontown storyboard scenes were videotaped and displayed on a monitor screen, while a separate videotape from the VistaVision camera filming the blue screen matted the actor over the storyboards' images on the monitor, allowing the production to evaluate whether the actor was being correctly placed into each shot.

The pressures of duty for ILMers were typified by the case of an exhausted Ed Jones, who, after working for months without a day off, went to a local coffee shop to order his usual toast and cappuccino and stood, frozen and befuddled at the counter, struggling to remember the word "toast." A fellow ILMer was nearby and, after a few moments of pantomime, helped Jones complete his order.

Zemeckis would later comment that working on *Roger Rabbit* was "like directing

a movie with the volume turned up to full blast." There were 751 credited members of the production, and the more than 82,000 frames of animation had all been hand-drawn, the thousand-plus shots all composited with traditional ILM optical printers. Although *Roger Rabbit* was a monumental

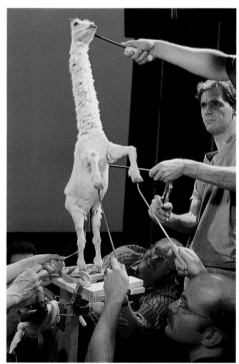

Left: The transformation sequence in *Willow* required a series of animatronic puppet creatures (with the transitions morphed). Here Wesley Seeds prepares a goat puppet.

Below left: Blue-screen filming for the transformation sequence began with the animatronic goat puppet, animated here by Bob Cooper (kneeling in foreground), Jeff Olson (kneeling in background, to the right), and Blair Clark (standing).

Below right: The goat puppet with its neck fully extended brought the physical animation to the ostrich stage of the transformation.

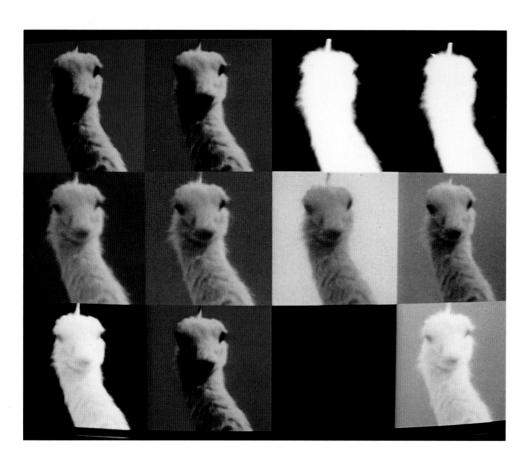

The ostrich caught in the digital realm.

achievement and a critical and box-office success, the production itself had been an ordeal and few who had worked on the film were talking sequel.

"The only reason to do another *Roger Rabbit* would be if you could push the technical envelope and do it all digitally," Jones observed. "It would be a more precise effort because in the digital realm you'd have more control over the individual elements and all of the edge characteristics. There would be no degradation or loss of quality in the compositing as you layer in all the separate elements. I believe computer animation paint systems and digital composites could capture the energy and authenticity of the original cartoons."

Who Framed Roger Rabbit? would win both the American and British Academy Awards for best visual effects, but Jones would create his own souvenir of the experience: a paperweight in the shape of a piece of toast, a personal reminder of the rigors of making movie history.

1988 (MGM/Lucasfilm Ltd.)
Development of Morphing Software

Willow is a film full of mythic visions: two-headed dragons, luminous fairies inhabiting enchanted forests, fairy-tale villages, and sinister castles. But the most unusual effects image of them all was the scene that unfolded when the hero, Willow, waved a magic wand and transformed a bewitched possum back into the human form of his ally, the sorceress Fin Raziel. To accomplish the scene ILM had to perform a little magic of its own, and the new computer graphics department got its first taste of big-time filmmaking—and achieved an image-processing breakthrough in the bargain.

The scene would call for Willow, a novice with the wand, to set off a succession of metamorphic effects, from goat to ostrich to turtle to tiger, before Raziel was restored to her human form. Executive producer George Lucas, director Ron Howard, and Dennis Muren (who cosupervised the effects with Micheal McAlister and Phil Tippett) wanted to produce a truly visionary effect, avoiding the traditional mechanical and optical tricks or camera cutaways. Muren felt that despite the unknowns it was time to give the fledgling CG group a shot at creating the effect.

Digitally creating each creature and the stages of metamorphosis was initially considered, but early 3-D tests proved unsatisfactory and the sequence became an image-processing challenge. "We quickly realized creating completely computer-generated animals was too much of an R and D project," recalled CG supervisor Doug Kay. "It would have required us to do work in 1987 at the level of *Jurassic Park*, and we wouldn't have been successful given the time frame and budget. So instead we got the idea of photographing either live-action animals or puppets, digitizing the elements, and then distorting the pictures from one to the other."

The resulting metamorphosis software created by programmer Doug Smythe would

become known as the "morphing system." The final strategy for achieving the shot involved shooting blue screen of the creatures and an actress playing Raziel, scanning the elements into the computer, and then digitally blending each image into the other. "Image processing means altering an image mathematically," Muren noted. "For *Willow* we decided to try to match the movements and the shapes of two different characters and compute the blend from one 2-D image to another to another, merging the images into one continuous synthetic image."

PUPPET ELEMENTS

Although a real tiger and the actress would be filmed, it was decided that the goat, ostrich, and turtle would be creature shop creations because those stages had to be specially articulated to segue to each successive transformation. The sequence was designed by Dennis Muren and David Allen, and artist Dave Lowery executed the storyboards. After prototype sculptures and storyboards, the creature shop produced rod puppets indicative of "a freestyle approach that would be analogically repeatable" rather than more complicated motion-control or go-motion setups,

according to rod puppet supervisor Allen.

The armatured goat puppet, designed by Tad Krzanowski, was the key puppet in the sequence. Special foam was needed to allow the goat's neck to be telescoped from its compressed starting width of one inch to the eighteen inches needed to bridge into the ostrich transformation. The foam was covered with actual goat hair, and the goat's head was equipped internally with vacuum hoses that would collapse and fit tightly over a smaller ostrich head hidden within. Lucas requested the added touch of a plume of colorful peacock feathers for the ostrich puppet, which was accomplished with a low-tech effect—fanning out attached umbrella spokes decorated with real peacock feathers.

GEARING UP FOR DIGITAL

Meanwhile, the CG department, faced with its first major assignment, had to take a variety of preparatory steps before even attempting any morphing magic. A commercial Eikonix—a single-frame, laser-based film scanner—had to be upgraded for feature-film scanning, which required adding transports to move the motion picture film through the scanner, filters, lenses, a light source, and

Above left: Some of the transformation stages were best staged with the real thing, such as this tiger that took the ILM bluescreen stage.

Above right: Once the puppets and live-action elements were shot, they were scanned into the digital realm. Here Lincoln Hu (left) and Doug Kay (right) monitor a now digitized tiger.

Above: The transformation sequence originally was to include a live-action cut with a half-human, half-tiger figure, but this idea was dropped in favor of a seamless morphing effect. Here David Allen points out a detail on the sculpted tiger headpiece to Richard Miller.

Below: The humanoid tiger, realized as a creature suit, is prepared for blue screen by Anne Polland (left), Jean Bolte (middle), and Tony Hudson (right).

separate each scanned-in blue-screen element from its blue background and create mattes for the final composite. Called "blue-screen extraction," the technique was a traditional practice in the optical department. But to create *digital* blue-screen extraction software required ILM's optical department to sit down with CG programmers and review how the department pulled mattes off the original negative from a blue-screen element.

MORPHING

Once the blue-screen backgrounds had been digitally extracted, it was time to discover if Smythe's morphing program could meld each digitized figure into one seamless metamorphosis. While digital artists performed the work with pressure-sensitive tablets or a mouse and viewed the results on a high-resolution computer screen, the work itself was being processed in the digital realm as a geometric distortion of each two-dimensional image. The elements were melded into each other and key frames (representing the major poses in a sequence) selected, allowing the programmer to manipulate grids of points and curves, spatially distorting them over each input image so that edge and internal features could exactly overlap. For generating realistic-looking motion-blur for puppets, the morph imitated the one forty-eighth of a second in which a real movie camera would allow light to expose a frame of film; this was created, again, by spatial manipulation of grids along select key frames.

The only effects step in the process that did not involve new digital technology was the use of a Pixar output film scanner. The completed transformation element and its matte were scanned directly onto film, and the two elements were delivered to optical for compositing with the background live-action plate.

The *Willow* transformation effect was a technological breakthrough that caused an immediate sensation in the entertainment industry. Although it would become a common effect in film, music videos, and television com-

other optical and mechanical adaptations. Revisions to the original Pixar painting program were also needed to allow CG operators to use a digital brush to paint out any visible rods and cables from the scanned-in puppet elements rather than relying on the hand-drawn, frame-by-frame articulate matte process traditionally used in opticals for wire removal.

Most important in gearing up the CG operation was the creation of a special software to mercials, it would be almost two years before any ILM competitor could duplicate the technique. In 1992 Doug Smythe was honored, along with Tom Brigham (who had conducted his own pioneering morph work at MIT in the early 1980s), with a technical achievement award by the Academy of Motion Picture Arts and Sciences for advancing technology with the morph computer software program.

The morph process introduced the CG department as a player, not a mere dabbler, in the art of effects. The transformation sequence also marked a threshold moment for the old photochemical process of traditional opticals, which was fast giving ground to the growing power of the digital realm. With *Willow* the CG department had taken steps toward engineering a higher level of input scanner and had begun duplicating such traditionally photochemical techniques as blue-screen extraction. Lucas's decade-old dream of all-digital opticals was now in sight.

In retrospect, Muren's decision to go with a computer graphics solution to rescue the

"Donovan's Destruction," the grisly comeuppance for Indy's Nazi foe Walter Donovan in *Indiana Jones and the Last Crusade*, was the first all-digital composite. As with the sequence in *Willow*, separate foam latex puppets capturing separate shots in the disintegrating transformation were created, scanned, and morphed through the stages.

Below: In the climax of *Last Crusade*, Donovan thinks he's drinking from the cup of immortality but instantly ages and is blasted into eternity instead. The sequence required careful planning, including these three-dimensional studies for one of the destructing stages.

Bottom left and right: Marc Thorpe works one of the life-size, foam latex Donovan puppet heads.

sorceress Raziel from her bewitchment seems a risky gamble given the tight production schedule and the relatively unsophisticated state of digital tools at the time. But Muren had a different perspective: "I had no Plan B in case Plan A failed, but there's always some sort of solution available. Computer graphics is like a chess game; you maneuver your way around the board, planning ahead but adapting to new situations, always moving your pieces to win."

INDIANA JONES AND THE LAST CRUSADE
1989 (LUCASFILM LTD./PARAMOUNT)
The First All-Digital Composite

Adolf Hitler's reported interest in talismans of supernatural power has been the subject of inquiry for both scholarly papers and the fantastic imaginings of true-fact pulp magazines. Hitler's mystic bent would provide the "Macguffin" (Hitchcock's word for the plot device that drives a story) for the first and third episodes in the Indiana Jones trilogy: In *Raiders of the Lost Ark*, Indy must find the sacred Ark of the Covenant before Nazi pawn René Belloq does, while in *Indiana Jones and the Last Crusade*, the sacred talisman Indy and the Nazis chase after is the Holy Grail, the chalice Christ shared with his apostles at the Last Supper.

In *Crusade*, the Grail is described as having the power to impart immortality to whoever drinks from it. Hitler's agent, a Nazi-sympathizing industrialist named Walter Donovan, does not plan to share the mystical

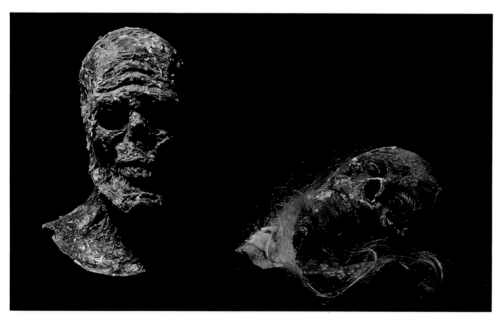

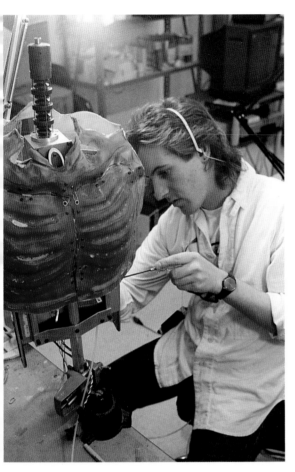

Far left: A torso piece was designed for Donovan that, when moved by a motion-control rig, would simulate the villain's death throes. Here Mike Jobe prepares the torso section.

Left: The completed Donovan on the motion-control rig.

Below: The finale, in which Donovan's skeleton smashes to bits against a wall, was created with a skeletal figure composed of brittle polymer material suspended on wires and blown apart with pyro charges.

prize with his Führer, and, like the villain of *Lost Ark*, comes to discover that the ultimate price is exacted for those who profane the sacred.

Donovan meets his fate in the inner chamber where an ancient knight guards the Grail. With gun drawn, Donovan selects an ornate silver goblet from a table filled with cups, dips it into a font of water, and drinks. In seconds Donovan realizes something is horribly wrong. Grabbing onto his partner, the sexy Dr. Elsa Schneider, he begins to age in seconds, his skin shriveling, his eyes disappearing in their sockets, his final skeletal face and form disintegrating into ash.

DONOVAN'S DESTRUCTION

The sequence, dubbed "Donovan's Destruction," was similar to the grisly end of Belloq and his Nazi cohorts in *Raiders*. In that film, the payoff for opening the Ark was accomplished with a series of cutaway shots of melting wax heads and a final pyro shot of a wax Belloq head exploding. But director Steven Spielberg didn't want a traditional approach in the latest Indy movie and insisted that the aging and disintegration be accomplished in one continuous shot. "I didn't want to do a series of cutaways so the actor could be advanced in makeup," Spielberg said. "We've all seen that, and I think people have a high level of expectation with these movies. I think the ILM crew would've been disappointed in me if I didn't offer them some new challenges every time out."

ILM assigned effects supervisor Micheal McAlister and his team to meet Spielberg's challenge. The effect would be attempted with a twofold approach: three motion-control puppet heads showing Donovan in advancing stages of decomposition would be filmed, and a seamless blending of the heads would be attempted using the digital morphing technique pioneered in *Willow*.

"We took a head cast of the actor and made a latex rubber head with motion-control mechanics," ILM makeup effects supervisor Stephan Dupuis explained. "Programmed moves made Donovan's cheeks suck in and his nose go back. We then took a cast of this head in its most decayed position and made a second head in which the nose went completely inside, the eyelids shriveled up, and the mouth curled back even more. He looked like a mummy at that point, and from this we cast the third head. The final head had to shrivel down to a skeleton."

All three heads were placed on the same motion-control rig so that they would go through the exact same motions in the frame. To avoid making it look like a head-on-a-stick shot, the heads were attached to a special motion-control rig representing Donovan's torso and neck. Not only could a more realistic head movement be achieved but the motion-control operators could make the torso shrug, bend, and shake, simulating the agony Donovan would feel as his body was torn apart.

All of the puppets were photographed in front of a blue screen, and the footage was scanned into a Pixar image-processing computer so that the morphing system could blend the stages of disintegration. The morphing was complicated by the need to use the first puppet's hair and background throughout the shot. Seamlessly integrating the second and third puppet stages required texture mapping over the master head.

Unlike *Willow*, in which specific elements were digitally manipulated and later optically composited, all the main elements of the sequence would be manipulated and composited in the digital realm. Once the shot was digitally composited and scanned back out to VistaVision, the image still required the traditional optical touch to be reduced to the four-perf standard. A few months later, the CG group would accomplish two more all-digital composites in the water creature sequence of *The Abyss*. But *Crusade* would be on record as the first full-frame, major-effects shot in which all the elements were scanned in, digitally composited and scanned back out to film.

"At the time, *Indiana Jones and the Last Crusade* didn't seem like a dramatic break-through," observed Doug Kay. "But, in fact, it was. We had finally realized a goal George Lucas had set way back, when Ed Catmull started the first computer graphics group at Lucasfilm. We put it all together on this shot to create our first totally digital composite."

DIE HARD 2: DIE HARDER
1990 (Twentieth Century-Fox)
The First Digitally Manipulated Matte Painting

The final scene in *Die Hard 2* had detective John McClane (Bruce Willis) and his wife, Holly (Bonnie Bedelia), happily reunited after another harrowing adventure battling terrorists. As the two are driven off, the camera pulls back to reveal a snowy runway crowded with jets, ambulances, military and police vehicles, and dozens of bystanders. The scene fades to black, and the credits roll. Director Renny Harlin had used a similar pull-back shot in *Nightmare on Elm Street 4*; in this film, a character dreams he's surrounded by junked cars, and the scene is given a disquieting jolt as the camera pulls back to reveal the junkyard world of dream demon Freddy Krueger.

For *Die Hard 2* the airport scene presented too many logistical and budgetary problems to attempt practically. At great expense a runway thick with snow would have had to be rented and filled with planes, vehicles, and people. Since it was a night shot, the director of photography would have had to engineer a herculean, if not impossible, lighting setup to capture the massive scale of the jumbo jets and all the vehicles and actors.

The shot was tagged as an effects challenge by the film's ILM visual effects squad. It was decided to best realize the airplane-filled runway as a matte painting that would incorporate live-action elements of actors and real vehicles. The shot, labeled "MP-4" on ILM's storyboards, would present its own unique challenges for the effects artists to overcome.

THE CHALLENGE OF MP-4

The prospective matte painting would have to be on-screen for some thirty-five seconds—much longer than the three-to-five-second window considered optimal before an audience might suspect the trick. A particular problem was integrating live-action elements into the painting, including six plates featuring actors and vehicles, separate passes for blinking lights, steam, and atmospheric haze. Although live-action plates were usually composited using rear projection, the scale required for the pull-back camera move would have resulted in a giveaway parallax view of a two-dimensional painting.

"When you use rear projection, you're projecting from the back [of a glass-painted surface] onto a piece of frosted glass," effects camera supervisor Bruce Walters explained. "If you move side to side from the glass you can see what's called 'the hot spot' moving with it, as you move off-center from where you've lined up your camera lens. So you don't want to move the projector because you can see that shift. Well, there was no way we could have shot a move with that kind of zoom on it with rear projection and make it look good. But sometimes when people are bidding [for] movies they say, 'We'll figure it out, even if it's impossible.' That's how these things get started. If we can't do it one way we have to find another way."

Walters estimated that in order to accomplish the shot with a traditional approach, a painting would have to be thirty feet long and fourteen feet wide. At sixteen times the size of a normal matte painting, it wouldn't even physically fit into ILM's twenty-four-foot-wide matte painting room. Considering that the average matte painting took three weeks to complete, Walters estimated that the *Die Hard* airport runway scene conceivably could have taken forty-eight weeks for the painting phase alone.

Walters began to consider the digital option, but that, too, had its problems. Digitally manipulating and compositing a

MP-4 was a thirty-five-second shot (much longer than the few seconds a camera would normally hold on a matte painting) that began as a tight, live-action shot with a camera pull-back revealing the matte-painted expanse, with live-action elements.

Left: The completed painting was photographed and scanned into a Macintosh II—along with six live-action plates, lights, and atmospheric haze—allowing Uesugi to blend all the elements into a final shot that could then be outputted to film.

Below: Those long, long hours can make artists do funny things—like this frog symbol on the side of an MP-4 vehicle.

matte painting and live action had never been attempted before and would require tremendous image-processing power. Walters then envisioned scanning in the painting by dividing it into a grid form of sixteen squares. As the camera moved progressively back, however, the amount of film resolution needed for each stage of the pull-back would increase to one hundred times film resolution, requiring so much data that the shot would be prohibitive. But Walters was still convinced the shot was doable in the digital realm. The answer to the riddle of MP-4 would come to Walters in a dream.

THE DREAM SOLUTION

"Often when I'm working on a problem, I'll have a dream in the middle of the night where the answer comes to me," Walters revealed. "It happens to me all the time, but unfortunately it's a very painful process because it always seems to happen at the last minute. These dreams are not symbolic; I'll just see myself solving the problem. In my MP-4 dream I saw that instead of dividing the painting up into a side-to-side, top-to-bottom grid, I could divide it up like a bull's-eye made out of four rectangular shapes. So instead of painting at one hundred times film resolution, we'd only need four paintings at

Above: To create the finale image of a jet-crowded runway for *Die Hard 2*, matte artists Yusei Uesugi and Paul Huston plotted the composition and scale with model planes.

Top right and opposite page: The painting, dubbed "MP-4," which took artist Yusei Uesugi five weeks to complete, was finished on a canvas thirteen feet wide and five feet tall—four times the size of a normal matte painting. In the foreground of the top right photo are photos of the live-action plates used to prepare the painting.

four times film resolution. When I dream up these ideas my buddy John Knoll helps tell me if they'll work or not. So the next day I met with John and Doug Kay, and we worked out the idea on a chalkboard, and they helped technically figure out what I had conceptualized in my dream."

Matte artists Yusei Uesugi and Paul Huston sketched out the final look and perspective for the painting itself by placing on a board small model planes and nails to simulate the people in the scene. Uesugi, who would paint the matte shot, then took a single frame of film of the mock-up. The still image was then projected down with a rotoscope camera, and a drawing made that could be used as a grid to align the cameras. The grid was then loaded into an Automatte camera and projected onto the painting surface, marking the points where people would be placed.

After the live-action plates were filmed, photographic prints representing all six of these plates would be pasted onto the painting's surface area. The painting itself, although considerably less than the sprawling canvas envisioned earlier, was still thirteen feet wide and five feet tall and would take five weeks to complete. With brush and oils

Uesugi painted with the most detail at the foot-wide bull's-eye center, since this was where the camera would begin, and worked a rougher, more impressionistic style to the edges of the canvas. Meanwhile, effects cameraman Pat Myers programmed the overall move for all the plates as well as the four views that would comprise the final pull-back effect.

Four photographs of the final painting were taken and scanned into a Macintosh II. A thirty-five-second move that normally would have required 840 frames of information would be accomplished in the digital realm with only four frames. The bull's-eye approach allowed the painting to be scanned in and manipulated without wasting precious computer memory. Uesugi could then view the painting in its computer environment by monitor and, with the aid of Photoshop soft-

ware and an electronic pen on a digital tablet, work the colors and blend lines between images.

MP-4 would be the first time digital techniques had been used to blend a painting with live-action elements. The shot was also hailed as one of the most memory-intensive CG projects to date. At thirty-five seconds it was the longest continuous shot the department had dealt with to that point, and it required fourteen or fifteen Macintosh disks, each holding about six hundred megabytes of information (roughly the memory of ten thousand normal Mac disks).

For the computer graphics department, MP-4 represented another giant step in the art of image processing. For Bruce Walters it was a dream come true.

BUILDING THE VISTAFLEX

The wide-screen VistaVision format of the 1950s, resurrected by George Lucas and ILM for the optical compositing advantages it would give its *Star Wars* production, had once been used for such feature films as *The Ten Commandments*, *North by Northwest*, and *White Christmas*. When it was decided that *Roger Rabbit* would be filmed in 35mm VistaVision to provide the highest-quality first-unit images for the unprecedented amount of opticals ILM would have to produce, it was the first time in some thirty years that the eight-perf format would be used to shoot an entire feature. ILM was charged with designing and building two new live-action VistaVision production cameras, which needed to be delivered to waiting live-action plate crews in England within only six months.

Production cinematographer Dean Cundey and his camera assistants drew up a wish list and discussed the project's goals with ILM. It was of major importance that the camera have all the freedom of a normal four-perf, 35mm live-action production camera. The new cameras would have to synch with sound, run quietly, and be mobile, light, and able to hold one-thousand-foot film loads (instead of the standard four-hundred-foot loads). A breakthrough aspect of the new camera technology was its design for shooting moving backgrounds for optical compositing instead of using the typical locked-off camerawork on background plates.

"We built two cameras, one high speed and one sound speed," said electronics technician Mike MacKenzie. "They couldn't have shot this movie without them because there were no other VistaVision cameras at that time which were soundproofed and lightweight. The cameras were not only quiet, but their ease of use was a hundred times better than any other VistaVision camera. If you look at the old cameras when they get blimped [made soundproofed], they look like a motorcycle sidecar. Having to use them would have made an arduous shooting schedule much worse and much slower."

The entire engineering staff had to work around the clock for a final three-month stretch to machine the two cameras. Time grew so short that the crew only had time to test the cameras with a mere four hundred feet of film. They had time to do no more; the day after that initial test, the cameras (dubbed the VistaFlex) were on a flight to the first unit production in London. The cameras made it to England and cleared customs just hours before they were needed on the set.

ILM's VistaFlex camera records the antics of two *Willow* brownies, with the performers clambering on an oversized set representing a secion of a runaway cart. Eyeing and lining up the action from above are visual effects supervisor Micheal McAlister (left) and camera assistant Pat McArdle (right).

The VistaFlex cameras worked perfectly. Dean Cundey, in a letter to chief engineer Mike Bolles, later praised the VistaFlex as "one of the most significant (and also underrated) advances in camera technology in the past ten years."

"We were half insane by the end of production," MacKenzie recalled. "I remember when the driver came to pick up the camera cases. All that morning we had been working like crazy and then, suddenly, the cameras were gone. They were as ready as they were ever going to be. I remember breaking open a bottle of champagne and pouring it into paper cups. I think that's the closest I'll ever feel to being a woman who's just given birth—except [in this case] someone swooped in and took away the baby before we even had a chance to admire our work."

CHAPTER SEVEN

ILLUSIONS OF REALITY

It is testament to the power of modern effects magic that some critics have derided the "effects movie," claiming the effects overpower subtleties of plot and character. George Lucas disagrees: "The people who saw *Star Wars* and said 'spectacular special effects' just never understood it. The same thing with *Indiana Jones*: 'It's high adventure . . . just one cliffhanger after another.' Some people look at those movies and they don't see the intricacies of the character and story because they're overwhelmed by the whole thing. You can see so many movies released in the wake of those two movies, just loaded with special effects and stunts, but they don't make very interesting movies."

Although Industrial Light & Magic has earned its renown for achieving fantastic visions, less heralded are the company's contributions to movies in which audiences might not suspect any effects at all. In Steven Spielberg's World War II–era epic *Empire of the Sun* (1987), the CG department digitally generated a squadron of Japanese fighter planes flying over Shanghai. In *The Last Temptation of Christ* (1988), a scene in which a lion appears before Jesus Christ as he sits in a sacred circle was accomplished by using a split-screen effect to integrate separate photography of the lion and actor Willem Dafoe. In *The Doors* (1991), matte paintings helped director Oliver Stone stage a desert location where a young Jim Morrison has a mystical experience. Spielberg's acclaimed black-and-white-filmed *Schindler's List* (1993) was given a few poetic dabs of color—a red candle flame and the red coat of a little girl—by ILM digital artists who scanned in special color footage for the sequences, created mattes for objects in color, and dropped everything else to the black-and-white tones in which the rest of the movie had been shot.

Effects that re-create everyday reality are one of the most difficult of movie illusions. A planet exploding in space is obviously an effects shot (although the realism of the effect and the power of the story must still allow audiences to suspend disbelief), but a great deal of moviemaking requires effects work to fabricate reality (such as the matte-painted mansions of *Gone With the Wind*).

During ILM's second decade the company had a number of assignments placing airplane models in location environments—effects as complex as creating spaceships in orbit. Beginning with *Always*, ILM developed a realistic, in-camera approach (as opposed to motion-control, blue-screen stage work) to airplane model work, flying and shooting airplane models in open-air locations. For *Die Hard 2* and *Alive*, ILM would not only have to simulate airplanes in flight but crash them as well.

DIE HARD 2: DIE HARDER
1990 (Twentieth Century-Fox)
Flying Through Storms

Big-budget moviemaking doesn't require filmmakers to move heaven and earth—but sometimes it just feels that way. *Die Hard 2* was a film that required herculean efforts to accomplish the special and visual effects.

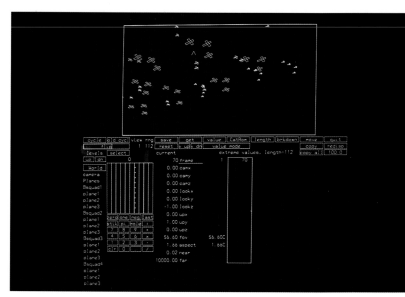

Clockwise from left: A squadron of World War II Japanese fighter planes buzz Shanghai, a subtle CG effect added to director Steven Spielberg's *Empire of the Sun*.

In the first *Die Hard*, New York detective John McClane had an explosive Christmas season battle with terrorists inside a high-tech skyscraper in Los Angeles. For the sequel, also set during the Christmas season, McClane would have to save Dulles airport in Washington, D.C. Renegade U.S. military officers had shut off runway lights and contact between the control tower and the planes in a bizarre plot to liberate a Central American military figure being flown in under extradition for drug charges. For the filmmakers the logistics of realizing the story included the need to show nighttime blizzard conditions, airplanes forced to circle the airport on dwindling fuel supplies (including an L-1011 craft bearing McClane's wife, Holly), and several spectacular crashes.

Thanks to its breakthrough live-action airplane model work for *Always*, ILM was awarded the task of creating shots of planes flying through the blizzard and crashing on snow-slick runways. A few of the shots were calm-before-the-storm scenes of airplanes flying through blue sky and would be accomplished by filming models blue-screen and matting them into sky plates. But blue screen was impossible for the storm scenes since any smoke effects would have contaminated it. And, of course, there were fiery plane crashes to produce.

For *Die Hard 2* director Renny Harlin's first unit and special effects coordinator Al DiSarro's crew, the production got off to an inauspicious start at the first location shoot in Moses Lake, Washington. Their arrival at evening had seen a countryside nestled under a blanket of snow, but by the morning sun the snow had melted away, a harbinger of what would prove to be one of the warmest winters on record.

Harlin, DiSarro, and the production

chased after snowbound locations to no avail. With the entire movie hinging on a winter storm to keep planes circling and the hero in peril, the production decided to manufacture what nature had failed to provide. Although falling snow could be simulated with plastic

Above: John Goodson works a pattern for the C-130 military transport, one of the thirteen-some airplane models for *Die Hard 2*. The model department had only two months to create a complex mix of perfectly scaled and detailed military and commercial aircraft.

Left: Model maker Kim Smith paints an F-4 Phantom military jet model, which measures six feet in the fuselage and four feet in the wingspan. All the models were constructed of fiberglass and aluminum and required interior wiring and paint jobs.

Pat Sweeney lines up a military transport model for a blue-screen shot that would be composited in a blue-sky background plate. Most of the film, however, featured planes flying through a blizzard or getting blown up, which precluded further blue-screen adventures.

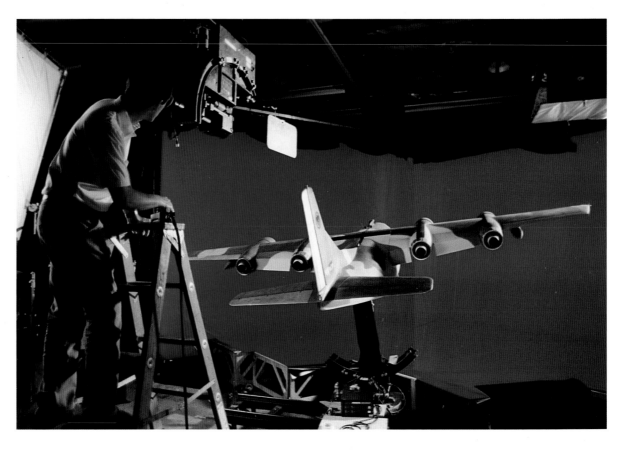

flakes, there were ecological concerns about releasing plastic into open location shoots, and so that option was relegated to sound-stage shots. Biodegradable soap flakes were the next best option for the open-air work, but the soap industry had switched from flakes to granular soap fifteen years before. Creating a biodegradable soap flake required DiSarro to retool an East Coast factory, with crews working round the clock to produce almost 100,000 pounds of old-fashioned soap flakes. To provide a ground-snow effect, as was needed for location shooting at Denver's Stapleton Airport, multiton ice crushers were trucked to the location to produce hundreds of pounds of ice for the camera nightly.

Meanwhile, back at ILM, *Die Hard 2* visual effects supervisor Micheal McAlister and his crew had decided to do their own location work in the style of a live-action second unit. ILM's work was geared for a realistic look; Harlin had impressed upon McAlister that the film's success depended on audiences believing real jets with real passengers were in deadly jeopardy.

ILM decided to film its models flying and crashing at a lonely airstrip in the vastness of Southern California's Mojave Desert. There were westerly winds roaring through the Tehachapi Pass into the valley that kept electrically generated wind turbines spinning on the mountainsides—providing power enough to naturally fan the navy fogger smoke needed to create the storm clouds through which to fly the model planes (a technique used in *Always* to simulate smoke from forest fires). The logistics for ILM's location work included erecting a tent city at the airstrip to accommodate tons of cameras, lights, models, riggings, foggers, food services, and other supplies. The team would be able to smoke their airstrip set, fly and film their models by night, and spend their days at a hotel a half-hour drive away. To assure that their work matched the principal photography, Paul Huston, ILM's art director on the film, would join the main unit on location, taking notes and pictures and reporting back to McAlister.

Model shop supervisors Charlie Bailey

and Jeff Olson and thirty model makers began work in January 1990. The model makers had only two months to build a mix of military and commercial aircraft, including one F-4 Phantom jet, a modified C-130 military transport craft, one 727, three 747s, five DC-8s, and two L-1011s. The sizes ranged from 747 models measuring twenty-three feet long and forty inches high from belly to cockpit to the F-4's six-foot fuselage and four-foot wingspan. The models, constructed of standard fiberglass and aluminum, also required internal wiring for radio-controlled lights, landing gear, access panels to rig pyro, and special paint jobs to emblazon the hulls with the logos and paint schemes of such fictional companies as FujiAir and Northeast Airlines. To meet their production deadline the shop had to contract out the DC-8s and 747s, although ILM still was responsible for their paint jobs and internal wiring.

LOCATION WORK: BATTLING THE ELEMENTS

By early March McAlister's sixty-member crew—nicknamed "Crash and Burn Productions"—journeyed south from Marin County in several forty-foot truck trailers full of models and equipment for nearly a month of shooting model planes with live-action practical-effects photography. Awaiting the Crash and Burn crew were weeks of hot desert sun, bitterly cold nights, and vortices of wind screaming down from the mountains.

"A few of us went down there to prerig three days before the main crew arrived," model rigging expert Dave Heron remembered. "We were out there in howling sandstorms, pounding stakes to hold the tents down, but Mother Nature was killing us. We'd escape into our vans when it got real bad. When the main group pulled up, the sand was blowing so hard we couldn't even get out of our vans to greet them."

"It was hell revisited—terrible, blizzard-like wind conditions blowing dirt and sand everywhere," assistant effects director Ed Hirsh grimly recalled. "We looked like World

War Two desert rats with goggles and scarves on for protection. The mess tent was the worst in terms of deafening sounds. The wind made it sound like people were standing around banging garbage can lids together. Most people just ate in their trucks to avoid that noise. On the set, both the space heaters and the smokers would be making a huge racket, so the noise level was deafening wherever you went. Because we were out in the middle of nowhere, we needed to be self-sufficient. We had ten snorkel forklifts, a huge generator, and enough lights to illuminate a football field. It was the biggest stage show we'd ever done in terms of the amount of lighting and rigging equipment we needed. We'd shoot from sundown to sunup. The shift would end at dawn with Bushmills and beer at the camera truck."

The production team would set up their shots utilizing storyboards and Huston's morning telephone reports from the principal photography locations detailing the live-action weather conditions that would have to be matched on the airstrip set. (The Crash and Burn crew settled on gypsum rock for a ground-snow effect.) Cranes rising twenty

This little-used airstrip in Southern California's Mojave Desert was perfect for the film, as it had room to fly the large models and continual winds to blow the fog machine smoke.

CRASH & BURN PRODUCTIONS

Above: *Die Hard 2* effects supervisor Micheal McAlister and his sixty-member crew spent a month in the desert flying, crashing, and blowing up model planes, which made this self-proclaimed title an appropriate one. (The words are emblazoned over one of the pyrotechnic effects produced by the crew.)

Below: Since the story was set at night, that's when ILM worked. For shots where the airstrip needed to be in camera view, the airstrip set was dressed with gypsum rock to simulate snow.

feet off the ground suspended the lights and radio-controlled camera and models, and the foggers filled the open-air set with clouds of smoke.

In a scissor-lift high above the man-made clouds, McAlister and his assistants and tech people could direct the flying scenes that McAlister called "a nightly aerial ballet." The radio-controlled camera was operated by director of photography Kim Marks from the perch in the scissor-lift. The models, suspend-

ed by wires attached to wings, nose, and tail, were controlled by radio-controlled rigs capable of tilt, bank, and other movements.

The foggers were mineral-oil vaporizing units measuring four feet long by three feet square. When heated up, they produced clouds that extended a hundred feet wide and a quarter mile long. A wind force of only five to ten miles an hour was needed to blow the cloud bank. On a few occasions production was halted when the wind gods of the Tehachapi Pass were too generous: flurries set the cranes to swaying and the aerodynamically designed models bucking at the wires, fighting to fly free.

CRASH AND BURN PRODUCTIONS

The most difficult challenge facing the Crash and Burn crew was staging the fiery crash of a DC-8 passenger plane and the explosion of a 747 commandeered by the terrorists. In the story the terrorists, in order to demonstrate to authorities their supreme control of the airfield, establish radio control with the plane and guide the pilot through the blizzard to a fiery end, the crash and fireball consuming the plane and 230 passengers. The plans for the shot had touched off a debate between Harlin and Twentieth Century-Fox executives, who were concerned that the scene might be too grisly for sum-

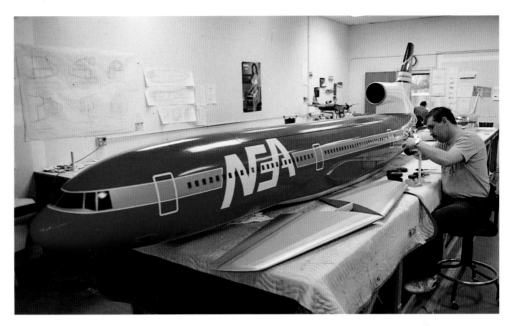

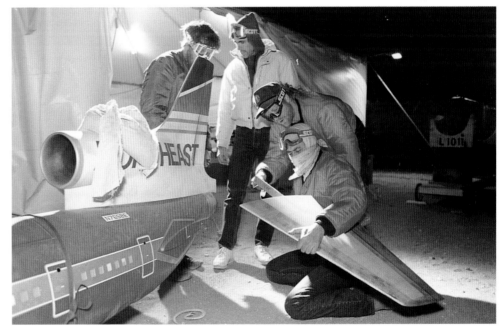

mertime audiences. Harlin stuck to his guns, convinced that the shot was necessary to convince audiences of the ruthlessness of the villains. However, shots of the passengers' frightened reactions to the initial impact, which had been shot on a set and originally cut into the movie, were so terrifying (made all the more authentic by preproduction research of Federal Aviation Administration test crashes and data from real plane crashes) that they were ultimately cut before the film's release.

ILM's crash of the twenty-three-foot-long DC-8 model would require three separate shots, the first showing the plane's nose pulling up prior to impact (simulating the pilots' last desperate effort to avoid a crash), the second the plane skidding along the runway, and the finale a pyro shot with three separate explosions consuming the doomed jet.

For the impact and skid, one of the five

available models was held aloft from a forklift and rigged to slide down two main cables that ran diagonally down 150 feet from the forklift's base and were attached to a pair of two-foot spikes pounded into the ground. The cables themselves were laced through pulleys attached to the wings, and a third cable was laced through the tail to control the up-and-down nose positioning. A tow cable, attached to the nose of the plane, extended down to the trailer hitch of a pickup truck set to pull out at forty mph and drag the jet down its cable

Top left: An L-1011 "Northeast" passenger model is lifted by the cranes that would "fly" the models.

Top right and bottom: The Northeast model, which in the film is carrying detective John McClane's wife to Dulles International Airport, receiving final fuselage detailing at ILM by model maker Joe Martinez . . .

. . . and further attention at the Mojave Desert location.

ramp and into the shot. But the model, as an accurate miniaturization of a real craft, needed to fly, not crash, and at first glided twenty to thirty feet beyond camera range. To solve the problem, the tow cable was laced through an eyebolt attached to the exact impact spot so the cable could drag the huge model into the ground.

The pyro shot of the DC-8 would be a dangerous effect given the vagaries of timing and the wind. The model, stuffed with gunpowder, kerosene, and flammable liquids, had to be timed to explode at a precise mark. To extend the action, the pyro unit, headed by John McLeod, rigged the explosives to detonate in sequence: the engines erupting in flame, one wing exploding, the other wing exploding, the fuselage detonating in a final fireball blast. To trip the pyro a rope was attached to a detonation switch inside the plane. The coiled rope, which would unravel as the plane was towed, would act as a ripcord, pulling the switch and setting off the explosive sequence at its designated spot.

Top: Foggers produced smoke (a nontoxic vaporized mineral oil) that, when whipped by the mountain winds, looked like storm clouds.

Middle and bottom: The Northeast airliner is flown through the cloud effect.

"There were three of us on forklifts getting knocked around pretty badly by the wind," Dave Heron recalled of the first pyro shoot. "We were bumping right into the plane which was fully loaded and rigged with pyro. We finally just came down and waited for the wind to die down. But once a model's full of pyro and gasoline, you can't back away from it. We did manage to blow it up—I felt the concussion from seventy-five yards away when the DC-8 blew."

The pyro unit had another challenge in the climactic shot of the 747, its seats jammed with escaping terrorists, exploding on liftoff. In the film the villains have seemingly made good their escape. But the scrappy McClane, who has managed to open the jet's fuel tank, uses a cigarette lighter to light the gas streams, setting off a fire trail that catches up to the plane and blows up the jet as it lifts into the sky.

For the 747 shot the ILM crew had to dress the set with gypsum and control the

Left and below: In the finale, the bad guys attempt a getaway in a 747 cargo carrier. (At twenty-three feet long, the three 747 models were the biggest in the production.) Here, a sixty-foot crane lifts the mighty model into position for an explosive finish.

Right and below: Quick-thinking detective McClane manages to ignite a fuel leak that catches the wing of the departing cargo plane. For the resulting series of explosions, the model was held in a secured, stationary position and detonated by remote control.

Far right: Climax of 747 pyro blast.

smoking units to match the live-action shot of a real jet taxiing down a runway at a location shoot in Alpena, Michigan. The Alpena film would also serve as the background plate into which the fire trail would be composited. The fire trail itself would be shot at ILM's Marin County back lot using a long pipe loaded with propane gas and lit at one end. The fire effect was then rephotographed by camera on a pin-block mechanism under an animation camera, with animated fire reflections added to realistically marry the composited fire trail to the live-action plate.

For the 747 blast McLeod's unit packed

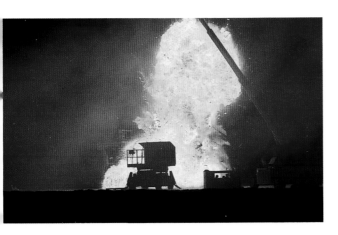

the model with hundreds of pounds of explosives. The pyro was rigged to explode in three blasts, using a combination of primer cord to tear the plane apart, gunpowder for the big explosion, and kerosene for a final fireball effect. Unlike the DC-8 explosion, the 747 would be detonated electronically, each blast timed a few hundredths of a second apart. The night of the shot the pyro-packed 747 was wheeled out by dolly and wired to a sixty-foot construction crane that lifted the model fifteen feet into the air. The trip wire ran from the plane's nose to a bunker fifty yards off-camera where McLeod was hunkered down, ready to touch the wire to a battery and set off the blast.

When the explosion went off, it created a mushroom cloud that lifted hundreds of feet into the air. The blast could be seen miles away, prompting calls to the airstrip by distant onlookers who had glimpsed the blast from a freeway and were concerned that a real plane had crashed.

The logistics of the production—manufacturing special effects snow; flying and crashing models in the desert—escalated the estimated *Die Hard 2* production price tag to a then-record $70 million. The design and execution of the film's spectacular action effects did, however, prove to be a crowd pleaser, and the film was one of the top-grossing movies of 1990. For ILM's Crash and Burn Productions the experience would ultimately be remembered for the painful battle against the elements of the vast Mojave Desert.

ALIVE
1992 (Disney/Paramount)
Plane Crash at 11,000 Feet

For a film based on a true 1972 account of survival in the remote, snow-covered Andes, ILM had to open the movie with a terrifying plane crash that had to look completely realistic. ILM's work for the eighteen-shot sequence was divided into three segments: a plane above the daytime clouds, its descent

Left, top to bottom: To heighten suspense and audience anticipation as to its outcome, the crash of the Windsor DC-8 was achieved with these shots: hitting the runway, sliding down the runway, and this final fatal explosion. A complicated ripcord mechanism triggered the series of blasts that took out one of the five nearly twenty-three-feet-long Windsor models in the second cut of the crash sequence.

through the clouds, and the subsequent crash at the mountain's 11,000-foot elevation.

"We initially thought about crashing the plane into a mountain on a computer and did some tests in CG," said ILM effects supervisor Scott Farrar. "But you need to see all the debris in a physical sense. Trying to figure out the physics of such action would be mind-boggling. We ended up using cables to drag the plane and crash it into a model of the mountain. We used CG wire removal and major rig removal and painted in some of the missing spots on the frame, and filmed it out—a perfect marriage of old and new techniques."

For the aerial background plates the Canadian Rockies were designated as stand-ins for the Andes. Farrar and a three-person crew spent a week shooting the VistaVision footage with a camera mounted to a heli-copter. It was "very scary," Farrar recalled of flying along the ten-thousand-to-twelve-thousand-foot elevations of the glacial face and fighting the unpredictable weather to make a number of perilously close approaches to approximate the flight crew's point of view of the approaching impact.

CRASH DESIGN

The approach-and-crash sequence, de-signed by art director Bill George, had been designed and storyboarded to be the most

Above: Scott Farrar (left), John Goodson (middle), and Jon Foreman (right) inspect the *Fuerza Aerea Uruguaya* plane model that will simulate the true-life Andes plane crash dramatized in *Alive*.

Right: The Andes crash would be created with full advantage of ILM's back lot, natural light, and a sculpted Andes set.

Left: Tony Sommers (middle), and Lorne Peterson (right), loom above the Andes as they make the set ready for the eight-foot breakaway model.

Below, left to right: As the cameras roll, a tower rig (digitally erased later) rides the plane into its prealigned impact point.

realistic airplane crash ever simulated. The concerns throughout, from background plates to the impact of a model on a miniature mountain landscape, were that the shot-to-shot look relate to what a camera would actually capture in a real situation. Unlike a *Die Hard 2* crash, where a spectacular nighttime explosion concealed the effects, the *Alive* plane would crash in daytime and be ripped apart by the mountain, making it a risky effects shot since audiences would be able to scrutinize every detail.

The crash called for the plane's midsec-

tion to tear apart and then lose its tail and wings while plowing through snow and rock. An eight-foot breakaway model was designed with the front end and tail section heavily reinforced and a nonreinforced midsection built up of plastic, foil, wire, and metals so that when it broke open it would have the layered metal look of a real plane crashing. The task for Dave Heron, the key rigger in charge of the miniature physical effects, was to engineer two separate shots, the first with the midsection blowing open, the second with the plane losing its tail and wings.

The miniature mountain set, sculpted from plaster and foil and dressed with baking soda, was erected in an area of the ILM parking lot. A cable drive system designed by Dave Heron was rigged to fly the model, which was mounted on an aligned track, into designated crash points on the mountain set. Before each take the model had to be pre-aligned so it would hit the mountain at the break-point "sweet spot," a weakened area barely three inches in length. A continuous loop cable that ran through a series of sheaves was able to pull the plane to impact at twenty-five mph, fast enough to crack the plane at its break points without causing any telltale model jiggles or bounces. Adding to the realism and scale was a background consisting of plaster and foil mounted to a steel framework and dressed and detailed, with a canvas backing painted to match the location.

"Director Frank Marshall knew the plane crash at the beginning of the film had to be extremely realistic and frightening because it was the main action sequence that would literally throw the audience into the story," Scott Farrar concluded. "Because the story was being told from the survivors' point of view, Marshall wanted the audience to feel like they were on the plane with them. The design of this sequence is a perfect example of how the marriage of visual and mechanical effects can create an extremely realistic sequence."

PHOTOSHOP: CREATION OF A SOFTWARE SYSTEM

Photoshop has helped ILM's CG department function with more freedom in the digital realm. Since its first major motion picture use in 1989's *The Abyss*, ILMer John Knoll's software has been an integral part of any ILM project requiring image processing.

John Knoll describes himself as one of those whose lives were changed by *2001* and *Star Wars*; after seeing these films, he wanted to be in the business of making movies. A model maker as a kid, Knoll was naturally drawn to the effects crafts. "It was completely fascinating to me that in special effects, part of the frame might be a painting, part a model, and part live action," Knoll said. "I decided to go to college in Los Angeles, study filmmaking at USC, and try to get a job at ILM."

Although Knoll would eventually be using and developing motion-control and computer technology, he never studied those disciplines during college. Luckily he had a knack for developing interests in complex technologies and became a self-taught expert on the subject. As a final USC project Knoll, who had become fascinated with motion control, bought a used Apple II computer and a four-channel CNC milling machine controller, bolted it onto an old Oxberry animation stand, and shot an experimental slit-scan movie (in which streaked images were produced by filming a subject through a slit in a foreground barrier, a technique that produced the streak photography in the famed "Stargate Corridor" sequence in *2001*).

After being hired at ILM in 1986 as a motion-control cameraman, Knoll found himself searching for a new hobby. He had begun working with the Pixar image-processing system and found it a cumbersome tool requiring a lot of typing of commands to work. Intrigued with the notion of developing a new image-processing

John Knoll watches the water pseudopod of *The Abyss* take shape.

tool, he hooked up with his brother Thomas, who was working on a doctoral thesis in vision systems for computers at the University of Michigan. His brother's researches in computer vision, for example, how computers can "see" materials coming down an assembly line and recognize and remove any defective parts, had its roots in image processing.

Photoshop had actually been targeted for the publishing industry. "Photoshop was primarily intended for the print industry, for preparing images to be printed on four-color offset presses," Knoll said. "I'd say ninety-five percent of its use is for prepress, and a much smaller percentage are using it for animation video and special effects kinds of things."

Knoll describes software as composed of millions and millions of instructions for the computer. Since it would be too time-consuming and complex to write every single

processor instruction, a programmer writes software in an intermediate, symbolic language, a code that a computer can translate and turn into the actual instructions to be executed by the computer.

"When you're writing this intermediate language typically what you do is write a few pieces of the code and run it to see whether it works and test it until you're satisfied. The art of computer programming is basically a divide and conquer process," Knoll explained. "You analyze the problem, what it is you want the computer to do, and you break that problem up into smaller pieces, and each one of those smaller pieces gets broken up into even smaller pieces, and you tackle them all one at a time and make all the pieces work."

One of the major advantages with Photoshop was that the ILM team working on such CG-intensive projects as *Terminator 2* and *Jurassic Park* could take flawed shots

The magic of Photoshop, with its capacity for electronic painting and seamless cut-and-pasting of elements, helped ILM provide *The Young Indiana Jones Chronicles* television series with the kind of lavish production values normally seen on the big screen. For this shot, Photoshop expands a simple art gallery set into a sumptuous art museum by seamlessly integrating a Paul Huston painting of a long hallway (which includes the painted patrons in the distance), duplicating and extending the set floor, and pasting onto the walls a variety of painted images. This shot represents an early example of the use of Photoshop technology for matte paintings, according to matte painter Yusei Uesugi. In the ensuing years digital tools and techniques have been perfected and expanded to produce even more seamless works.

and use the software to paint themselves toward a solution—which provided a quantum leap over the traditional image-processing method of photochemical optical printing.

"In traditional opticals what used to happen is we'd always have to remake the dreaded 'BC'—the black center," Knoll recalled. "You'd have a background plate and you're going to composite, say, an airplane into the shot. Well, you can't just double-expose the airplane over the background; you want to make a hole for it, the matte. So you use what's called a holdout matte—a clear piece of film with a black silhouette where the object's going to be, and that's bipacked with the background plate so that it makes a little hole. Some of these elements would just eventually wear out, and any problems with the BC would be immediately evident. You thread them up through the optical printer enough times [that] they start getting scratches or other problems. In an optical composite if there's some flaw, and if the shot is ninety percent of the way there, there's not too much you can do. What's really nice about digital manipulation is you can paint your way to a finished shot and see your work right on the screen as it

happens; you don't have to wait around for film to be processed. When you have a digitized picture it's putty in your hands, and you can do anything you want with it. I haven't gotten bored with computers because they're such a flexible tool and there's almost unlimited possibilities. I think of computers as a kind of brain amplifier, a tool that amplifies your abilities. It allows you to take your ideas and go a lot farther."

Knoll observes that now he's essentially returned to doing what he loved as a kid: building models. Only now the models

belong to the digital realm, not the physical world. "Building computer models is much the same skill as building models with real materials, but there are some big improvements. When I think about a pie chart of my day as a model maker, about half the time was spent sanding. You don't have to sand stuff in CG. Writing software is the same kind of introverted, concentrated work that building models was. It satisfies the same creative desire. When I'm writing a piece of software, it's craftsmanship—crafting this really complex and beautiful thing."

CHAPTER EIGHT

SPELLS OF ENCHANTMENT: FANTASY EFFECTS

"**F**orget . . . counties overhung with smoke, Forget the snorting steam and piston stroke, Forget the spreading of the hideous town," socialist William Morris wrote of the industrialized London of the Victorian era in the prologue of his book of enchanted poems, *The Earthly Paradise*. Or, as painter Sir Edward Burne-Jones put it: "The more materialistic science becomes, the more angels shall I paint."

Prior to the arrival of cinema, those who wished respite from "snorting steam and piston stroke" could indulge themselves in the fantastic visions produced by fantasy-book illustrators. Advances in printing and image reproduction allowed the flowering of art charged with an enchanted atmosphere: The very clouds took supernatural shapes or gnarled old trees a human face, evil creatures trolled the dark woods at night while winged fairies slept in moonlit boughs, knights on steeds journeyed on their mystic quests and battled a dragon or two along the way.

Upon this foundation of dreams, the movies built their own fantastic visions in films such as *The Thief of Bagdad* and *The Wizard of Oz*. Of course, what an illustrator could create with pen or brush required teams of artists, craftsmen, engineers, and optical technicians to realize as a live-action movie. As visual effects technology became less cumbersome, so the images on screen could attain a nearer reflection of the mind's imaginings.

Two of the most ambitious projects of ILM's second decade—*Willow* and *Hook*—had the fantastic visual themes reminiscent of the fantasy illustrators of old. *Willow*, a Lucasfilm project that executive producer Lucas had first conceived during the making of *Star Wars*, told the tale of Willow Ufgood,

Woodland study for *Willow*.

a farmer in the land of Nelwyn who must deliver to safety in a distant kingdom a baby girl with the potential to end the evil rule of Queen Bavmorda. In *Hook*, director Steven Spielberg took J. M. Barrie's Peter Pan story and updated it—the boy who never grows up has left Neverland and aged into a workaholic acquisitions attorney, an unhappy state of affairs that is remedied by a magical return to the land of Lost Boys, pirates, and fairies.

These fantasy films were achieved through a variety of techniques: matte painting shots establishing the fanciful Nelwyn countryside in *Willow* and the "Neverland Reveal" of *Hook*; computer graphics techniques, such as the breakthrough Raziel morphing sequence and the texture-mapped Neverland painting of the Peter Pan flyover (and even a digital prop of Captain Hook's hook that Tinker Bell shakes). Both films were populated by those enchanted creatures of the fantasy world: magical, tiny, winged fairies.

For *Willow*, ILM would create the fairy queen Cherlindrea, a glowing, ethereal figure who inhabits a dark forest along with her fairy subjects. The effect would require shooting separate flying footage of Cherlindrea (Maria Holvoe) and a group of gymnasts that comprised the fairy contingent. To emphasize

her special, ethereal qualities, Cherlindrea would be hung from wires on an ILM stage and filmed against a black background, while the other fairies would fly blue-screen.

The magic touch for Cherlindrea included backlighting the actress, filming at forty-eight frames per second and overexposing by four stops, and adding optical enhancements that gave a vaporous quality to the final image. The fairy queen could also materialize and disappear through the magic of John Knoll's special effects photography. "I rear-projected a moving plate of Cherlindrea and took two pieces of ripple glass on motorized movers," Knoll said. "As I lifted the glass away from the image, it started to get more distorted. Two pieces of ripple glass moving at slightly different speeds and one moving upward created the effect. Right at the end of the shot we did a quick optical dissolve to the real elements of Cherlindrea."

All the fairy effects entailed shooting the actors full-frame and then rephotographing the filmed images on an animation stand, sizing them in relationship to the background plate. After some initial thought of cel animating each character's wings, it was decided to create separate model elements and attach them with pin-block techniques. Animation department head Wes Takahashi constructed

Below left: The creative brain trust (left to right: George Lucas, director Ron Howard, Phil Tippett, Dennis Muren) contemplate an enchanted brazier that will come to life in a climactic sequence in *Willow*.

Below right: Cameraman Bob Hill shoots the brazier, which was animated as a stop-motion blue-screen element.

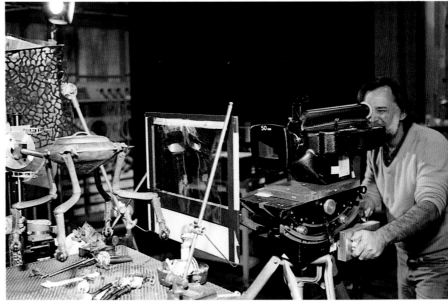

three-inch wing miniatures out of clear plastic with etched membranes for texture and covered them with a diffraction grading film to create a spectrum of colors when light hit them. Knoll created a motion-control "wing flapper" device that allowed the wings to flap. Effects-camera supervisor Bruce Walters then took over and photographed the wing flapping under an animation camera equipped to tilt and roll in any axis. Walters also wrote the motion-control moves that would keep the

Tinker Bell but Peter's triumphant flight over Neverland island. For the rough flying choreography, Brevig assembled a crew of ILM's most experienced stage and camera people, including Dave Heron, Ed Hirsh, and Kim Marks, whose approach was to fly the actors and stunt doubles with the same approach used for blue-screen spaceship photography.

"The essence of model spaceship photography is that you move the camera past the model, which remains stationary," said

Left: The fairy queen Cherlindrea (Maria Holvoe) hovers over the child destined to bring about the downfall of the evil Bavmorda.

Below: Willow (Warwick Davis) encounters a forest fairy in a magical shot from the film.

wings attached to the character elements that had already been shot.

While Cherlindrea and the other forest fairies made only a brief appearance in *Willow*, the fairy Tinker Bell (Julia Roberts) in *Hook* would be on-screen for more than one hundred shots and require storytelling flourishes in the effects. "The character of Tinker Bell that Spielberg had in mind," according to visual effects supervisor Eric Brevig, "had the power and speed of Mighty Mouse, translucent wings that needed to emote, and a glow that would interact with the scene and reflect the essence of her energy. On top of that, Tink was generous with the fairy dust. There were no easy solutions; Tinker Bell needed to be a complex effect."

The flying for *Hook* not only involved

Brevig. "As the camera moves past the subject, it looks to the camera like the subject is doing the flying. For [Tinker Bell and Peter Pan flying] we used this approach on a giant scale with some very sophisticated mechanical rigs to fly the camera. Because the actors were not physically traveling through space they didn't have to struggle to maintain their balance in the flying harnesses, thereby enhancing the sense of effortless flight. We also oriented the actors in the wire rigs so they could perform any aerial acrobatics with the most freedom of motion. For example, Steven loved the look of barrel rolls while flying, which is impossible in a normal horizontal flying harness. So we frequently oriented the actors in a vertical position with the wires in line with their bodies. By positioning the camera on its side, the actors still appeared to be horizontal in frame but had no restrictions of movement."

For Tinker Bell, the original negative blue screen was just the starting point. Animation effects cameraman Pat Myers photographed Tinker Bell's five-inch wings as a separate element under an animation camera using a wing-flapping go-motion rig similar to the one used in *Willow*. For every one of the thou-

sands of frames, each wing element needed to be perfectly attached to Tink's body. To achieve optimal wing movement, Myers moved the wings between exposures in classic stop-motion animation style, while the go-motion rig provided the necessary motion-blur when filmed. At the same time, the blue-screen footage went to motion-control effects cameraman Charlie Clavadetscher and Peter Daulton, who used pin-blocking techniques to choreograph and plot the flight paths for the final shot. The programmed moves were then transferred to the optical department, where they were used to shoot the elements during the compositing process.

"We didn't exactly break the law, but we rewrote it on *Hook*," observed opticals supervisor John Ellis. "The law was that you couldn't do motion-control moves on the optical camera because you'd have to do a preliminary composite and lose a generation of quality. We shot Tink against blue screen, and normally if you wanted to add shake or movement, you would have to do a precomp with the separations and add the shake to the precomp. [A precomp, or "preliminary composite," is the use of the principal elements of a shot, such as the background and primary

Below left: Chief model maker Lorne Peterson prepares a one-third-scale redwood forest set for *Willow*.

Below right: An interactive Cherlindrea light element is prepared on the miniature forest set.

foreground, as a reference for the creation and placement of additional elements.] The new motion-control optical cameras we had built enabled us to do moves on the separations. We first attempted this for George Lucas on *Willow* because he wanted to do a tilt-up from a plate to a matte painting. We had a motion-control printer built for that shot, [which we] really refined and used on *Hook*. The whole intent of a motion-control optical printer is to make it easier to create elements. If they shoot five ships onstage, we can rephotograph those to fill the frame with forty that all look different. We can do moves, zooms on original negative. Shooting the moves directly on the motion-control printer, rather than on the animation camera, allowed us to save one duplication step—thereby sav-

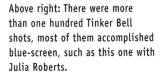

Above right: There were more than one hundred Tinker Bell shots, most of them accomplished blue-screen, such as this one with Julia Roberts.

Above: Tink starts to pull Peter, who doesn't realize he's the fabled Lost Boy Pan, back to Neverland. For the live-action background plate, Williams's bow tie was pulled by an off-camera wire to integrate the final composite and the Tinker Bell effect was enhanced by animated glow elements.

Right: Effects animator Pat Myers utilized a combination of traditional stop motion and go-motion to animate Tinker Bell's flapping wings. Thousands of resulting wing elements were then tracked, frame-by-frame, to the Tinker Bell character.

Far right: Although Tinker Bell was played by Julia Roberts, many of the flying scenes required the use of a stunt double in a flying harness, such as pictured here. (Note the blue set piece that was built to conform to the final placement of Tink in the scene.)

ing film generation—so the image quality would be that much better."

With wings added to the blue-screen image, Tink was nearly complete. The glow that would surround the character while flying was created in the optical department using various diffusion filters and matting techniques. To provide the look that the glowing fairy was interacting with the world around her, a lens flare effect was added by photographing a tiny lightbulb on an animation stand.

For Tink's pixie dust, Spielberg wanted a sense of floating particles. The dust also had to interact with subjects, such as the faceful of

dust Tink tosses at a grown-up Peter, who responds with a sneeze. Since it would be too time-consuming for computer graphics to figure out the interactive elements and for the animation department to draw individually thousands of particles per frame, the two departments joined forces to produce the magical effect. For the CG side, the particle-generating program that had provided the sub wakes and sea debris for *The Hunt for Red October* was used to create and track the particles. The cel animators worked with photostats of each frame of pixie-dust action, tracking their hand-inked particles to the live action.

Top left: Peter Banning (Robin Williams), an acquisitions attorney in London with his family, is visited by Tinker Bell in this early scene from *Hook*.

Middle: The ensuing scene of Tink walking up Peter's dress shirt—after having stepped onto an ink pad and thus leaving inky footprints along the way—would be realized as a digital composite.

SUPERNATURAL TENNIS

Willow and *Hook* evoked otherworldly time and place, but a modern setting for supernatural action can be more disquieting than a locale that is clearly fantasy. For example, the town of Eastwick was seemingly one of those bucolic burgs families grow up in or folks retire to—until the day the devil came to town. A highlight for ILM's work on *The Witches of Eastwick* (1987) was a sequence in which three women of the town play a little game of tennis with Satan (Jack Nicholson). It's a supernatural game, as the tennis ball moves in strange ways: drifting across the net in slow motion, stopping and spinning in place, shooting up into the sky.

"As originally storyboarded, the special effects shots were intended to show the abilities of the players to manipulate the ball in rather extraordinary and magical ways," observed visual effects supervisor Michael Owens. "However, due to the fact that not all the actors were experienced tennis players, it became necessary to use visual effects to create normal game play as well. So every gameplay shot we shot for the live-action plate, except for a few close-ups, was filmed without a ball actually in frame. The live-action plate of the tennis game had to be intricately designed and choreographed so the actors would be able to pantomime their play. Later, an actual tennis ball was photographed on an animation stand and optically inserted into the shots. Considerable time was spent on calculating and plotting the movements of these

Bottom: The final composite, with Tink's shadows produced as pencil animation and digital, not opticals, providing diffusion and density to the animation. The tiny footstep depressions on Peter's dress shirt were also added digitally.

Above: Tink transports Peter over Westminster Bridge on the way to Neverland. Trails of fairy dust were produced here using computer graphics. Hand-drawn fairy dust animation was also created for scenes in which particles had to interact with people or objects. (In a sly cameo, glistening droplets of fairy dust will cause a kissing couple—George Lucas and Carrie Fisher—to float into the air.)

Right: Animator Gordon Baker conjures up some fairy dust, at thousands of hand-drawn particles per frame.

animated balls, as it was necessary to be responsive to the discrepancies of the actors' timings and body attitudes as well as the expected physical properties of the ball in flight. It all resulted in a single visual effect that aided in developing the dark, comedic playfulness of the scene."

THE INVISIBLE WORLD

For *Ghost* (1990) and *Memoirs of an Invisible Man* (1992), ILM had to create some spectral characters to haunt the modern world. For *Ghost*, director Jerry Zucker was adamant that the film not be overwhelmed by the effects—of which ILM would have more than one hundred, including scenes of the ghost (Patrick Swayze) passing through earthly objects. In *Invisible Man*, ILM would have to make star Chevy Chase disappear altogether.

Zucker knew exactly what he wanted for the effect of the ghost passing through objects. "I met Jerry on the set, and he went over to the coffee and snack table, took a napkin, dipped it in coffee, and said, 'This is the effect I want when our ghost passes through solid objects,'" explained effects supervisor Bruce Nicholson. "He wanted the object to be

absorbed by the ghost form in a bleeding-liquid look, so when the ghost character passed through any surface he blended into it, absorbing color and texture. He wanted an organic and dimensional quality to the effects."

Many shots involved a unique teaming of animation and rotoscope specialists. The rotoscope department made a frame-by-frame "cutoff matte" that represented the plane of a door cutting off a ghost's arm as it pushed through the door, while the animation department generated an "absorption matte" that worked in conjunction with the cutoff matte to soften the edges and create the

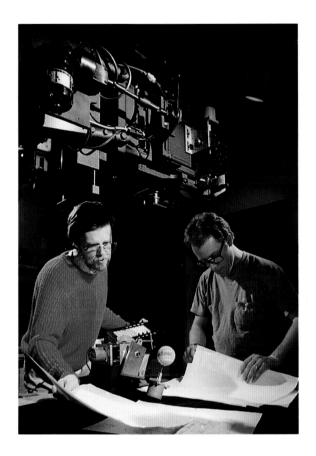

absorption quality to the effect. Frame-by-frame hand-drawn cel animation worked on those shots in which the ghost form (which had been photographed on a motion-control animation stand) needed to interact with complex shapes.

For a subway sequence in which the ghost leaned into a passing train, separate blue-screen elements of the actor and a miniature subway as a background plate were photographed. The two elements were then delivered to the animation department, where rotoscoped mattes could be generated for the split area where ghost and object intersected.

The subway sequence required model supervisor Lorne Peterson and his crew to build one-fifth-scale miniature subway cars and a tunnel realistic enough to hold up in tight close-up shots. Because there was almost no model budget, the model makers were forced to be especially inventive: subway-car wheels were recycled from the time-traveling DeLorean car used in *Back to the Future 3*, and leftover miniature lightbulbs from the

tunnel sequence in *Indiana Jones and the Last Crusade* were used as subway tunnel lights. The cost concerns also kept the miniature set too small to allow for a VistaVision Empire camera to get the needed angle of the train roaring out of the tunnel, so an ILM Nikonflex (a Nikon camera adapted to hold a motion picture film magazine) originally built to shoot the mine-car chase sequence in *Indiana Jones and the Temple of Doom* was cantilevered to one of the subway cars.

The challenge for the optical department was to achieve the transparency Zucker desired at the cutoff line of the composites, which required optical artists to create simultaneously hard-edge and soft-edge matting. "It was hit-and-miss method; there was no formula to do it," Nicholson remembered in frustration. "We had to do a lot of guessing, a

Clockwise, left to right: Effects cameraman Bruce Walters and head animator John Armstrong team up to produce the "Tennis" sequence for *The Witches of Eastwick*. All the tennis balls—from scenes of normal play to magical ball movements—were optically inserted into the choreographed movements of the actors. Here Jack Nicholson addresses the ball, while Michelle Pfeiffer ponders the next move.

Far right, top to bottom: Director Jerry Zucker told effects supervisor Bruce Nicholson that scenes of the ghost (Patrick Swayze) passing through solid objects had to have the bleeding look of a napkin dipped in coffee.

Right: Peterson inspects the tunnel set interior.

Below: For a scene of the ghost interacting with a passing subway train, the model shop produced scale cars that would be propelled by cables through a tunnel set. Here Brian Gernand (left) and supervisor Lorne Peterson touch up the vacuform plastic roof of one model car.

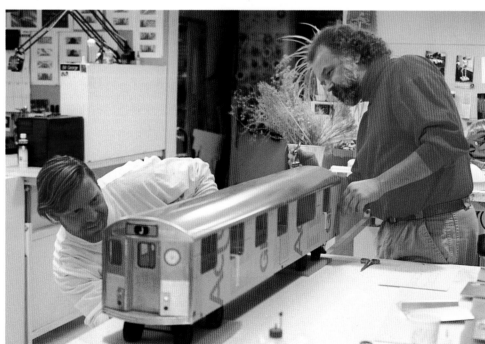

lot of trial and error. Finally, something would work. These shots took an average of six takes each—double or triple our usual number of takes. It raised my blood pressure forever."

"Ironically, this film was done in ILM's last phase of being primarily an optical house," visual effects producer Ned Gorman observed. "We had to torture the techniques to get what Jerry wanted. In digital, you could do a palette of changes for the director. He'd be able to sit down with the guys and dial it in to fine-tune it. The finessing that took us forever in optical would have been much easier to do in digital."

Two years later the advances in digital made possible the disappearing act in *Invisible Man*, which was an important film in laying the groundwork for the upcoming CG triumphs of *Terminator 2* and *Jurassic Park*. Creating the illusion of invisibility was Dennis Muren's Mac Squad, which, equipped with Macintoshes and Photoshop software, also went to work on *The Rocketeer* and *Hook*.

"*Invisible Man* was an extension of *Ghost* both conceptually and technically, but this time I had digital technology at my command," said Nicholson, who was also effects supervisor on this film. "As a matter of fact, I wouldn't have even tried this movie without digital painting and compositing capabilities. Digital solutions didn't make the effects easy; they made them *possible*."

During principal photography on *Invisible Man*, ILM's plate crews used VistaGlide motion-control cameras, with their capability for repeatable dolly and other moves, to shoot in real time at twenty-four frames per second. Two plates were shot for each effects scene: one without the actor, one with the actor in a blue bodysuit. The elements were then scanned into Macintoshes for 2-D image processing using the Photoshop painting program to accomplish the traditional jobs of rotoscoping and optical compositing.

Above: Director Zucker checks out the final miniature subway track and train that will serve as background plate elements.

Left: The final composite, with the blue-screen element of Swayze. According to producer Ned Gorman, this production marked the close of ILM's traditional opticals phase and the dawn of the company's conversion to all-digital compositing.

Digital manipulation allowed the effects artists to create invisibility as a three-dimensional reality—the viewer can actually see the back label of the shirt and the inside of a sweatband when worn by the invisible character, or the surrounding court and hedges through the invisible legs, arms, and head. The inner elements of clothing were scanned in as separately shot prop elements that could be animated to match the movement of the real clothing shot for the actor plate. With the actor wearing blue on areas of the body to be rendered invisible, digital artists could then paint over those isolated areas with the background-plate photography.

Right: For the vanishing acts in *Memoirs of an Invisible Man*, supervisor Nicholson credits the digital innovations made in the wake of *Ghost*. *Invisible* effects began with both live-action and blue-screen photography, with actor Chevy Chase wearing blue material for those areas that would be rendered invisible.

Below: Once in the digital realm, blue material could be isolated, with painting programs used to complete the clean background plate areas.

KUROSAWA'S DREAMS

Akira Kurosawa, the famed director, had need of some ILM effects magic for *Akira Kurosawa's Dreams* (1990). During his illustrious career Kurosawa had crafted epics based on Japanese history, martial tales of masterless samurai, psychological thrillers set in modern times, and poignant character studies, but he had never directed an effects-filled film. *Dreams* was a movie in which only effects could adequately realize his vision: eight short stories based on actual dreams the director had experienced throughout his life. ILM would produce effects for two of the sequences: "Sunshine Through the Rain" and "Mount Fuji in Red."

The opening dream, "Sunshine Through the Rain," was based on the Japanese folktale tradition that an elemental concert of rain and sunshine meant the fox's bride was going to her husband's house. In the segment a little boy, fascinated by the rain falling on a sunny day, ignores his mother's admonishment that this ritual of the animal world was not meant for human eyes and slips out into the forest to observe the wedding procession. He is spotted by the animals, and when he escapes back to his house his mother is waiting—with a knife. For the sin of violating the privacy of the foxes he must either kill himself or go to the place underneath the rainbow where the animals live and beg their forgiveness. ILM's shot would be the final scene in the segment: the little boy walking across a field of flowers toward misty mountains bridged by a rainbow.

"Mount Fuji in Red" was an apocalyptic vision in which six nuclear power plants that ring the sacred mountain suddenly explode. As the sky turns red and the mountain turns molten, a crowd of doomed, screaming people crowds the road below in a fruitless escape. "Man's stupidity is unbelievable," a scientist dryly notes as radioactive clouds waft down from the mountain. It would be ILM's assignment to produce the atomic conflagration, capturing both the look of the mountain and what Kurosawa requested as "angry clouds."

"At ILM we'd receive these very impressionistic line drawings over the fax and try to figure out what they meant," explained Peter Takeuchi, visual effects producer for *Dreams*. "Kurosawa would draw the outline of Mount Fuji, and then he would draw these little squiggles in the sky above and describe them as 'angry clouds.' The language thing became very difficult, and for the next six months things would go back and forth by fax to try to get more of a description about these 'angry clouds.' Did he want nuclear mushroom clouds or clouds like storm clouds?"

Then Takeuchi, visual effects supervisor Ken Ralston, and the rest of the ILM *Dreams* production crew flew to Japan to shoot their background plates. The hardest location work was for the Mount Fuji sequence, which would be filmed above a resort town at the foot of the mountain. The action was set to film on a hill facing Fuji and a valley in the distance, with the hilltop camera crews overlooking an American football-size field on which a thousand extras would enact the panic of the Fuji meltdown.

The first day of filming was hectic. When the ILM crew bus pulled up at seven-thirty in the morning, its passengers were greeted by the sight of buses at the foot of the hill unloading the thousand extras for the big Fuji meltdown scene. The extras were divided up into specific groups that assembled under different-colored flags. "Once each group had gone through wardrobe and been given suitcases, toys, bicycles, and other props, the ADs would take the group and march them up the muddy road to the location," said Takeuchi. Kurosawa soon drove up in a Jeep, the camera crews took their positions on the platform facing Fuji in the distance, and the thousand extras and vehicles were assembled in the field below them. Then the director faced the crowd with an amplified microphone in hand and called for a rehearsal.

"Kurosawa said, 'Action,' and everybody started running around like crazy and screaming. This went on for about thirty seconds until Kurosawa blared out, 'Stop,'" Takeuchi recalled. "Then it was interpreted for us that Kurosawa was concerned that the people weren't running fast enough, that they didn't have enough panic on their faces, that they were too much looking at him and the cameras instead of looking at Mount Fuji. That's all blared out to the crowd, and [then] they did it again, and what a difference! So then he said they were going to roll film, and we did six takes and it took probably forty-five minutes. We were framed up for our plates and the live-action crew was shooting close-ups of the crowd and the principal actors. After he said, 'Cut' for the sixth take, Kurosawa thanked the crowd and asked the crew to applaud all the extras. So we stood up and applauded, and they, in turn, bowed to us, and they all broke out in applause."

The Mount Fuji sequence was, however, a major problem, both in creating the image of the mountain changing colors and the surrounding imagery of the nuclear blasts. One

problem was that a controlled burn in a forest at the mountain's base had been conducted during filming, unbeknownst to Kurosawa's crew, and smoke from the burn had drifted across ILM's close-ups and ruined those plates. To produce the wide shot of the crowd scene and the mountain beyond, the crowd-scene parts of the plates were combined as a soft-edge split with a Fuji matte painting in the distance.

To add realism to these invisibility effects, elements of inner clothing (which would normally be concealed by skin) were scanned and matched to the real clothing shot in the original plate.

Right: Famed director Akira Kurosawa's own dreams inspired his *Dreams* film. The director's own concept paintings would be used to guide ILM's work on two key tableaus. Kurosawa had been creating his own concept art since 1977 when, frustrated that some of his scripts were unable to attract backers, he began to communicate his vision with his own dramatic artwork. Kurosawa's *Dreams* art included this rainbow vision for the "Sunshine Through the Rain" sequence.

Below: The final "Sunshine" scene ILM created was composed of many elements: a plate of a little boy walking across an open field in Japan, separate rain elements, and a Mark Sullivan matte painting for the sky, mountain, and rainbow.

Opposite page, top: "Mount Fuji in Red" concept painting by Akira Kurosawa. In this nightmare vision, power plants ringing the sacred mountain begin an explosive meltdown, terrorizing the antlike mobs in the foreground.

Opposite page, bottom: Final composite, with live-action shot in Japan, a matte-painted mountain, and explosive effects that combined cloud tank elements, pyro, and animation.

For the close-ups of Fuji, ILM had originally built a fourteen-foot model rigged so a
snowcap would melt. This was a painstaking
re-creation of the sacred mountain. Unfortunately, film of the model element did not
meet with Kurosawa's approval; he wanted a
stylized Fuji that evoked the tapered slopes
created by the artists of Japan's old wood-
block print tradition. At that point ILM went
to all-matte paintings for Mount Fuji. The
hellfire of the exploding nuclear reactors was
another problem.

"Originally we shot pyro elements of explosions for composite, and Kurosawa said, 'No,
that's too real,'" Takeuchi recalled. "So we
scrapped all of that, and we went to the cloud
tank and shot a bunch of cloud tank elements
of billowing liquids and paints inside the
water tank and composited that, and he said:
'More angry.' So we shot different speeds of

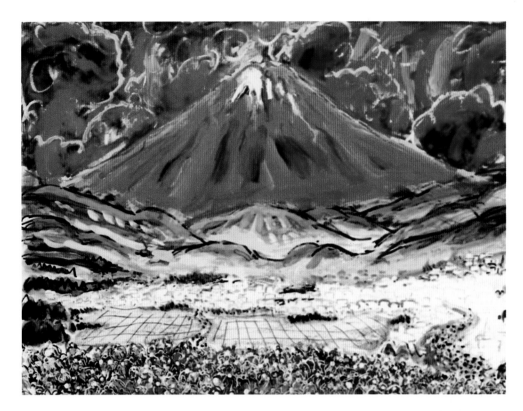

ILM visual effects supervisor Michael Owens designed this desert vision for *The Doors*, director Oliver Stone's film based on the life of rock star Jim Morrison.

that, and he still didn't like it, so then we started comping all kinds of different things for him as tests, and he picked one which was a combination of the real pyro and a little bit of cloud tank elements and some animation, and that's what wound up in the movie: a mishmash of everything."

The "Sunshine Through the Rain" shot was also shot in the Mount Fuji area, in the open countryside of a military station at the base of the mountain. The empty field of the military base had to be dressed with real

and plastic flowers to create the appearance of a countryside in springtime bloom. Instead of the complex logistics of the Mount Fuji scene, the shot required only a little boy on his way to make peace with the foxes that lived under the rainbow. The plate had the little boy walking across the field toward a destination that would be realized later with a rainbow, mountain, and sky matte painting produced by ILM artist Mark Sullivan back in Marin County. Composited into the shot would be a light rain element created with soap crystals dropped against a black background and shot high-speed with the rainbow matte painting double-exposed over the whole image with a slow, sweeping wipe move.

Kurosawa happily received the shot of the boy and the rainbow, an image that would be used to advertise the film. "Kurosawa seemed to really love the 'Sunshine Through the Rain' shot" Takenchi explained. "He said he liked the Mount Fuji final, but after a while you could tell when he really liked something and when he was just being polite. I felt he was just being polite about the Mount Fuji stuff. All the changes with the sky—'Angry, make it more angry'—I never really figured that out."

CHAPTER NINE

MAXIMUM IMPACT:
THE ART OF ACTION

The Jones boys—Henry Senior and Indiana Junior—are driving at top speed as a Nazi fighter plane on their tail swoops down and fires away; New York cop John McClane is trapped in the cockpit of a C-130 airplane as his foes riddle the fuselage with bullets and toss a few grenades through the hatch and into his lap; The Rocketeer and his girl are aloft with nowhere to run atop a burning Zeppelin that's about to explode. When it comes to deadly dangers, our heroes look to ILM for a little saving grace.

The action film, dating back to the old slam-bang Saturday-matinee serials, has always been about good guys versus bad guys, of perilous predicaments and thrilling escapes, of final face-offs and justice triumphant. But too often the genre has been bereft of mythic spirit, reduced to big guns and explosions. But as with any good movie, story and character are what matters, and they are what make an audience care.

Indiana Jones, a rogue combination of brains and brawn, style and sweat, has from the beginning been a character audiences have cared about. Audiences were hooked from that first sight in 1981 in *Raiders of the Lost Ark*, when Jones turned and surveyed a

Producer George Lucas and Harrison Ford, preparing for the third installment of the Indiana Jones saga, check out a prototype model plane for use in a death-defying Indy chase scene.

Right: Pat Sweeney (left) and Michael Fulmer (right) size up the plane on the blue-screen stage.

Below left: To down a pursuing Nazi plane, Indy's father (Sean Connery) opens up an umbrella and stirs up a fateful flock of seagulls. A bird element shot against a black background was created with hundreds of windup toy birds that, when released, could flap and fly.

Below right: A quarter-scale miniature plane and pilot, dusted with a cloud of feathers, was used for a subsequent cut of the plane stalling out.

jungle scene, eyes intense and alert for lurking dangers. By the 1989 release of *Indiana Jones and the Last Crusade*, the character had achieved icon status, and Harrison Ford was donating one of Indy's trademark fedoras and leather jackets to the Smithsonian Institution in a special ceremony in Washington, D.C.

To create an action character who becomes more complex through a series of installments is no easy task. Even the best first movies lose their edge in the follow-up. For the third Indy adventure, executive producer George Lucas, who created the character and cowrote the three stories, struggled with director Steven Spielberg to conceive of an adventure worthy of his character.

"The third Indiana Jones movie was supposed to be more of a haunted house movie, but Steve [Spielberg] had done *Poltergeist*, and he didn't really want to do another movie like that," Lucas recalled. "I originally wanted to do one of the Holy Grail—which was actually the idea for the second Indiana Jones movie—but Steve at first didn't like the Holy Grail idea. So I came up with another idea, which took place in Africa—we actually went over to Africa and scouted locations. But Steve was ambivalent about it. So I went back and developed a draft based around the Holy Grail that was good enough and convinced Steve I could make this Grail thing work and be tangible. A major leap, I think, was [made]

by introducing Indy's father as a character."

Indiana's scholarly father (Sean Connery), whose life's work was trying to locate the Passover chalice used by Christ on the eve of his arrest and crucifixion, was the key premise that unlocked the story.

Above: At the beginning of the chase sequence, the Jones boys try to drive for freedom while two Nazi planes dive in pursuit with guns blazing. One plane crashes into a mountainside; the resulting explosion was provided by some location pyro work.

Left: As Indy and his father drive into a tunnel, the second Nazi plane crashes behind them, the impact shearing off its wings and sending burning fuselage hurtling after the speeding car. Bluescreen shots of the driving Joneses would be composited with live action of an ignited quarter-scale plane model rocketing through a quarter-scale tunnel set.

Right and below: The 180-foot-long tunnel set was composed of ten sections, each one hinged on top to open for access. Scale models of both the plane and car were pulled on hidden cables at speeds approaching thirty miles per hour. After the test phase, the model plane would be set afire and a separate cable-pulled camera system would film the action at high speed.

INDIANA JONES AND THE NAZI FIGHTER PLANE

For *Last Crusade*, the perils faced by Indiana and his father are, as usual, meted out by Nazis as the chase is on with the Grail as the prize. A centerpiece of the action was a ten-minute chase sequence featuring almost three minutes of visual effects. A highlight of the chase had a Nazi fighter plane diving for the car driven by the Jones boys. The car turns a corner of a mountain pass and enters a tunnel just as the fighter, which can't come out of its dive, hits the tunnel entrance. The wings are cracked off and the plane's burning fuselage skids past our heroes, exploding at the tunnel's exit.

The sequence combined live-action plate work and ILM blue-screen photography, models, pyro, and opticals. For the opening of the shot of the plane hitting the tunnel entrance, a model plane was filmed as a motion-control blue-screen element, its aluminum foil wings animated with stop motion to break away. The interior tunnel shots then required a nearly two-hundred-foot tunnel model, which was built in ten sections with lighting concealed inside the tunnel walls and hinged on one side so the top could be lifted up, like a canopy, for access. Set out and filmed in the ILM parking lot, the tunnel model had a track along which a model plane, as well as a camera sled, could be pulled. Timing was paramount for shooting the flaming model plane, which had to move through the tunnel at twenty to thirty miles an hour and be filmed at high speed to keep the fire in scale.

Top: Indy and Henry Jones feel something gaining on them in this blue-screen shot.

Middle: Shot of the flaming, quarter-scale plane hurtling through the tunnel set.

Bottom: The fiery plane closes in, final composite (with the car's grimy windshield shot as a separate element and optically inserted into the action).

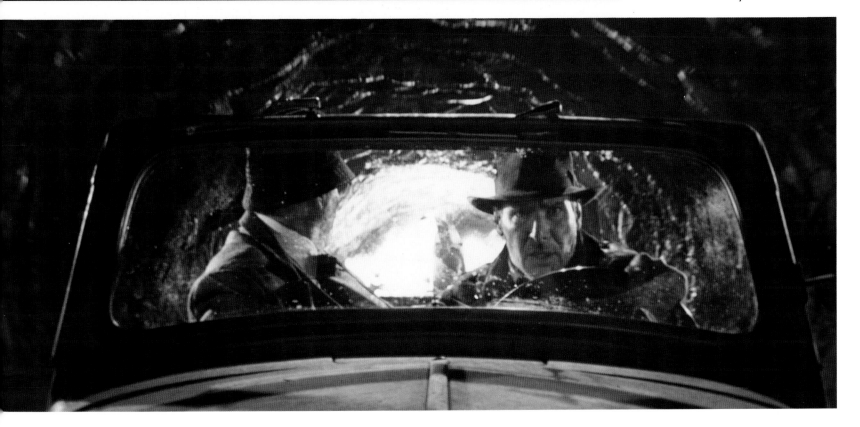

Top: The burning plane passes Indy's car and explodes beyond the tunnel exit. A tunnel in Spain, where the live action was staged, was shot as a background plate to composite this shot of the model, which exploded at ILM (with additional pyro and animation effects added to the mix).

Bottom: Live-action shot at the tunnel in Spain, with stuntmen driving the Jones car through the debris of the exploded Nazi plane.

For the shot of the plane passing Indiana's car, a separate blue-screen element of Ford and Connery in their car was shot. In one of those little touches no one would ever expect as an effect, the car's previously dirtied windshield, deemed unworthy of blue screen because it wouldn't have photographed well, was shot as a separate element and optically inserted. For the shot's finale, a background plate at the actual tunnel at the location in Spain was shot, complete with pyro work. Shots of the miniature Nazi plane emerging and exploding ahead of Indiana's vehicle were then cut into location footage of a stunt-driven car exiting the tunnel through a practical plane debris effect.

DIE HARD ESCAPE

In *Die Hard 2*, the signature scene is played out in an episode in which John McClane is stuck in the cockpit of a grounded C-130 aircraft. His enemies pepper the fuselage with assault-weapon fire before tossing grenades through an opening in the cockpit. Desperately, McClane straps himself into a parachute ejection seat and blasts off, flying into space as the plane explodes below him.

To create the shot, ILM's optical effects work had to cut in with live-action practical effects. The opening, staged on a snow-slick runway, involved special effects coordinator Al DiSarro and weapons specialist Mike Papick rigging a full-scale fuselage mock-up (built from a mold of a real C-130) with three thousand bullet hits. Each hit had to be drilled, loaded with a charge, tapped, and wired to discharge in the sequence director Renny Harlin wanted. When the bad guys opened fire (shooting blanks in actuality), the bullet hits were detonated.

The actual escape as storyboarded called for the camera to be looking down as McClane, securely strapped to the ejection seat, flew ostensibly hundreds of feet up toward the hovering camera with the C-123 exploding below and McClane then drifting away. The shot would require a blue screen of actor Bruce Willis composited into a shot of a rough plane mock-up being exploded. The shot would be a textbook example of the problems in making separate elements blend into one scene with traditional optical compositing.

The actual pyro work was accomplished with the mock-up in Indian Dunes, California. A high-speed, four-perf camera was positioned on an overhead crane looking down on the mock-up. As the blast was also designed to send up a fireball to engulf the camera view, the camera itself was safety-shielded to protect the lens.

A problem for the blue-screen work was that to accommodate Willis's schedule, ILM had to shoot its blue-screen footage prior to the Indian Dunes pyro work (usually the main background plate would be shot first to determine lighting and other factors). The lighting of the blue-screen subject, and how it would match the exploding plane element, would be a matter of guesswork.

The actual blue screen required strapping Willis into an ejection-seat facsimile attached to a motorized rig. As the rig slowly rotated the actor in place head over heels, an illusion of movement was supplied by the camera moving down a one-hundred-foot track and dollying into a tight close-up of the actor's face.

The actual compositing required a range of optical techniques. Since the mock-up pyro had been shot in standard four-perf and the Willis blue screen in VistaVision, the four-perf film had to be unloaded into an eight-perf camera to finish the shot. The department also skip-printed (printed every other frame) the ejection-seat element to give a more realistic sense of speed. Because the elements had

been shot in reverse of the normal process, the lighting on Willis did not match the background plate. Neutral-density filters (which equally absorb all light wavelengths, reducing the color exposure of an element) were added

Above: One of the cliff-hanging thrills of *Die Hard 2* is a scene in which John McClane (Bruce Willis) jettisons himself from the cockpit of a grounded military transport plane. The hero element was shot blue-screen with Willis in an ejection-seat rig that slowly tumbled as a track camera dollied in.

Left: Final optical composite. Although the lighting was somewhat off on Willis—because of scheduling problems the blue screen was shot first and couldn't account for the light from the background explosion—the scene's raw, explosive energy still made it a crowd-pleasing success. (The digital breakthroughs to come would allow filmmakers to correct such imperfections without having to reshoot elements.)

to provide an after-the-fact lighting effect. Both elements had also been shot very sharp, and since Willis was supposed to be blasted high in the air, opticals changed the focus on the background explosion during compositing to provide a more realistic depth of field.

But even though the shot wasn't a textbook optical composite, *Die Hard 2* visual effects supervisor Micheal McAlister was still satisfied. With the action coming fast and furious, audiences would be caught up in the thrilling momentum of the sequence. Optical ace John Ellis recalled a similar action shot that was not textbook but good enough: "Our visual effects supervisors all have a lot of experience in not only knowing how to make a shot better but also when it's good enough to leave it alone. The absolute king of that is George Lucas. I'll give you an example. We were all in the screening room with George on *Raiders of the Lost Ark*, looking at the chase sequence where Indiana has control of a truck and crashes it into a Nazi Jeep, which sends the Jeep over this cliff. It was a composite of a matte painting of the cliff and background, a miniature car, and little puppets that come tumbling out that had been shot blue-screen. Well, we're all excited, but the color timing's not real good and the contrast isn't the best— there's a bit of a matte line—and George goes: 'I'll take that as a final.' And everybody says, 'But, George, the contrast isn't right, and the painting isn't finished, and there's a couple of matte lines.' And George goes, 'I know all that. But I know where the audience will be. The audience will cheer at this shot.' And the man was absolutely right: The audience cheered at the shot. Making the shot any more than it was wasn't necessary because it told the story he wanted to tell."

In director Ron Howard's *Backdraft*, a modern firefighting saga, it was originally planned to produce a series of arson fires as a malevolent character, not as merely a natural phenomenon. A few ILM "brain flame" shots were achieved optically, while most of the film's fire effects were done practically.

This page: One of ILM's major visual effects shots in *Backdraft* was of a burning chemical plant, with firefighters running across the burning roof as it began to collapse. The spectacular effect began with a forty-foot-long, quarter-scale rooftop model set that filled ILM's main stage. A computerized control board set off the pyro charges while a camera filmed at seventy-two frames a second to keep the conflagration in scale.

THE BRAIN FLAME

When firefighters have to enter a burning building, either for a rescue attempt or to combat a blaze, they enter a hellish world of raging flame. Although *Backdraft*, Ron Howard's 1991 fire-fighting adventure, used breakthrough practical fire effects to actually place its stars (including actors Kurt Russell and William Baldwin) into the heart of several burning interiors, ILM was still needed for five shots, notably some "brain flame" images that visualized a wrathful persona for the fires. Since the digital age was dawning, with fire and other organic matter too problematic to create CG, visual effects supervisor Scott Farrar and his crew shot flame against black on the main ILM stage and optically composited the fire elements into the background plates.

"The flame elements were very hard to composite, the matte edges had to be fiddled with," Farrar noted. "In one shot, where the brain flame comes up on Billy Baldwin [the scene pictured at left] a real hose was spraying water in the scene, which created some tricky matte edges. It required some delicate frame-by-frame rotoscoping to achieve a soft-edge blend on that shot."

This page: The exploding rooftop set is further enhanced with a Mark Sullivan matte-painted foreground. The firefighters were photographed from the actual distance of the rooftop scene itself and digitally "difference-matted," a process by which differences between image elements allowed specific elements to be isolated and matted into the final scene without the need for blue screen.

FIERY FINALE: EXPLOSION IN HOLLYWOODLAND AND CRASHING A ZEPPELIN

The Rocketeer finale was another face-off between good and evil, typified by plucky American Cliff Secord and Nazi Neville Sinclair. In the story, the Nazi has kidnapped Cliff's girlfriend, Jenny, and is spiriting her away in a Nazi zeppelin, the *Luxembourg*, that has been touring the U.S. (the film is set prior to the U.S. entrance into World War II). As the airship lifts off from its mooring at Griffith Observatory in Los Angeles, Cliff dons his Rocketeer helmet and rocket pack and jets up to the zeppelin. During a furious fistfight between Secord and Sinclair a fire breaks out in the control room. In the confusion, Sinclair picks up the rocket pack. The Nazi triumphantly straps on the flying device, fires it up, and steps out into space, unaware that the pack has caught a bullet and is leaking. As the rocket pack bursts into flame, the Nazi falls like a burning meteor, exploding into the famed Hollywoodland sign and knocking out the "Land" letters. Meanwhile,

Cliff and Jenny, pursued by a Nazi thug, race to the top of the burning zeppelin as the airship begins to explode. At the last moment an autogiro piloted by Howard Hughes and Cliff's pal Peevy swoops down, and they toss out a ladder that our hero and heroine grab

This page: In *The Rocketeer* an elaborate battle sequence between evil Nazi Neville Sinclair (Timothy Dalton) and the Rocketeer (Bill Campbell) in a burning zeppelin takes an explosive turn as Sinclair steals the rocket pack, revs it up, and steps into space—unaware that a fuel leak is about to make him a human meteor. Impact point is the old Hollywoodland hillside, created as a tenth-scale set on the ILM back lot.

Near right and right: Blue-screen element of Dalton reacting as the rocket pack catches fire . . .

. . . and the animated flame element to be composited with the blue-screen shot.

Below: Timothy Dalton is flown by wires as he acts out his character's flaming demise. All the rocket-pack flames in the sequence would be hand-drawn and optically composited.

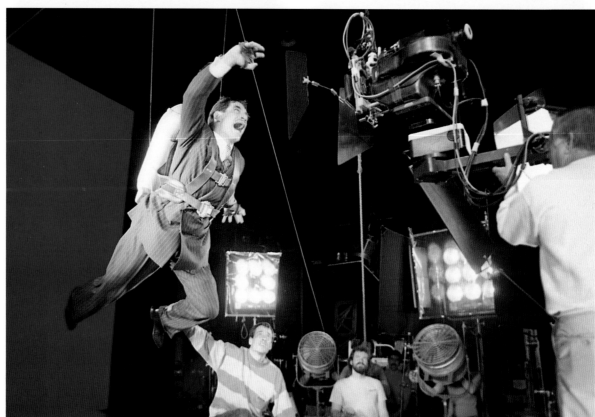

onto and fly away on as the *Luxembourg* explodes.

For the Nazi's fiery fall, ILM shot blue-screen elements of actor Timothy Dalton hanging from wires. Showing the Nazi consumed by flames was a complex task for opticals. According to John Ellis, the shot required using an overriding zoom on animated film elements to track the actor's image

combined with animated interactive light passes. The holdout matte of the actor, which isolated that element, was printed out of focus, causing the matte to go soft around the edges and thus allowing the composited flame pass to appear to consume the actor. The Hollywoodland explosion was created in ILM's parking lot, as a pyro hit on a tenth-scale re-creation of the hillside and letters.

Left: Sinclair engulfed by the flames. A variety of traditional optical techniques were used to put the character into the fire.

Below: A direct hit! Sinclair's fiery crash into Hollywoodland, an ILM pyro hit that topples the last four letters.

(The five-foot-tall set letters were in scale to the real fifty-to-sixty-foot letters.)

Blowing up the zeppelin proved to be one of the ILM crew's most challenging sequences. The inspiration for the *Luxembourg* was a real-life German zeppelin that was touring the States in 1937 when it met a fiery fate. The *Hindenburg*, an eight-hundred-foot-long transatlantic dirigible, exploded as it was being moored at its landing site in New Jersey. In a fantastic coincidence, longtime ILM stage technician Dick Dova had actually been pres-

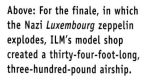

Above: For the finale, in which the Nazi *Luxembourg* zeppelin explodes, ILM's model shop created a thirty-four-foot-long, three-hundred-pound airship.

Near right: Scale mockups, such as this tail section, were utilized throughout the sequence for various shots of the zeppelin.

Top right: The thirty-four-foot zeppelin being lifted into position for the explosive effect, based on the 1937 explosion of Germany's transatlantic airship, *The Hindenburg*.

Bottom right: The zeppelin pyro work misfiring. When the explosive effects fired out of sequence, ILM, which had been contracted to build only one zeppelin, had to scramble to build and blow up a new airship.

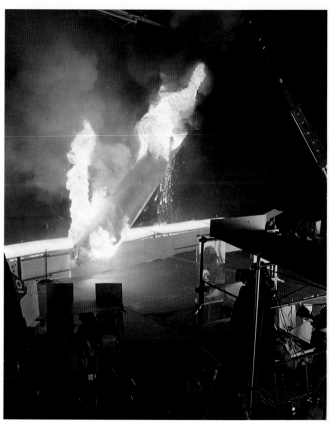

ent at the historic disaster, waiting at the landing site with his mother for his dad, who had just arrived in the seemingly indestructible airship. The senior Dova had a movie camera with him that was running as the explosion began to rip through the zeppelin's envelope, and he took as much footage as he could before tossing the camera out the window and leaping after it. Escaping unhurt,

Dova was one of many indirectly described in the Movietone newsreels, which had exclusive footage of the disaster and announced at the time: "Frantic passengers leap to the ground from a roaring inferno and in one brief minute the once proud Queen of the Air is reduced to a red-hot mass of twisted metal."

"Dick brought us a video transfer from film that his father had taken of the

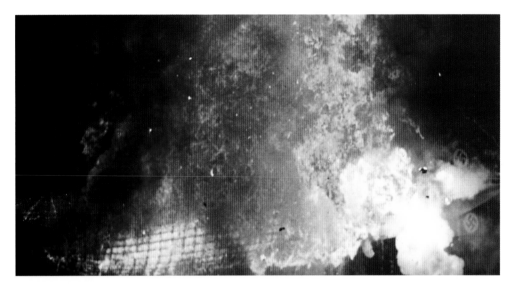

Hindenburg explosion, an actual point of view of someone on board," said producer Patty Blau. "What you saw was a huge hangar on the ground with people looking up. Then you see this wash of light, and you realize that the guy is standing there filming the *Hindenburg* as it's exploding. It was an incredibly valuable reference for our shot."

To model makers and pyro technicians, the footage provided some insights on the stages of destruction for a burning zeppelin: The skin would first burn off, exposing the steel structure, the structure would then collapse, and, with the hydrogen that kept it aloft escaping, the airship would crumble and fall.

The *Luxembourg* was a complex project from the start for Steve Gawley and his model crew. Just assembling the materials for the thirty-four-foot-long, three-hundred-pound model was a challenge. The skinning material, a heat-shrinking polyester substance known as Solartex, was only available from England and, since it was the time of the Desert Storm military operations in the Middle East, the

Top left: Exploding airship element.

Middle left: Holdout matte of the Rocketeer, his girlfriend (Jennifer Connelly), and ladder.

Bottom left: . . . final composite.

Top right: Zeppelin pyro blast.

Bottom right: The final shot was a composite that included the zeppelin blast shot at high speed, an eighth-scale autogiro model-shot motion control, blue-screen elements of ladder and actors, and a matte painting for background.

This page: Another Nazi villain bites the dust in *The Last Crusade*. In the storyboard, and a closing image in the film, Indiana Jones and Elsa witness the final moments in the destruction of Walter Donovan, an evil schemer who lusted for immortality but instead met a hellish end.

British army had commandeered much of the desired silver Solartex material for its military operations. Obtaining large quantities of white Solartex led to an eight-week delay because of special wartime postal inspections. Another concern was that in a cost-cutting move, Walt Disney Studios had ordered only one zeppelin model, despite ILM's urging that a spare be contracted due to the risky nature of miniature pyrotechnics.

The pyro work was staged at Hamilton Air Force Base, a Northern California military installation. The *Luxembourg* model was wheeled out and lifted up on a forklift to give the pyro crew access for rigging the explosive charges, which would be detonated by remote control. Once the access holes were sealed up, the model, in a nose-down position, was raised twenty feet in the air by crane. As the five VistaVision cameras began shooting at a range of different speeds as high as three hundred frames per second, the model was detonated, and what happened next was a production crew's worst nightmare: The bombs went off out of sequence, with the tail exploding before the nose, rendering the footage unusable.

With the production deadline bearing down, Gawley and his crew of nine model makers had to build another zeppelin within five weeks—as compared to the four months they had to build the first ill-fated

Luxembourg. The retake would have no room for error; the second pyro try was scheduled a few weeks before the film's scheduled June 21 release. If the pyro work failed a second time, the production would be forced to composite optically a fire effect using a foot-long zeppelin miniature, a far cry from the spectacular finale a large-scale model explosion would provide.

"The day we were going to blow up the second zeppelin model, I glanced at an event calendar and discovered that very day was the actual anniversary of the *Hindenburg* explosion!" visual effects supervisor Ken Ralston recalled. "I took it as a bad omen, a very weird coincidence. We blew it up, shooting at high speed, so it was over in about five seconds, but the next day they had to drag me into dailies."

The second pyro work had done the trick, producing realistic footage of the zeppelin exploding and falling out of the sky in a slow burn, making for a fitting end to the Nazi quest for the rocket pack.

BREAKTHROUGHS:
CREATURES FROM
THE DIGITAL REALM

In 1985, ILM's original computer division managed to summon the very first dimensional creature from the digital realm for a feature film: a stained-glass image of a sword-wielding knight that came to life in *Young Sherlock Holmes*. The computer-generated stained-glass figure had been created at the nexus between the departure of the old Lucasfilm computer division and the gearing up of ILM's CG division, a time of transition from purely research and development to actual motion picture production.

Although the Pixar hardware of that period was capable of working 80 million polygons—the basic building blocks of a three-dimensional creation—computer-generated characters and environments then required an enormous output of resources. Scanners required sixteen hours to scan and store one *minute* of film, while it took 720 disks to store a single two-hour movie. *The Adventures of Andre and Wally B.*, a 1984 1.8-minute short, required sixteen computers (including the Cray XMP-2 and XMP-4, then the most powerful computers in the world) to process data for months. (In *Industrial Light & Magic: The Art of Special Effects*, Tom Smith described a discussion in which it was concluded that if the effects in *Return of the Jedi* had been accomplished digitally an entire warehouse would have been required to store the data.)

But computer hardware and software grew in processing power and memory capacity. Although new digital-image-processing techniques—such as the morphing sequence in *Willow* and the composite shots in *Indiana Jones and the Last Crusade*—provided the initial ILM breakthroughs on the digital front, it was a succession of 3-D computer-animated creations that would generate the most talk among audiences and media worldwide.

The 3-D imaging breakthroughs of the late eighties and early nineties would convince a skeptical film industry that computer graphics *had* arrived as a cost- and time-effective production tool. The resulting technological revolution would hit with a suddenness that had many traditional effects artists converting to computer graphics and digital-image processing.

THE ABYSS
1989 (GJP Prod./Twentieth Century-Fox)
WINNER OF ACADEMY AWARD FOR BEST VISUAL EFFECTS
Nonterrestrial Water Pseudopod

The element of water, a transparent liquid composed of hydrogen and oxygen, can be as sublime in appearance as a lake holding the moon in its reflection, as majestic and powerful as the crushing force of a waterfall, as fearsome as a flood that sweeps away everything in its path. It takes many forms, from raindrops to rivers to ice floes to the oceans that cover most of the planet's surface area. Humans drink, bathe, and play in water, and couldn't live without it.

In *The Abyss* ILM would be faced with the challenge of imitating the elemental mystery of water to create a life-size, pseudopod creature composed entirely of seawater. In the story, the crew of Deepcore, an underwater oil-drilling operation that becomes involved

A strange, nonterrestrial seawater pseudopod rises from an open pool to explore Deepcore, an underwater drilling rig in director James Cameron's *The Abyss.*

in the search for a sunken nuclear submarine, encounters nonterrestrial creatures living at the bottom of the sea. To make contact, the aliens create a saltwater optic probe that enters Deepcore through an open pool and, to the astonishment of crew members Lindsey Brigman and Bud Brigman (Mary Elizabeth Mastrantonio and Ed Harris), rearranges its watery tip into the exact likeness of their faces.

The Abyss was a monumental undertaking for director Jim Cameron and his production team. To stage the underwater work, the largest freshwater filming tank in the world was created in the reactor containment building of an uncommissioned South Carolina nuclear power plant. The postproduction creation of the watery pseudopod would be in concert with the production's grand ambitions, requiring ILM to venture out into the far frontiers of 3-D computer effects technology.

PLANNING THE CREATURE

Cameron, who had a very clear idea as to how the creature should look and move, had considered various options, including stop motion, sculptural replacement animation, and hydraulic water systems. He was still searching for the right effects team to attempt the watery creature when he agreed to a hurried meeting with Dennis Muren at ILM to discuss the possibilities of attempting the effect as a 3-D computer creation. When Cameron arrived for the meeting, not only was George Lucas sitting in but Muren had ready a computer graphics sketch of a water snake that animator Jay Riddle had generated the night before. The quick turnaround on the CG water-snake image helped allay Cameron's concerns that computer graphics would be too slow or unable to duplicate the image in his mind. Doing the shot digitally was still a leap into the unknown, but Cameron liked the chances and awarded ILM the job.

The pseudopod effects team would be led by Muren, John Knoll (who handled supervisor duties during the period when Muren was overseeing the effects effort for *Ghostbusters II*), and CG artists Mark Dippé and Jay Riddle. The CG department was ecstatic at the chance to mimic nature but sobered by the scale of the project. It would be ILM's largest 3-D order to date, requiring twenty separate shots and seventy-five seconds of three-dimensional imagery. "There was no way we could have produced the sequence without a major commitment to expand the CG department in every way," explained ILM president Jim Morris, then the *Abyss* effects producer.

To create their creature the ILM team needed powerful new tools. They got their tools (and ultimately a strategic business alliance) with the purchase of powerful computer workstations produced by Silicon Graphics. At the time of *The Abyss*, SGI, with an estimated $167 million in sales in 1988, was just beginning its spectacular rise. By 1993 the company had generated more than a billion dollars and its workstations had helped ILM artists produce the imaginative computer effects for *Death Becomes Her*, *Terminator 2*, and *Jurassic Park*. The digital toolbox for *The Abyss* was also enriched because of an agreement with Alias, a Canadian software company that provided CG with a proprietary modeling and animating software package.

BUILDING THE CREATURE

Before the pseudopod could be sculpted in the digital environment, the creature's spatial and textural qualities were developed with clear resin maquettes produced by the model shop. Having a physical, three-dimensional model that could be held, lit, and examined from various angles was important for later determining the form that would be developed in the computer.

The digital work began with the construction of a pod spine on which the basic tubelike shape would be built. Animation programs

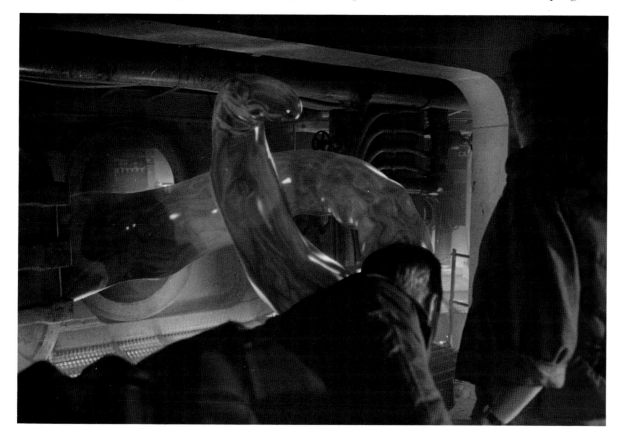

The serpentine pseudopod discovers Deepcore crew members Bud Brigman (Ed Harris) and Lindsey Brigman (Mary Elizabeth Mastrantonio). The computer-generated creation was a leap into the unknown for the CG department.

Far and near right: Director Cameron had a clear idea of the look for the pseudopod: a snake-like, organic form composed entirely of seawater. Before constructing the creature in the digital environment, concept sketches worked out the basic form . . .

. . . while physical, three-dimensional models helped CG artists imagine the textures and dimensional qualities they would be creating (note the facial features at the tip).

Below: Steve Williams and Mark Dippé watch the pseudopod take shape in the computer.

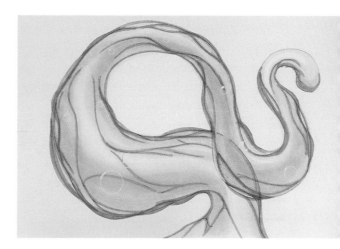

helped lock in the creature's fluid, serpentine moves. It was decided that the pod's surface would not be dripping seawater, which would have complicated matters, but would be created through a rippling effect accomplished automatically through a computer program filter.

"It [the creature] had to be living; you had to feel that it had a mind of its own and was moving and rippling purposefully," explained Mark Dippé. "Each ripple had to

be hand-adjusted. We spent a lot of time watching and studying waves. Then, we'd set some wave generators up—using experience, divination, a few incantations—and would have to wait all day to see if it worked [the computers took some time to process all the instructions]. By trial and error we created a library of ripple effects that seemed to work, and then we'd go in and recycle them throughout the sequence."

REFLECTIONS OF LIGHT

"Water reflects ten to fifteen percent of light and refracts the rest of it," observed John Knoll of the need for the water creature to reflect and refract light realistically. "Because water is transparent, some of the light that hits it will reflect off and some will pass through it. But the path isn't perfectly

straight because water and air have different densities. When light hits a medium of higher density it is bent in toward the 'normal' [a geometric computer graphics term meaning an imaginary line that runs perpendicular to the given point on the surface of an object;

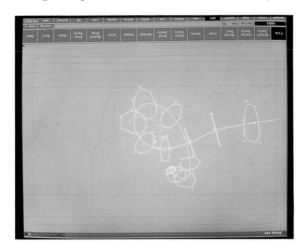

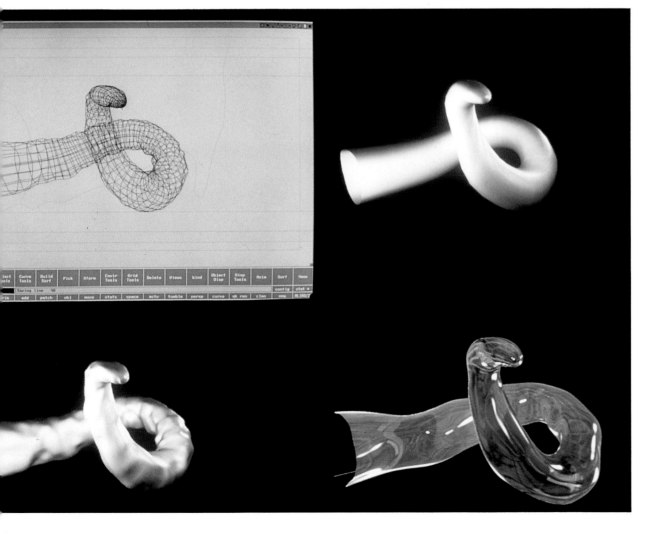

This page: Starting with a digital spine, the pseudopod evolved from a basic tube shape to a rippling, reflective surface.

Right: For the sequence in which the pseudopod communicates with Bud and Lindsey by transforming its tip into the facial likeness of each, ILM utilized a laser scanning device to capture data from each performer. Unlike the laser scanner used to create physical sculptures of the Starship *Enterprise* crew in *Star Trek IV*, the new-generation Cyberware scanning equipment (owned and made available by Disney Imagineering, the R and D arm of the company's theme park division) recorded raw numbers that could be inputted into ILM's CG system and then manipulated.

Below: The pseudopod transforms into Bud, as Lindsey tentatively reaches out in response. The CG artists had a range of laser-scanned expressions to draw from—some twelve for Lindsey and eight for Bud—with the morphing system developed on *Willow* utilized to transition from one expression to another.

used to calculate reflection and shading information]. There is a law that defines the index of refraction, and you can calculate what this bend angle is. I did a little bit of experimentation to figure out what the refracted image would look like through water. I concluded that the angle of how much of the scene you would see behind it was small enough so that we could cheat and derive all of the refraction information just from the background plate. It was a cheat and not technically accurate, but we wanted to do something that could be done quickly. To be perfectly accurate we would have had to do actual ray tracing, which is a time-consuming and tedious process, to measure the actual refraction of light rays."

The background plate photography into which the pseudopod would be composited would be complicated by the creature's reflective character. "When you want to simulate an object in computer graphics that's highly reflective, you're seeing [on the screen] a distorted view of its environment, because in reality shiny objects are reflections of the world around them," Knoll observed. "So in

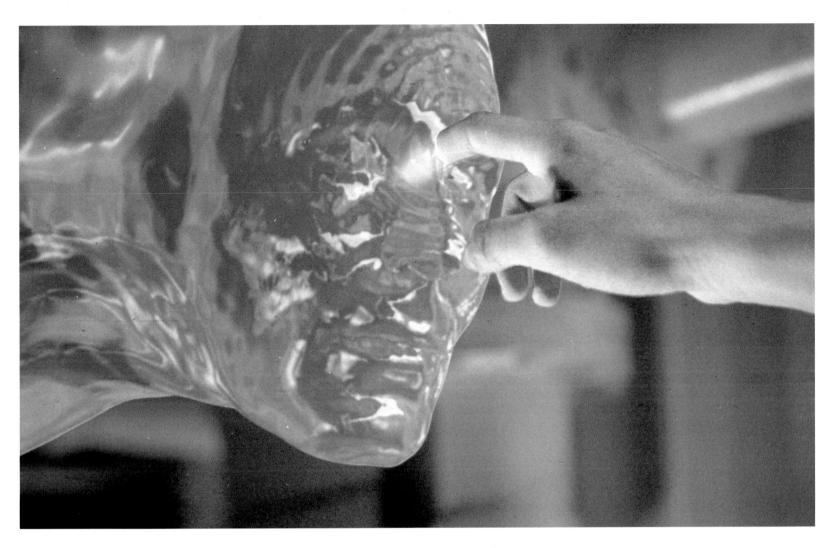

order for the computer character to adequately represent that, you have to give it [the computer] a description of the world around it, and a common way to do that is by making what's called a 'cubic reflection environment.' This digital cube is six-sided, and all six sides can represent the particular set or environment around the object. When it's rendered the computer can figure out in what direction an incoming light ray would be reflecting and what part of the cubic environment you'd be seeing; it then can shade the pixel."

To create the digital environment, Knoll traveled to the location to still-photograph every inch of the Deepcore set. But as on any busy movie set, a perfect document wasn't possible: Some parts of the set's ceiling and walls were missing, and actors, crew, props, and lighting equipment were often in the way

of a clean photo. It was in perfecting the digital environment for the water creature that Knoll got the first feature-film opportunity to test his Photoshop image-processing program.

"When I got back to ILM I had this huge pile of pictures. I got them all scanned into a Macintosh, and then I used Photoshop to piece all these pictures into a cubic environment," said Knoll. "I could make sure all six sides of the cube blended together so there weren't any seams and so that it was all color-balanced. With the software I could also paint out any light stands and people, or make up any part of the set that didn't exist, and gradually piece the whole thing together. With this photo cube we could play the camera and lights exactly in the same position they were in during actual shooting of the plate and create the reflective element which was a com-

Contact! The entire pseudopod sequence, which required twenty separate shots and seventy-five seconds of CG, was a breakthrough in its creation of a synthetic character. The highest praise came from James Cameron himself: "With the pseudopod, what you see in the film is exactly and precisely what I visualized."

ponent of the pseudopod creature."

When the pseudopod was a completed element—animated form, watery rippling surface, light refraction and reflection—it was decided that the optical department would do the compositing honors. To composite digitally the lengthy sequence would have required a time-consuming one to four hours per frame (a minimum of seventy-five full days), and Knoll estimated the output scanner reliability was then about forty hours between breakdowns.

The ILM effects team unanimously credited Cameron for his strength of vision in the pseudopod sequence. "So many effects scenes are used as placeholders for the big action, but Cameron used effects very differently in the pseudopod sequence," Jim Morris observed. "He designed it to be an elegant, graceful moment which allowed a lingering and mystical response in the viewer. The audiences I saw it with seemed awestruck: they actually gasped when they saw this creature."

Most significant for ILM was the impact the sequence had on its growing computer graphics department. To CG department manager Doug Kay, *The Abyss* represented the crossing of another threshold, this one a defining moment. "Instead of just producing quiet little elements or wire removal and things you didn't see, the pseudopod was the key featured sequence, and it got great publicity," Kay recalled. "There was tremendous pride felt inside the department, and it was the high point of my professional career when ILM picked up the Academy Award for this work. It was a culmination of all the work of building this department and getting the tools on line."

The Abyss not only accelerated the evolution of 3-D computer graphics, but the water creature was visible proof to the film industry that computer graphics was a feasible new tool for creating cinematic illusions. The breakthrough gave Cameron some visionary ideas about how to approach the sequel to

The Terminator, his 1984 hit film about a cyborg killing machine from the future.

"Jim kept telling us that if the pseudopod didn't work out, he could always cut the whole sequence out of the movie," Dennis Muren remembered. "On *Terminator 2*, however, he committed himself to computer graphics by designing a main character, the T-1000, who was entirely dependent on computer graphics and who couldn't, under any circumstances, be cut out of the movie."

For Muren, accustomed to the high stakes and pressures of big-time effects production, *T2* represented a winner-take-all roll of the dice, a challenge to call forth the most fantastic creature yet from the digital realm.

TERMINATOR 2: JUDGMENT DAY
1991 (Carolco)
WINNER OF ACADEMY AWARD FOR BEST VISUAL EFFECTS
WINNER OF BRITISH ACADEMY AWARD FOR BEST VISUAL EFFECTS
T-1000 Cyborg, Liquid Metal Prototype, c. A.D. 2029

The first *Terminator* film faded to black with a shot of a pregnant Sarah Connor (Linda Hamilton) driving off into the wilderness, armed with the knowledge that Skynet, the computer system that controlled the nuclear arsenal, would eventually achieve intelligence and release its nuclear firepower on the entire human race. The new life growing in her womb would be a son, John Connor, the man who would lead humanity back from the brink in the prophesied war against the machines. His father, a human soldier sent from the future to protect Sarah, had died in the victorious battle against an assassin from the future, the metal-cyborg Terminator (Arnold Schwarzenegger).

In *Terminator 2: Judgment Day*, the apocalypse had not yet arrived and Sarah, wound tight from years of steeling herself for the coming conflagration (and recurring dreams of Los Angeles leveled in a nuclear blast), had snapped and landed in a state mental hospital. John Connor, ten years old

The liquid-metal T-1000 strides out of the fire. In one unbroken shot, the cyborg from the future metamorphoses from chrome man to human form. ILM's forty-four CG shots in the film would again push the boundaries of the impossible, not only in the computer-generated figures, but in digitally compositing CG and live-action plates.

and in the care of foster parents, was bitter and edgy, having been raised on Sarah's ravings of Skynet, nuclear holocaust, and time-traveling Terminators. But mother and son would be reunited by an unlikely comrade—a Terminator reprogrammed by human forces to serve as protector against a new cyborg killer on the way from Skynet.

James Cameron originally conceived the battling Terminators as looking exactly like the assassin of the first film, an 800-series class of metal cyborg. Since that entire series of machines would look like assembly-line figures of *Terminator* actor Arnold Schwarzenegger, the star would have had to be duplicated, either by a stunt double or split-screen effects, whenever the two cyborgs had to be in frame together or during face-to-face encounters.

But Cameron abandoned the idea and came up with a fantastic new creation: the T-1000, a liquid-metal cyborg with the ability to assume the shape of surrounding objects of equal size, heal its own bullet wounds and other injuries, and even reconstitute itself after being blown apart. The director was counting on ILM computer graphics to create the kind of fantastic visuals usually dreamed up and drawn for a superhero comic book but never realistically realized in a live-action fea-

ture. "I honestly felt that eighty percent of the CG effects in the script were impossible to do," admitted B. J. Rack, Cameron's coproducer and a veteran of such effects pictures as *Total Recall*.

But visual effects supervisor Dennis Muren realized that the challenge of providing forty-four CG shots was an opportunity to develop new tools and achieve the next level of digital imaging. "It was extravagant enough to give us a kick in the ass, but it wasn't asking for the impossible," Muren confidently observed. "Cameron wrote it smart; he wrote it for what we could do with our tools. It was all doable."

The digital assignment would require 100 elements and 7,965 frames of three-dimensional imaging. It would also be the first time all effects work was composited entirely digitally. The computer graphics department, however, had an advantage going into the *Terminator* challenge: The old laser-light ILM-Kodak prototype input scanner had been replaced by the new Trilinear Multicolor High Resolution CCD Digital Input Scanner, which had begun being developed in January 1988 and received its first feature-film workout for *Die Hard 2*. The new scanner would not only help produce *T2*'s breakthrough

effects and become the department's main scanning device through 1994 (when a second, new-generation scanner would go online) but in the process allow for computer graphics and image-processing breakthroughs that would remove many of the physical barriers that traditionally kept filmmakers from realizing their vision.

BREAKTHROUGH IN DIGITAL SCANNING

The new CCD scanner was the first high-end digitizing device able to output a multicolor, high-resolution image capable of being intercut with production footage. The scanner could scan in and digitize all standard 35mm formats, including four-perf frame and eight-perf VistaVision; original negative film; an intermediate positive (also called "interpositive," an image on an original negative that represents an element for composite); or a final positive piece of print film. (To film final

Above and below: The T-1000, a cyborg assassin with shape-changing powers, assumes the appearance and uniform of an L.A. police officer throughout much of the film. The creature's metamorphic cycle would range from its "chrome man" form to a humanoid appearance.

Left: Thanks to ILM's CG artists, the T-1000 could take full-on shotgun blasts and keep on ticking—such as in this shot, a combination of live-action footage with actor Robert Patrick composited onto the computer model.

Below: A particularly surrealistic effect was this image of the T-1000 passing through bars in its relentless pursuit of Sarah Connor.

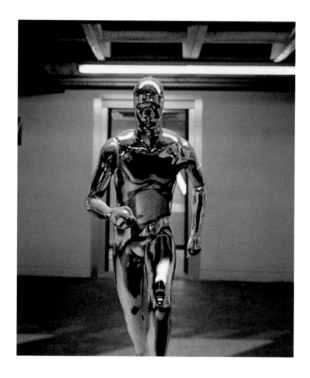

This page: Just as traditional cartoon cel animation often utilized rotoscopes of live photography for realism, so too does CG incorporate live-action references into the digital realm. To produce a realistic moving chrome figure, a black grid-painted Robert Patrick was filmed and the reference footage scanned in. The resulting digital skeleton was used as a guide in creating the T-1000 animation.

work out of the computer realm, ILM used commercial Solitaire output film recorders with Oxberry cameras.)

The new CCD scanner was the centerpiece of the synergistic means by which ILM could enter, work in, and exit the digital realm with a high-resolution image for recording back onto clean negative. The *T2: Judgment Day* duty also required ILM software engineers to develop new programs and a hardware setup of some thirty-five high-powered Silicon Graphics workstations. (In fact, the capacities of SGI hardware were growing every year—effectively doubling in power and speed from year to year—thereby allowing high-end clients such as ILM and NASA to process the highest-resolution images.)

The volume of digital work also necessitated CG department expansion, which involved not only installing the new SGI units but increasing the staff from eight to more than forty animators and software engineers. CG coordinator Judith Weaver recalled that "nothing this big had ever happened in the department. There was a mad rush to set up, and three weeks later it was humming." CG animator Steve Williams remembered it as

"like a mass warfare effort. Teams changed and people reconfigured as talents emerged. It was a manic, energy-filled production with incredible deadlines and pressures."

The main design team, led by Muren and art director Doug Chiang, refined the storyboards and locked down the design of the T-1000 character. As with *The Abyss* and other big 3-D projects, T-1000 puppets were created as a physical aid for visualizing the look to be created in the digital realm. The actual animation work for one of the T-1000's full-form shape changes would require five separate metamorphic stages, progressing from an amorphous blob of liquid metal through chrome-man stages and finally into a realistic-looking human.

THE HUMAN MOTION GROUP

The shots, defined by CG producer Janet Healy as being "difficult, very difficult, most difficult, and miraculous," were divided among six teams. One of the teams, "The Human Motion Group," was assigned the ambitious animation assignment of generating the T-1000's chrome form, the next-to-final stage before the cyborg assumed the appearance of actor Robert Patrick.

"Our intention was to duplicate human motions and mannerisms realistically, believably, as opposed to the previous attempts [in other movies]—all of which tended toward a cartoony look," commented team leader Lincoln Hu. "You have to follow the laws of physics. A walking chrome creature, even though it's an abstraction, needs to reflect and move correctly, or it'll look phony to the audience."

In order to build digitally a chrome man from its wire-frame spine to a full-motion figure with skin and musculature, the Human Motion Team first had to record photographically Robert Patrick's motion characteristics. A black grid, which would help the computer assimilate the physical data, was painted on the actor, who was then filmed by front and side cameras. Next, the reference footage was digitized and a frame-by-frame digital skeleton built. In an echo of reality, the computer-generated character's motion would include a barely noticeable limp, the result of an old athletic knee injury suffered by Patrick.

BODY SOCK SOFTWARE

To create a humanoid creature, one of the long-standing problems in generating complex forms had to be overcome: The points where polygons and patches (the building blocks of 3-D digital imaging) met often resulted in creases and overlapping, which destroyed an image's continuous quality. The answer was "Body Sock," a breakthrough software program created by ILM that smoothed out and blended together the edges of a digitally modeled surface.

According to Stefen Fangmeier, a technical director on the Human Motion Team, "Separate body parts or patches have always been the bane of traditional computer graphics. The Body Sock program was a big mathematical software challenge met by Lincoln Hu, Michael Natkin, Angus Poon, and Eric Enderton. They solved the problem of taking pieces of geometry which don't fit together

and making them look like one smooth, continuous surface. This was the biggest software breakthrough on *T2*, and it quickly became an essential tool in our arsenal."

MAKE STICKY SOFTWARE

Another *T2* software breakthrough, termed "Make Sticky," helped move several shots from the "miraculous" category to the "difficult" column. The software allowed CG

Left: One of the breakthrough tools developed on *T2* was the "Make Sticky" software program, which allowed scanned-in, two-dimensional background plates to stick to a 3-D form as it was animated, as in the "Checkerboard Floor" scene of the T-1000 rising out of a hospital-floor pattern behind an unsuspecting security guard.

Above: Having risen from the floor, the T-1000 begins to undergo the molten stage of a transformation cycle.

artists to project the 2-D images from a live-action plate onto 3-D computer models. According to Tom Williams, one of the main designers of the software, when the computer model moves, the software "will pull the projected imagery along with it."

Make Sticky was originally developed for the "Checkerboard Floor" scene inside the

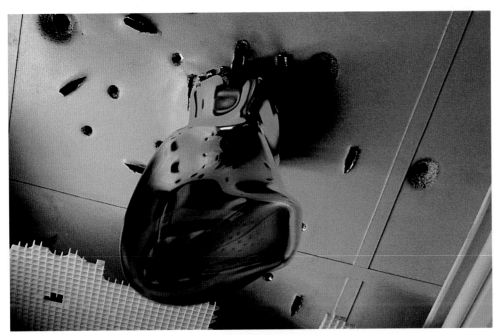

mental hospital where Sarah was incarcerated. In the shot a doomed security guard is getting his last cup of vending-machine coffee while behind him a section of the checkerboard floor begins to mutate and a head, and then the entire cyborg form, pulls up out of the surface. In creating the amazing footage, CG artists scanned in the live-action plate of the checkerboard floor and projected the two-dimensional image onto the 3-D form of the rising T-1000. The Make Sticky program then, as its name implied, held the projected plate imagery in position as the head and body emerged from the distorting floor.

Make Sticky also helped create an illusion later in the sequence, as the T-1000 passed through metal bars that locked off a section of the hospital's hallway. The surrealistic effect was achieved by filming two plates, one a pass of the empty corridor with the bars in place, the second a shot of the actor in position with no bars in the shot. Both plates were scanned into the computer, and a 3-D computer model of Robert Patrick was match-moved to the live-action footage of the actor walking through the area where the bars would be in

The T-1000 in its liquid-metal state as it descends from the roof of an elevator . . .

. . . and later in the film, as it does its transforming thing in a helicopter cockpit.

Another transformation sequence as John Connor (Edward Furlong) and his protecting Terminator (Arnold Schwarzenegger) retreat into a steel mill for the final battle.

the final shot. When Patrick started walking through the bars, CG substituted the digital model of the actor, and the Make Sticky software held the projected bars in place as the face distorted through the bars.

The death-pit sequence, a showdown between Terminators in front of a steel mill's molten pit, was one of ILM's most difficult scenes, and it ran the playbook of CG techniques. It was the only sequence in the movie not tightly storyboarded by Cameron, who gave Muren and his team relatively free rein in developing concepts.

The battle ended with the T-1000 falling into the pit. In its death throes, the creature flayed around in a hellish frenzy, splashing about in the molten steel and going through a series of transformations that showed the cyborg slipping in and out of the human forms it had stolen throughout the film. To supply CG with the plate elements, the live actors were filmed in the "molten" vat, a three-foot-deep acrylic tub filled with water and mineral oil and rigged with lighting effects. CG then provided splashes to comp on top of some thirty different elements, ranging from digital morphing shots of the cyborg shape-changing into the other characters to foreground smoke and heat ripples. CG added a slight movement to the original locked-off photography to give the subtle look of the scene being documented with a hand-held camera.

PAINTING WITH FILM

Another key component of ILM's digital arsenal, which Janet Healy called "our secret weapon," was Photoshop and other draw-and-

paint software systems. No longer were potentially days of delay necessary to correct a shot; by rerendering that shot in CG, an artist armed with painting software and a digitizing tablet could simply paint the solution in the computer. The painting programs became extremely important as the production deadline neared and there was not enough time to write special problem-solving software.

"One of the biggest problems we face in creating effects is that our magic doesn't always work," Muren observed. "A complex miniature explosion can be ruined by a piece of flying debris that looks as small as it really is, or a flying person can be seen hanging from wires that were supposed to be invisible. Sometimes accidents will happen, and a shot will be scratched, or a crew member will appear reflected in a car window. But what would have been a costly reshoot a few years ago is now an invisible digital fix using paint. Paint programs allow an artist to add or subtract, cut and paste any part of a frame over another using digital brushes.

"On *T2* I realized we didn't need to think in three dimensions all the time, that the images for film are really two-dimensional

This page and opposite: The T-1000 finally corners Sarah (Linda Hamilton). But not to fear, Arnold comes to the rescue, and the cyborg meets its end in a molten pit.

and flat. Once I realized that we could paint on the individual film frames using the 2-D paint programs, I realized we could do anything. I reasoned if we could get a shot ninety percent right, our artists could take the shot, go into Macintoshes, and use Photoshop to paint out any flaws. They could go for the final polish that would take us to one hundred percent. For example, in a shot where the T-1000 runs out of an elevator and into a parking garage, we could not prevent the computer model's shoulders from separating from the body due to the extreme positions they had to move through. These 'tears' lasted only a few frames but were enough to ruin the shot. What we did was to paint in the gaps with a chrome color, and we got the shot. I used this on thirty percent of our CG shots as our secret weapon to getting finals."

The high point of the *T2* experience for Muren was watching the morning dailies of the previous day's work. Seeing a fantastic humanoid creature with the ability to transmute from a chrome figure to a man, or take on surface textures, reminded him of the excitement he felt watching the breakthrough images of *Star Wars*.

The film's box-office success—and the press and television news shows praising the wizardry of ILM—marked a new era for the effects company and the entire film industry. It was now clear that 3-D digital work was not a science fiction fantasy. Even more so than *The Abyss, T2* showed that digital could, in fact, be the star of a show. The once uncharted frontier of the digital realm was now being mapped out, the first trails cut, and wider explorations were now possible.

DEATH BECOMES HER
1992 (Universal)
WINNER OF ACADEMY AWARD FOR BEST VISUAL EFFECTS
WINNER OF BRITISH ACADEMY AWARD FOR BEST VISUAL EFFECTS
Digital Manipulation of the Human Body

"Everybody is an expert on skin; it's something everyone's intimately familiar with," observed Judith Weaver, ILM's CG effects production supervisor for *Death Becomes Her*. Therein lay the challenge of the movie: to manipulate digitally body parts and render skin that didn't appear to be computer-generated.

In the film, directed by Robert Zemeckis,

DIGITAL BREAKTHROUGH: CCD INPUT SCANNER

When an image is "digitized," it's been introduced into a computer as an array of binary numbers, the units of information by which a computer can then manipulate the image. To introduce images into the digital realm requires an input scanner. Until a team of six ILMers (digital experts Lincoln Hu, Joshua Pines, and Jeffrey Light, mechanical and optical experts Mike MacKenzie and Mike Bolles, and visual effects supervisor Scott Squires) and two researchers from Eastman Kodak (Mike Davis and Glenn Kennel) built and introduced the CCD scanner in 1990, there had been no effective and reliable input scanner for feature-film production.

The CCD team has championed the device for changing the way movies are made and with good reason: The CCD scanner was the breakthrough device that allowed the film industry to manipulate digitally film imagery. The CCD, first used in 1990 for *Die Hard 2* and *Back to the Future 3*, handled the digital-image com-

positing for such breakthrough films as *Terminator 2* and *Jurassic Park*. Able to digitize a variety of film formats—from eight-perf VistaVision to standard four-perf 35mm—the device meant that ILM no longer needed to be concerned with exclusive use of large-format VistaVision film for digital compositing.

CCD is an abbreviation for "charged coupled device," a light-sensitive electronic chip. Light strikes an assembly of CCD chips, which function as image-recording devices, converting the information to an array of binary digits that provide meaningful information to a computer. The trilinear array of the ILM/Kodak scanner is able to provide high resolution at a maximum of eight thousand pixels in a horizontal direction.

The physical device consists of a standard 35mm film transport, a custom lamphouse, a special fiber-optic bundle for illuminating the film gate, an imaging lens, the CCD sensing array and related electronics, a custom-made mechanical system for moving the transport and film across the CCD array, and custom software to operate the system.

The CCD scanner, along with the computer graphics and digital software tools and output capabilities, formed the triumvirate system for entering into, working in, and exiting the digital realm. The scanner itself had been a technological dream, an evolutionary leap from the Pixar laser and off-the-shelf scanners

Output scanner (with George Gambetta).

in use through *Indiana Jones and the Last Crusade*. "I got interested in computers and electronics, and subsequently image processing, because I could see the potential," said Scott Squires. "But to work we had to be able to input the film, store it, manipulate it, and output it. All of those issues had to be addressed. But input scanning was probably the biggest stumbling block."

By 1994, with almost no optical printing available and nearly every frame of ILM work requiring some form of digital work, a backup CCD scanner was built along the lines of the original. Although the new generation scanner could provide for additional through-put as needed, the original (which would continue to evolve, upgraded with new software and electronics) would remain the workhorse device. In 1995 the Academy of Motion Picture Arts and Sciences honored the breakthrough scanner with a Scientific and Engineering award.

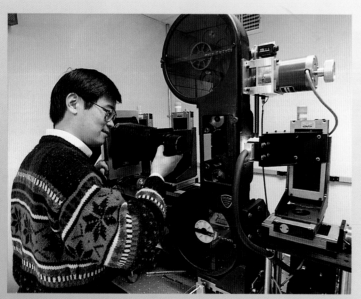

ILM/Kodak Input Scanner (with Lincoln Hu).

fading actress Madeline Ashton (Meryl Streep) and her rival, Helen Sharp (Goldie Hawn), drink of a mysterious elixir that promises them youth and immortality. On their journey into eternity the women experience physical mishaps that would slay mere mortals: Madeline suffers a broken and literally twisted neck, Helen a shotgun blast that opens a hole in her gut. By the end of the film the two tumble down the steps of a church, literally shattering into pieces.

A year earlier the digital technology did not even exist to meet the *Death Becomes Her* challenge, according to visual effects supervisor Ken Ralston. But each year the power of hardware and software was increasing, and so ILM was able to create the desired effects. Of the 140 visual effects shots in the film, 45 required computer graphics, some clocking in at a minute of continuous digital action. The number of frames that would be handled by the relatively new CCD scanner totaled 56,504 (compared to 55,330 *Hook* frames, 7,965 for *T2*, and even the 12,695 frames that would be handled in *Jurassic Park*).

ILM's Digital Advances

Death Becomes Her also benefited from ILM's gearing up for the computer effects challenges of *Jurassic Park* and other anticipated future CG needs. Consultations with SGI led ILM to reconfigure its digital setup and add new hardware, dramatically increasing processing, rendering, and through-put.

During the making of *Death Becomes Her*, the Mac Squad unit of roto, optical, and animation experts (who had been providing digital work for *Hook* and *Memoirs of an Invisible Man*) formally transitioned from Macs to SGI hardware. "It was the completion of the integration of the digital group into CG," digital artist Doug Smythe observed. "Mac was the bridge to get them into the computer world, the training wheels. We had some really big teething pains transitioning to SGI computers; it was difficult trying to learn so much and under such hard deadlines. One

of the greatest things for me was helping these people learn and seeing the lightbulb going on in their heads."

"There's a learning curve when you shift from traditional tools, but I really enjoyed learning new stuff after ten years of just using the same tools," added cameraman Pat Myers, one of the Mac Squad who had for years worked the traditional craft of effects camera and pinblocking. "But regardless of the tools or the technology, there is no magic button."

During this period a software development team was also building software tools outside the crisis atmosphere of a production schedule. "After *T2* the software group started setting long-term priorities and goals," said Tom Williams, an ILM programmer who was promoted to executive in charge of digital effects after *DBH*. "We didn't work to solve the problems for just one shot or just one production, but tried to find a way to fix it for the future."

The physical contortions to be suffered by the main characters as scripted in *Death Becomes Her* walked a fine line between the fantastic and the grotesque. To get a dimensional quality right at the visual-concept stage, Doug Chiang scanned a photo of a model and manipulated it in Photoshop to great effect.

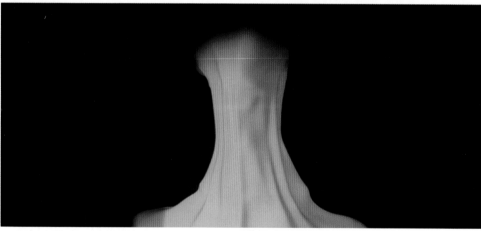

Top: Unlike the fantasy realms of watery sea creatures and chrome cyborgs, the CG challenge of *Death Becomes Her* was to duplicate the look of human skin. Unlike Walter Donovan in *Indy 3*, fading actress Madeline Ashton (Meryl Streep) gets to drink from an elixir of immortality—and the results get curiouser and curiouser.

Bottom: Computer-generated neck element for the Madeline shot.

According to Doug Smythe, *Death Becomes Her* "became a kind of guinea pig" in developing both commercial and proprietary software, much of it in anticipation of *Jurassic Park*. SoftImage, an animating software package developed by a company in Montreal, was tested on *Death Becomes Her* to see if it would work for *Jurassic Park*. The CG department also integrated a new program called Colorburst, a painting and digital rotoscoping package developed by Parallax, an English company. C-Bal, an ILM program developed by Smythe, improved digital blue-screen matte extraction and allowed artists to adjust easily the color saturation of elements

and final composites, which was a critical need for matching the many multiple-element *Death Becomes Her* composites.

MM2, a 2-D match-move tool that could accomplish digitally what was once an effects camera and pin-blocking technique, "changed our lives," according to software manager Michael Natkin. The software, written by John Schlag and John Horner, had been first developed and tested on *Hook* and *Invisible Man*, but it was given a thorough workout on *Death Becomes Her*. The software animated or tracked 2-D images, allowing elements to be rephotographed using the match-move program so that all the elements, and the background plate, could move and interlock together. "The director is now completely free to move the camera without compromising for visual effects," Smythe noted. "We could scale our elements up or down and match specific elements to fit any camera move. We were matching every single frame with the subtlest little bounces and moves."

DIGITAL ART DIRECTION

Although *DBH* was a testing ground for new programs, Doug Smythe recalled the effort as "methodical and organized. There was never a sense of 'How the hell are we going to do this?'" An important factor in keeping matters on track was the development of an extensive digital concept design stage conducted by visual effects art director Doug Chiang under Ken Ralston's direction. Whereas a pencil sketch or painting of an effect could be open to interpretation when the effect was developed in the digital realm, working on the design directly in the computer "proved indispensable for the later execution of the sequences because nothing is left to interpretation," according to Chiang.

One of the most difficult design challenges was creating the look of an immortalized Meryl Streep, who takes a tumble down a winding staircase and suffers a series of neck injuries that leave her neck completely twisted around, with her head either facing backwards, dangling, or grotesquely elongated.

"After extensive research into the anatomy and physics of this effect, I arranged several photo shoots to provide the base for digital artwork, as well as painted photorealistic artwork," Chiang noted. "I then scanned the concept artwork into a Macintosh and used Photoshop to work out the subtleties. By

digital concept art to determine the amount of modeling and animation that was necessary."

THE MOTION-CONTROL WOMAN

The twisted-neck scenes required neck and upper back 3-D computer graphic and blue-screen elements to be match-moved together with the background plate and filmed out as a digital composite.

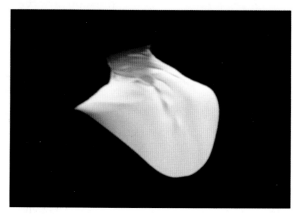

digitally altering to allow for texture, lighting, bone protrusions, bruising, and other factors, we could develop concept art that was closer to the final product. Also, because the twisted-neck sequence was going to be computer-generated, which is typically time-consuming and difficult to alter, we were able to use the

Left: In *DBH*, Madeline discovers that immortality has its problems, such as taking a fall down a flight of stairs and experiencing some twisted results. As in such films as *Memoirs of an Invisible Man* (in which making an actor invisible required isolating those areas that would digitally disappear), a blue mask was used to set apart the areas on Streep that would be manipulated.

Bottom left: CG element for the twisted-neck area.

Below: Streep was photographed blue-screen and the head digitally attached to a headless body. The art direction phase, in which 2-D photos of models were scanned and altered in the computer, were vital in working out the designs for the misshapen physiognomy of the immortal characters.

For the blue-screen work Streep traveled to ILM, where photography could isolate just her face and head as a separate element (as well as a blue-screen element of a dangling ponytail wig). For the precise way Streep repeated actions during her blue-screen work, she won the praises of CG supervisor Smythe, who called the actress "the closest thing to a motion-controllable person I've ever seen."

Smythe recalled the day the actress came to ILM for her blue-screen shoot: "It was at the end of a really long and tedious day. No one wanted to break more than Meryl, but we needed her to stay after the main crew wrapped for some additional reference shots. I reviewed our needs with her, and then we were ready to go. The camera starts to roll, the cameraman yells, 'Speed' . . . and I waited. There was total silence. Meryl finally glances over, confused. Finally, Bob Zemeckis leans over to me and says, 'Usually someone says "Action" about now.' No one had told me they were expecting *me* to be the director! We burned off a good forty or fifty feet of film before I finally said 'Action.' My first directing experience—and the crew will never let me live it down."

Smythe needn't have felt so chagrined; for that year's Academy Awards, he would win a Technical Achievement Award for his development of the morphing software system, and *Death Becomes Her* would win American and British Academy Awards for its visual effects work.

Death Becomes Her marked a major advance in simulating living organisms in the digital realm. While the water creature of *The Abyss* and the liquid-metal and chrome man of *T2* were realistically animated, they were pure creatures of the imagination and more forgiving in terms of realism. But the macabre physical contortions created for *Death Becomes Her* had to simulate human skin and anatomy. In meeting the challenge the CG department developed tools that later would be used to create the *Jurassic Park* dinosaurs.

"With *Jurassic Park*, CG has entered its adolescent phase; the hormones are acting up, and it's strutting all over the place," Dennis Muren would declare. "The viewers will see something they have never seen before: dinosaurs that look as if they are actually in the shot. This is not the usual effects trickery, this is another level of experience."

JURASSIC PARK
1993 (Amblin/Universal)
WINNER OF ACADEMY AWARD FOR BEST VISUAL EFFECTS
WINNER OF BRITISH ACADEMY AWARD FOR BEST VISUAL EFFECTS
Digital Dinosaurs

ILM, which always prided itself on creating realistic-looking effects, got its greatest challenge on Steven Spielberg's *Jurassic Park*, the big-screen adaptation of the Michael Crichton bestseller. Crichton's story of genetic engineers extracting dinosaur DNA from an amber-trapped prehistoric mosquito and cloning the ancient creatures for an island amusement park was given a truth-is-stranger spin when, two weeks into the movie's production in September 1992, it was announced that California scientists had extracted the DNA of an extinct bee that had been preserved in amber for 25 million years. Although scientists only managed to determine the molecular makeup of the ancient

Below: Bringing the *Jurassic* dinosaurs to life required advances in animatronic and robotics, with the Stan Winston Studio creating the mechanical versions for live-action sequences and former ILMer Phil Tippett's own shop working with ILM to produce a fusion of CG and stop-motion animation. But ILM's CG breakthroughs were so breathtaking (as well as being unencumbered by the limits of physical materials) that Spielberg upped a planned handful of shots to six full minutes of computer-generated creations. The breakthroughs began with this T-rex skeletal test by Steve Williams.

The fully sculpted and animated T-rex test creation composited into a background plate of the Marin County countryside.

insect, offering clues to the biological clock of evolutionary time lines, the news showed the suddenness with which modern sciences had overtaken subjects once securely in the realm of science fiction. Creating the dinosaurs for *Jurassic Park* would require a high degree of authenticity to capture the imaginations of audiences that had witnessed televised moon walks and space-shuttle launches, not to mention the cinematic wonders of the effects age.

Spielberg's ultimate goal was realistic creatures, not cliché movie monsters. The dinosaur team was originally organized with Stan Winston Studios producing full-scale animatronic puppets, ex-ILMer Phil Tippett's shop crafting miniature puppets and stop-motion animating them, and ILM computer graphics generating a few digital dinosaur herd shots and digitally adding motion-blur to, and compositing, Tippett's animation elements.

Only a few CG shots had originally been planned for ILM because of the great unknown in creating a living creature. "We'd done a water creature and a chrome man, but a living, breathing animal was another level of complexity altogether," Muren recalled.

"No one wanted [the opportunity to create breakthrough CG work] more than me, but I had to be responsibly cautious. We had to prove it internally before we could go sell the idea to Steven [Spielberg]."

SECRET CG TESTS

ILM CG animator Eric Armstrong and CG supervisor Stefen Fangmeier had been working on tests of a gallimimus herd galloping through an African savannah, but animators Steve Williams and effects supervisor Mark Dippé wanted the department to contribute more than a few herd shots. As Williams recalled, the duo wanted to show that CG could create "a full-screen, in-your-face, Tyrannosaurus rex."

Spielberg agreed to fund a testing phase to see if photorealistic, CG dinosaurs were possible. Muren traveled to Spielberg's Amblin offices in Southern California to show the director and his production team video tests: two shots of a stampeding gallimimus herd. "Everyone went nuts when we showed the tests," Muren recalled. "Steven was thrilled and put a stampede sequence into the script. This was the test that made the differ-

Right: Modeling stage of a T-rex that has broken loose to attack one of the tour vehicles. The sequence was cut with Stan Winston's mechanical effects as well. ILM's full-motion work generally took over when an entire figure needed to be displayed. In this scene, the CG dinosaur would be attacking a computer-generated vehicle.

Below: Wire-frame beginnings of the park's tour vehicle. The final shot would include a blue-screen element of two children trapped in the overturned car, as well as a completely CG back wheel that would move with the motion of the CG T-rex's ferocious attack.

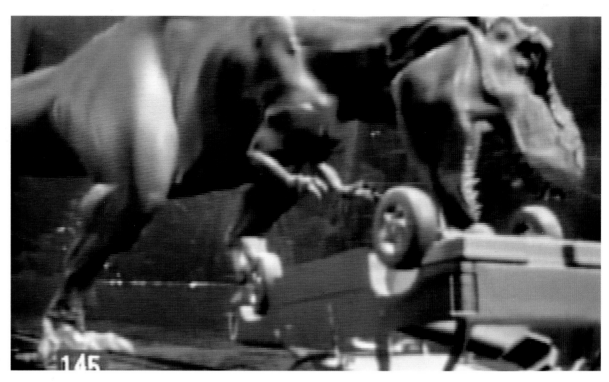

ence and gave us the confidence and funding to move forward."

The workload shifted suddenly after that screening. Traditional stop- and go-motion photography was eliminated from the schedule, and the responsibility to create the dinosaurs for more than fifty scenes was transferred to the realm of computer graphics.

ILM's charge was to create digitally three-dimensional, full-body creatures—a Tyrannosaurus rex, a couple of brachiosaurs, several velociraptors (or "raptors"), and herds of gallimimus—that would be digitally composited with live-action plates and that could cut perfectly with Winston's animatronic creations. This new form of computer-generated movie creature, credited in the production as "full-motion dinosaurs," would be featured in scenes of the T-rex attacking tour vehicles on the island's main road, a herd of gallimimus in the wild, the raptors stalking the children in a kitchen area, and a final battle between the T-rex and the raptors in the Jurassic Park visitor's center.

STOP-MOTION ANIMATION PHASE

Phil Tippett's creature shop was not, however, cut loose from the production. Realizing that everyone was embarking on a new era of realistic computer imaging, it was decided that Tippett's crew would work with ILM on the characteristics of creature animation. To connect the two facilities ILM set up a *Jurassic Park* transmission network, a video and audio microwave path to the Phil Tippett

The dinosaurs return in Steven Spielberg's *Jurassic Park*. The extinct creatures—such as the CG Tyrannosaurus rex—were so convincingly resurrected that they awed audiences worldwide and made the movie one of the biggest international hits of all time. As Dennis Muren, ILM's "full-motion" dinosaur creator, puts it: "This was the best project I've ever worked on and something that probably won't happen again. It was the right people together on the right film when the technology was ready to explode."

Ian Malcolm (Jeff Goldblum) finds his visit to Jurassic Park a little too exciting as he looks to escape from the T-rex that has broken loose. (This shot did not appear in the final film.)

Studio across the Bay in Berkeley. (A similar communications setup would link ILM with Spielberg's Amblin Studios.)

To interface with the digital realm, ILM and Tippett created a Dinosaur Input Device (DID)—later referred to as "Direct Input Device"—which was a fusion of computer animation and stop motion. "The DID was made because a third and final test showing the T-rex chasing the gallimimus herd had a serious jerky animation problem our animators couldn't fix," Muren explained. "Phil and I were very worried. Our solution was to build the DID as an alternate animation approach to ILM's soft-image animation, which would give us a choice for the best animation tool and personnel. Ultimately, our animators fig-

ured out how to fix the jerky problem, and Phil's animators used the DID for the animation of fifteen or so shots. So both worked." The device was a basic armature built with encoders at pivot points that translated typical stop-motion manipulations into a wireframe figure in the computer. Concurrent with the DID development, Tippett and his longtime animation collaborators, senior animator Randal Dutra and Tom St. Amand, spent four months completing animatics for all the major dinosaur action in the film. The animatics, which utilized traditional stop-motion photography of armatured puppets, provided an essential previsualization tool, a moving storyboard that worked out the choreography that would be duplicated with both mechanical and CG dinosaur creations. The stop-motion animation roughs could be filmed and played back on video.

"Artistic realism was the goal on all of the animation," according to Tippett. "We worked to get rid of all anthropomorphic actions. We wanted the dinosaurs to be as naturalistic as possible. It was the subtlety and all the refinements to the animation that allowed us to make those creatures look like real animals and not like movie monsters. All animation is similarly grounded, whether the medium involves a computer mouse or a physical armature. Good animators can't be *told* how to move something; they have to feel it with their own bodies. Cerebral communication can only go so far. The best animators I've seen are the ones who initially block out their puppet's performance using their own bodies. I myself tend to grunt and groan a lot. Working things out with real materials is an ancient form of communication. It involves working in real space, in a physical world with consequences—if you slip, you cut yourself. I felt it was real important for communications that we get everyone on some common ground."

During preproduction, Tippett directed a team of eight ILM animators and two animators from his shop in an active course of study to prepare them for their roles as dinosaur performers. They observed animals at wildlife parks, zoos, and marine exhibits, participated in dance and movement classes, and attended stop-motion classes where traditional armatures were used as a teaching tool. "Before this intense training for *Jurassic*, I tended to just move my little mouse around and not use my body," admitted Eric Armstrong. "All of the classes helped break the ice; we would get really loose in front of each other. It was definitely physical. Everyone got up and out of their chairs to act out the motion. It helped people get uninhibited."

"We were establishing character traits and movements for the dinosaurs, all of which made up what we called a 'movement bible,'" explained Dutra. "There's always going to be some dramatic and artistic license, especially in film, but speaking for myself, I certainly made a big point to study what a lot of paleontologists had found, what the bones had told them, what the parameters of movement that some of the joints allowed were. I think it's real important for whoever is going to be doing this kind of motion work to have a real feel for some of these creatures and to feel in your head just how these creatures moved."

One of Dutra's main assignments was designing the animation for the sequence in which the two children in the film are stalked in the kitchen by a pair of hungry raptors. The basic moves—what Dutra called "the dance of the whole thing"—were first worked out with storyboards, animatics, and discussions with Spielberg, Muren, and Tippett.

"After you get a general idea of the floor plan, the real test for the animator is to make it all look real, to put in the all-important pauses and action," Dutra noted. "For example, the movement of the raptors jumping on the tables in the kitchen had to be broken down so that all the muscles, joints, and posings could go into a smooth, believable sequence. In this production we were actually afforded some research time on actual move-

ments, and that made the big difference because this wasn't going to be rehashes of old dinosaur movies with monsters on the loose. What was so seductive about animating these creatures was giving them realistic power and grace, so you could actually believe they were living and walking around. The raptors were incredibly designed predators. They had these arms with fingers that ended in nails that were like grappling hooks, so whenever they grabbed onto something they would hook in, like a lion would do to a wildebeest. I can't think of one predator today which would stand a chance against them."

After establishing the basic movement through key-frame poses, layers of refinements—from eyes blinking to tails thrashing—were added to further enhance the realism of movement. The modeling of the creatures began, as with most such realizations, with sculpted maquettes. The *Jurassic Park* maquettes were measured by lasers to generate a digital blueprint for each model, data that would help modelers establish proportion and detailing. While the DID system handled the primary motion for one quarter of the workload, the majority of shots relied on CG animators directly manipulating the digitized model on SGI computers with the aid of SoftImage company software that allowed them to create moves that would automatically be incorporated into the entire motion of a CG model.

BUILDING A DINOSAUR: WIRE FRAMES, SKIN TEXTURES, AND MUSCLES

After Tippett, Muren, and Spielberg were satisfied with the animation on any given shot, the wire-frame dinosaur moved forward to the next stage in the CG process: the painting of texture maps for the skin surface. Artists Carolyn Rendu and TyRuben Ellingson provided most of the texture maps that contributed significantly to the animal's complex skin-surface characteristics. Viewpaint, a new, in-house software program written by John Schlag and Brian Knep, rev-

One of the steps in integrating a CG creature with live action requires compositing the background plate with the three-dimensional wire model.

olutionized the way artists created the surface-texture maps by allowing the artist to paint the surface of the dinosaur as if it were a real sculpture. With the new program, instead of painting an image, the digital artist could look at a 3-D model rendered on-screen and add the color with texture-map coordinates, bending it around complex finished shapes.

"Viewpaint was a critical technique for us," explained CG supervisor Alex Seiden. "We couldn't have gotten the look and the detail on the dinosaurs without it. We wanted to make it as easy for an artist to paint on the computer as it is to paint on a real model. Usually, texture mapping is real indirect—you have a flat square that gets applied in a distorted way like wrapping paper. Viewpaint lets you paint right on the sculpture as you look at it, so the interaction and results are much better."

"Traditionally in CG, the artist had to

paint the flat surface and assimilate what it would look like wrapped on the 3-D object," effects art director Ellingson added. "Viewpaint allows you to see maps on the geometry of the sculpture as you paint. The most difficult transition for me was that I had to compensate for shadows and paint everything flat because the shadows are created afterwards by the technical director in the rendering phase. We would make a bump map [by which a CG object is given a rough surface texture] that would be as if the computer were reading my bump map like braille."

One of the biggest breakthroughs on the animation front was Enveloping, an in-house tool ILM developed specifically to enhance the dinosaur animation. Working in conjunction with Body Sock, the program developed for the T-1000 in *Terminator 2*. Enveloping allowed animators to make the computer-generated flesh move with all the realism of

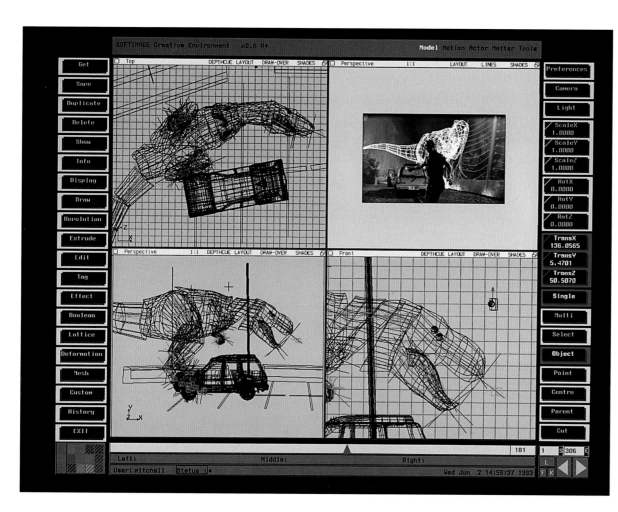

ILM modeled its computer-generated dinosaurs with Alias and SoftImage software, producing three-dimensional, wire-frame skeletons and later adding moving muscles and skin textures.

actual skin moving against muscle and bone. A primary "Enveloping" pass gave the sense that the skin and muscle were moving realistically with the animal's skeleton, a second pass would add sways or jiggles to body parts in tune with the shot's primary movement, and additional passes could add such effects as the expansion and contraction of flesh that would occur during breathing.

BACKGROUND PLATE BREAKTHROUGHS

The various software breakthroughs, building on the advances pioneered during *Death Becomes Her*, would allow for unprecedented freedom in the digital compositing of CG creations and live-action film. For the first time in ILM's history all restrictions on camera movement in background plates were removed, thanks to such tools as SoftImage, which allowed CG artists to create 3-D match-moves for any live-action plate

and weave those shots with complex and hand-held camera moves.

"We pulled out all the stops on every dimension of the plate photography," recalled Stefen Fangmeier. "Spielberg was able to go wild. There was almost no blue screen in this film. No motion-controlled dolly moves. Locked-off camera shots were eliminated. For the first time, the effects required no restraints or restrictions on any of the live-action photography. We went in there with no strings attached."

ILM had first used SoftImage for a *T2* test and for a few shots in *Death Becomes Her*, but *Jurassic Park* would be the first major use of the commercial 3-D animation package. "SoftImage is really focused on creating character animation, and the tools in that package are the type a traditional animator would use," noted Tom Williams. "For example, if you're building a creature's limb, it lays out the skeletal structure, so if you move the wrist, the rest of the arm—the forearm, shoulder, and everything—will move naturally, rather than in a normal software program in which you'd have to specify the exact angles for every single joint. It makes it very easy for animators to create key poses. It's very interactive."

For the live-action plates, shot on location on the Hawaiian island of Kauai, such props as bright-green tennis balls and luminous glow sticks placed at equal distances throughout the geography of the background plate served as reference points to create the match-move programs. Once scanned in, all reference props could be digitally removed.

"Our job was to create a computer camera move that matched what the cameraman did on the set," explained Charlie Clavadetscher, who was part of the 3-D camera match-move team. "If there were reference points such as tennis balls or glow sticks, we'd match-move to them. Otherwise, we'd use blueprints and measurements from the actual set or location to build rough 3-D models to represent people and props in the plate. The idea is to move the computer camera around until it locks into the actual cameraman's view of the set. When we had an accurate match-move program, we'd deliver that information to the animator, who would use it as a guide to lock the choreography of the creatures to the live-action plate."

T-rex attacking the tour vehicle (a still from the film combining both the CG dinosaur and CG vehicle).

DIGITAL ROTO

The venerable art of rotoscoping was also used to integrate the digital creatures into a scene. If a dinosaur needed to walk behind the leaves of a tree in a live-action plate, then an articulate matte would be produced, carefully outlining and isolating each leaf per frame so the creature could be composited behind them. For *Jurassic* the traditionally hand-drawn art of rotoscoping would be accomplished digitally, with Parallax's Matador software.

"*Jurassic Park* has the most extensive rotoscoping ever done at ILM," observed George Murphy, CG supervisor for 2-D effects and matte work in the film. "Matador was a big improvement over previous matte-generating systems. Instead of hand drawing each outline, rotoscopers could put down points and digitally generate curves and lines for key frames. The computer automatically does the frames in-between. The rotoscoper

then goes in and fine-tunes each frame as needed. The efficiency of roto has increased tenfold with this software. Ninety percent of the mattes in *Jurassic* were rotoed frame by frame using Matador. Only ten percent were extracted. But each matte required customization, and so many shots needed four, five, or more separate mattes to be generated. Roto overlapped into the compositing arena because frequently we'd end up combining multiple mattes so that we could hand over just one or two precomposited elements to the technical director (TD) on any given shot. But the new tools make the rotoscoping cleaner than you've ever seen before. Chattering mattes and matte lines are completely a thing of the past."

FINAL COMPOSITING

After the modelers, animators, painters, and rotoscopers had created their elements, the job of the technical director was just

A computer-generated raptor poised for the kill (a still from the film).

Near left: One of *Jurassic Park*'s wonders is this full-size brachiosaur introduced early in the movie. The photorealistic realism was achieved with various software programs that laid skin, muscle movement, textures, and other detailing over the wire-frame skeletons.

Middle: CG brachiosaur detail (shot did not make the final film).

Opposite page and bottom: John Hammond (Richard Attenborough), Alan Grant (Sam Neill), and Ellie Sattler (Laura Dern) marvel at creatures out of time. Aside from a rampaging T-rex and a deadly group of velociraptors, the film attempted to portray the various creatures as living animals, not mere movie monsters.

Far right, top to bottom: Alan, Alexis (Ariana Richards), and Tim (Joseph Mazzello) watch a galloping gallimimus herd. The pastoral wilds of Jurassic Park were created on the Hawaiian island of Kauai, although background plates for the end of this sequence (in which a hungry T-rex attacks the herd) had to be relocated to Oahu because of the destruction in the wake of Hurricane Iniki, which tore through Kauai toward the end of location shooting. When the herd becomes a dangerous stampede, motion-blur on the CG dinosaurs add frightening realism.

Right and below: Back in California, ILM plotted out the shot with reference footage that duplicated the background plate photography.

beginning. TD Joe Letteri described his job in relation to the production pipeline: "After the 3-D CG is rendered, we're still only halfway there; you don't really know if the shot is working until you comp all the elements together. There are people who model the creature and animate him, there are the painters who create the surface textures and the roto people who generate all the mattes. The TDs are responsible for technical issues involved in all of these processes. We pull the pieces together."

"The finishing touches made all the difference in the effects for *Jurassic Park*," stat-

This page: Alan looks on as the
T-rex pounces on the passing herd.

ed George Murphy, who served as a TD on several of the sequences Fangmeier supervised. "Images and elements generated on the computer tend to look too clean, too mechanical, so we added blur to every shot. We blended the edges on all of the 2-D mattes and all the 3-D elements. We spent a lot of time adding defects that real-location photographers work so hard to get rid of, such as added film grain for a more organic and natural look. We frequently used the match-move software MM2 to add 2-D camera movement to any shot that seemed static. When a dinosaur clomps through a scene, we'd add camera bounce as if the photographer were responding to the earth-shaking impact of the creature as its foot hit the ground. Even just the slightest move helps give the impression that there's a real person behind the camera. We added grass and dirt and rain splashes to help blend our elements into the plate. It's always that last ten percent of finessing that takes a pretty good comp to the level of a photorealistic comp."

Dennis Muren stressed the benefit of being able to see a composite of every shot, every day, during the process of producing the imagery: "The importance of seeing the visuals continually, and tweaking them until they look right, cannot be overestimated. This ability gives us a tremendous advantage over the traditional method of opticals, where you'd get maybe two or three chances to see your shot composited. Also, all the disciplines and parameters that make up a CG dinosaur are separate and repeatable. A model is really separate from its movement, which is separate from its surface detail, which is separate from its lighting. We can change all or part of the image at will. We can tune each process until it's perfect—and that's the biggest difference between CG and traditional effects."

The final step in many of the composites in *Jurassic Park* involved the stroke of an artist's electronic paintbrush. If a shot seemed marred by some detail, effects supervisor Muren would often turn to the secret weapon that had finalized shots in *Terminator 2*: painting on the final composite. Digital artists Dave Carson and Barbara Brennan corrected many of the small imperfections that still existed on the comp by using Photoshop or Parallax's Matador software to paint a solution, thereby allowing the shot to be considered finished. For one shot, the head of the child actress who played Lex was digitally attached to the body of an adult stuntwoman and the blends were painted to match to make it appear that the child had done the stunt herself. The stunt of a car falling through trees toward Grant (Sam Neill) and Tim (Joseph Mazzello) was done in safety: The car hung from cables and was lowered by a motorized winch. The cables were digitally painted out. "Probably half of our shots were cleaned up

this way," recalled Fangmeier. "Part of me says that a painting touch-up is a cheat—it's not the solution of a CG purist—but let's face it, everything in effects is a cheat. Painting is probably the most efficient clean-up solution available nine times out of ten."

JURASSIC PARK COMMUNICATIONS

The full-motion dinosaurs were not the full extent of ILM's breakthroughs. Fiber-optic and satellite communications systems were required that would deliver visual and audio dailies to Spielberg at his Amblin studios in North Hollywood and later at his *Schindler's List* production location in Krakow, Poland. According to effects producer Janet Healy, "We couldn't have made the film Spielberg wanted without our communications system in place; we would have been in the dark. Communication was the key to giving Spielberg what he wanted. Immediate feedback from the director was essential, and we got it without wasting any travel time."

The fiber-optic path laid between ILM's Marin County facility and the Amblin post-production suite was transmitted via SONET, a digital data network operated by the Pacific Bell telephone system in California. The device that enabled ILM to transmit *Jurassic Park* video and audio data along the fiber path, and for Amblin to receive the information as digital data, were CODEC boxes at both ends of the line that allowed the sender to encode images while the receiver's CODEC box decoded the transmission.

The fiber-optic path between ILM and Amblin worked perfectly until March of 1993, a full two months ahead of the finals deadline for *Jurassic Park*, when Spielberg had to depart for Krakow to begin filming *Schindler's List*. Fred Meyers of ILM took charge of linking ILM's fiber-optic transmissions, encoded from the point-of-origin CODEC box and sent along multiple satellite paths beamed to the decoding CODEC box in Spielberg's lodgings in Krakow, a villa dubbed "Hotel Kalifornia."

Unlike the ferocious T-rex, the
gentle brachiosaurs evince a gentle temperament. In this idyllic
scene a CG herd was combined
with blue-screen elements of the
performers and a Chris Evans
matte painting (which was digitally enhanced by Yusei Uesugi).

The ferocious, flesh-eating raptors (here stalking the children in the park's kitchen) provided the thrill of danger. Both mechanical and CG raptors were used in the sequence, with ILM effects for the full-body shots.

To protect *Jurassic Park*'s satellite pathway from anyone who might monitor and intercept the signal, the images were scrambled using a digital encrypting system called BMAC. The scrambled signal was uplinked to a domestic satellite from SF Satellite, a facili-

ty in San Francisco, California, downlinked in Virginia at Washington International Teleport, and turned around to an international satellite (Intelsat K) that transmitted the material to Europe. The Intelsat signal was received by the Hotel Kalifornia satellite dish and decrypted into video and audio for presentation on monitors in Spielberg's editorial suite. The international link also allowed ILM and the Krakow unit to view and comment on the same transmitted images simultaneously.

Jurassic Park was the kind of breakthrough film that generates major changes within a company. The film's digital challenges were so immense that during the nearly yearlong effects preproduction period the computer graphics department streamlined or updated its capacities: A group reconfigured hardware to maximize through-put and rendering speed, new and improved software tools were prioritized and developed by a software team led by Tom Williams and Michael Natkin, and a new database (dubbed "Scene Kit") was built by programmer Eric Enderton to better interface all programs uti-

A complex web of fiber-optic and satellite communications systems linked ILM to Amblin offices in Los Angeles, a production suite in Poland (where Spielberg was filming *Schindler's List*), and Phil Tippett Studio across the Bay in Berkeley. Here ILM effects producer Janet Healy and Dennis Muren link up with Phil Tippett to discuss the raptor kitchen sequence.

lized by CG for *Jurassic Park* and future digital projects.

Jurassic Park would become the most popular global box-office hit ever, with nearly $1 billion in grosses. The story, either praised as the ultimate resurrection of a fifties-style science fiction movie or dismissed for having cardboard characters in a plotless tale, was universally praised for its dinosaurs. Audiences could not resist being awed by the seemingly photographic evidence that dinosaurs had returned to again walk the earth. "It's as if I had gone back sixty-five million years with a thirty-five-millimeter camera and hid behind a tree and shot a brachiosaur walking by," Spielberg said. "It's extraordinary, and it's also frightening."

Perhaps no other film so illustrates the power of visual effects: ILM's digital dinosaur work that so thrilled the world accounted for a mere five to six minutes of the film's 126-minute running time. But the startling realism of ILM's digital creations would generate controversy over the power of the computer in the creative process.

"When I saw *T2*, I felt the tide pulling at my calves, but it wasn't until those first T-rex tests on *Jurassic Park* that I saw the tidal wave on the horizon," animation director Tippett recalled. "I'm excited by the new technology, and it's very stimulating to ride on the crest of this technological wave. If it's paramount that these things look real, then we now have the ability and the technology to make things look photorealistic using the computer. But this revolution is going to surpass the industrial revolution, and there's going to be a lot of blood on the floor. From the perspective of the traditional artist, I feel like we've all been bombed, and there's bound to be a huge displacement of people as this computer tool replaces many types of craftsmen by its sheer speed and miraculousness. But the computer demands that you be very procedural and use specific language to communicate and control it. It's not the same thing at all as having a relationship with materials. My concern is that in the technical realm, things can be very monolithic and one can tend to lose touch and sight of the real, physical world.

"Most of the people I grew up with in the effects business were all attracted to this stuff as kids. We started as ten-year-olds, building things in our garages and photographing them. We became professionals as a calling, not just a career choice. Our life and our work aren't separate; they're the same thing. I feel like the world has changed around us with a suddenness that no one could have predicted—and right now, we're experiencing future shock!"

"It's clear that computers have initiated a revolution as dramatic as the industrial revolution," Muren observed. "To me, *Jurassic Park* was a major, major step. After *T2*, CG was still wide-open in terms of challenges. But *Jurassic* covered so many areas—lighting, performance, creature, skin, motion. We still haven't done realistic humans, but after all, humans are just another variation of a living thing. Now we've got to search for the next challenge—maybe natural phenomena? I don't want to limit it to fire and water—I think it's bigger than that. The results we achieved on *Jurassic Park* exceeded my wildest expectations. Computer graphics is now the most potent tool we have."

THE COMMERCIAL WORLD

Although Industrial Light & Magic is famed for its feature-film work, the company's work in commercials and videos had been quietly expanding since 1987 when Jim Morris, then a producer, prepared a company business plan underlining the importance of a commercials division. The successive administrations of general managers Warren Franklin and Scott Ross spurred the development of the new department, with producers Tom Kennedy and Clint Goldman instrumental in expanding the department's size and creative goals.

"Without diversification, ILM may very well have had significant business difficulties," explained Morris, who became general manager in 1991. By the time Morris was named the first-ever president of the company in August of '94, the division would be producing some twenty to thirty commercials a year and generating a large portion of ILM's business.

ILM's commercial division expanded further in 1988 when Tom Kennedy, with a background in electronics postproduction work, and Clint Goldman, with his own background in computer graphics, were hired to expand the new department and offer services to Lucasfilm Commercial Productions, ILM's commercial live-action sister company. While Goldman and other ILM producers took on most of the line producing, Kennedy began developing the production capabilities, marketing, and client outreach.

"One of the challenges starting out was that there's a much longer production cycle in features—usually six months as opposed to six weeks," Kennedy explained. "Also, ILM didn't have the kind of longstanding relationship with ad clients that it had with feature-film producers and studios. When we first began contacting ad agencies, we emphasized how ILM had pioneered unique processes in features, and that we could bring these capabilities into the commercial realm."

One of ILM's first ads, created for Saatchi & Saatchi in New York, was for a "Kid's Club" Burger King campaign. The spot, directed by Matthew Robbins with visual effects by Michael Owens, featured a film editor working on a burger commercial who is pulled into his moviola and a film environment in a mad chase after an elusive hamburger. "Up until then nobody had attempted a commercial that complex and photorealistic,"

A surface-peeling wind reveals a new Dodge Daytona in this spot directed by Steve Beck, with the help of visual effects supervisor John Knoll.

Kennedy noted. "The spot showed off Matthew's storytelling abilities with Michael's expertise in visual effects."

Another of ILM's key early ads was for Heinz ketchup, in which a trail of computer-generated ants raid a picnic for the foodstuffs liberally doused with the ketchup. The 1990 ad, which was directed by Jim Money and produced by Clint Goldman with visual effects by Dave Carson, predated by five years the CG performance animation technology ILM would bring to such feature film projects as *Casper* and *Dragonheart*. "Because we were working in a low-resolution format, it gave people the ability to animate things quickly," Kennedy observed. "At that time it allowed us to develop animation skills and do more experimental, less photorealistic work, such as the Heinz ants."

TV commercials, with their low-resolution, interactive video-production environments, have always been fertile ground for imaginative image makers. ILM's own recent work has spanned a range of artistic and technological techniques. Highlights include an Acura Integra automobile racing

Giovanni Donovan puts the finishing touches on this miniature Christmas-themed set for an Old Spice spot (directed by Dave Carson).

CG ants have a picnic with Heinz ketchup.

through a desert valley along an expansive, "Hot Wheels"–style racetrack (featuring a mix of live action, miniatures, and digital work); an Aurora automobile driving into a piece of modern art, cornering and accelerating over swaths of oil-painted brushstrokes in a complex digital composite; and an encounter between Darth Vader and the Energizer Battery bunny, who keeps on going as Vader's own lightsaber, powered with a less reliable battery, sputters out (produced as a live-action piece).

According to Kevin Townsend, who was named executive producer of ILM Commercial Productions in 1994 (after Kennedy transitioned to the features side of ILM), the breakthroughs in image making, which have allowed for both bombastic (*The Mask*) and subtle (*Forrest Gump*) visual effects, have given his division the ability to take commercials beyond their ostensibly product-pushing nature.

"When I came on board, the commercial division was an offshoot of the features side, primarily doing visual effects intensive spots with no humanity in the work," Townsend recalled. "For example, we did an AT&T message center spot in which three answering machines were stop-motion-animated, with no people or appreciable dialogue. But the marketplace has shifted, and now there's a push in the advertising community to combine live action, dialogue, and visual effects. So where once there were either live-action or effects commercials, there's now a combination of techniques to produce a variety of work, from grand effects to subtle storytelling."

Unlike movies, in which ILM's work has to fit into the grand scheme of a feature-length production, the process of making a commercial allows for a higher degree of creative autonomy, according to Townsend:

"The commercials side is responsible for creative content from beginning to end. The process begins with an advertising agency hiring ILM as a subcontractor. The agency will send us a storyboard detailing the commercial, and we take those boards and figure out direction, do production-cost estimates, and provide all aspects of the creative execution. For example, for the Darth Vader spot for Energizer Batteries, the agency had originally come to us with the idea of using *Star Wars* footage with the bunny composited in as a blue-screen element. But rather than do a visual effects shoot, we said it would be more cost-effective to just reshoot it in-camera, with the lightsaber as a blue-screen element. So the first three to four shots were lifted directly from the movies, with our new live action beginning with the appearance of the bunny."

ILM's feature-film fame has been a powerful draw for clients interested in breakthrough visuals. The company is often hired

Some magic toys receive a sparkling water shower in this Perrier spot.

The advantages of the Acura Integra are illustrated during a breathtaking drive through this fantastic stretch of track, a homage to the Hot Wheels toy racing set, with CG supervisorial work by Stephen Rosenbaum.

Charles Barkley strides through ILM's Toyko set to meet Godzilla in this high-concept Nike shoe commercial.

cials are tantalizing, given that an artful spot can be viewed by as many as a billion people who are simultaneously tuned in to a global television event. Whether or not a spot is beamed via satellite around the world, commercials are an international medium. An influential ILM ad aired in the United Kingdom was the British Petroleum "Elevator" spot, in which a pizza delivery boy making a stop at a BP research and testing facility watches as the door to each floor opens up to reveal some outlandish vista, from a jet-testing hangar to an astronaut floating in space who awaits his order on the "final floor." Rock-and-roll maestro Paul

for event commercials, those big-ticket, high-powered spots that air during Super Bowl or Academy Award telecasts (the number one and two biggest ad days of the year), or to be part of unusual promotional packages (such as ILM's Nike Godzilla spot, which previewed as a theatrical trailer). "We stay away from the hard-sell, product-oriented approaches, like people holding up bars of soap," Townsend explained. "That doesn't utilize what our strengths are: to create images that, in the real world, are uncreatable. We want to tell good stories, to move the story forward by any means necessary, whether with or without visual effects."

The commercials division has also provided a niche for traditional ILM effects departments rocked by the expansion of computer technologies. "Commercials have such a short turnaround that there usually isn't time for computer graphics," observed former model department head Jeff Mann. "The work we've done on commercials comprises over half of our model department workload at this point."

The high-profile possibilities of commer-

A magical high-rise elevator door keeps opening on a succession of strange images, such as this stop at the "Aviation Fuel Research Floor," in a British Petroleum spot.

McCartney was so impressed by the commercial that he phoned George Lucas and arranged for ILM to do the effects for his *Off the Ground* music video in which, through blue-screen wire work and Macintosh compositing techniques, he was made to fly over city skyscrapers, fields, and forests and into the sky. (Although ILM had used Macs extensively for matte painting work on the *Young Indy* TV series, McCartney's video was one of the few times the company had done all compositing and postproduction work on a Mac, as opposed to its normal high-end SGI systems.)

Commercial assignments have often led

Darth Vader versus the Energizer Battery bunny. Vader's lightsaber is about to run out of power, but the bunny will just keep going and going and going. . . .

ILMers to journey to far-flung location shoots. For producer Peter Takeuchi, a memorable trip was a 1988 spot for Japan's Suntory beer, for which ILM had been hired to provide an animatronic whale that would be shot motion-control and composited into background plates shot on an isolated New Zealand beach. The visual centerpiece had come to director Jiro Takasugi in a dream: Celebrants at a sunny beach party see a whale flying through the clear blue sky above the ocean and raise their glasses of Suntory to toast the magical sight.

The problem with the shoot was that the oceanfront location was being visited by fierce Arctic storms even as the twelve-van caravan of crew, extras, ad agency reps, and equipment arrived at the isolated coastal area. Rather than pack up and move to a balmier clime, the director opted to come to the location each day and ritually wait for the storms to blow over. "It was a mystical experience," Takeuchi recalled. "I found out the director was a Shinto priest and

nature watching was a big meditative thing. I got into it, too—standing on the beach, looking out over the ocean and watching the clouds pass over. We did this almost every day for a week, waiting for the sky to turn blue so we could shoot our shot. When it was suggested to the director that maybe we fly north and find another beach, he'd say, 'No, no, no. This beach is the one.' He was confident that no

matter how long it took, he was going to get the weather he wanted. And he got it."

No longer a mere offshoot of the feature-film side, the department has seven full-time directors and a sixty-person support staff. But with all the pumped-up production values, breakthrough visual effects, and intricate story lines, does the product itself get lost in the process? "I take it as a compliment when people are entertained by one of our commercials and have to think hard to remember the name of the product," Townsend explained. "Everyone's so ad-conscious these days, and there are many factors as to why people buy certain products. We know when we've been successful because there's a sense of satisfaction. It's by being good storytellers that we've opened up to more product categories and expanded the types of work we can do."

Rocker Paul McCartney, impressed by ILM's British Petroleum "Elevator" commercial, hired ILM to provide visual effects of him flying through the air for the title track music video of his *Off the Ground* album. The ILM team, headed by visual effects supervisor Scott Squires (who also supervised the BP spot), flew McCartney from wires at George Lucas's Skywalker Ranch and composited the famed musician in background plates that included green fields, forests, castles, and clouds. Rather than a Harry videopost tool, Squires opted for using the Macintosh in concert with FlipBook, a program he wrote that allowed for blue-screen composites, extractions, and manipulations on the Mac at full video or film resolution.

CHAPTER TEN

INVISIBLE EFFECTS

In *Star Wars* mythology the Jedi Knight was master of the Force and part of a lineage of spiritual warriors who helped keep order throughout the galaxy. The Jedi myth inspired the name for JEDI (Joint Environment for Digital Imaging), an alliance between Industrial Light & Magic and Silicon Graphic Images forged in April of 1993 and aimed at developing high-end computer graphics and image-processing capabilities. The partnership was a complement to a major restructuring of George Lucas's entertainment empire that made ILM a division of the newly formed Lucas Digital Ltd.

ILM's retooling for the digital revolution included the sweeping away of the archaic trappings of the industrial age. By the spring of 1994 Ted Moehnke, who had been property master for *THX 1138* and directed the building of ILM's San Rafael facility back in the days of *The Empire Strikes Back*, was combing the company's storage bays, cataloguing and auctioning off old props, industrial hardware, and memorabilia. The once mainstay and state-of-the-art equipment deemed expendable included the "Rama," one of ILM's first motion-controlled rigs, and the cloud tank, which had produced atmospheric effects for such films as *Poltergeist* and *Kurosawa's Dreams*. What wasn't being sold off was being dismantled, decommissioned, or, like the venerable Anderson optical printer, put on display.

The new technowave was felt with brutal suddenness in the halls of ILM. The old matte painting department, which had once held easels for brush and oil work, was replaced with computer hardware and painting software systems. The old motion-control camera and thirty-foot track that had been used to shoot matte paintings since the days of *Empire* had been removed and replaced by some twenty CG workstations. The optical printing department, once the final stop for assembling into a final image all the effects elements produced for compositing, had been virtually eliminated by the CCD scanner and the rest of a digital through-put system.

"*Jurassic Park* is the thing that made the film industry change, that showed computer production had become reliable and dependable," observed former optical dog John Ellis, who had twice headed up the old photochemical-based department but had made the transition to digital-operations manager. "In the past you'd give a digital assignment to a bunch of laser-brained computer experts and hope to god they'd get it done in eight months when you needed it. I'm a believer in the digital world, yet I spent seventeen years perfecting a craft at which I was very good, blue-screen extraction, dealing with edge characteristics, and color timing. But I could also see the limitations of trying to make film do something it just can't do. You can pull exposures, you can shrink mattes, you can enlarge mattes, you can do a number of cheats to make things a little better, but when it comes right down to it, if the character is blurred in front of a blue screen, and the film can't see the resolution, there's not much more you can do. In digital you can say, 'No, be here, or there!' But I don't think anybody really thought the digital advances would happen as

Above: The computer-generated creatures produced by ILM—the watery pseudopod, the shape-changing cyborg, the photorealistic dinosaurs—garnered most of the glory in the mass media. Often overlooked were the breakthroughs in compositing, the creation of synthetic sets and props (such as the overturned vehicle in *Jurassic Park*), and the digital replication of performers. One of the early CG props was this digital composite of Tinker Bell striking a deal with Captain Hook and shaking his hook—a computer-generated creation.

Right and below: To provide a reference for the CG animators, actress Julia Roberts shook a blue-screen set piece . . .

. . . while a computer-generated hook was created and tracked to the stage motions.

quickly as they did. I knew it was coming, but I thought it'd be more of a four- or five-year dissolve. Instead, it seems like a jump cut."

For George Lucas, who had directed the assembling of ILM's old industrial infrastructure and had resurrected the old VistaVision process from oblivion, the triumph of the new digital order did not occasion teary reflections. "I don't like technology much, so I have no emotional ties to the technology whatsoever," Lucas stated. "I care about the images on the screen, and I'm really not enamored with the process at all. As a matter of fact, technology mostly gets in the way, and therefore you're constantly trying to get a better tool. With digital I think you end up with a different kind of person doing the work as opposed to the old ways, and I'm not sure if that's better or worse. But on the practical side of moviemaking, I don't think anybody really likes to stand out in the snow at three o'clock in the morning when it's forty degrees below zero and load celluloid, which is brittle and breaks, into a camera. Most people have to work under difficult conditions, and if they didn't have to do that, they'd say, 'Great!' "

Above: Forrest Gump (Tom Hanks) meets President John F. Kennedy, one of the many wonders worked by ILM in one of the most successful films of all time: top five on Hollywood's all-time box-office list and winner of six 1994 Academy Awards, including Best Picture, Best Actor (Tom Hanks), and Best Visual Effects for Ken Ralston and his ILM team. Accepting his Best Actor Oscar, Hanks's emotional acceptance speech had this effects analogy: "I feel as though I'm standing on magic legs in a special effects process shot that is too unbelievable to imagine and far too costly to make a reality."

Left: Invisible effects abound in *Gump*, including the Vietnam sequences, which were staged in South Carolina and were augmented with ILM digital matte paintings, rain, smoke, tracer fire, jets, bombs, and explosions.

POST–*JURASSIC PARK* VIRTUAL FX

The digital dinosaurs of *Jurassic Park* were exemplary for the stunning breakthroughs in computer graphics imaging. Audiences worldwide were awed by the sight of snarling, rampaging, photorealistic creations that once had been only as real as artist's renderings or fossilized reconstructions in museums.

But CG was only half of the magical possibilities of the digital realm. The breakthroughs afoot also allowed filmmakers to produce seamless invisible effects that ranged from the creation of synthetic (or "virtual") sets to the replication of a dozen extras into a cast of hundreds. Of course, invisible digital effects had been in limited use at ILM a few years prior to *Jurassic Park*. There was, for example, a *Hook* shot of Tinker Bell shaking Captain Hook's hook, a CG composite effect accomplished by shooting blue screen of Tink actress Julia Roberts shaking a reference set piece and combining the image with a CG hook tracked to match Roberts's motion. But the new generation of seamless effects allowed for greater wonders than the occasional CG prop.

One of the earliest such breakthroughs was a virtual pirate ship test for a movie that never received the green light for production. "This synthetic sailing ship we created [in

Above: The set for the alien spaceship interior in *Fire in the Sky*.

Right and below: ILM flew actor D. B. Sweeney from wires to simulate weightlessness. Any wires visible on film could be completely removed digitally.

Left: The talking Dictabird puppet from *The Flintstones*, created by Jim Henson's Creature Shop.

Clockwise from bottom left: In a key scene, a scheming Bedrock executive (Kyle MacLachlan) attempts to grab the Dictabird, who knows too much. Rather than concealing puppeteers on the set, the production opted for hiding nothing, with ILM digitally removing rods, rigs, even puppeteers, for the final.

1993] looked so much like a real ship it was mind-blowing," Jim Morris observed. "We also photographed some extras sword fighting and placed them in the rigging with cannons firing. Since we were dealing with a 3-D object in computer space we could affix the characters to the rigging. You could never do that before."

The ability to scan live-action elements into digital environments also allowed film-makers to place actors in scenes that would have been prohibitively dangerous to attempt

Opposite page: Matte painting at ILM transitioned to a digital medium during production of *The Young Indiana Jones Chronicles*. For a *Young Indy* shot of a train chugging across a bridge (far right), a live-action train element shot by Lucasfilm was composited with a one hundred percent digital environment created by Yusei Uesugi using Photoshop software on a Macintosh computer, the third image created by the new digital matte painting department. (Although Western Images did the final composite for the episode, the image here represents Uesugi's pre-comp of the train and his painting.) The new digital-painting tools also came to the rescue on a *Young Indy* episode in which producer Rick McCallum, after some seven fruitless months of trying to gain permission to shoot a scene at the Spanish riding school in Vienna, achieved an approximation of the actual location with what he hailed as "our first breakthrough painting on *Young Indy*." The shot digitally composited live action filmed in a building in Prague (top right) with a Yusei Uesugi painting (bottom right). Uesugi was able to paint half the balcony and, with the aid of Photoshop software, flip the image to complete the upper story. (The framed painting in the middle is a Uesugi original—a painting within a painting.)

by practical means. One such shot, a Vietnam battle sequence for *Forrest Gump* in which Gump carried fallen comrades to safety as explosive fireballs erupted around him, was safely and effectively rendered as a digital composite.

In the 1994 release *Baby's Day Out*, a variety of separate elements, including a baby, other actors, models, and traffic, were shot and composited in a three-dimensional computer graphics city that was completely photorealistic, down to the digitally painted shadows of a computer-generated sun. "For *Baby's Day Out* I'd say more than half of our shots were in a computer-generated city, and we're putting this baby in perils that, of course, could never be done in real life," noted art department manager Mark Moore. "The city is so realistic, with all the three-dimensional angles, weird perspectives, and lighting, that some people will not see that it's an effect because it's so good."

A major breakthrough was the creation of a feature-film digital compositing and editing process that duplicated the interactive, real-time production systems used for years in the video world. Previously, time had been a major constraint for filmmakers: The old photochemical process usually had to factor in a day's wait for developing filmed elements before they could be optically composited on a printer, while digital-image processing also took hours to render an image.

But in the post–*Jurassic Park* age, filmmakers had the power to manipulate complex composite shots digitally and see the results rendered and visible on their workstation monitors within seconds. "There's a real synergy happening between video tools and film tools," explained ILM producer Clint Goldman. "It's a cross-pollination of three disciplines: film, video, and computer graphics."

At ILM the digital breakthroughs were revolutionizing the means of production. *The Young Indiana Jones Chronicles*, an ABC-TV series first produced by Lucasfilm in 1992,

would, within the low-resolution medium of television, provide the perfect testing ground and launching pad for developing interactive, real-time image-processing technologies and techniques applicable for high-resolution film work. At the same time, Lucasfilm would bring to TV the kind of motion picture production values rarely seen on the phosphorescent screen.

THE YOUNG INDIANA JONES CHRONICLES
1991 (Lucasfilm Ltd./ABC-TV)
TV Production Breakthroughs

George Lucas had conceived *The Young Indiana Jones Chronicles* as a vehicle for turning American kids on to the wonders of history and the thrill of exploring the world. After all, as a fictional construct, the adult Indiana of movie fame, with his globe-trotting adventures set in the World War II era, was squarely in the time frame of the formative events of the twentieth century. In the series, the young Indy (as he was affectionately known around Lucas enterprises) would be engaged as both witness and participant in history, from the hellish trenches of World War I battlefields to the smoky nightclubs where jazz was born. Along the way Indy would meet such historic figures as Albert Schweitzer and Pancho Villa.

For *Young Indy* Lucasfilm set up a production suite at Western Images, a San Francisco–based video postproduction facility. Working in television meant the production could utilize such interactive digital compositing and editing systems as the Harry, a commercial system produced by Quantel. At the same time, *Young Indy* took the standard video technologies out for a spin, bringing big-movie production values to the series while staying within a tight TV-show budget. Most of the audience in TV land would be unaware that much of what they viewed— rugged wilderness environments, the city streets of European capitals, or bustling crowd scenes—were invisible effects. All the digital tools were put into play to create syn-

thetic sets, produce matte paintings for establishing shots, replicate extras, and composite images.

"*Young Indy* took the very best of all the usable technologies and put them to work to support story lines using digital and video tools in a synthesis that was unlike the ways they'd been used before," explained Jim Morris. "They would routinely do hundreds of shots in a show, most of which would be invisible, such as wire removal, rotoing out a character that wouldn't be in that particular scene, or painting out a billboard in the background instead of going to the trouble to take it down during shooting. It allowed George to do things like shoot a scene at noon and repaint it at a digital workstation to make it look like a sunset shot, so he'd never have to worry about losing his light. The digital technologies allowed for seamless splits, so George could take, say, ten extras, quickly shoot ten splits of them in different positions, and split them together so you'd have one hundred extras in the scene, which saved a lot of costume and other costs and gave the show a lot of scope. The production became very facile at using these digital tools. While many of these techniques had been used in limited ways before, it really brought out their promise in terms of supporting narrative."

One important effects technique transformed into a digital medium for the making of *Young Indy* was the venerable art of matte painting. The technological transition had begun with MP-4, the shot of an airport runway crowded with planes that had been produced for *Die Hard 2* in 1990. But that shot had been produced with traditional brushstrokes, and the final painting photographed, scanned, and then manipulated. The complete digital makeover would shatter these old constraints, providing painters with a creative freedom about which they once only dreamed.

DIGITAL MATTE PAINTING

"*Young Indy* was a great opportunity for us to make a smooth transition from the old ways of creating matte paintings to the new technology," observed Yusei Uesugi, who along with *Star Wars* veterans Paul Huston, Eric Chauvin, and Bill Mather comprised the new digital matte painting department. "One reason was *Young Indy* was made at TV resolution, and as these shots could be processed much faster than doing it at film resolution, we could try a bunch of different techniques and get used to the new technologies. Also, in every episode we'd have to apply the new techniques to different situations: painting jungles, buildings, all kinds of environments."

Matte painting had always been a resource for providing an expansive establishing shot or extending the physical limits of a set. But the two-dimensional nature of the medium had always prohibited camera moves and often made problematic the seamless blending of painted image with live-action

elements. With digital matte painting, however, the old restrictions didn't apply.

"One artist working on a personal computer can now handle an amount of work that in the old days required a matte painter, a motion-control cameraman, and the optical department," Uesugi explained. "Now we can do a painting, composite it, do some animation—basically everything needed to create a matte painting shot. We still can create a single element and give that to another department, but sometimes it saves time if we do everything in the digital matte department and skip all the data transfer."

The digital technology now allowed artists to utilize different software programs to manipulate scanned-in reference photos or create outright dimensional images in virtual space with the aid of 3-D modeling tools. "We have more choices, more options now," Uesugi noted. "For example, in the traditional compositing of matte paintings with live action, the basic rule was the actor could not go beyond where the matte line would be, the blend line between the painting and live action. But now we can have an actor go beyond where the matte line would be and digitally rotoscope later on, which provides for a tremendous amount of believability and reality for a shot."

On *Young Indy*, the new digital matte department became adroit at combining live-action elements with painted environments that could be manipulated to mimic a three-dimensional subject. One such shot, of young Jones riding horseback and grabbing the reins of another horse before it could gallop over the edge of a canyon precipice, took the live-action element of the actor and horses (shot under natural sunlight without need for blue screen), pulled a different matte in postproduction, and composited the live action into a digitally painted environment. The canyon environment was painted, with the rocky walls distorted in virtual space to simulate a camera push-in move, while an animation effect for a snaking river below was used to

simulate the frothy crash of rapids (although in keeping with the traditional matte painting approach of not putting in more details than necessary, only the part of the river instantly discernible to the viewer's eye was animated). What would have been a dangerous stunt, with actor and horses riding to a cliff edge, was not only safely realized, but the incorporation of natural sunlight on the live-action elements, with the environment painted to match, made for a completely realistic-looking final shot and a triumph of invisible effects.

Digital paintings could also easily be produced from scanned-in reference photos. One such *Young Indy* shot was a night scene of characters boarding a steamboat on the water from an old junk. Lucas had thought of the shot postproduction, when he realized the story called for an establishing shot at that point. Live action of actors walking a gangplank from the junk to the steamboat were shot blue-screen and composited into a digital environment of synthetic water, and the boats were produced from scanned-in reference photos shot on the San Francisco waterfront.

The Young Indiana Jones Chronicles was an opportunity for ILM to develop in the new low-resolution medium of television some of the tools and techniques that could be adapted to feature film postproduction. As with the before-and-after images pictured here, in the brave new world of digital the bare minimum set could be easily and seamlessly expanded with digital matte paintings. Examples of this digital magic are the cityscape (above left) and the ocean liner (above right) that were conjured up into bare minimum sets.

Meanwhile, the digital production tools developed during the *Young Indy* series finally transitioned to features with the 1994 Lucasfilm production *Radioland Murders*. The film, featuring one tumultuous night at a radio station during radio's golden age, would employ all the magical digital techniques used for *Young Indy*, including matte painting, replication of sets and extras, and real-time compositing.

The new digital production suite inaugurated on *Radioland* was dubbed the "Sabre System" at ILM. It had all the effects, compositing, and editing features of a video Harry but could function at the high speed and high resolution required for feature-film work. With Sabre, some one hundred *Radioland* shots could be delivered at a bargain for a feature production. The system was also used for nearly a third of the composite shots on *Forrest Gump*, as well as for a 1995 video foray into HBO's *Tales from the Crypt*.

DAWN OF THE SABRE SYSTEM

The Sabre (not an acronym but a metaphor evocative of the mythic power of a Jedi Knight's lightsaber) developed during a time of technological breakthroughs in real-time, interactive motion picture compositing and editing.

Quantel, producer of the Harry, had brought out its own interactive commercial production suite for features work: the Domino, which provided full through-put, painting, compositing, and image-processing tools and was first used extensively on the 1994 MGM science fiction release *StarGate*. Although ILM found Domino a superior film-making tool in many respects, the system was too limited for its creative tastes. According to Jim Morris, the Domino was a "closed architecture" system, meaning outside and proprietary software couldn't be added to it, a hindrance for an FX house accustomed to creating software to overcome specific problems and advance their technological arsenal.

ILM designed its Sabre as an "open archi-

tecture" system that could accept both off-the-shelf and proprietary software. The Sabre was designed with eight SGI Onxy super-processors and featured the interactive, features-friendly "Flame" and "Inferno" software packages (produced by the Canadian company Discreet Logic). "In addition to Flame and Inferno we brought in a variety of other commercial, painting, and match-move software and some proprietary software of our own," Morris explained. "We can add to it as need be, which makes the Sabre, in the aggregate, a much more flexible system than most of the other systems available. The Sabre is also resolution-independent, so you can dial in whatever resolution, whether it's TV resolution, features, or an Imax show. And it's probably four to six times faster than our conventional rendering approach.

"It was also important for us to have a system that was user-friendly, instead of the old script-based approach where a computer person had to actually type in all the commands. Sabre is very interactive, with icons you can point to and click on. Now, the script-based types of programs continue to have their place because they allow for a customizing of each shot using script that you can't necessarily do using an interactive point-and-click interface. But what an interactive system does is bring traditional artists, whether they're animators or painters or whatever, into the digital environment and have them do good work."

According to Dan McNamara, the manager for both electronics editorial and the fledgling Sabre department, the new system, with its high-powered SGI processors, was a fruitful early result of the JEDI alliance between ILM and Silicon Graphics. But the artist-friendly Sabre, which could be utilized for a variety of compositing needs—from digital matte painting work to editing and image processing by a feature-film director—had not immediately replaced traditional methods of digital compositing.

"Before Sabre people would work on dif-

Director Robert Zemeckis was a perfect director for *Forrest Gump*: an accomplished storyteller with an eye for dynamic visual compositions and a flair for effects, particularly the invisible kind. The visual effects would be helmed by Ken Ralston.

Top right: For *Gump* many of the effects would be as seamless as the blue-screen feather illusion that opens the film.

Top left: Gump is waiting at a bus stop as the feather softly floats down. Some twenty-five different feathers shot in front of blue screen were made to seem as one.

Bottom left and right: To allow Gump to pluck the fallen feather from his shoetop, a real feather was attached for the live-action photography and digitally erased later.

ferent monitors on different aspects of a shot—and they still do," McNamara observed. "CG still has a 2-D group that produces excellent composites [using the traditional script-based interface]. We're trying to take the best of both and create a new way of dealing with our 2-D compositing. In traditional 2-D compositing, the effects supervisor might say, 'I want this matte blurred a little more,' so you type in a script and you have to come back the next day to see the change. With Sabre it's interactive; you can see and position objects onscreen very quickly, as opposed to having to crunch all the numbers. We're putting a lot more computing power under the control of one person, which is not the way we've traditionally worked."

ILM's showplace for the evolving state of invisible digital effects was *Forrest Gump*, a production that utilized Sabre System compositing, digital matte painting, and some of the production techniques (such as replication of crowds and sets) developed on the *Young Indy* series.

It was, however, one particular ILM *Gump* effect that generated a considerable prerelease buzz: the appearance of Gump seemingly interacting in old footage with such historic personages as Presidents John Kennedy and Richard Nixon. "The old footage was nothing," shrugged visual effects supervisor Ken Ralston. "It was the easiest in some respects because it's the most obvious."

The real wonders of *Gump* were, after all, invisible.

FORREST GUMP
1994 (Paramount)
Image Processing Breakthroughs

Forrest Gump, the tale of a slow-witted Southern boy whose good-natured pluck and blessed luck take him on a path from college football star and Vietnam War hero to world Ping-Pong champion and millionaire founder of Bubba Gump Shrimp, did not seem the stuff of big box office prior to its release, although with director Robert Zemeckis at the helm and Tom Hanks as star, there was some anticipation that the movie could be a sleeper hit.

It was a shocker, then, when the film passed $300 million in domestic grosses alone, attaining stature as one of the five biggest hits in box-office history, while the picture of Gump sitting on a park bench, his face heavy with an inward gaze, became an iconic film image (along with the likes of King Kong swatting fighter planes from atop the Empire State Building or Rhett Butler taking Scarlett in his arms for a passionate kiss). *Gump* had rocketed into the rarefied air of a cultural phenomenon.

"I know Bob [Zemeckis] was totally flabbergasted [by the film's success], but it was a happy surprise," Ken Ralston observed. "*Forrest Gump* was the same as *Star Wars* for me, which is you're doing a lot of work, try-

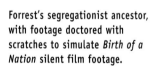

Forrest's segregationist ancestor, with footage doctored with scratches to simulate *Birth of a Nation* silent film footage.

ing to stay ahead of your deadlines, and you have no idea how it's ever going to work. In fact, while we were shooting, Bob said to me, 'You know, this could just be a grand experiment.' The shots on *Gump* were absolutely the hardest I've ever been involved with because of their subtlety. Effects shots with spaceships or where everything's blowing apart are easier to do than the kind of really beautiful, subtle, naturalistic touches that *Gump* is absolutely riddled with. There's no way to distract an audience to get you past the weaknesses because everyone's familiar with the natural world. So if there's a problem with how you're presenting it, the audience may not understand what's wrong, but it'll feel wrong [to them]."

One of the film's many invisible effects was the opening and closing shot of an airborne feather dreamily floating through blue sky and over small-town rooftops before drifting over the park bench where Gump sits and softly settling to rest on his shoe.

Although a CG effect was originally considered, it was finally decided that the floating feather illusion would be created with some twenty-five different feathers shot bluescreen and digitally blended together (after tests showed they could be matted against a sunny background). A monofilament line held a single feather in place as blowing fans ruffled it and a camera shot at seventy-two frames per second, producing "a lilting, dreamlike" visual quality, according to Ralston. The end of the sequence, when Gump plucks the feather from his shoetop, was produced with a real feather affixed to Hanks's shoe, which allowed for matching the falling blue-screen feather into its final position with the seamless illusion of Gump picking it up (but which also necessitated digitally erasing the practical feather from the live-action plate).

One astonishing, telltale invisible effect was the transformation of able-bodied actor Gary Sinise (who plays Gump's Nam commander, Lieutenant Dan Taylor) into a man who loses both legs during a fateful battle. While some classic movie tricks—such as a wheelchair with a false bottom—simulated the disability, there were several photorealistic scenes in which Sinise's Lieutenant Dan was clearly a double amputee. To allow the team of computer artists, led by computer graphics supervisors George Murphy and Stephen

Top to bottom: During a fateful battle in Nam, Gump's commander, Lieutenant Dan Taylor (Gary Sinise), lost his legs. The requisite blue material assisted ILM digital artists in creating mattes and seamlessly removing the legs, although any background object obscured by the blue leggings also had to be replaced.

A host of invisible *Gump* effects involved replication of crowd scenes (a technique first extensively explored by ILM in the video-resolution lab that was the *Young Indy* TV series). On this page, a single-tier football stadium in Los Angeles with one section full of extras becomes, after an image-processing makeover, a big-time University of Alabama football contest.

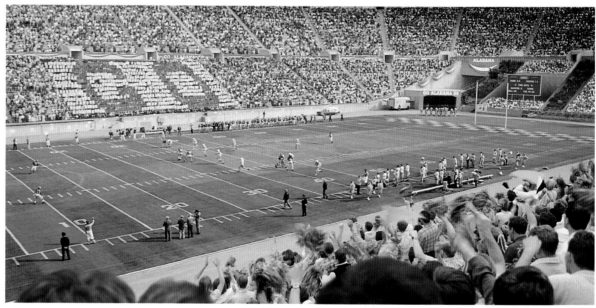

Rosenbaum, to remove his legs digitally, the actor wore blue leggings so mattes could be generated. But the blue stockings produced "holes" in the plates, which ILM digital artists had to fill by piecing together whatever in the shot had been obscured by Sinise's legs. The shadows of his legs had to be erased and the shadows of his stumps had to be added.

Invisible digital-effects work allowed filmmakers to conjure up entire environments: A frenzied University of Alabama football game was created by filming a small crowd of spectators in a single-tier stadium in Los Angeles, digitally replicating the stadium into three tiers, and multiplying the dozens of extras into tens of thousands (complete with one section flashing red "GO" signs); a re-creation of a D.C. antiwar rally had hundreds of extras digitally replicated and placed around the Reflecting Pool in front of the Lincoln Memorial (with reflections of the Washington Monument's spire also added to the pool); and

A scene of Forrest, fresh from Nam, addressing an antiwar rally before . . .

. . . and after a clutch of extras has been replicated around the Lincoln Memorial's Reflecting Pool and a reflection of the Washington Monument added. Unlike the defined structure of an easily filled stadium, replicating crowds in the outdoor park was among the most difficult shots in the film, according to Ken Ralston.

a Ping-Pong match in a set of a Red Chinese hall was completed by digitally adding a CG ball and stands filled with spectators (while Chinese flags, mistakenly hung upside down during the live-action shoot, were digitally flipped back into the correct position).

Digital matte paintings were utilized to create seamless effects for the Vietnam War sequences. A scene of American GIs fanning out over rice paddies was created with live-action plates shot on location in North Carolina, craggy mountain peaks constructed from photographic elements of Marin County's Mount Tamalpais (taken by Yusei Uesugi), and two different sky photographs digitally blended together, resized, and color-corrected. In a shot of Gump staring up at the Nam night sky, in which a 180-degree camera move during a nighttime location shoot revealed a background lighting rig, visual effects art director Doug Chiang took the original plate and replaced the back-

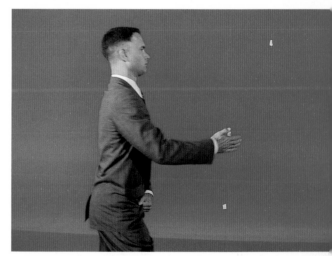

matte painting shots because the cameras were very loose [for the live-action elements] and we had to track the perspective and make sure everything worked."

The tremendous amount of digital work

Top: Forrest's Ping-Pong match in Red China was also played, like the tennis match in *The Witches of Eastwick*, without a ball. But whereas the tennis ball was added using motion control technology, the Ping-Pong ball in *Gump* would be digitally inserted.

Bottom: In the final shot, not only was a set expanded into an indoor stadium but the Chinese flags (mistakenly hung upside down for the background-plate photography) were restored to their rightful position.

ground, adding palm trees, clouds, and a moon overhead.

"What the art department does [when] the effects have to be very subtle is usually wait until we get the actual plate. I'll take an image and scan it in, add all the enhancements, and then print it out to show Ken Ralston and Robert Zemeckis to see if it's enough," Chiang explained. "Zemeckis wanted different skies, different lighting conditions, so we would be creating whole new environments, giving more life, more magic. Digitally enhanced shots, like the night sky in Nam, were very complex

for *Forrest Gump*, and other features in production at the time (including *The Flintstones*), actually brought ILM's computer-processing power to the breaking point. "Our SGIs just gave up; they stopped talking to each other across the network because the people who had written the [commercial] software to make the networks run quickly never anticipated that level of usage," noted digital effects chief Tom Williams. "The Silicon Graphics people were so shocked that we'd put so much strain on their equipment. We've had that problem historically, but when you start on a project you're going to want as much detail, realism, texture, and motion for the animation as possible. All of the stuff required to create an effect is information, information, information. During the time we were working on *Forrest Gump* and *The Flintstones* we had so much information going back and forth in our system. We had between two hundred and three hundred computers, each trying to pull a five-second shot of high-resolution imagery across the network. When you think about it, that's two hundred

Opposite page, top: The most famous scene in the film is when college football star Forrest meets and shakes JFK's hand at a White House reception honoring the All-American football team. Instead of digitally inserting Hanks into archival footage (as was the case with a scene involving Governor George Wallace), it was decided to shoot a new background plate of the Oval Office and digitally composite both a blue-screen image of Hanks and a JFK element lifted from this historic footage.

Opposite page, middle: For his blue-screen work Hanks had to be positioned so the resulting image element could line up with the archival footage of the late president. (Note tape marks suspended by string to help line up Gump's eye line and handshake.)

Opposite page, bottom: JFK element extracted from the archival footage.

This page, top: Background plate of an exact Oval Office replica, filmed during principal photography in Los Angeles.

This page, middle: Gump meets Kennedy, rough comp. Although Hanks had matched the handshake positioning of the archival footage visitor, in the final composite the two hands, photographed decades apart, would have to come to grips.

This page, bottom: Final composite, with morphing software sealing the shot with a handshake.

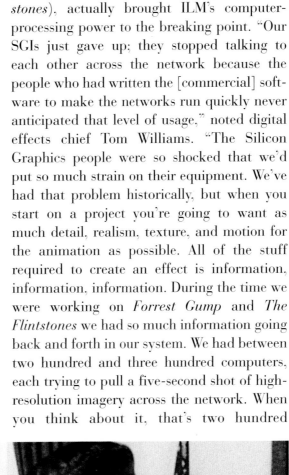

Right: Other celebrity encounters included this shot of Forrest receiving the Medal of Honor from President Johnson. One shot of Johnson was created by digitally removing LBJ's head and attaching it to footage of a present-day stand-in.

Middle: The thanks of a grateful nation, in the form of a plaque from President Nixon, goes to Forrest for playing Ping-Pong in China. Archival footage was utilized, with a young man painted out so that a blue-screen Hanks could be inserted, with additional digital manipulations for the president's expressions and lip movements.

Bottom: Gump's Ping-Pong champ laurels are crowned with a visit to *The Dick Cavett Show*. The talk show host himself, made up to look twenty-some years younger, was filmed with Hanks on a simulation of Cavett's talk show set. Both of them were then seamlessly dropped into an old *Cavett* episode—the host back in his interviewer's chair, Hanks filling out the seat once occupied by Yoko Ono. John Lennon, waiting all the time, coolly lights up another smoke.

machines multiplied by about ten megabytes of data, which is two gigabytes [a gigabyte is one thousand megabytes, or one billion bytes] at any one time on a network that can handle probably about ten megabytes a second—so we were overloading it by a factor of two hundred. But the people who write software, and even those who build our SGI computers, can't anticipate what ILM will use it for. That makes us a very scary test site for a lot of people, but, fortunately, it's worked out well. Our vendors realize that if they solve the problems we have they'll be solving the kinds of problems people will have later on, which makes for a good marketing spot to be in."

CREATURES TO CHARACTERS

The opposite of invisible effects, which pass unnoticed by moviegoers if done correctly, are the fantastic, crowd-pleasing visions of computer-generated imagery. The dimensional creations previously produced at ILM, including the water pseudopod and the liquid-metal T-1000 Terminator, were pure creations of the imagination, with no semblance to the normal flesh-and-blood world. With *Death Becomes Her*, digital artists began experimenting to produce human skin. *Jurassic Park*, with its photorealistic dinosaurs, was a creative peak for ILM's computer graphics artists.

The stunning upward curve of computer graphics had, within some five years, transformed ILM in particular and the film indus-try in general. "I've seen a complete revolution in the world of visual effects—a Brave New World," said Patty Blau, a seventeen-year ILM veteran producer and currently executive in charge of production. "This is an amazing time to be living in this world. The technology allows the artistry to blossom; it's allowed directors to bring out scripts which they had put away as impossible dreams—for they're no longer impossible. I can't think of something that we cannot solve now. Time and money are our only limits."

Instead of showstopping CG creature effects, ILM's post–*Jurassic Park* age would witness the coming of a new breed of CG creation: synthetic characters that would have to act. "Digital characters will become a specialty of ours, a kind of imagery that wasn't fea-

In *Congo*, the big-screen adaptation of the Michael Crichton novel, ILM had to produce the full fury of an erupting volcano. In this shot (which did not make the final cut), a real balloon filmed over a river and valley in Costa Rica has been digitally composited with a completely synthetic mountain and 2-D digital matte-painted environment, which included animated smoke and painted lava that seemed to actually be flowing. "It's a superb application of what we did on the *Young Indy* TV series, but for features," observed producer Ned Gorman. "This whole shot was done by two people within a month, as opposed to the months it would have taken to physically create, film, and composite the lava and other elements."

Right: In *Congo,* the hero (played by Dylan Walsh) and Amy the mountain gorilla (a performer in a suit) try to escape the earth-shaking lava flow gutting the Lost City of Zinj (this image did not make the final cut). The complex action sequence, which lasted several minutes, required digital comping of different elements (such as the tree exploding into flame) and intercutting between the soundstage set and scale miniatures to accommodate the areas of lava flow.

Below: Unlike the balloon shot of animated lava, the close-ups of the lava cutting a fiery path through the Lost City were created using practical effects. "We had our model makers take precise measurements of the live-action set, then build 6th and 8th scale Styrofoam miniatures and paint them blue for extraction purposes," explained Ned Gorman. "In the miniatures we'd built trenches through which we poured this white sludge largely composed of methacil—we used 1,000 gallons of it during the production. We overcranked to 96 FPS and top lit so the white would look hot and digitally colorized it to give it a self-illumination."

sible even a few years ago," Jim Morris noted. "In a certain regard we've become more like an animation house, but an animation house that can create photorealistic-looking characters for film and video and television. This goes beyond the old blue-screen shots of an actor composited into the burning building or animatronic characters. We're getting called upon to create principal actors for the movies. And that's a pretty dramatic change."

"HERE'S LOOKING AT YOU, BOGEY": SABRE SYSTEM MAGIC

During the climax of *The Maltese Falcon*, private investigator Sam Spade (Humphrey Bogart) wearily explains to his lover, the woman who murdered Spade's partner during the hunt for the jewel-encrusted golden falcon, the code of honor between partners that compelled him to turn her over to the authorities.

The voice and image of Bogey from that 1941 scene, as well as other scenes gleaned from his starring roles in such films as *Casablanca*, *Key Largo*, and *Dead Reckoning*, would be digitally extracted and inserted into "You, Murderer," a February 15, 1995, episode of HBO's *Tales from the Crypt*. Directed by Robert Zemeckis, with ILM visual effects supervised by Ken Ralston, the strange story had Bogart as Lou, a murdered man who returned from the dead to exact revenge on the wife and the plastic surgeon who had betrayed him. The twist was that the TV episode would be filmed from Lou's point of view (which would also be the audience's point of view) and the Bogart character would only be revealed when he looked in a mirror, or otherwise saw his reflection.

The idea had come to Zemeckis during a *Tales from the Crypt* story session. The director wanted to tell a tale from one character's point of view, and when the talk turned to the possibilities of revealing the character in reflections, Zemeckis had a brainstorm: Since it was a *Crypt* tale, why not bring a famous actor back from the dead to play the reveal scenes? And since the story was in the film *noir* tradition (and the point-of-view storytelling device had been featured in Bogart's 1947 release *Dark Passage*), the discussion settled on Bogart for the part—a mere thirty-eight years after the actor's passing.

First, permission to use snippets of past

Bogey performances had to be obtained from the copyright holders. But Zemeckis also wanted to bill the "You, Murderer" episode as "starring Humphrey Bogart," which led the production to forestall any possible future legal problems by also obtaining permission from Bogart's heirs.

In order to resurrect Bogey digitally, ILM scanned in plates of scenes featuring stand-in actor (and Bogart lookalike) Robert Sacchi seeing his reflection, and digitally grafted onto Sacchi's body specific Bogey heads taken from the scanned-in footage of his old movies. The complex compositing work was a major workout for ILM's new Sabre System, which had been similarly utilized in *Forrest Gump* to add President Lyndon Johnson's head onto a stand-in's body digitally. Since the *Crypt* episode was for a TV program, the Sabre operators did have the advantage of working at lower resolution, although the challenge of the project required a full complement of the system's painting and compositing tools, while the production deadlines—seventeen shots that needed to be delivered in three weeks—would test the system's vaunted real-time, interactive capabilities.

One of the major problems involved in joining the two plates—one the head of an actor filmed decades before, the other the stand-in actor's body—was in digitally matching the two elements into one seamless figure. For a shot of Sacchi looking into a mirror and adjusting his tie, the Bogart neck, which was thinner than Sacchi's, at first was disappearing and leaving a gaping hole in the stand-in's collar area, which required morphing and stretching manipulations of the old footage image to fit. Time warping was sometimes required to stretch out the archival image and dialogue bits to synch in with the

Crypt plates. In other shots, Bogart's eyes in the original footage did not face the audience, necessitating the creation and insertion of a pair of digital eyes that would maintain Lou's point of view.

Performing most of the work on the Sabre for the HBO show was Sheena Duggal, an ILM newcomer who had worked on high-resolution digital paintbox systems in London and on the first feature application of the interactive Flame software (for *Super Mario Bros.*). One of her major challenges was colorizing the old black-and-white images before they could be integrated with the new plates. "When you're coloring black and white you're basically dealing with luminescence, and if you try to put color into it as it exists it'll just look flat," Duggal observed. "To get over that we had to paint all kinds of mattes to give different contours, color, and tonal areas in Bogart's face. Then, tracking those mattes to the motion can get very complicated indeed.

"It's hard to learn some aspects of computers if you come from an art background because artists aren't used to dealing with things in a mathematical way. Personally, I prefer to stay on the artistic side and as far away from that aspect of it as I can." The Sabre did allow for an artist to concentrate on the work, not on the intricacies of technology. On the system's twenty-four-inch color monitor Duggal could call up elements or whole images of the work in progress and view them separately or simultaneously.

Resurrecting old Bogart performances and inserting them into the different dramatic context of "You, Murderer" was, of course, opening up a Pandora's box of vexing new questions, seemingly fulfilling dire prophecies of synthetic actors starring in

Lucasfilm's *Radioland Murders* was the first feature to utilize ILM's new Sabre System, which brought into the high-resolution filmmaking world the same real-time compositing and editing freedoms long enjoyed in video's low-res post environment. One *Radioland* shot that got the Sabre treatment has Roger (Brian Benben), harried hero and suspected murderer on the run, riding the teetering call letters of radio station WBN. The shot began with a stage element of the actor that was composited into background plates to dizzying effect.

future features, even the danger of mass media or unscrupulous governments transmitting digitally altered photorealistic images. Ken Ralston, who with Zemeckis had pushed the creative and technological envelope on such films as *Who Framed Roger Rabbit?* and *Forrest Gump*, was philosophical about having Bogart act in *Tales from the Crypt.*

"I think years ago I was a lot more adamant about not doing things like this, but what we did with *Gump* and *Crypt* are relatively benign uses of this [technology]," Ralston said. "If it's legal, and all the people who own this stuff or the heirs to this material can't get it stopped, I have no problem with it. And Bob isn't doing anything terribly miserable with it. But it's like Zemeckis said; he's sort of the Oppenheimer [J. Robert, director of the Manhattan Project] of these kinds of effects, and he's building the bomb . . . and dropping it the first time. What others do with it is up to them. You can't unin-

vent it. It's going to take something really awful and crude done with this before they pass some laws to stop it."

During an HBO press conference prior to the airing of the installment, Zemeckis and fellow executive producer Joel Silver answered questions about the deeper meaning of bringing departed movie stars back to life. "This is all new, so there's no real Screen Actors Guild rules about this," Silver said. "I remember at one point Bob said to me,

'I can see the time when you call up an agent and they just send you a floppy disk of their actor.' And you just keep putting the floppy disks in and say, 'Maybe we should go to Richard Widmark.' "

CHAPTER ELEVEN

THE COMING OF SYNTHETIC ACTORS

Puppets, masks, and costumes have been used to great effect in producing movie creatures, from the stop-motion Kong puppet used by Willis O'Brien in *King Kong* to the foam latex puppet of Jedi master Yoda (brought to life with voice and movement provided by master puppeteer Frank Oz in *The Empire Strikes Back*).

But just as such traditional creature work required the sculpting of clay, machining armatures, and casting foam, a CG process, unencumbered by physical materials, had taken shape: Alias modeling software producing the wire frame skeleton (what Tom Williams calls the "digital clay") of a character, SoftImage animating the figure, and Pixar's Renderman software producing the computer picture itself. For ILM, such commercial software provided the production foundation, while the ambitions of the company—which routinely took it into unexplored creative frontiers—necessitated breakthrough in-house CG software.

"The programs we developed between *T2* and *Jurassic Park* were absolutely critical for producing the type of imagery we created for those movies," explained Williams. "For each part of the process we have a different tool, such as the basic animation, a tool for skin and muscle movement, painting tools necessary for providing wrinkles or skin folds or coloration on an animal, lighting that will match what was on the set [for the background plate], a tool to match the live-action camera exactly, a tool to make the picture. Then you put the computer picture into the live-action background scenes. That makes it sound like simple discrete components, but in reality it's this organized spiderweb of different proprietary tools that we depend on that, if we didn't have, we wouldn't be able to produce our films. We have a dozen people just working on that [in-house software]. We had to build up this whole process of doing these types of productions, and we've received a huge response to our character work. Back on *T2* we were almost developing bit parts, and by *Jurassic Park* [the CG creations] were major supporting characters. Now, in *Casper*, *Jumanji*, and *Dragonheart* we're working on leading roles in films."

But betwixt the digital dinosaurs of *Jurassic* and the 3-D cartoon ghosts of *Casper* would be a seemingly human character, an unassuming bank clerk named Stanley Ipkiss, whose body would become a kind of Silly Putty capable of erupting into explosive bits of visual mayhem every time he donned "The Mask."

THE MASK
1994 (New Line Cinema)
The Cartoon Human

The comic-book cover was a lurid one, appropriate to the first issue of a magazine titled *Mayhem*: a green-suited figure up against a bullet-pocked wall, his hands and skull-like face dripping with blood, a swath of perfect teeth grinning through the gore, the jagged word balloon above asking "Who's laughing now?" Such was the first appearance of the Dark Horse Comics character "The Mask," an urban loser who, after don-

The wild transformations of *The Mask* were based on the classic cartoon mayhem of animator Tex Avery. This whirling dervish effect was both the Mask's mode of transportation and the transition state between transformations. Here, in need of a little carrying around money, the Mask exits a bank with a sack of cash, scattering some ruffians who planned their own unauthorized withdrawal.

ning a strange mask purchased at a curio shop, transforms into a cackling, magical being who cuts like a buzz saw through any miscreant who might have abused him.

Although *The Mask* had its comics debut in 1989, a mere two years later a movie script featuring all the ultraviolence of the comic was circulating in Hollywood. The screenplay would ultimately lose the mean-spirited quality of the source material and become an effects-filled, romantic comedy-adventure. Steering the creative fortunes of the project would be director Charles (*Nightmare on Elm Street 3*) Russell and actor Jim Carrey as Stanley Ipkiss, the nice guy with the mask who was tired of finishing last. New Line Cinema, the film's production company, committed to making the 1994 summer release a breakthrough visual effects extravaganza.

The ILM team hired to provide the digital visual effects would include supervisor Scott Squires and animation director Steve Williams. *The Mask* consciously set out to produce, with complete photorealism, all the histrionics of an old Tex Avery animated cartoon.

"We had read a number of different scripts that involved live-action characters which had comic-book ramifications in the 'realistic' world," noted Patty Blau, executive in charge of production. "*The Mask* walked through the door at an advantageous time for them [the producers] because they were ready to go and we had a window of opportunity. We thought the script was terrific, and the technology was available. We thought we could take the element of a computer graphics character as a major character in a film, which we could see was a coming vision in the industry, and produce a real showcase piece."

The CG work featured a range of unprecedented photographic animation flourishes, including such classic Avery-esque riffs as an amorous Ipkiss salivating over a sultry nightclub singer, in the process going through literally eye-popping and jaw-dropping convulsions which climaxed in his transformation into a randy wolf. Even Ipkiss's dog, Milo, turned into a hound from cartoon hell after getting his paws on the magical mask.

"The zany action in this film probably

overshadowed some of the technical feats," said Squires, whose honors in 1995 included an Oscar nomination for *The Mask* and an Academy Technical Achievement Award for pioneering work on digital technology in film-making. "For scenes where the character first puts on the mask, new software had to be written to animate and stretch the tentacles of the mask over Jim Carrey's head and to dig into the mask as his fingers moved on it. For the scene in which the Mask swallows dynamite and his stomach explodes, we had to create a perfect blend/match of color and skin texture since only part of his face was animated. Other scenes required seamless transitions to or from the live action. And no motion control was used because, with forty-five shooting days, it was a tight shooting schedule. Every scene with a moving camera required a 3-D match-move on the computer. All the scenes with computer graphic masks for Jim or the dog had to be tracked frame by frame in 3-D space so their CG heads would match. *The Mask* helped lay the groundwork for CG animation films such as *Casper* and *Dragonheart*."

In addition to the cutting-edge high tech, there were practical effects and the usual fun and games. "For a scene in which the cops stop the Mask and begin pulling things out of his pocket, the plan was to have CG enhancements make the objects inflate as they came out of the pocket, similar to the early shot in which we created a computer-generated mallet to smash a clock in his apartment hallway," Squires said. "However, when we framed the actual shot, I suggested instead that we cut his pants and have people below Jim and off-camera pass items up through his pants. This had just as much impact without the cost or time in making an effects shot.

"For the clock sequence I just mentioned, we had finished shooting a shot with Jim and we'd started shooting a reference of the clock moving in the scene. I was on my hands and knees moving the clock through its motions when Jim leapt on my back and started riding me like a cowboy. The computer graphics crew at ILM were a bit surprised to see this in the reference dailies."

Despite the over-the-top ambitions of the

The cops spot the Mask, yell "Freeze," and, in perfect cartoon fashion, he does exactly that, an effect created with a plate of Carrey and a CG overlay of icicles and frost.

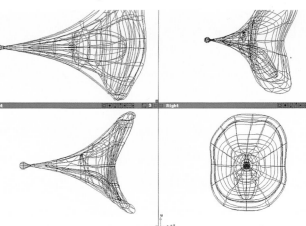

This page: You're crossing the street when a motorist slams on the brakes and leans on his horn. What do you do? If you're the Mask, you can turn a little bicycle horn into a windshield-shattering loudspeaker. The construction of the cartoonish image began with these wire-frame images.

effects, ILM's work still had to walk a fine line. While the sight of a cartoon animation character's eyeballs expanding and popping out of their sockets might be a sidesplitting sight, the same antics performed by a photorealistic figure could be horribly grotesque. As such, the preparatory visual effects design stage headed up by ILM art director Benton Jew was vital in shaping the final animated character.

DIGITAL CHARACTER DESIGN

"What we're finding is that current directors are very aware of the technology and are very specific as to what they want," observed art department veteran Doug Chiang. "We've found that hand-drawn sketches aren't quite good enough, so we've had to go back and digitally alter photographs to get the characters correct so that the director knows photographically the image that we're re-creating is exactly what he's going to see in the film. In some ways it's changing the art department, in that we're helping directors previsualize their films. Our designs are becoming more specific to the actual look of the film."

Chiang himself had pioneered the use of a computer in developing design concepts on

Death Becomes Her in which (as with *The Mask*) there was the danger of producing a grotesque effect. In order to create *Death Becomes Her* designs that would best simulate the 3-D reality of the final effect, and not be limited by two-dimensional animated pencil tests, Chiang photographed some models, scanned the photos into a Macintosh, and with Photoshop software digitally worked out a dimensional final design for director Bob Zemeckis.

"The advantage of digital art is you can just cut something out or replicate it as many times as you want, add atmosphere or blur, or go back to a previous version that you liked better," Chiang said. "We still have our traditional tools—paints and markers and pencils—but now we're also doing about half of our work on the computer (mainly the Mac, with Photoshop for the 2-D work). Sometimes we do 3-D, but that's still in the

"Smokin'!" When Stanley Ipkiss (Jim Carrey) dons a mysterious mask, he becomes more than a mere bank clerk—he becomes a super-hero!

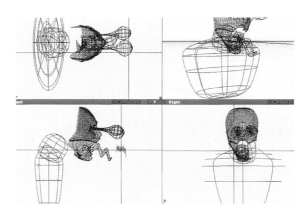

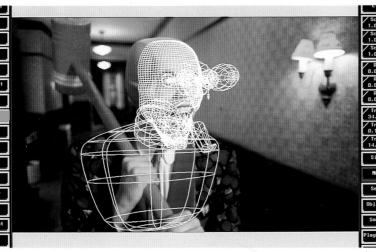

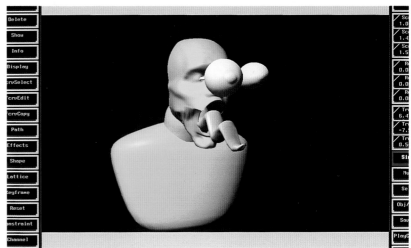

Top, left to right: The CG magic begins with a background plate of actor Carrey (with the Mask makeup effect produced by outside Oscar-winner Greg Cannom). In this scene ILM prepared a startling Avery riff with a wire-frame construction in Alias software.

Middle left: With SoftImage software, CG artists composite the wire frame over the background plate.

Middle right: A quick rendering of the CG animation and the background plate figure.

Bottom: Final composite. As with *Death Becomes Her*, art direction helped design physical contortions that were fantastic but avoided the grotesque.

At the swank Coco Bongo Club a sultry torch singer brings out the beast in Ipkiss. The wolf transformation began with Carrey miming the final cartoonish effect, digital removal of the actor's head, and the insertion of the final CG animation.

very early stages and we haven't used it in concept work yet. A lot of times we'll scan in a photograph that's really close in lighting and texture and use that, or if we can't find the actual photographic reference, we'll shoot it ourselves or have the creature department create a sculpture and photograph, scan it in, and then colorize and put the texture on it."

The significance of *The Mask* was that CG effects could now produce photorealistically all the distortions of reality de rigueur in the world of cartoon animation. The illusion was

Milo, Stanley's faithful dog, manages to get into the act and is transformed into a whacked-out superdog.

also advanced by the contortive effects produced by Carrey himself, with the blips of CG action reserved for the kind of eye-popping mayhem impossible for the actor to achieve physically. Those synthetic moments, basically distorting and embellishing the scanned-in images of Jim Carrey, were the seminal beginnings of a purely computer-generated character. It would not be a long wait before the arrival of completely computer-generated performers—and they would include a happy-go-lucky ghost, a menagerie of animals, and a fire-breathing dragon.

CASPER
1995 (Amblin/Universal)
3-D Cartoon

In filmdom's predigital days, a feature based on the likes of Casper, the friendly ghost of Harvey Comics fame, would have been best realized with traditional, hand-drawn cartoon animation. With the new CG tools a strange new world of effects possibilities had been opened up, as ILM created Casper and the Ghostly Trio as synthetic

beings having both cartoon elasticity and three-dimensional forms.

"On *Casper* we were dealing with this really weird hybrid medium," observed animation director Eric Armstrong, who was concerned with performance issues (he was one of two directors, the other being Phil Nibbelink, who directed the animatic roughs at Amblin that guided ILM's animators). "It's like traditional animation in that you're working with a drawn line and you can be free to break the rules of gravity, of volume, of anything, with the only limits being the artistic and acting skills of the animator. But it's also like stop motion that requires physical puppets or models to be built with armature and skin, with animators trying to get the best performance dependent on what a joint can do, how far a puppet can move, how flexible it is. Well, we've got a strange new medium where we really have the flexibility a traditional animator has because we can do anything, but yet we have limitations like a stop-motion animator because we have to know ahead of time what [the CG character] has to do, so we can build it to do it."

Casper was a huge challenge for ILM's CG department, requiring a team of thirty animators working on some four hundred shots, many running at 1,700 frames (or more than a minute of continuous CG animation). Unlike past CG efforts, the virtual cast had to carry the film with convincing performances.

BUILDING A VIRTUAL BEING

In the early days of *Casper* production, Amblin had hoped to create some shots of its ghostly cast using mechanical puppets, an effort that Dennis Muren recalled as "a total failure." Mechanical servos did not allow for the subtlety of facial expressions and fluidity of physical movement required for a convincing performance.

Although some thought had been given to creating Casper as a realistic-looking child, producer Steven Spielberg opted for emulating the look of the original comics character. Since ILM would be creating the major characters as well as providing their performance, the effects house had considerable input on their design. ILM was cognizant throughout the art direction phase that 2-D design sketches (and even a prototype puppet created to help the CG animators) would not completely translate to the realities of the digital realm. "Unlike hand-drawn animation, if there's a flaw in a CG character it's always there, so we had to try and fix those flaws so the characters would work from every angle," Armstrong noted. "The modeler has to build certain things so the animator can get the animation he or she wants, which takes a lot of preplanning."

To conjure up their characters from the digital realm, ILM's animators utilized such commercial software tools as Alias for modeling and SoftImage for animation, along with a package of in-house tools. The most important proprietary tools were "BuildShapes" and "ShowShapes," which provided an interface library of different face shapes that

animators could morph and blend into a rendered final image. To produce an ethereal, ghostlike effect (and avoid the look of a rubber prop floating around), Casper's form was rendered so that some of the background plate was visible through the character.

Breakthroughs during the roughly year-long CG production schedule were such that the first *Casper* scenes produced (with the cheerful wraith whipping up some breakfast for some mortal friends) paled in comparison to subsequent shots, in particular a soul-searching moment as the little ghost recalled

Casper was another ILM CG breakthrough for character animation. Here the friendly ghost haunts the dreams of a young girl (Kat, played by Christina Ricci) and later invites her to explore the secrets of Casper's haunted house.

Above: Rounding out the computer-generated creations in *Casper* are the Ghostly Trio (here putting a scare into Halloween pranksters Amber (Jessica Wilson) and Vic (Garette Ratliff Henson). Where Casper is gentle, these three spooks are obnoxious troublemakers. Let's meet them (pictured to the right in test stills):

Fatso . . .

Stinkie . . .

Stretch.

his own death. Unlike live-action acting (in which a flesh and blood actor could reach into his or her heart and experience to bring forth a performance), putting a synthetic actor into the mix required specific, physical manipulations of the character to convey emotions. As such, both the creation of the character and its performance were inextricably connected.

PERFORMANCE ASPECTS

Since the task of producing CG characters was a new art form, and the talent pool of available CG artists limited, ILM conducted a global talent search to assemble its *Casper* team. "You'd like to be able to cast the animator to the character, and we sort of did it on this film, but the schedule was such, and the number of animators in the world who can do this kind of work so limited, that we weren't able to do it through the whole show," observed *Casper* supervisor Dennis Muren.

Casper was also the beginning of a new creative environment, one in which ILM's work went beyond effects and into the province of pure, emotive performance. "Something that none of us anticipated is [that as] Casper's the star of the movie, and then there's the Ghostly Trio, the director [Brad Silberling] was not about to let any-

Left and below: Unlike previous CG effects, *Casper*'s ghostly creations were not mere visual extravaganzas but synthetic performers. "We had never done full-blown character animation before, and it was a huge learning experience for all of us," supervisor Dennis Muren explained. "My criteria was that a dialogue shot had to work without sound. The face and body movements alone needed to communicate what the character was feeling. Achieving this level of computer animation was much more difficult than we anticipated."

Bottom: Very early CG Casper figure in development.

body else direct his stars, which makes total sense," Muren pointed out. "So Brad had to direct our animators. It's amazing that Brad was able to figure out how to do this. With actors a performance comes from within them, so a director gets into discussing performance with actors all the time, but nobody can really talk to a computer. And it's tough talking to the animators because they're learning this as fast as anybody else. To figure

Right: Ghosthunter Dr. Harvey (Bill Pullman) and Kat in breakfast sequence with Casper and the Ghostly Trio.

Below: Casper and Kat share a moonlit moment atop a lighthouse.

The synergy of animation and performance necessitated a film-optic link with video pictures of the work in progress between ILM and Amblin's Los Angeles–area *Casper* production suite (similar to the transmissions that relayed *Jurassic Park* shots), as well as frequent visits to the effects facility by Silberling to work on the intertwined performance and animation questions on a frame-by-frame basis. Along the way, the *Casper* art department provided ILM with rough-posed animatics (usually for every eighth frame of the scene) illustrating the performance aspects the director desired.

Having a cast of virtual characters meant Silberling was dealing with performance issues long after the completion of first-unit filming (along with the score, sound effects, dialogue dubbing, and other traditional postproduction work). *Casper* was a seminal effort for ILM, a production that had to break new ground every step of the way but a project still consistent with ILM's creative purpose according to Eric Armstrong: "*Casper* was no different from any other film I've ever been involved with at ILM. It's always been a matter of taking an element

out how to get expressions and feelings essentially out of nothing has been a real challenge. At the beginning we didn't think we could move Casper's face too much without all sorts of bizarre artifacts showing up—seams showing and things tearing apart. And then there's the sense of life in the eyes, which are sort of photoreal with glints in them, which originally we didn't think we could manage."

and putting it into a live-action environment, making it look as real as the things that were shot for the actual plate. That's what we specialize in, that's what we do best."

JUMANJI
1995 (Tri-Star)
CG Mammals

In *Jumanji*, an award-winning children's book written and illustrated by Chris Van Allsburg and published in 1981, two children named Peter and Judy are left home while their parents attend the opera. The bored siblings go to play in the park across from their house where they discover a boxed board game with the legend JUMANJI: A JUNGLE ADVENTURE GAME. The mysterious game turns into a supernatural experience as each roll of the dice brings to life chattering monkeys, stampeding rhinos, a monsoon, and even a burst of lava. Only after the kids wend their way along the board's snakelike path to the "Golden City"—and shout *"Jumanji"*—is all restored to normal.

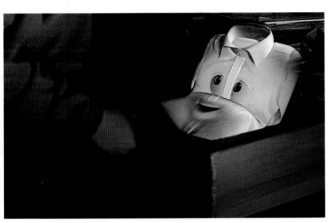

Top left: There were many CG models for our friendly ghost. Here Casper takes the form of a dress shirt.

Above: Casper's just a party guy.

Left: The Ghostly Trio strike a spooky pose in this startling effect.

Above: Casper immortalized on Mount Rushmore. For ILM's CG artists, *Casper* was ILM's biggest CG production to date, with some 418 separate shots and 52 minutes of on-screen time.

Right, top to bottom: In this showdown, Fatso's protoplasmic form gets vacuumed up by the good Dr. Harvey.

In the film version realized by director and ILM alumnus Joe Johnston the game has begun, with the young Alan Parrish (Robin Williams) sucked into the boardgame's jungle. Twenty-six years later, the game is rediscovered by Peter (Bradley Pierce) and Judy (Kirsten Dunst), and the renewed play once again summons forth the creatures and natural forces from the Jumanji jungle. ILM's major task was to create some one hundred 3-D, photorealistic shots of monkeys, rhinos, lions, and other creatures that would invade the streets of the normally quiet New Hampshire township that serves as the setting for the film.

The greatest challenge in creating the jungle creatures was in capturing the look of fur, one of many organic materials traditionally difficult to achieve in CG. "Creating realistic fur has always been a big problem because the computer likes to think in very hard-edged terms," observed ILM *Jumanji* art director Doug Chiang. "In nature there are a lot of unusual shapes, and it's difficult to program in all those shapes as opposed to something that has one surface, such as a chrome object. Flame, for example, is very lively, and to cap-

ture that life you have to go in and animate a lot of different parameters; you can't just plug in a number and say, okay, this is flame. *Jurassic Park* was leaps and bounds over anything that had gone on before and was quite an accomplishment, but re-creating the hard skins of reptiles is a little bit easier than re-creating the soft textures of feather and fur. Something like hair has a lot of surfaces, and that's just one of the issues. Every strand of hair has its own characteristic, so we can't just model one hair and replicate it."

The *Jumanji* lion's mane, with both its

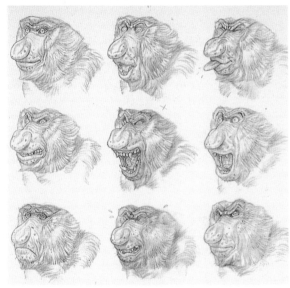

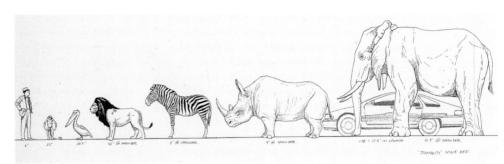

flowing short and long rasta-styled hairs, proved the biggest CG challenge, according to visual effects producer Mark Miller who credits CG supervisor Carl Frederick and software writers Jeff Yost and David Benson with the animation breakthrough. "Each hair was modeled individually in the computer," said Miller. "The hair not only had to lay on the surface but there had to be a certain amount of recoil when the lion moved. The SoftImage animation tool, that moves an arm or leg, moved whole clumps of hair."

According to Chiang, the success of the *Jurassic* creatures had been a vital step toward re-creating ever more complex animals: "Gradually, through the whole creative process,

you find solutions, you have happy accidents, you modify and use ideas that have worked on other shows. On almost every show I've worked on there's something we didn't definitely know if we could do, but we went in knowing that somehow we'd pull it off."

Top left: *Jumanji* rhino model sculpted by Richard Miller. With the new digital tools, such detailed, physical 3-D sculptures can be cyber-scanned into the digital realm, with the resulting data used to construct the animated, virtual character.

Top right: For *Jumanji*, art director Doug Chiang provided this scale reference illustration as a starting point for ILM's CG animators.

Middle right: *Jumanji* monkey concept art by Claudia Mullaly.

Middle left and left: Baboon expressions, style sheet, and colored marker image by Terryl Whitlatch. "With this film we were creating real animals digitally for the first time," said ILM supervisor Steve Price. "We also had to integrate these animals into improbable scenes. So we [had to] develop new software systems as well as use programs, such as particle systems, in ways that extended their potential."

Right: Draco the dragon, very early *Dragonheart* concept sketch by Steve Price.

Below: Draco the dragon, rough CG model. Creature creator Phil Tippett initially produced a four-foot-long model that was scanned in and used as a basis for the construction of the virtual dragon. Once in the digital realm, skin coloration and other details were worked out.

DRAGONHEART
1996 (Universal)
A Living Dragon

In some future time, when synthetic movie characters are commonplace, film buffs will debate which was the first completely CG performer: the ghostly characters of *Casper*, Pixar's animated *Toy Story* cast, or Draco, the fire-breathing dragon and star of *Dragonheart*. A possible distinction is that the CG cast members of *Casper* and *Toy Story* were three-dimensional cartoons, while *Dragonheart* produced a photorealistic creature.

Draco represented a natural, if fantastic, evolutionary leap from the dinosaurs of

Jurassic Park. The dragon, designed by director Rob Cohen, former ILMer Phil Tippett, and visual effects supervisors Steve Price and Scott Squires, had a host of problems that had to be hurdled on the way to the creature's ultimate creation.

In *Dragonheart* a dragon-slaying knight named Bowen (Dennis Quaid) teams up with the last of the dragons (voice supplied by Sean Connery) to battle an evil ruler. To capture a Dark Ages atmosphere, the live-action location work was staged from summer through early winter of 1994 in the wilds of Slovakia, an hour's eastward drive from the salons of Vienna, much of it along rough one-lane roads.

The location work included building sets, from the mud huts of "Swamp Village" to a waterfall. But it was for the photographic wonders of the countryside itself that Cohen and his first unit had come: Expansive fields of wheat open to the horizon without a power line in sight, forested mountains, working mills, the ruins of medieval castles. But rough weather conditions also went with the rugged terrain. "We were shooting out in the middle of wheat fields during a heat wave that was breaking all records—it was like 108 degrees," Squires recalled. "Then came November, and we were atop a castle while it was snowing, with the ground below covered with a quarter inch of ice."

The ILM team had come to Slovakia to shoot the all-important background plates into which ILM would, months later, digitally insert the synthetic dragon. Working with special effects supervisor Kit West and his crew, Squires also supervised the staging of practical, on-location effects that would provide a realistic, interactive touch for the time when the CG dragon was later composited.

Both the interactive touches and performance requirements of *Dragonheart* were a level beyond the animalistic actions required of the *Jurassic Park* dinosaurs. As a virtual actor, Draco had to engage in stretches of conversation; this required special timings during the location photography for which dragon dialogue would later be added. Cohen often recited Draco's lines to work on timings in scenes in which live actors had to "act" with the dragon. In-camera placement of the creature for the plate photography was also vital, particularly for the conversations between Draco and Quaid, which demanded correct eye lines to seal the illusion that the dragon and knight were in the same scene together.

Storyboards and a posable dragon model (built by Phil Tippett) placed in front of the camera helped rough out shots for ILM's plate photography, but composing the dragon shots accurately required scale dimensions for the proposed CG creation, as well as a method of measuring the areas in the plate in which the dragon would later be composited. Prior to the location work, Draco's dimensions had been established at forty-five feet long and seventeen feet tall, which made the dragon big, yet not big enough to completely dwarf the actors. Reference markers (which had also been utilized for *Jurassic Park*) helped establish on location the creature's height range, which varied from Draco raised to full height to settled down on his haunches (with any references digitally painted out later).

But the breakthroughs in camera freedom that had begun during the making of *T2* allowed for the shooting of background plates without the need for locked-off cameras, so it was vital that accurate camera measurements be established during the location work for the later match-moves of the CG character with the plate photography. Shots of such complexity called for something more than merely "holding up a monster stick," according to Squires.

"On something like *The Mask* I would be there taking tape measurements and working out some of the rough marks for doors and windows, which worked pretty well," said Squires. "But with *Dragonheart* we knew that with so many shots in organic landscapes, measurements would be problematic. You couldn't just measure from this blade of grass to that tree branch. So I got together with Charlie Clavadetscher, one of our head people in match-moving, and said, 'There's got to be a better way of match-moving than tape measures.' So we bought digital surveying equipment, which we called 'electric transit.'"

The tripod-set surveying device matched up with reference markers by sending out an infrared signal that bounced back and forth from the markers. "The Transit knew electronically how far away a reference was, what the pan and tilt angle was, and from that I could calculate the relative height with a program I wrote on the Macintosh and Power-Book to tie in to it," said Squires. "So instead of two or three people roughing things out, you could record [the references] and the Transit system would plot it out for you. We took measurements up to half a mile away, taking readings on cliff tops and things like that. One day we measured a castle from at least a quarter mile away, and when we came back later for a

A

B

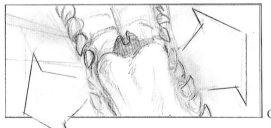

C

'DRAGONHEART'   FF 19

Left: *Dragonheart* storyboard sequence by Benton Jew.

TYRUBEN ILM MAT:

Above: Milo the dog (transformed by the magical mask); color-marker concept art for *The Mask* by Benton Jew.

Above right: "Nessie," concept art for *The Flintstones* by TyRuben Ellingson. Nessie and Dino the dinosaur were among six CG creature characters produced for the feature-film version of the classic TV show.

reshoot, we took the same measurements and we were only half an inch off."

Practical effects for interactive scenes, dialogue timings, exact measurements for the plate work—all were prerequisite to the enormous challenge of bringing to life a photorealistic, fire-breathing creature. "The fact that the dragon is a realistic-looking character and has a lot of close-ups pushes the demands on the animators and technical directors to another level of detail and complexity," noted co-CG supervisor Alex Seiden.

DRAGON DESIGN

While Squires was finishing his location assignment in Slovakia, his CG team had already begun to model Draco the dragon. Early CG tests utilizing *Jurassic Park* digital dinosaurs were stretched and manipulated to ascertain such subtle design aspects as the appropriate length of Draco's snout and mouth. And with close to two hundred shots (as opposed to some sixty shots on *Jurassic Park*), the animation demands of *Dragonheart* would take photorealistic CG creature work into a new dimension. (Seiden estimated that Draco's head alone was at a level of complexity

half that of the entire T-rex in *Jurassic Park*.)

"When we were doing *Jurassic Park* we found we could get a lot more close-ups on the T-rex and the raptors than we ever expected, but *Dragonheart* was scary because we went a step beyond that, with longer close-ups, plus we had to make him talk," Seiden noted. "It's a big creature, so there's a lot of places to add paints—we had to make him feel big and powerful yet scary—and when you add wings there's a whole other set of issues around motion that you have to make work. And, unlike *Jurassic*, he had to be as subtle and powerful an actor as Sean Connery. But *Jurassic* had to have been there for us to do this; we definitely built on the technology of *Jurassic*."

Some of the proprietary tools used to build Draco included the Make Sticky texture map software developed for *T2*, Viewpaint software for painting the surface textures (a *Jurassic* breakthrough), and the animation-enhancing Enveloping program (yet another *Jurassic* tool). The design work included 2-D production sketches of the dragon based on the mouth and facial movements of Connery (who had long before recorded his Draco dialogue) to help the CG crew develop shape keys for the dragon's mouth, as well as new software tools for quicker and easier facial animation. As with *Casper*, it would require all the acting and animation abilities of the ILM CG crew to render a believable character.

"With a lot of shows, if you get one shot that's not at one hundred percent, it's not much of a problem; the film still works," Squires observed. "But with this, if it doesn't work, or even if you have one bad scene with the character, the audience will go, 'Wait a minute!' Any problem with either the rendering, the modeling, or the animation stands out. You can't do any cheats with this. The animators have to be full-on actors, revealing themselves through the dragon. But this film, like *The Mask*, was evolutionary. In *The Mask* we had character animation, and we had to meld all these things together of [Jim Carrey] changing into a Tex Avery character and coming back. With *Dragonheart* we had to create a fully realized dragon, make him talk and be believable as a real character. But the chance to try something new is why I do these projects. I'd rather not just go through the steps. Even if I have a project that's similar to something I've done before, I like to look at how, technically and creatively, I can do it better. Things are evolving in the world of visual effects, and I hope we at ILM can continue to tap into the huge potential."

DREAMS OF FUTURE FX

At the dawn of moving pictures, scenes of the real world were enough to put people in the seats. In the virtual age of movies, filmmaking had seemingly come full circle, from reflections of reality to the modern public fascination with the *simulation* of reality. And on the creative CG horizon lay the possibility of producing synthetic humans. "I have a running bet with an animator here for the deadline by which a photorealistic human is created," Eric Armstrong said with a smile. "But my feeling about that is, if you can have an actor to do it, why do it in CG? What's the point?"

The talk of synthetic humans, in Dennis Muren's view, was perhaps no different from a sculptor carving from marble a perfect human form, although he, too, was reserved about the potential benefits of such a breakthrough. "I had a director call me a few years ago who wanted to have a CG character in his show for the publicity—it might get people into the theater," Muren noted. "I never heard back from him. Now we are a lot closer to it [creating a CG person] if we have to do it. To me, it would be a challenge, but if you want it to be unique, it shouldn't be an actor—something like an android could be pretty interesting. But I don't know why people are getting so excited about computers. People aren't aware that it's people who are doing all this on computers. But this attitude is temporary. It'll pass and computers will be recognized as just another tool."

Most ILMers, so hands-on and familiar with computers, indeed viewed the technolo-

gy as a tool. For them, future musings often gravitated to possible permutations of existing technology—or the evolution of new ones.

IMAX: THE BIG UNKNOWN

Imax, the largest film format in history, had always represented the great unknown for effects artists accustomed to 8-perf VistaVision and the conventional 35mm final film. The medium's 70mm, 15-perforation film frames required not only special photographic and projection systems (geared, like VistaVision, to run film horizontally through the camera), but special theaters equipped with giant screens rising the equivalent of eight stories.

In 1995, ILM accepted the challenge of producing visual effects for *Special Effects* an Imax-format documentary produced by NOVAMAX/WGBH Boston, a large-film-format division of the PBS "Nova" series established in 1984. *Special Effects* (directed by Ben Burtt, a Lucasfilm veteran beginning with dialogue and sound effects duties on *Star Wars*) would not only document the history of film effects, but explore the nature of human perception that can be so beguiled and tricked by cinematic illusions. "In the film we'll show ILM artists creating an effects sequence in the Imax format, which hasn't

The third-generation ILM scanner, which became operational in January of 1994, can enter any film format into the digital realm—even Imax footage, the largest film format in history. The brain trust who led the way on developing the breakthrough scanner are (left to right): Michael Bolles, Mike MacKenzie, Jeff Light, Lincoln Hu, Udo Pampel, and Josh Pines.

Lincoln Hu gets under the hood with the new ILM scanner.

been attempted before," noted NOVAMAX senior producer Susanne Simpson. "In the past, conventional 35mm optical effects images couldn't hold up in the Imax format; there'd be film grain six feet tall."

In 1992, when Simpson first approached ILM regarding the unique project, the technology didn't exist to produce effects that could be exhibited at ten times the size of normal 35mm motion pictures. To work in the Imax format, a third-generation scanner would have to be designed and built. The first scanner had been built in 1985 and provided breakthrough digital work for *Willow* and *Indiana Jones and the Last Crusade*. That prototype was replaced in 1989 by a second-generation scanner, jointly developed by ILM and Kodak, which was the first dependable feature-film digitizing system. In the *Jurassic Park* year of 1993, for example, that workhorse second-generation unit digitized some 123,500 frames of film.

Although the second-generation scanner had been running consistently since 1989, ILM's scanning technology would continue to evolve. The new scanner would handle both the growing digitizing workload and such exotic formats as Imax. A seven-person ILM team, headed up by Lincoln Hu and Josh Pines,

worked for seven months developing the third-generation system, which became operational in January of 1994. "The new scanner employed the same trilinear CCD imaging technology as our second-generation scanner, but we introduced new electronic, optical, mechanical, and illumination designs to improve scan speed, image quality, and flexibility," Lincoln Hu explained. "We made our components to be easily serviceable and interchangeable between 35mm and 65mm formats. We can switch to a mechanical assembly to accommodate the Imax format in two hours, after calibrating and realigning the system for 70mm.

"We had to do proof of concept to satisfy NOVAMAX, our client, that we could handle the format without any loss in image quality. When we were ready to shoot our tests in spring of '94, our confidence level was high; we knew we could handle the images. We shot tests of people in the back lot at ILM and scanned them. Once an image is in the digital realm, the format doesn't matter; you're not restricted by the originating format. When we scanned out to the Imax format, there was no image degradation. No one had done that before."

Producing visual effects in the large format would, however, pose tremendous challenges for ILM's *Special Effects* team. "When you're digitizing high-profile visual effects in 65mm, the sheer size of the Imax frame multiplies processing time by a factor of four," explained ILM executive producer Ned Gorman. "We've always been expert at integrating visual effects into live action for 35 and even 75mm film formats—matching grain, color timing, and resolution to the surrounding footage. In Imax that's always been the big unknown. But we wanted to try and work in this format."

The format itself received a jolt of publicity in 1995 with the release of Sony Pictures' *Wings of Courage*, a tale of brave pilots flying mail runs into the Andes. The 45-minute Imax feature, produced in 3-D for good measure, was an attempt at classic movie storytelling, although the spectacle of 3-D images blown up big as buildings and viewed through wrap-around goggles seemed to overshadow the story. Adding to the problem of mass acceptance of the new medium was a paucity of venues, with only some 125 special theaters worldwide.

But the typical Imax production did offer visions impossible to experience at the local multiplex. "Imax images fill your peripheral vision," Hu enthused, "but for the effects artists that means there's no place to hide—any image defects are as large as a house. But an Imax image is incredible to see. In 1994, NASA took an Imax camera aboard the space shuttle when it went to do some repair work on the Hubble space telescope, and I saw the film, *Destiny in Space,* at an Imax theater in L.A. It was pristine footage; there was no atmospheric distortion. It made you feel like you were in outer space. The projectionist at the theater said that watching that film was the closest thing [he had] to a religious experience."

Tom Williams's future techology dream was of an interactive experience that would enable participants to explore virtual worlds or even inhabit the form of computer graphics characters, controlling the action with a joystick. Players from all points on the planet could be linked through TV screens, computer modems, or game pods in arcade settings. Williams saw such a breakthrough as offering the nearest thing to a tactile, hands-on experience in a virtual age.

"Even though I'm in charge of all this computer work at ILM, I still have a bit of longing for the old days," Williams admitted. "I can go into the [Lucasfilm] archives and pat R2-D2 on the head, or see all those amazing costumes. You can't share something like that on a computer. I'd be excited to have these pieces of art be shared by people; it'd be nice if something was out there for everyone to touch, that would enable you to explore [a virtual landscape] from a nonhuman perspec-

tive, from inside one of these creatures that we've made. You can imagine kids hopping onto some network and flying through a *Casper* set and pretending they're one of the Ghostly Trio or someone hopping into the brain of a T-rex and moving across these computer-generated environments."

George Lucas, famed for his own visionary meditations, had an idea of future technological scenarios that would make theatrical, narrative-driven movies as quaint as an old silent reeler. "I see true environments being created and combined with a lot of the biotech things going on, in terms of manipulating people's senses through drugs," Lucas imagined. "This combination will have the most powerful effect on the kind of storytelling we're doing today. It's too far off for me to worry about, and I'm not interested in virtual reality at its current level because it's just too crude. But the interface will improve dramatically, and if you can program virtual reality or simulator rides with biotech you will have a very interesting nonworld. The first step would be to take the simulator-ride part of an environment with the [biotech] part so that you believe the room is shaking or moving, that you're in a situation. At some point they may do away with the mechanical part of it, but that's serious biotech, where you can just implant the story in a pill and live it. That's not outside the realm of possibility. You'd take the pill and go to sleep. It'd be like a dream and you'd have an actual, real, physical experience of something completely imaginary. What that'll mean for society I have no idea and how you'd get there from here is way beyond me, but I know enough to know it's within the realm of possibility. Because they're already going there—creating images without actually making them, just as you create them in a dream."

EXPLORING THE EFFECTS FRONTIERS WITH DENNIS MUREN

The visual effects career of Dennis Muren, from his role as second visual effects cameraman on *Star Wars* to his acceptance of his eighth Academy Award as visual effects supervisor for the full-motion dinosaur effects of *Jurassic Park*, has been a journey from mastery of traditional crafts to pioneering digital and computer graphics technology. But for Muren the technology of moviemaking is simply part of the process; achieving the final image is the goal of the creative journey.

Question: When did you first become interested in making movies?

Muren: I don't know where it came from, but I've been doing it since I was a kid. I remember looking over and over again at the same movies. I saw *The 7th Voyage of Sinbad* about eight times. It was hard getting my parents to drive me to the theater to see it that many times, but I had to figure out what I was seeing, how an effect was done and how it fit into the whole picture. And then, one of the hardest things I learned was how to view something and imagine part of it changed and how that would affect something. Like, how would it be different if [the stop-motion] character moved at a slightly different speed or turned his head half a second later—how would that affect the audience response to it? And that has nothing to do with how you even get the head to turn at all, which is something you maybe had to deal with ten minutes before. It's that capacity—to be able to view [in an] extremely detailed and extremely global [way]—that's one of the most important things an effects supervisor can bring to a project.

Q: What kind of images are you interested in creating?

Muren: I've always liked things that somehow have to do with spectacle and the impossible, where things are defied—gravity is defied, things are out of scale—and there's some sort of artistic sensibility which makes for a dynamic combination.

Q: What are the most important qualities an effects artist needs?

Muren: That ability to see both the details and the global view. That's the hardest thing to learn, and some people never pick it up. You've got to be able to have a grasp of the whole subject because you've got a vision you've worked on with the director, which has to do with an aesthetic response at one tiny moment in a two-hour movie. You've got to know how it all fits together so you can control everything.

Q: What prompted you to explore digital technologies?

Muren: I knew all the traditional tools and how something could be best done traditionally. I just started getting bored with that toward the mid-1980s—I thought we [had] hit a wall. All we were doing was variations on stuff, and it couldn't ever get any better, and digital had always been sort of a promise. But my biggest interest has always been the imagery and the result, not the process. Digital often gives you a better image and result when it's all over with. It's still very difficult to work with, and there are very few people who know how to do it very well, but the result, for me, makes it worth the effort. In CG the motions are separate from the lighting,

Dennis Muren catches up on *Life* (in a cameo role as a mysterious Nazi spy tracking Indiana Jones in *Raiders*) . . .

which is separate from the surface texture, and you can work on any one of those components without having to start all over again—as you would with traditional effects. So, you can choose any number of ways to view a scene, and once you've made up your mind, you can hone in on making the final image pretty much what you want.

Q: You took a year's sabbatical from ILM after *The Abyss* in 1989 to explore computer technology. Could you describe your research?

Muren: The work on *The Abyss* was so astonishing because it offered a possibility of images that could be perfect. I decided I wanted to learn more about computers. I bought a Macintosh and explored the world of digital music, 2-D imagery, and compositing. I bought a scanner and took it completely apart to understand how it worked. My overriding feeling was that it was time to commit to digital and make it work on a larger scale. In some cases you can solve problems on the fly, in a panic. But I don't know if we ever would have made that jump if it had been me working; you can get so buried in the pressures of production that you don't see the forest for the trees.

I felt there was a triangle that had to be completed—the ability to scan in film, manipulate it, and then get it out in a reasonable amount of time and on budget. The computer graphics part of *The Abyss* was so strong it seemed we had to lick the digital part, and that's what I set out to do. I spent a lot of time around the Bay Area, Silicon Valley, and L.A. trying to figure out if it was possible to make this triangle work.

We [the CG team] solved it one at a time. We managed to get some stuff scanned in on our new Kodak CCD scanner. I found out about Solitaire [a film output device used to convert digital images into film] and managed to get an L.A. company to film out one frame of film that I'd managed to input from one of the *Back to the Future* movies. I had a lot of people tell me

the thing would never work, that there'd be an effect called "blooming," in which if you had something white or bright in the shot, it'd bounce around on the inside of the phosphor tube and flash the frame. Well, sure enough, it did flash the frame, but it wasn't enough to make it not work. So it was a matter of it not being perfect but being good enough. And the trade-off was phenomenal because now we had a tool that completed the triangle. It took a lot of persuasion to get people at ILM to realize this is the way we should be going, but we managed to get a Solitaire output device in here [ILM] and our Kodak CCD scanner locked in for *Terminator 2*, which [turned out to be] a real breakthrough film because with the output all figured out we could scan in everything, make all the computer graphics creations and digitally composite everything, then scan out all the completed shots.

Q: You also created the "Mac Squad," which helped introduce some of the other

departments into computer technology using Macintosh computers.

Muren: What the Macs managed to do was get everything out of the sort of rarefied R and D side of ILM into the place where the effects supervisors and the optical guys and others could work on it. We also had them use Photoshop software, which was a very user-friendly tool. We used the Mac squad on *The Rocketeer, Memoirs of an Invisible Man*, and a few other shows where we did some of the opticals digitally on the Macs.

Q: How would you describe your working relationship with the rest of the computer graphics artists?

Muren: In digital I'm working with many people who have four to ten years' worth of experience and have gone through graduate school in computer science. In the half decade since *The Abyss* we've really come together. It's been an education on both sides—for me to learn about the new tools, for them to understand filmmaking. I can bring a fresh viewpoint. I don't have the bias that a lot of computer folks do, who want things to be pure and perfect. In school they were trained to write bulletproof programs that could work perfectly over and over again. But in movies we're making one shot, and if a shot only gets 90 percent successful, then I'm all for using a painting software or other program to finish the shot off.

Q: Could you describe the complexities of digital effects?

Muren: It's like the very nature of writing software—it's almost unlimited what you can write and the degree of complexity. That's one of the big problems—no matter how you solve something, someone will walk in and tell you another way to

... and brainstorms on *Jurassic Park*.

Thumbs up! Muren and company celebrates ILM's *Jurassic* success in "The Pit" (the colorful office of CG artist Steve Williams). Clockwise from left: Muren, Mark Dippé, Eric Armstrong, and Steve Williams.

Q: What about the database of images ILM has been creating?

Muren: We have a record of all our finals from films. The digital images don't belong to us—they belong to the particular studio—but there may be some time in the future where they'll want to do a rerelease or a sequel, and we'll have the digital record of a shot and computer graphics models.

Q: Will film become obsolete?

Muren: Eventually. They're still working on getting the digital cameras down. Theaters would be able to use an electronic or laser-light projection system, which is not a new thing; it's been around for a long time. The hard part will be getting the thousands of movie theaters across the country to upgrade and install a new $200,000 projection system.

Q: What about the interest in interactive media and virtual reality? Will these new entertainment technologies replace movies?

Muren: I think people always want to be told a good story with images, and that's the movies. There's going to be another audience that might want to interact with a story or be in a dark ride, but I personally don't think that's something that's going to grow huge. I could be completely wrong, but I think stories and actors are what make movies what they are, and that's what people want to see. Five or ten minutes in a simulator ride might be fun. But instead of seeing a simulation, it might be more fun to just get out on the bay in a sailboat.

make it better. So I didn't want to make it [digital technology] perfect.

Q: There are a lot of concerns about where all this new technology is taking us.

Muren: I think about the technological concerns a little bit, but I think most of it will blow over in the next few years. It's like, so what? We're just now going through something we've never gone through before, which is the clarity of this image that, whether it's on TV or theaters, can be faked. I think part of the mystique of the computer is it gives a false stamp of approval to certain things. But people control all that stuff. Eventually the public will come around to

see the computer for what it's always been: just a tool.

Q: What is the current stage of computer graphics, in terms of what you can do as a filmmaker?

Muren: We're completely free of restrictions of costumes and materials, stop motion or go-motion, of nature holding things up. All those things are out the window, and we can now think more in terms of how they [computer-generated or digitally manipulated images] move. We have this wonderful ability now to make these images move with the freedom of a cartoon. We can figure out the essence of a character and how it would actually be moving.

CHAPTER TWELVE

MYTHIC VISIONS

"*Star Wars* is not a simple morality play;
it has to do with the powers of life as they
are either fulfilled or broken and suppressed
through the action of man."
—Joseph Campbell

As chairman of the governing board of Industrial Light & Magic, Lucas has seen his effects house grow from that first decade, when revenues from the *Star Wars* and Indiana Jones movies sustained the operation, to ILM's present stature as a self-sustaining creative entity.

The recipe for ILM's kind of success seems absurdly simple: "The idea is you put together a team of people who are extremely good and you always have the highest quality people," Lucas said. "ILM is also a company where it has to make enough money to develop the state of the art. So everything has to be done extremely efficiently, and they have to generate enough money year after year to be able to buy new equipment. It's a very capital-intensive business, so that means a huge amount of money is reinvested every year after year after year. And most companies can't do that. In most places someone wants to take money out of a company and put it someplace else, or people can't develop enough resources to do that. It's like anything else: you build up an organization with capital and equipment and all that kind of thing to a high level so it can function."

"When ILM started there was no effects industry—now there's an industry beyond ILM," president Jim Morris observed. "I'm sure there are people who feel ILM has become too corporate since the early *Star Wars* days. Well, we are working on major Hollywood motion pictures, so it's certainly not a free-for-all. But we are still kind of funky when you compare us to a business like IBM or Xerox. I also feel there's a creative freedom here that's actually similar to how it was when the company started. We've got a new breed of young people working here who happen to be computer savvy instead of camera savvy. Dennis Muren actually remarked to me recently that there's a feel at ILM now that's not unlike how it was when the company first started to do *Star Wars*."

ILM's impact can be measured by the effects industry that grew in the wake of the *Star Wars* films. As time has gone by, many ILMers have struck off on their own, setting up their own shops, which include Pixar's features animation, creature and stop-motion expert Phil Tippett's own studio, and Matte World, which was formed by ILM's original matte department group (Craig Barron, Chris Evans, and Michael Pangrazio).

But despite the inevitable personnel departures, the increased competition, and the pendulum swing of fortune that can weaken the strongest of companies, ILM remains the effects industry leader. Morris gives a ballpark estimate that in feature-film billing alone, a typical year will see the movie industry spend $80 to $100 million on visual effects for A pictures and an additional $30 to $40 million for B movies—and ILM will control 50 to 80 percent of the A market.

George Lucas and Silicon Graphic Images president Ed McCracken at the April 7, 1993, press conference announcing their JEDI partnership. The strategic business partnership would seek to maintain ILM's status as effects industry leader with cost-effective image processing, software development, and other digital advances. In remarks published in the *San Francisco Chronicle*, McCracken also observed that the alliance with ILM would "produce a revolution of technology that within ten years will find its way to the $5,000 home computer."

In ILM's second decade the capital, growth, and creative energies have been in computer graphics and image processing. During this period other effects techniques have been used as well: Real model planes have been built, flown, and crashed; actors have zipped themselves into Godzilla monster suits; puppets have been crafted for stop-motion manipulation; miniature set environments have been built; photochemical opticals have wed animated cartoon figures to real-world environments; and blue-screen work has been used to create the elements for composite shots.

But moviemakers have ventured too far into the digital realm to turn back from the possibilities of computer graphics characters, virtual sets, and the filmless future. The ability to composite and image-process seamlessly in the digital realm as well as create such powerful creatures as a watery pseudopod, the shape-changing T-1000 cyborg, and digital dinosaurs has made the computer the most potent tool in the arsenal of effects. The decommissioned Anderson optical printer is testimony to the changes wrought by the new technology.

The wonders of computer graphics and image-processing technologies were also pointing the entire movie industry toward a possible filmless future. Although industry-wide it was still the "film" industry, ILM's digital makeover had gone far toward eliminating the old sprocket mechanics of shooting and projecting film.

"Once we have everything digitally composited, we have to film it back out to negative to turn over to the studio, so they can make their prints and distribute it, but we could just as easily deliver digital data shots on exabyte tape or some kind of disk," Jim Morris explained. "Internally we're a digital company. We still do a lot of stage photography, but we could just as easily use some electronic capture medium. I would imagine we're still a few years away from proven production electronic capture and distribution. While the technology exists, there isn't agreement on which specific standard and technology everybody wants to invest in. There's also a lot of tradition in Hollywood. There are still people cutting on upright Moviolas because they like it that way. There are people who love the physicality of film, and it's difficult for them to get cozy with electronic data. But in my mind it's not about film versus digital. At this point in time digital is a processing and an image-creation medium, and when it's done correctly the results are imperceptible from any other film process."

The ILM logo—the magician in top hat and tux rising through a gear wheel and with a wave of his wand making a lightbulb float and illuminate—now seems a quaint image of that old industrial age of machined tools and optical hardware. Today that magician lurks in the computer as binary data. If called up on a computer monitor that magician would be a three-dimensional figure able to morph, contort, expand, and contract, that floating lightbulb might explode into rainbow rays of light, and that gear wheel might be set spinning in a realistic, virtual environment—any of an endless series of 2-D and 3-D computations, the designs of which would only be limited by an artist's imagination.

The original *Star Wars* opticals sometimes featured only two or three element layers, typically because the inevitable grain buildup of successive layering would take the image further away from first-generation quality. But working in the digital realm for the film's twentieth-anniversary special edition, ILM could layer multiple elements without any generation-loss problems and enjoy virtually unlimited control over CG creations, such as in this shot of the Rebel fleet lining up in formation for the Death Star attack. The final digital composite, which replaced an old optical composite of the same scene, boasts a CG starfield, Death Star, and X-wings. To create the new fighters, texture maps were taken off the original -wing motion-control models, ith ILM effects artists (led by sual effects supervisor John oll) able to exert fine-tuned ntrol over the wing motion and neral animation of the final models.

To George Lucas the new technological tools represent an emancipation from the limits of the physical world. The rub is that a computer is so much useless hardware without an artist's touch on the keyboards. So the artist who might have painted a matte or built a creature or worked a printer now channels his or her creative impulses into crafting images in the digital realm. And as the magicians of old had their workshops where they built their trick props and devices, today's effects magicians utilize specially built software and hardware to create their illusions.

For the practical near future, the evolving capabilities of computers are taking filmmaking beyond the sole province of effects work, according to Lucas. "It's not a matter of special effects, it's a matter of production, and they're both going to merge at some point," he observed. "ILM is now a separate entity, but eventually it'll be absorbed into the process of production and there won't be anything like postproduction visual effects. Companies like ILM will be the producers of the films, or film producers will absorb companies like ILM, but there won't be that much difference between them."

Entering their third decade Lucas and

ILM are coming full circle, moving into production on the next installments of the *Star Wars* saga. When Lucas and ILM were creating the first *Star Wars*, the film seemed a perfect mirror for the real-life quest for space. "*Star Wars* first came out at a time when the space program was a much newer and exciting kind of thing," said Lucas. "But I still think people's imaginations and mythology always has to relate to the great unknown, whatever that is."

Because of *Star Wars* the Lucas enterprises will always be linked to the promises of the space age and faith in the future. A highlight of the 1992 Academy Award ceremonies occurred when Lucas appeared onstage to accept the Irving G. Thalberg award, which Steven Spielberg presented with the words, "Like his creation Luke Skywalker, George Lucas continues to look into the future and dream." The Lucas salute continued as the stage curtains parted and images from outer space appeared on a screen—a taped greeting from the crew of the space shuttle *Atlantis*, who had been in space for a week.

"The imagination and ingenuity that have turned dreams into the reality of space flight are no different than those which turn ideas and inspirations into motion pictures," remarked *Atlantis* flight commander Charlie Bolden in the message from space.

RETURN OF THE FORCE

In 1995, with the twentieth anniversary of *Star Wars* two years away, Lucasfilm announced plans for a trilogy of new *Star Wars* films which would comprise the first three chapters of Lucas's unfolding saga. The prequels, set some forty years prior to the Galactic civil war period of the original films, would be played out against the twilight of the Old Republic, which had benevolently governed for more than a thousand generations before suffering the corrosive rot of political and civic corruption. The new films would essentially be the story of Anakin

George Lucas gathers his *Star Wars* creations in the countryside near Skywalker Ranch. (Photo session for the Japanese ad agency Dentsu, August 1987.)

Skywalker, the Jedi Knight and father of Luke, who would eventually heed his soul's sinister stirrings, embrace the dark side of the Force, and transform himself into Darth Vader.

Ushering in the new *Star Wars* era would be a twentieth-anniversary theatrical rerelease of the film that started it all, to be followed by *The Empire Strikes Back* and *Return of the Jedi*. But unlike the typical rerelease, George Lucas would have his ILM team (comprising some 150 persons) to make over *Star Wars: A New Hope* as a special edition. The ongoing two-year production effort would utilize traditional model work as well as the full arsenal of digital tools, including CG creations, digital matte paintings, and Sabre System image processing. The 100-some shots ILM would prepare for the special edition included CG ships, creatures, and digital stuntmen inserted into the original footage, digital fixes of the old photochemical technology, and some entirely new footage.

The special edition had its roots in the filmmaking realities Lucas had faced back in 1975, the year production on his space saga began in earnest. Back then *The Star Wars* (as the production was first called) had to contend with a tight budget, deadline pressures, the limits of predigital visual effects, and numerous special effects snafus during the tough first-unit shoot in Tunisia and EMI–Elstree Studios in England. Two decades later, Lucas could return to his masterpiece to enhance *New Hope* in ways not possible in those early rough-and-tumble production days.

"It's like a virtual director's cut," laughed TyRuben Ellingson, *New Hope* visual effects art director (along with Mark Moore). "Dennis Muren told me that George really wanted this to be the archival version, the one that went down in history. It's a very romantic notion. In a way, he's adding some missing pieces to the puzzle. The things that are being changed are not frivolous at all but very specific to what George had originally envisioned for the film but wasn't able to do because of budget

and technology. Now we can do it digitally and retain image quality. It's interesting that ILM was created to do *Star Wars* and after all these amazing pictures the company has worked on, the new technology that's being developed is being folded back into the original picture."

But while the 1995 rerelease announcement was generating some anticipatory excitement among the moviegoing public, the mood was not celebratory behind the scenes at Lucasfilm and Twentieth Century-Fox. Toward the end of 1994, Fox executives had been hit with a shocker: The original *Star Wars* negative, the template from which thousands of pristine rerelease theatrical prints would be struck, was discovered to be in such a deteriorated state it would be impossible to release in theaters. The once-vibrant color had faded away (10–15% overall, according to Leon Briggs, a former veteran of the Disney lab who had worked on such restoration projects as *Fantasia* and *Snow White* and was called in to help rescue *Star Wars*), and dirt embedded in the six reels of negatives had produced scratches and pit marks that would appear larger than life when projected onto the big screen. "It was my determination that all the backing didn't get washed off originally and became stuck onto the negative during the final solution stage [of the developing process]," noted Briggs.

The color-fade problem was particularly troublesome as the original *Star Wars* negative had been stored, along with thousands of other films from all the major studios, in Kansas, far from the potential earthquake catastrophes in Los Angeles. Out in the heartland the studios had their vaults hundreds of feet underground, in the miles of man-made caverns dug out by long-gone salt miners. Besides its impregnable nature, the subterranean vault had another main advantage: it held a constant 50–53 degrees, the optimum temperature for preventing the irrevocable fading of original color photography. *Star Wars*, however, had been produced during a decade of increased location shoots, staged in all kinds of lighting and weather conditions, that demanded fast new film stocks to be developed. One of those color stocks, known as Color Reversal Intermediate (CRI) #5249, was so prone to fading that Kodak discontinued making it in the early eighties. Unfortunately, sixty-two different shots in *Star Wars* had been made utilizing the CRI stock.

In 1994, Ted Gagliano, Twentieth Century-Fox senior vice president for feature post-production, had first seen a print struck off the original negative at DeLuxe Labs in L.A., and had soon thereafter arranged a screening at Fox for Lucasfilm's Rick McCallum and Tom Christopher. Upon returning to Skywalker Ranch McCallum gave a full report on the original negative problem, but Lucas had already had a premonition about the quality of the film. "Originally the challenge was getting the film back to the glory of what it was," said McCallum, "but by the summer of '94 George said, 'I'm worried about the negative because every print we get is bad.' That's when we got really scared about the presentation of this film."

"When I had first seen the print at De-Luxe, I was shocked," Gagliano recalled. "I was a Marin [County] high school student when I first saw *Star Wars* and it had been so spectacular—it was the reason I ultimately went into the movie business. But after seeing the dirt and the problem of fading it didn't have the same feeling. It looked like an old movie. At the ILM screening I had prepared everybody for what they were going to see, and afterward Lucas said to me: 'Well, the speech was worse than the viewing.' I think he was disappointed but slightly relieved. He could tell it was fixable. The challenge was to integrate the new [special edition] footage into a good negative."

The actual restoration work would be undertaken by a team comprising Lucasfilm (with Tom Christopher as editor-in-charge) and Twentieth Century-Fox, Pacific Title (for recompositing of opticals), YCM Labs (to

provide the color timings), and film restoration consultant Leon Briggs (who helped supervise the overall process, including the cleaning of the original negative).

Although a master interpositive (IP; a positive image made from an original negative) had been made in 1985 for the purpose of video releases (including a 1993 THX laser disc release of the *Star Wars* trilogy and a boxed THX video set released two years later), making prints entirely off IPs wouldn't provide the highest-generation release print. No pristine prints befitting a grand anniversary release existed either—any available prints had suffered their own scratches and general damage from the wear and tear of shipping and exhibition. Even if an acceptable print was available, a negative from a print would still fail to produce the best possible big-screen visuals. "The original negative is the best, which was Lucas's whole scheme: to make it look as good as it possibly could," noted Pacific Title optical supervisor Chris Bushman.

"We could only go back to the original negative," summed up Rick McCallum. "It's our source, the only life-force we have."

RESTORING *NEW HOPE*

Although the restoration battle plan would utilize scanning technology to make needed repairs in the digital realm, the prohibitive costs of doing the entire negative that way (many millions of dollars) led to a strategy of utilizing master elements, such as the IP, to restore the original negative. A major part of the restoration process was cleaning off the dirt in a special 100 degree–plus bath solution (although two of the four film stocks that comprised the original negative couldn't be subjected to those temperatures and had to be addressed separately). "After selectively cleansing the negative they'd remove and send us those sections of the original negative for which we were doing the special edition work," explained *New Hope* visual effects producer Tom Kennedy. "We'd scan it and

Left: This explosion of an X-wing during the fateful battle along the Death Star trench was one of six explosions that underwent a digital fix for the special edition rerelease. Originally the model pyro had been shot against blue screen and the explosion matte had not been completely extracted in the final composite. By scanning in the original negatives, ILM was able to create a digital composite and fully extract the matte for a seamless "explosion fix."

Below: Another special edition explosion fix along the battle zone of the Death Star trench. Here R2-D2, fitted into the exterior shell of Luke Skywalker's X-wing, takes a hit of laserfire from Darth Vader's pursuing TIE fighter.

match it to the new print as we did our work. For parts of the film that were too damaged we went back to the interpositive struck from the original negative, which was the closest we could get to the original negative."

Part of the problem with *Star Wars*, faced by both the restoration and the special edition teams, would be that the film encompassed many different photographic styles, from location and soundstage work to complex motion-control shots and simple opticals, with the four film stocks scattered throughout. While the in-camera, live-action, and special effects work was cut in as original negative, all the opticals, rephotographed using old optical printers, were dupe negatives.

Thankfully, the original negatives that composed the final composite elements had been safely stored at the Lucasfilm archives. In a ironic touch, the old optical printer technology used to create *Star Wars* but abandoned years later in ILM's conversion to digital technology would be utilized again to restore the many wipes, the skip frames, and the rest of what Pacific Title vice president Phillip Feiner called "the bread and butter opticals." Pacific Title's work involved taking the original elements from Lucasfilm and recompositing them, utilizing the company's eleven state-of-

the-art optical printers. With modern lenses and the latest, best Kodak film stocks, the old-fashioned printer technology delivered new comps boasting "a boost in resolution and color saturation," according to Feiner.

The restoration team also had recourse to such master elements as the YCM (yellow-cyan-magenta) separation masters, a process that essentially uses primary-color light sources to convert color film into three separate black-and-white film records for each reel. The black-and-white separations, with their metallic silver composition, aren't prone to the fading fate of original color dyes. "You

Right: One of the early *Star Wars* sequences had four Imperial stormtroopers searching the sand dunes of Tatooine and discovering the escape pod that had delivered R2-D2 and C-3PO to the desert planet. Originally shot in the arid spaces of Tunisia, the scene was plagued by both the limits of technology and special effects problems (such as a failed creature effect standing, still as a statue, on a distant sand dune). The special edition contains snippets from the original scene, including some of the Tunisian sands and two stormtroopers, but the sequence itself was expanded with new plates and stormtroopers shot in the desert outside Yuma, Arizona. In the foreground of the photo at right, ILMer Tom Kennedy sets up the electric transit surveying equipment—the same tool first used by supervisor Scott Squires during the location work on *Dragonheart*—that provided the background plate measurements necessary for later match-moving of computer-generated elements. (The special edition filming was documented for director Ben Burtt's *Special Effects* Imax film by an Imax camera crew hidden from view.)

Bottom right: The photo-realistic, dinosaurlike dewback, which would roam in the desert spaces of Tatooine and the crowded streets of Mos Eisley, first took form as a sculpture, and was further developed with texture studies, such as this Terryl Whitlatch concept painting.

know the original negative will fade, so you can turn to the separation masters; it's the record of what it'll look like and it'll last forever," explained Gagliano. "So the negative you make off your YCMs should be just as good as the original negative."

Also coming to the rescue were two prints done in the vibrant colors of the "three-strip" Technicolor process, which had been introduced in 1932 but had become an almost lost art soon after the making of *Star Wars*. One of the prints that had used this venerable process had come from George Lucas himself. "George had a private [Technicolor] print in the basement of his home," Gagliano noted. "For the color timing he told us to go for that look: 'That's the *Star Wars* I made,' he told us."

At the end of more than a full year of restoration work, the team had a renewed appreciation for what Gagliano called the "fragile medium" of film. In many ways the mere act of developing exposed film was one of moviemaking's greatest magic acts. "I could send a film to five or six different labs and it'd come back as totally different images; that's how bizarre, and magical, this film process is," McCallum noted. "Film has been proven to be inherently unstable, like any chemical process. It's alchemy, the temperature of the bath. It comes with intense feelings. The saga

of what happened to the *Star Wars* negative is you've got this process that's so fundamentally incomprehensible for us to deal with—the alchemy of what happened to these stocks."

VIRTUAL CUTS

In late 1993, before the *New Hope* original negative problems had been discovered, ILM's special edition work commenced with a brainstorming session between Dennis Muren (who along with John Knoll, Joseph Letteri, Alex Seiden, and Steve Williams supervised the project) and art director TyRuben Ellingson.

Lucas's major interests had been in expanding the desert town of Mos Eisley and

adding original footage of a Jabba-the-Hutt-confronting-Han-Solo scene that had been dropped from the original film. The special edition was also an opportunity for *Star Wars* veteran Dennis Muren to address a slate of fifteen to twenty shots that had always troubled him. "I suggested to George that we expand the vision and he was open to it," Muren recalled. "Motion issues, particularly in the space battle scenes, were my main concerns. Then Tom Kennedy and others contributed their own ideas for redoing shots."

The initial art direction stage began with Muren, using a *Star Wars* videotape of the film as a guide, describing the proposed shots as Ellingson dashed off a quick succession of storyboards. "Dennis told me I had fifteen seconds a board to get down the rough concepts," Ellingson recalled. "He was making a point that *Star Wars* was first done with a young, savvy crew and things had happened really quickly. By the end we had twenty-some numbered storyboards that could start dialogue about how the shots were going to be done."

Soon after, an available *Star Wars* print was screened at ILM's main screening room with Lucas pointing out the special edition changes to Muren, Ellingson, and Ned Gorman (who would share visual effects production credit with Tom Kennedy). "George might say, 'Mos Eisley wasn't big enough; I want to make it more of an urban center with some spaceships in the sky and more buildings visible,'" Ellingson explained. "In certain shots it would be adding a new creature, in others it would be an entirely new shot that would intercut with the existing sequence. I was amazed at how quickly George could articulate what he wanted. Within a twenty-minute period I had enough information to do all the artwork that was subsequently approved."

On the creative side there were concerns that ILM's new generation of tech-driven cybersurfers wouldn't be grounded in the material reality of the *Star Wars* universe. "In the virtual world you don't have to worry about materials, or drilling holes and putting

Stormtroopers scan the Tatooine sands in this frame from a Yuma sequence. Besides the new stormtroopers (in foreground), the shot was enlivened with a CG Imperial landing craft coasting low on the horizon and a synthetic trooper and dewback moving along the dunes.

Luke jets along the ground in his landspeeder, a scene originally accomplished by driving the craft with a tricycle rig, a mirror attached to the bottom to reflect the sandy ground (providing the illusion of being suspended in midair), and an animated shadow. It was a nice bit of magic in its day, but to sell the shot to modern audiences, ILM digitally freshened it up, erasing any telltale evidence of the suspended mirror and providing a softer edge to the animated shadow effect to better blend it into the plate.

things together, but everything about the first *Star Wars* was very much about putting things together in the real world," Ellingson noted. "For the special edition I'd done some concept sketches for this low-rider motorcycle that flies through Mos Eisley, and the CG modelers working on it created something that looked soft and interesting, but it didn't feel like it came from the *Star Wars* universe. So I went out and got a box filled with shower heads and threaded pipes and stuff and showed them: 'Look, this is the kind of stuff the *Star Wars* universe was made out of—very mechanical and real-world. You can't let your CG aesthetic get in the way of that.'"

A key to the special edition work would be that the new CG elements not jump off the screen in contrast to the original footage. ILM had to contend with such artifacts of the bygone optics age as a diffusion look created by panty hose stretched over camera lenses (for the bright wastes of the Tatooine sand dunes). "The challenge was to seamlessly put our synthetic images into the image space from the original footage—to enhance and not change," explained CG supervisor John Berton. "Not only were we working with twenty-year-old footage, but a lot of the shots chosen for improvement were not VistaVision.

There was a lot of work in funky 35mm four-perf with filters and artifacts that required us to write special image-processing software to duplicate the look of the original photography. It was a lot more complicated than just dropping in a CG image."

A particularly challenging shot in the Mos Eisley portion of the film was a sequence in which the droids observe stormtroopers conducting a search for Obi-Wan and Luke. For the special edition the scene would be augmented with two CG dewbacks, including a synthetic stormtrooper dismounting from one of the creatures. The challenge in integrating the new footage was that the original Mos Eisley street scene filmed in Tunisia had not only been photographed in four-perf but with what Berton recalled as a "very wild" camera move. Although the film's original camera notes were available (indicating that the particular shot had been made from a truck platform), the CG crew still had to figure out whether the actual camera move had been a pan, zoom, or dolly.

"That was a major hurdle, to take a twenty-year-old film and rebuild the camera moves to allow us to put in the CG elements," Berton said in summing up the match-move challenges. "Computers work well with smooth curves, but real cameras have vibrations and minute adjustments. The new cameras are steadier, and normally we'll take measurements [at background plate shoots]. Sel Eddy and Terry Chostner, who handled the camera match-moves on the special edition, did a tremendous job allowing our virtual camera to match the real camera."

A major shot involving both original footage and new, computer-generated elements was the excised scene of crime lord Jabba the Hutt confronting Han Solo over a botched smuggling operation the cocky pilot had undertaken for Hutt. The scene, set in the Mos Eisley docking bay where Solo's *Millennium Falcon* was stored, had been scripted to feature Hutt as "a fat, sluglike creature with eyes on extended feelers and a huge ugly mouth."

The production couldn't physically create that fearsome creation, and scenes shot with a human actor proved woefully inadequate to the image of a vicious crime lord. But the missing Jabba scene had always been troublesome. After all, Solo's run-in with the crime lord would be a major plot point in the trilo-gy, with bounty hunter Boba Fett taking Solo, encased in a living prison of carbonite by Darth Vader, to the crime lord's lair at the conclusion of *The Empire Strikes Back*. By the third film a gargantuan, sluglike Jabba would finally appear, created as a full-scale, foam latex, animatronic creation. With the digital advances available to the special edition team, it was finally possible to take the original docking bay footage and replace the actor with a CG Jabba.

"Jabba wasn't finally designed until the third film, so now you're seeing the result of that whole period of time retro'd back in," art director Ellingson noted. "Every attempt was made to make Jabba look like the same character, although a little younger. You see him move faster and under the power of his undulating organs, which is amazing because it takes this kind of computer technology to deliver that kind of freedom.

For many ILMers the restoration and special edition work was an opportunity for a little time traveling back to a vanished optical age. It also had been a more primitive era for animatronics and physical effects.

On the streets of Mos Eisley, Imperial stormtroopers conduct a search for Obi-Wan and Luke as the worried droids look on. This shot is as it appeared in the initial release, but has been enlivened with the addition of two CG dewbacks and the completely synthetic stormtrooper dismounting at left. "This scene was shot in Tunisia in four-perf," explained visual effects producer Tom Kennedy. "It was never imagined that it would be a visual effects shot." Integrating in the new elements required matching the original lighting scheme and the yellow-hued color timing, as well as old and virtual camera moves.

"Nothing worked" was how Rick McCallum explained the English crew's first-unit work. "It was sort of a missing link period of film history in England, and George entered into that filmmaking landscape at the worst possible time. To be fair, [in England] there wasn't a lot of experience with that kind of science fiction movie. Nobody was doing robots. Just to get R2-D2 to move was like a miracle. The radio controls were constantly failing, so there were cables pulling R2-D2 through the scenes, which had to be painted out later [with garbage mattes or some other optical technique]."

"In *Star Wars* there were a tremendous amount of opticals just to make the practical effects work," added Tom Kennedy. "Clever techniques like step printing and jump cutting—things we take for granted today because of the ease of digital painting and rotoscoping. Back then the opticals were obviously painful. The first film was more matte

paintings and motion control and blue screen in its early days. Then there's this huge, fast step forward in the art of rotoscoping and rig removal on *Empire* and *Jedi*."

Although the restoration and special edition work on *New Hope* was initiated to finally accomplish the director's original vision, the project was also approached as "a dress rehearsal for building the *Star Wars* prequels," according to CG supervisor Berton.

"By *Return of the Jedi*, George had tapped out, in a way, the ability to create a universe with the density he wanted," Berton noted. "Of course, you don't want to fall into the trap of the technology driving your vision. It's easy for people to look at CG dinosaurs and shape changers and virtual reality, but Lucas always has storytelling at the heart of any film he wants to make. Now we have the technology [to accomplish it]. The special edition work has provided us with information on how to make ourselves more efficient for the next *Star Wars* films. I know there's a lot of

Below: The Rebel armada, final special edition composite, produced by John Knoll on a Mac. The scene had originally been envisioned by George Lucas as one shot, with a 180° camera move following the armada's approach, but it proved too complicated for the motion control technology of the day and was realized as two cuts. In the digital realm, utilizing CG ships, ILM could create Lucas's original one shot composition.

An Imperial TIE fighter swoops down on a speeding X-wing during the Death Star trench battle sequence. This and other trench shots required scanning and recompositing of the film's original VistaVision elements.

talk for the next trilogy about digital creatures and aliens that can move with total freedom and not have the constraints of puppets or a guy in a suit, and the sweeping grandeur of a total environment. That's possible now. One such special edition shot was a vista-shot of Mos Eisley seen as Luke's Landspeeder enters the city. Yusei Uesugi built this entire city in 3-D and painted on top of it, all completely CG. This gives us the digital back lot, an interactive digital set in which you can put real actors. This kind of shot really stretches our muscles. This is a harbinger for the future."

It's appropriate that the next *Star Wars* chapters will not only mark the beginnings of ILM's third decade but take audiences worldwide into the new millennium. The creative force of ILM, with both a century's worth of special effects tradition and a decade of discoveries in the digital realm behind it, will create those mythic visions, will once again transport audiences into the mystery of space and back to that story of "a long time ago in a galaxy far, far away."

"There's an anticipation of the new *Star Wars* trilogy, that we'll see a whole other evolution and a whole new set of technical changes," said visual effects supervisor Mark Dippé, who along with ILMer Steve Williams was hailed as among the "shock troops of digital Hollywood" by *Premiere* magazine (January 1996). Dippé had been living in Los Angeles when *Star Wars* was unleashed and he recalled a rock concert–like energy crackling through the Westwood area theater where he first saw the film. "*Star Wars* was a visual revelation. It was unbelievable how they achieved that dynamic camera movement. Seeing it was like, 'Who the hell is this guy George Lucas?' The film just stood apart. It still does. I think George Lucas's films had a big influence on changing the process and vocabulary of filmmaking. The legacy of *Star Wars* is that at ILM we get a chance to work on creating things that haven't been seen before, and we also create the technology to do it."

A few hardy veterans of that first *Star Wars* voyage still work at ILM. The following are reflections from those who were there.

STEVE GAWLEY

(model maker on *Star Wars*, currently an ILM model shop project supervisor): "On *Star Wars* everyone was multitalented, not so specialized. We were young, enthusiastic, and making these neat spaceships. I started out doing three-view drawings of spaceships, and Joe Johnston would make pattern drawings for the model shop to build from. I then did the detailing of the models after head model maker Grant McCune and his guys had done the basic shapes. Across the street from our facility was this government surplus store, and we'd go buy things we needed, pennies to the dollar. The fans we used to cool the lighting system on the *Millennium Falcon* were brand-new but bought from the government surplus.

"There was a bit of panic a few times. One time we had finished the *Millennium Falcon* model, and word came back from England, where they were shooting the first-unit work, that George didn't like it, that we'd have to build a new spaceship. It affected the live action because they'd need our model and any full-scale ship to match. It took a few weeks, with all hands on deck, but we came up with a new design. The original *Millennium Falcon* model actually became Princess Leia's ship—the Rebel Blockade Runner that is being chased by the Star Destroyer in the opening scene.

"I remember thinking the film might be special during a screening of three trailers for the film we had about five months before the release. Our screening room was furnished in early Goodwill, with old furniture and a mattress with springs coming out of it. It was called the screening room only because it had a screen and a projector. One trailer I really liked had dark space and this light in the distance that kept coming at you until you could see it was the title: *Star Wars*. Three days before the film's general release, we had a cast and crew screening in L.A., and it was wild. I'd worked on the film about a year and a half, but when we wrapped we all thought it was over. Now I've been with ILM pretty much straight through twenty years. In that time ILM has won fourteen Academy Awards and I've worked on models for ten of those films.

"I also got a chance to be in the *Star Tours* ride at Disneyland, which was neat because all our model work is up on the screen. I play the Red Leader who comes on the video view screen after the ship has gone into hyperdrive and landed in this battle. I'd worked in projects, and everybody around me had got the chance to do some fun bits in the movies—Lorne Peterson had done one, and Joe Johnston—but up until then you couldn't have a beard and be bald. So I said, 'Hey, guys, the Red Leader guy has a helmet and a chin strap, so let me have a chance!' I even have some speaking lines: '*Star Tours*, do you realize you're in a battle zone? We'll get you out of here!' There are Disneylands in like three corners of the world, so every minute of the day that thing is playing. It was quite a ride."

BRUCE NICHOLSON

(optical camera assisant on *Star Wars*, currently an ILM visual effects supervisor): "When George Lucas was finished with *Star Wars*'s principal photography in England and got back to L.A., the effects weren't up to speed. Only three or four shots had been completed out of hundreds [an estimated 984 scenes involved optical composites]. He later told me [that] his heart sank at the time, it was so disheartening. I think he got physically ill. He thought, 'Oh my God, what have I created?' Fortunately, things picked up. I don't know all the behind-the-scenes permutations, but I think people realized, 'We better get our asses in gear or we're out of here!' It was about that time that they went to night crews, with people like Ken Ralston and Dennis Muren as part of the effort to get things on track, and the studio brought in George Mather as production manager who helped get the work flow moving. When I came on, [only] thirty shots had been done, so we had a huge way to go.

"One of the challenges was that at the time effects films like *Earthquake* and such were done with tried-and-true, old-time effects people. We had a very hang-loose atmosphere—we were a bunch of hippies, really—but highly motivated. *Star Wars* was so technically ambitious we *had* to invent techniques. We had to build an effects facility from scratch and design camera systems. A lot of the technology was new, applying computer technology to our photographic systems. It was a brand-new ball game, and the price we paid was we didn't get much work done in the beginning. But there was a tremendous amount of innovation. A lot of it came out of that rebellious, cavalier attitude."

DENNIS MUREN

(second cameraman on *Star Wars*, currently ILM senior visual effects supervisor): "Around 1975 there were three big effects films that had been released: *Earthquake*, *The Towering Inferno*, and *Island at the Top of the World*. I'd heard they were really hard to work on, with big committees, and you had [just] one job; it didn't seem like much fun. I was ready to get out of the film business, to find some other way to earn a living, when I got the opportunity to work on *Star Wars*. That film was sort of my last chance to do something. What might

have been a big, boring Hollywood studio film instead turned out to be this neat little group of whiz kids working with a terrific director who had a vision. It gave me a new faith in films: that big features didn't need massive committees to get made.

"A lot of people who come to work here at ILM are incredibly starry-eyed; they're here because of the *Star Wars* series, although now we're also getting people here because of the later work, such as *T2* and *Jurassic*. I don't see the *Star Wars* trilogy quite the same way [as they do] because they were a tremendous amount of work. But that first film was really an education in being able to understand the palette of the big screen, the biggest canvas there is. Fortunately, because of John Dykstra and everyone else on the production who set it up, we were free to do everything, which was so foreign to Hollywood. I could light and shoot my own shot, and even paint a model a little bit if it needed it. It wasn't that much different from what I did as a kid."

LORNE PETERSON

(model maker on *Star Wars* and chief model maker on *The Empire Strikes Back*, currently an ILM model shop project supervisor): "For the Rebel base George wanted the look of a civilization buried in the jungle. He'd looked at *National Geographic* pictures of the pyramid of Tikal in the Guatemalan jungle and wanted to send a crew down there to get shots of this Rebel guard at the top of the pyramid, with the *Millennium Falcon* composited in later. Fox tried to get George to shoot at the jungle ride in Disneyland, but he didn't want that, so they sent Richard Edlund, Dick Alexander, and myself down to Guatemala. Nowadays if they wanted to go to Tikal, they'd send twenty to thirty people. But back then the studio didn't seem to have a lot of faith in the film. We were all pretty young, so we had this feeling of man against the machine.

"The Rebel guard you see in the film is me; I'm standing at the top edge of this three-hundred-foot-tall pyramid. Because we didn't take along a lot of props, I'm looking through field glasses that I made with a couple of light meters tied together with gaffer tape. Pretty funky. The pyramid was more than forty-five degrees, which is steeper than Giza, with steps that each went up twelve inches, with the flat spot being only six inches—not a lot of room; if you slipped, you'd go all the way down. I was selected to be the Rebel guard because I was the only one of us three who didn't have kids. At the pyramid's top was this building where, in the ancient days, the priest would come out. This was where they would cut out the heart of a human sacrifice, then throw the body down the steps.

"We flew down to Guatemala in March. The film was to be released that summer, so it was at the tail end of the production. We drove out to Tikal in this old Volkswagen bus with the photographic equipment we'd brought along in thirteen to fourteen aluminium boxes, each measuring two feet by two feet by eighteen inches. We hired four natives to help us drag this equipment with ropes to the top of the pyramid. Guys with machetes had to hack a way up for us because the old steps were just covered with jungle. The space at the top was twenty feet by twenty feet, with the priest's stone hut twelve feet by twelve feet with this six-by-eight-foot opening. At night we'd store the equipment in the priest's hut. We paid a native to stay up there in the priest's place, armed with a pistol and shotgun to guard the equipment while we slept down at the bottom in these grass-covered huts.

"The sky was supposed to be clear in the shot, but because the jungle is so steamy the sun would be rising out of this foggy haze. We were there a week because the sun wouldn't cooperate. Eventually we got as good a shot as we were going to get. Nowadays they'd just do the clear sky digitally. Richard and Dick would be set up at the priest's hut, shooting from behind me. We'd stay up there the whole day, from dawn to dusk, and never move from one spot, which is a very unusual, meditative thing. Every now and then I'd hear tourists coming through the jungle below. When they'd come by I'd be up there with my Rebel uniform and this big helmet and visor on and I'd shout out: 'Welcome to Pyramid Number Three, Temple of the Gods!' These tourists would be blinking, unbelieving, looking up like, 'Are you really there?'"

PAUL HUSTON (model maker on *Star Wars*, currently an ILM matte artist): "I got to work on *Star Wars* because one of my teachers at the University of Colorado architectural school, James Shourt, knew John Dykstra and recommended me to him. I was told that if I went to L.A. I could get a job on this show gluing plastic parts on spaceship models. At the time ILM was desperate for anyone they could get. They were even putting ads for model makers in the *Los Angeles Times*. I started as a storyboard artist, went to doing model making, and then helped Doug Smith shoot the models onstage.

"At the beginning we'd been set up as this kind of experimental unit by Twentieth Century-Fox and we were nonunion, with John Dykstra and his guys hired as independent contractors. There was all kinds of hearsay because of this—there was one rumor that there'd been a firebombing threat against us, which was scary. We were also hearing rumors that Fox was going to shut down the movie completely because of their uncertainty over the film. We'd been running almost a year and into a million dollars, but no shots had been finaled. The studio didn't realize the long start-up time needed to get all the machinery in place and running.

"Part of the initial problem surrounding the union issue was that the work we were doing, such as the motion-control photography, didn't exist before; it was like a whole new category. Also, studio craftsmen and guilds traditionally worked with such materials as wood, plaster, and steel. But we, and other model makers at the time, were getting into machining aluminium and experimenting with urethane, epoxies, and other kinds of plastics and silicone and injection molding. About six months into *Star Wars*, ILM did go union and the studio had to abide by it. Once the union question, which had been out of our control, was worked out, the tensions seemed to ease up. Then it became a question of getting the elements shot on time.

"The effect that movie had on people still amazes me. I've traveled around the world and seen the impact it's had. Once, I was in Sri Lanka for *Indiana Jones and the Temple of Doom*, shooting reference photos for the matte and model shop. I was going through this village and I met this family who existed by finding outcroppings of rock and breaking them down to gravel. The men would break the large rocks into small boulders, various family members broke these into smaller pieces and the grandmother sat under a tent at the side of the road breaking them down further to gravel size. I stopped to talk to them and I asked them about *Star Wars*. [In] India and Sri Lanka it's cheap to go to a show, so they do see a lot of films over there. When they found out I'd worked on the film, there was just this outpouring of warmth and enthusiasm. Then they brought their friends from the village around, telling them, 'He worked on *Star Wars*!' About the same time I was also working in the Ivory Coast, and I met these English-speaking refugees from Ghana who were nearly illiterate, disadvantaged, but as familiar with *Star Wars* as anybody.

"Maybe people around the world just enjoyed the spectacle of it, but there have been a lot of those kinds of movies made that didn't inspire the same kind of passion. I think George would say the film touches people at different levels of meaning—everyone's life struggle. My take on it is that most people around the world are oppressed by large, seemingly evil, impersonal forces and *Star Wars* is a rebellion picture, about the little guy winning out over the cruel powers that be. It stirred people's hearts."

ILM FILMOGRAPHY
AND ATTRACTIONS

Highlights and insights of two decades of visual effects achievements.

1977

STAR WARS

(Twentieth Century-Fox/Lucasfilm Ltd.)
WINNER OF ACADEMY AWARD,
BEST VISUAL EFFECTS

The visionary film that started it all, ushering in the effects era with such innovations as computerized motion-control technology.

1980

THE EMPIRE STRIKES BACK

(Twentieth Century-Fox/Lucasfilm Ltd.)
WINNER OF ACADEMY AWARD,
BEST VISUAL EFFECTS

"Getting the choreography of the space battles and asteroid sequence to be both exciting and clearly understood was very gratifying," notes Ken Ralston, then an effects cameraman.

1981

RAIDERS OF THE LOST ARK

(Paramount/Lucasfilm Ltd.)
WINNER OF ACADEMY AWARD,
BEST VISUAL EFFECTS

A highlight of this effects-filled film was the supernatural firepower unleashed during the climactic opening of the Ark.

DRAGONSLAYER

(Paramount)
ACADEMY AWARD NOMINATION,
BEST VISUAL EFFECTS

ILM refined the art of stop motion on this film with go-motion, which allowed motion-controlled devices to manipulate a puppet during exposure, allowing for realistic motion-blur.

1982

POLTERGEIST

(MGM/UA)
ACADEMY AWARD NOMINATION,
BEST VISUAL EFFECTS
WINNER OF BRITISH ACADEMY AWARD,
BEST VISUAL EFFECTS

The haunting atmosphere of this film was created with creatures, animation effects, and an imploding-house effect.

STAR TREK II: THE WRATH OF KHAN

(Paramount)

The computer-generated "Genesis Effect" sequence was the first all-digital CG sequence ever in a feature film.

E.T. THE EXTRA-TERRESTRIAL

(Universal)
WINNER OF ACADEMY AWARD,
BEST VISUAL EFFECTS

Of all ILM's work on this, one of the most successful films ever, one image stands out as an iconic movie image: the composite shot of Elliot and E.T. riding a flying bicycle past a full moon.

1983

RETURN OF THE JEDI

(Twentieth Century-Fox/Lucasfilm Ltd.)
WINNER OF ACADEMY AWARD,
BEST VISUAL EFFECTS
WINNER OF BRITISH ACADEMY AWARD,
BEST VISUAL EFFECTS

One of the most complex effects films of all time. In every respect it technically topped the work of the previous two films in the trilogy. Instead of the 50 and 100 models used for *Star Wars* and *Empire*, 150 models were utilized in *Jedi*. The dozens of creatures created by ILM ran the gamut from rod puppets and suits to animatronic creations and stop-motion puppets. And whereas a *Star Wars* optical shot might have thirty to forty separate elements, *Jedi* shots often required between twenty and eighty, with one space battle scene requiring more than three hundred separate elements.

1984

INDIANA JONES AND THE TEMPLE OF DOOM

(Paramount/ Lucasfilm Ltd.)
WINNER OF ACADEMY AWARD,

BEST VISUAL EFFECTS
WINNER OF BRITISH ACADEMY AWARD,
BEST VISUAL EFFECTS

For the film's famed mine-chase sequence, a fifty-foot miniature track was created and a mine car with puppets of Indy and friends was painstakingly moved with stop-motion animation and filmed with a special custom-built Nikon camera.

STAR TREK III: THE SEARCH FOR SPOCK

(Paramount)

In this third chapter in the *Star Trek* saga, ILM executed a major storypoint: the crash and destruction of the Starship *Enterprise*. The effect utilized the scale model built for the first film. It then would be resurrected, with minor alterations, for the next installment in the series.

THE NEVERENDING STORY

(Bavaria Studios)

For this Wolfgang Petersen production, ILM contributed matte paintings of an enchanted city and optically composited models and puppet elements that had been shot in Germany.

THE EWOK ADVENTURE

(Twentieth Century-Fox Television/ Lucasfilm Ltd.)
WINNER OF EMMY, BEST VISUAL EFFECTS

Among other effects, ILM's matte department produced an otherworldly latent-image matte painting of an Ewok caravan.

STARMAN

(Columbia)

A chrome spaceship created by matte painter Frank Ordaz was a centerpiece effect for this film.

THE GOONIES

(Warner Bros./Amblin)

A detailed galleon ship model was the ILM highlight on this production.

COCOON

(Twentieth Century-Fox)
WINNER OF ACADEMY AWARD,
BEST VISUAL EFFECTS

This show required the creation of a flying saucer and aliens, but what visual effects supervisor Ken Ralston most remembers is the joy of working with such veteran performers as Don Ameche, Hume Cronyn, and Jessica Tandy.

BACK TO THE FUTURE

(Universal/Amblin)
BRITISH ACADEMY AWARD NOMINATION,
BEST VISUAL EFFECTS

Getting the time-traveling DeLorean to lift up and fly was ILM's major achievement in this first installment of the popular series.

EXPLORERS

(Paramount)

For a shot of kids flying through clouds, ILM composited blue-screen footage of the children with a cotton-cloud effect.

MISHIMA

(Warner Bros.)

Although ILM only contributed titles to this biographical film, these titles effectively captured the ethos of the famed Japanese writer who committed ritual suicide in 1970. "We used a squeegee bottle that squirted ink on paper, which we composited with the title lettering, so it looked like a cut with bleeding," said effects cameraman Bruce Walters.

AMAZING STORIES

(Universal Television/Amblin)

Paul Huston and the matte department provided opening and closing background effects that featured a forced-perspective miniature.

EWOKS: THE BATTLE FOR ENDOR

(Twentieth Century-Fox Television/Lucasfilm Ltd.)
WINNER OF EMMY, BEST VISUAL EFFECTS

A forbidding castle was created with such traditional techniques as paintings and an in-camera matte shot.

YOUNG SHERLOCK HOLMES

(Paramount/Amblin)
ACADEMY AWARD NOMINATION,
BEST VISUAL EFFECTS

The knight that magically bursts from a stained-glass window was the first feature-film CG character.

ENEMY MINE

(Twentieth Century-Fox)

Matte paintings helped produce visions of an alien world; one work included a composite of a bright sun element.

OUT OF AFRICA

(Universal)

ILM's shot of a miniature train moving across a landscape was a departure from its traditional fantasy fare and so realistic it qualifies as an "invisible effect."

GENERAL CINEMA TRAILER

(General Cinema Corp.)

The first theatrical trailer ILM created entirely on an animation stand instead of a stage camera.

HOWARD THE DUCK

(Universal)

A highlight of this Lucasfilm production was the abundant animation department effects.

CAPTAIN EO

(Disney)

ILM had to achieve its visual effects magic in a 3-D, 70mm film format. "Combining live action, miniatures, animation, and matte paintings in 3-D is treacherous because you have to monitor the scale and placement of each element in three-space, not just in film," noted Eric Brevig.

STAR TREK IV: THE VOYAGE HOME

(Paramount)

In the story line, a new *Enterprise* was added to replace the venerable Starship destroyed in *Star Trek III* (actually this is the original *Enterprise* model, rewired, and restored).

THE GOLDEN CHILD

(Paramount)

ILM highlights include matte painting effects and the creation of Sardo, an animatronic puppet.

1987

STAR TOURS

(Disney/Lucasfilm Ltd.)

"As art director and co–effects supervisor, I remember how fun it was to try and design the hangar and boarding areas on-screen so they looked like a blend of *Star Wars* and Disneyland," recalls Dave Carson of this breakthrough Disneyland simulator ride attraction.

THE WITCHES OF EASTWICK

(Warner Bros.)

WINNER OF BRITISH ACADEMY AWARD,

BEST VISUAL EFFECTS

A magical tennis match was created with tennis ball elements optically added to a choreographed live-action match.

INNERSPACE

(Warner Bros./Amblin)

WINNER OF ACADEMY AWARD,

BEST VISUAL EFFECTS

To create a miniature ship cruising a human bloodstream, a blue-screen pod element was optically composited with such practical elements as a forty-foot-long translucent tube circulating water and blood cell effects.

BATTERIES NOT INCLUDED

(Universal/Amblin)

WINNER OF ACADEMY AWARD,

TECHNICAL ACHIEVEMENT

A technical breakthrough was Tad Krzanowski's special marionette rig used to fly miniature flying saucers.

STAR TREK: THE NEXT GENERATION

(Paramount Television)

ILM provided the series with an original *Enterprise* model, which would make its feature-film debut seven years later in *Star Trek Generations*.

EMPIRE OF THE SUN

(Warner Bros./Amblin)

In addition to a computer-generated squadron of planes, ILM's matte department provided shots that included a nighttime bombing raid and an exploding atomic bomb.

1988

WILLOW

(MGM/Lucasfilm Ltd.)

ACADEMY AWARD NOMINATION,

BEST VISUAL EFFECTS

ILM ran the universal FX play-

book on this Lucasfilm production, including matte paintings, miniature sets, stop-motion creature work, and blue-screen composites. To produce a magical transformation sequence, ILM broke new ground with the first use of digital morphing technology.

STAR TREK ATTRACTION

(Universal/Paramount)

Universal Studios tour ride.

WHO FRAMED ROGER RABBIT?

(Touchstone Pictures/Amblin)

WINNER OF ACADEMY AWARD,

BEST VISUAL EFFECTS

WINNER OF BRITISH ACADEMY AWARD,

BEST VISUAL EFFECTS

To integrate hand-drawn animation into live-action background plates believably was a herculean opticals project, requiring some 1,040 shots and ten thousand separate elements.

CADDYSHACK II

(Warner Bros.)

A cornucopia of tricks: digital golf balls, forced perspective miniatures, and an animatronic gopher.

COCOON: THE RETURN

(Twentieth Century-Fox)

For the first unit's shoot of the finale, Brian Dennehy could not be at the location, so ILM filmed him separately with blue screen and optically composited the actor into the scene later.

THE LAST TEMPTATION OF CHRIST

(Universal)

For a pivotal moment in a sequence of Jesus Christ's wandering in the desert, ILM created a shot of Christ sitting in a sacred circle as a lion materialized before him, an effect created with separate photography of actor Willem Dafoe and a lion joined with split-screen technique.

1989

THE BURBS
(Renfiel Productions/Universal)

ILM's highlight was an opening "Powers of Ten shot"—the generic name for a continuous zoom from infinitely large to infinitely small and vice versa—that descended from the depths of space into the Universal Pictures' planet Earth logo, through the atmosphere, and into a suburban neighborhood.

SKIN DEEP
(Blake Edwards Co.)

In this ribald film, ILM produced a takeoff on Luke Skywalker and Darth Vader's lightsaber battle with a dueling "glowing condoms" optical and animation effect.

BODY WARS
(Disney)

This Walt Disney World Epcot Center simulator attraction, a journey through the human bloodstream, featured thousands of computer-generated blood cells, "marking the first extensive use of computer graphics as composited elements," according to Dave Carson.

MICKEY-EISNER SPOT
(Disney)

Optical compositing of live-action footage of Disney CEO Michael Eisner and Mickey Mouse animation elements in the *Roger Rabbit* style.

TUMMY TROUBLE
(Disney)

More live-action/animation opti-

cal compositing to end this Roger Rabbit cartoon.

FIELD OF DREAMS
(Universal)

In this fantasy of an Elysium baseball diamond, ILM created effects-camera fireflies and optical work for the spectral ballplayers disappearing into the surrounding farm fields.

INDIANA JONES AND THE LAST CRUSADE
(Paramount/Lucasfilm Ltd.)

A breakthrough shot was ILM's all-digital composite for the "Donovan's Destruction" sequence, a transformation effect director Steven Spielberg wanted in one shot. "Steven once confessed to me on the set that sometimes he wakes up in the morning wondering if he will be able to come up with any good ideas," then FX supervisor Micheal McAlister noted. "I realized then that I was not alone—that all challenged people share this common experience."

GHOSTBUSTERS II
(Columbia)

"[With] two hundred effects shots in six months, it was very hard to organize and to maintain the ILM quality people expect from us," said Dennis Muren. "At one time we had nine crews shooting rubber ghosts, a river of slime, smoke clouds, the Slimer ghost character, and a walking Statue of Liberty."

THE ABYSS
(GJP Prod./Twentieth Century-Fox)
WINNER OF ACADEMY AWARD,
BEST VISUAL EFFECTS

The computer-generated pseudo-pod creature marked another milestone in the CG effects revolution.

BACK TO THE FUTURE, PART II
(Amblin/Universal)
ACADEMY AWARD NOMINATION,
BEST VISUAL EFFECTS
WINNER OF BRITISH ACADEMY AWARD,
BEST VISUAL EFFECTS

A breakthrough ILM digital-wire and rod-removal software program was first used extensively on this feature.

ALWAYS
(Amblin/Universal)

Creating realistic firefighting planes and flying them over miniature forests set ablaze were ILM's contributions to this Spielberg film.

1990

ROLLER COASTER RABBIT
(Disney)

Another Roger Rabbit animated short, with ILM contributing optical compositing of live-action and animation shots.

AKIRA KUROSAWA'S DREAMS
(Kurosawa Prod./Warner Bros.)

ILM provided effects for the sequences "Sunshine Through the Rain" and "Mount Fuji in Red."

JOE VERSUS THE VOLCANO
(Warner Bros.)

ILM provided a classic image: the miniature ship in a stormy sea effect.

THE HUNT FOR RED OCTOBER
(Paramount)

Although scale-model submarines were provided by an outside vendor, it was ILM's task to prepare the models, attach them to wire rigs, and fly them in a smoke-filled set that simulated an underwater world.

BACK TO THE FUTURE, PART III

(Amblin/Universal)

"Using our prototype Vista Glide motion-control dolly and camera gear head system to shoot our elements for the various split-screen shots was nerve-racking, and blending all those pieces together was more so," Ken Ralston recalled.

DIE HARD 2: DIE HARDER

(Twentieth Century-Fox)

Creating, flying, and even crashing scale commercial and military aircraft models was ILM's challenge for this successful summer sequel. The breakthrough effect, a matte painting known as MP-4, was the first digitally manipulated painting.

GHOST

(Paramount)

BRITISH ACADEMY AWARD NOMINATION,
BEST VISUAL EFFECTS

ILM work ranged from a miniature subway train and station (from the model shop) to spirits passing through physical objects (with optics magic).

THE GODFATHER, PART III

(Paramount)

For a shot of a mobster being gunned down in front of a glass door, ILM optically added bullet-hole hits on the glass.

1991

THE YOUNG INDIANA JONES CHRONICLES

(ABC-TV/Lucasfilm Ltd.)

This television series provided Lucasfilm with a low-resolution medium in which to develop the image-processing techniques and interactive digital editing technologies the com-pany would soon apply to high-resolution feature-film work.

MICKEY'S AUDITION

(Disney)

More live-action and animation optical compositing magic, as a cartoon-animated Mickey saunters in to see Disney chief Michael Eisner.

SWITCH

(HBO Films)

For a parable of a man dying and returning as a woman, an omnipotent spiritual effect—dubbed the "God column of light"—was produced with streak photography and an effects camera.

THE DOORS

(Tri-Star Pictures)

An ILM highlight was the visuals of rocker Jim Morrison's drug-induced hallucinations in a desert landscape. Working with Oliver Stone led FX supervisor Michael Owens to sum up the maverick director's unofficial mottoes as including "Be prepared to be spontaneous and travel light—meaning, 'Don't tie me down with technology.' In other words, seat belts not required nor encouraged."

HUDSON HAWK

(Tri-Star Pictures)

The Leonardo Da Vinci "Gold Machine" effects demanded extensive rotoscope work to trace light beams through practical elements.

BACKDRAFT

(Imagine Films)

ACADEMY AWARD NOMINATION,
BEST VISUAL EFFECTS

ILM's major shot, a tableau of a burning, collapsing rooftop with firemen racing across it, required minia-tures, a matte painting, and live-action elements.

THE ROCKETEER

(Disney)

The rocket-pack-powered Rocketeer effect included stop-motion puppet work and animation effects for the pack's jet flames. But creating and blowing up a scale zeppelin model was the most nerve-racking challenge.

TERMINATOR 2: JUDGMENT DAY

(Carolco)

WINNER OF ACADEMY AWARD,
BEST VISUAL EFFECTS
WINNER OF BRITISH ACADEMY AWARD,
BEST VISUAL EFFECTS

Breakthroughs in digital compositing and computer graphics allowed for the creation of a shape-changing, liquid-metal cyborg. "The great team of talented CG artists was brave enough to try anything thrown at them," recalled supervisor Dennis Muren, who counts this project a personal favorite. "And when I managed to figure out, after years of misfires, how to get our composites to be digital, there was no stopping us."

SPACE RACE

(Showscan)

The last all-opticals production at ILM, this outer-space film ride of funky, hot-rodding spaceships was filmed in Showscan, a process that films and projects at sixty frames per second to produce a heightened simulation of reality. Recalls producer Ned Gorman, "It was real *Jedi* tech, the end of an era. Track cameras, animation gags, opticals, with concept artist Ty Ellingson just pouring his heart out to give it an interesting look. Although it was the last all-opticals show, a lot of people will look at it and ask me how much was CG, which is very gratifying."

STAR TREK VI: THE UNDISCOVERED COUNTRY

(Paramount)

ACADEMY AWARD NOMINATION, BEST VISUAL EFFECTS

The computer effects touches included the Praxis moon blast and shock wave as well as ever-more-sophisticated morphing shots.

HOOK

(Columbia Pictures/Amblin)

ACADEMY AWARD NOMINATION, BEST VISUAL EFFECTS

Creating the Tinker Bell effect, magical fairy dust, and matte paintings (including a digitally processed painting that allowed for a dimensional perspective shift) provided magical flourishes for this Steven Spielberg fantasy.

1992

MEMOIRS OF AN INVISIBLE MAN

(Warner Bros.)

To create the effect of invisibility, ILM digital artists isolated and removed specific areas of the invisible man (Chevy Chase), while painting programs allowed for clean background plates to fill in the invisible areas.

DEATH BECOMES HER

(Universal)

WINNER OF ACADEMY AWARD, BEST VISUAL EFFECTS
WINNER OF BRITISH ACADEMY AWARD, BEST VISUAL EFFECTS

Another CG breakthrough: the replication of human skin for the immortal character played by actress Meryl Streep.

ALIEN ENCOUNTER

(Showscan)

Simulator ride attraction.

ALIVE

(Disney/Paramount)

"Photographing a miniature crash and painting out rigs proved to be a perfect marriage of digital and physical techniques," observed Scott Farrar.

1993

FIRE IN THE SKY

(Paramount)

ILM returned to its traditional-effects roots, producing the effect of a man (actor D. B. Sweeney) floating weightless in a spaceship by wires in a set environment.

THE METEOR MAN

(MGM)

For this superhero fantasy, ILM provided optically composited meteor elements and a blurring effect for the hero's whirlwind punches.

JURASSIC PARK

(Amblin/Universal)

WINNER OF ACADEMY AWARD, BEST VISUAL EFFECTS
WINNER OF BRITISH ACADEMY AWARD, BEST VISUAL EFFECTS

ILM's CG dinosaurs were a breakthrough in feature-film computer effects. From believable, organic lifeforms to digital-compositing breakthroughs, this was the film that finally convinced Hollywood that the digital era had dawned.

SCHINDLER'S LIST

(Amblin/Universal)

For director Steven Spielberg's Academy Award–winning Best Picture, ILM provided atmospheric splashes of color in several key scenes of the black-and-white film. "Technically, some of the difficulty came from the subtlety—under no circumstances were the effects to look like effects," noted visual effects supervisor Steve Price. "To complicate the challenge, the effects had to be rendered on color negative. This resulted in having to hand-cut into every black-and-white release print the individually timed color-effects shots."

RISING SUN

(Twentieth Century-Fox)

"Our work involved creating a sequence demonstrating how a surveillance videotape that looked completely real was, in fact, a doctored tape," said Mark Dippé. "This theme is very relevant to today's world; whether or not we can trust the images we see."

MANHATTAN MURDER MYSTERY

(Tri-Star Pictures)

Since director Woody Allen has often liked to work locations, particularly interiors with size limitations prohibiting the use of booms to catch live dialogue, stars in Allen's films are sometimes wired for sound. "Because they couldn't position a boom they had wired everybody for a particular shot," ILM producer Ned Gorman recalled. "In dailies they noticed this long wire was visible under Allen's shirt. We had to do a very complex digital blend to erase the wire."

1994

THE HUDSUCKER PROXY

(Warner Bros.)

To create backgrounds of the New York skyline that would be integrated into set backgrounds, matte paintings were created on Mac workstations and then scanned out and blown up to sixty-foot-wide and thirty-foot-tall photographic translight screens for the set backgrounds.

BABY'S DAY OUT

(Twentieth Century-Fox)

A real, blue-screen-filmed baby was digitally inserted into precarious situations on 3-D CG buildings. "The results were so effective that when the film was released there were protests that we had recklessly endangered the life of the baby," said John Knoll. "So Twentieth Century-Fox had us prepare a 'making-of' video to explain the process and show that the baby was never in danger."

STAR TREK VII: GENERATIONS

(Paramount)

An ILM highlight was the crash of the Starship *Enterprise*, which required a scale ship, miniature landscape, matte paintings, and blue-screen foreground trees to augment the environment.

DISCLOSURE

(Warner Bros.)

ILM provided a CG-crafted virtual reality sequence as a centerpiece effect to this tale of sexual intrigue and corporate politics.

RADIOLAND MURDERS

(Lucasfilm Ltd./Universal)

The digital production tools Lucasfilm developed in the *Young Indy* TV series were herein introduced into the high-resolution world of film in the form of ILM's interactive compositing and editing Sabre System.

THE FLINTSTONES

(Amblin/Universal)

Between the photorealistic creatures of *Jurassic Park* and the cartoonish character animation of *The Mask* was this transitional project. "We brought the fun-loving prehistoric creatures of Bedrock to life," said visual effects supervisor Mark Dippé. "Computer animation was the only way we could achieve these performances and still look real."

FORREST GUMP

(Paramount)

WINNER OF ACADEMY AWARD,
BEST VISUAL EFFECTS
WINNER OF BRITISH ACADEMY AWARD,
BEST VISUAL EFFECTS

From the seamless fall of a digitally composited blue-screen feather to crowd-replication scenes, this film was a breakthrough in "invisible effects."

THE MASK

(New Line Cinema)

ACADEMY AWARD NOMINATION,
BEST VISUAL EFFECTS
BRITISH ACADEMY AWARD NOMINATION,
BEST VISUAL EFFECTS

"*The Mask* represents another step in the evolution of computer graphics," noted visual effects supervisor Scott Squires. "Here was a rare opportunity to create a free animated computer graphics character within the confines of the live action."

1995

CONGO

(Paramount)

The major challenge was to create realistic lava flows, which was accomplished with scale miniature sets, a sludgelike mixture, and digital effects. Volcanic action from old movies served as an example of what not to do. "After viewing many volcano movies, I realized only red oatmeal lava had been made," said Scott Farrar, visual effects supervisor on the film.

IN THE MOUTH OF MADNESS

(Katja/New Line Cinema)

ILM only contributed eight or nine shots to this John Carpenter tale of a horror writer (played by Jurgen Prochnow) whose fictional fantasies begin to seep into the real world; the major effect was a surreal CG image of the character ripping himself apart as if he were an image on a printed page.

CASPER

(Amblin/Universal)

The friendly ghost and the Ghostly Trio had to be more than effects—they were computer-generated performers. "Rather than matching a prop on set or a scale model, we defined the ghosts entirely in our digital medium," noted digital character co-supervisor Stefen Fangmeier.

JUMANJI

(Tri-Star)

To help create believable CG jungle animals, ILM artists had to create realistic hair digitally. Hair was one of the organic elements previously problematic in the digital realm.

1996

DRAGONHEART

(Universal)

ILM's breakthrough in CG character animation was Draco, a synthetic dragon whose emotive qualities had to match the timbre of Sean Connery's recorded dialogue.

ILM AWARDS

1981

SCIENTIFIC AND ENGINEERING AWARD

The engineering of the Empire motion picture camera system.

RECIPIENTS:

Richard Edlund and Industrial Light & Magic.

SCIENTIFIC AND ENGINEERING AWARD

The concept and engineering of a beam-splitter optical composite motion picture printer.

RECIPIENTS:

Richard Edlund and Industrial Light & Magic.

TECHNICAL ACHIEVEMENT AWARD

The development of a motion picture figure mover for animation photography.

RECIPIENTS:

Dennis Muren and Stuart Ziff.

1987

TECHNICAL ACHIEVEMENT AWARD

The development of a wire rig model support mechanism used to control the movements of miniatures in special effects.

RECIPIENT:

Tadeusz Krzanowski.

1992

TECHNICAL ACHIEVEMENT AWARD

The development and the first implementation in feature motion pictures of the "Morph" system for digital metamorphosis of high resolution images.

RECIPIENTS:

Douglas Smythe and the Computer Graphics Department of Industrial Light & Magic.

1993

SCIENTIFIC AND ENGINEERING AWARD

The concept and development of the digital motion picture retouching system for removing visible rigging and dirt/damage artifacts from original motion picture imagery.

RECIPIENTS:

Douglas Smythe and George Joblove.

1994

SCIENTIFIC AND ENGINEERING AWARD

Pioneering work in the field of film input scanning.

RECIPIENT:

Scott Squires.

SCIENTIFIC AND ENGINEERING AWARD

Development work on a linear array CCD (Charge Coupled Device) film input scanning system.

RECIPIENTS:

Lincoln Hu and Michael MacKenzie.

1995

TECHNICAL ACHIEVEMENT AWARD

Pioneering efforts in the creation of the ILM digital film compositing system.

RECIPIENTS:

Douglas Smythe, Lincoln Hu, Douglas S. Kay, and Industrial Light & Magic.

GLOSSARY

AERIAL IMAGE PRINTER

A kind of optical printer capable of having an image projected into the air that is aerially in focus, meaning it is invisible to the unaided eye but visible to the lens of the taking camera and can be recorded on negative film. Early ILM aerial image printers (which were decommissioned in the 1990s) include the "Anderson," the "Work Horse," and the "Quad."

ANAMORPHIC

In this wide-screen exhibition format, special anamorphic lenses compress an image along a horizontal axis during photography, making it half as wide as it would normally be. When projected through the same-shaped lenses the film image becomes unsqueezed. This format was originally introduced in the U.S. under the imprimatur of CinemaScope and Panavision. ILM effects photographers have traditionally used VistaVision, a nonanamorphic camera system.

ANIMATIC

A simulation of a scene, used to work out compositions, timings, and other artistic and technical issues, traditionally accomplished by photographing storyboards, individual drawings, or 3-D mock-ups. With the emergence of computer technologies, such simulations can also be created with 3-D layouts in virtual space.

ANIMATION CAMERA

Animation cameras are usually mounted on a vertical stand (also called a "down shooter") above a table on which animation artwork can be centered. When shooting animation cels, the table is usually illuminated from above or below. This system can produce complex moves, with the camera moving up and down along its column support and the table itself capable of moving left to right and up and down and rotating horizontally. Modern animation cameras are usually hooked up to a motion-control system.

APERTURE

The rectangular opening behind the lens of a camera or projector (also known as the "gate"). In photography, aperture refers to the f-stop of the lens, which is the ratio of the focal length of the lens to the width of the opening through which light is allowed to pass.

ARMATURE

The skeleton of a stop-motion puppet, usually constructed of machined steel. Armature ball and socket joints allow animators to manipulate the puppet to create the illusion of movement. Although a stop-motion puppet's foam latex body will often wear out and be replaced during the grueling course of animation, well-made armatures normally outlast the production.

BACKGROUND PLATES

In optical photography, the background (usually a soundstage set or a location) over which foreground elements are composited.

BEAM SPLITTER

This semireflective mirror is placed in front of a camera lens at an angle to reflect the light striking it while transmitting the rest. It usually allows a camera to record simultaneously a foreground image that is partially transmitted into the camera along with the reflection of an image at the side of the camera. Also referred to as a "fifty-fifty mirror."

BEAUTY PASS

In multiple-pass photography, different exposures are used to capture separate elements in a scene, such as lights or smoke effects. The beauty pass is the exposure that captures all the subject's significant details.

BIPACK

Bipack cameras and projection systems are equipped to run two separate pieces of film simultaneously. A bipack camera system was used to photograph matte paintings for the first *Star Wars*.

Black center ("BC")

When compositing with an optical printer, the effects artist cannot merely double-expose foreground elements over a background. The goal is to make all elements look as if they were a single, photographed image. To create such seamless optical composites, a black silhouette of the foreground element, known as the "black center," is used to create a "hole" in the background into which the foreground image can then be optically printed. (Also known as the "male matte" and "holdout matte.")

Blue screen

Allows objects (such as the *Star Wars* spacecraft) or actors filmed in front of a blue screen to be photographed as foreground elements and optically (or digitally) composited into any background plate.

Body sock

A software system developed at ILM to help create the computer graphics liquid-metal cyborg of *Terminator 2*. The system allows animators to smooth and blend the edges of a digitally modeled surface.

Camera movement

The movement is the delicate, perfectly machined mechanism that allows film to be moved and positioned during photography. Components include the aperture, film gate, and registration pins. To appreciate the precision and durability required of this mechanism, consider: The movement of a camera must hold each frame of film perfectly still for 1/24th of a second before advancing to the next frame. The slightest imperfection in registering an image will ruin a final optical composite.

CCD (charge coupled device)

A light-sensitive electronic chip that converts color and brightness information to a small array of binary digits that form the basic unit of information used in computer technology. The system functions as a temporary image-storage device for the input scanners, which convert film images into digital information.

Cel animation

The clear acetate sheets on which artwork can be rendered and filmed under an animation camera. Each cel of an animated subject is drawn with incremental changes so that when photographed and projected the sequence has the illusion of motion.

Close-up

A tight, detailed shot of a subject as opposed to a distant, "long-shot" camera view in which an entire setting is captured. A "medium shot" is between these two extremes.

Cloud tank

A large tank of water commonly used to film cloud and other vaporescent effects. In 1994 ILM dismantled its cloud tank as part of its conversion to digital technologies.

Computer graphics

Computer graphics (or "CG") refers to three-dimensional computer images and animation completely generated in a computer, such as the lifelike dinosaurs of *Jurassic Park*, the ghosts of *Casper*, and the dragon of *Dragonheart*.

Cracker smoke

A nontoxic mineral oil base that, when vaporized, produces atmospheric smoke.

Cubic reflection environment

A dimensional environment, created in the digital realm, that represents how light will interact with a computer-generated subject and that ultimately enables the computer to shade the picture elements of the scene appropriately.

Dailies

The rough, unedited film usually viewed the day after filming. In the predigital days, dailies (or "rushes") were an almost ritual assembly for a crew of filmmakers. With computer graphics and image processing, works in progress can be viewed at any time, unlike film, which can't be viewed until it has first been photochemically processed in a lab.

Data

The information stored, manipulated, and transmitted in the digital realm as binary digits.

Digital composite

The compositing of separate elements scanned in and manipulated in a computer as opposed to the photochemical process of traditional optical printing.

Digital realm

All-encompassing term for the computer's internal data-based environment and the manipulations possible therein.

Digitizing

The process by which images are converted into the numbering system that a computer can manipulate.

Direct input device (DID)

Originally dubbed "Dinosaur

Input Device" when developed by ILM and the Phil Tippett Studio to help previsualize and plot out some scenes for the CG dinosaurs of *Jurassic Park*. The DID for that film was constructed in the form of a stop-motion dinosaur armature, with encoders at pivot points that allowed manipulations to be translated into the animation of a wire-frame figure built into the computer and visible on monitors.

DISSOLVE

A transition effect in which one image fades out and another simultaneously fades in.

DOUBLE EXPOSURE

The exposure of two separate shots on the same strip of film.

DUPE

When an original negative is copied, it's a dupe (short for "duplicate").

DYKSTRAFLEX TRACK CAMERA

The first motion-control track camera system, named for John Dykstra, ILM's first visual effects supervisor, who spearheaded its development for *Star Wars*.

EDITROID

The first digital editing system, developed by the first Lucasfilm computer graphics team. Other significant digital technology produced by that group included the Pixar laser scanner and the Renderman 3-D software system.

EFFECTS ANIMATION

Traditionally hand-drawn effects (such as cel animation or rotoscoping) used to produce such fantastic visuals as lightning bolts and fairy dust.

EIGHT PERF

In the VistaVision film format favored by ILM (and commonly used throughout the effects industry), there are eight perforations, or sprocket holes, per frame. The format provides twice as much area at higher resolution (because it has half the film grain) than the standard four-perf film frame.

EIKONIX

A commercial input scanning device for digitizing film. Eikonix is a trademark.

EMPIRE CAMERAS

The new generation of lighter, faster VistaVision cameras built for *The Empire Strikes Back*.

EMULSION

The light-sensitive silver halide material that coats the film surface. Color movie film emulsions have three layers, each sensitive to red, green, and blue primary colors, that are applied to a cellulose acetate or polyester base.

ENVELOPING

An ILM proprietary software developed to enhance the dinosaur animation for *Jurassic Park*, with the Enveloping pass providing the look of skin and muscle realistically moving with a creature's skeletal system.

ESTABLISHING SHOT

A shot that sets the scene, such as a close-up of a house or a wide shot of a city skyline. Matte paintings have been a favored resource for the creation of such environments.

FADE

Another scene-transition effect. When a scene "fades in," the screen starts out black but becomes lighter until the scene is revealed. To "fade out" means that a scene darkens and goes to black.

FILM FORMATS

Format is the aspect ratio of the projected image as well as the film measurement in millimeters across the width, such as 35mm and 70mm.

FILM GRAIN

The silver halide particles that make up the film emulsion can be visible as moving particles in the projected image. This visible grain increases with each dupe made from an original negative. The finer the grain the more desirable the picture. Because ILM's traditional optical work required elements to be filmed and rephotographed many times, the company went to the high-resolution VistaVision format to lessen the inevitable graininess. (To avoid excessive film grain and bypass the optical process altogether, traditional effects work often achieved first-generation quality images by working out shots in-camera.)

FORCED PERSPECTIVE

One of the secrets of set design and miniatures work is forced perspective whereby a realistic depth of field can be created in a limited space by placing smaller objects behind larger foreground elements.

FOUR PERF

The four perforations, or sprocket holes, for each frame of the standard 35mm film format.

FRAMES PER SECOND (FPS)

Film is exposed by a measure of frames per second. Live action is simulated by a frame formula of twenty-four frames per second (FPS).

FRONT PROJECTION

An in-camera effects technique for projecting background images into a live-action scene that is typically used in an enclosed soundstage set. Live-action foreground elements, such as actors or set pieces, can be stationed in front of a background screen, upon which filmed images are projected from the front; the entire scene is then photographed by a taking camera with the aid of a beam splitter. In ILM's predigital days, the process was often used to photograph matte painted effects.

GARBAGE MATTES

These animated mattes isolate and block out unwanted elements captured during the original photography, such as lights and cables.

GENERATION

The number of times an image is produced from the original, or first-generation, negative.

GLASS SHOT

In this classic in-camera compositing technique, a painting is made on a sheet of glass, with open unpainted areas left in which a background subject (such as models or miniatures) can be visible. When the background subject and foreground glass painting are perfectly lined up, the two elements can be photographed as a composite shot.

GO-MOTION

A problem of frame-by-frame stop-motion animation is that the technique, which cannot duplicate the blurring of normal motion, often has a strobing quality when filmed out. ILM advanced the technique in 1980 on *Dragonslayer* with go-motion, in which motion-controlled rods attached to stop-motion puppets could be programmed to move while the camera shutter was open, producing lifelike motion blur.

HARDWARE

The machinery and physical equipment used in computer work, as opposed to the software programs and binary data that run the computer.

HARRY

A commercial editing and compositing tool for video built by Quantel. The interactive, real-time capabilities of the Harry (a trademark) would inspire the development of similar digital compositing and painting systems for use in the high-resolution film world, such as Quantel's own Domino and ILM's Sabre System.

HIGH-RESOLUTION IMAGE

Because of the considerable computer memory and processing power required to create a digital image, it is faster to compute the work at low resolution. When completed, the digital image is then usually scanned out to film at the high resolution required for a feature.

IMAGE PROCESSING

The manipulations of an image in the digital realm. Generally, this is a 2-D process (as opposed to the 3-D constructs of computer graphics animation) in which input devices digitize film images so they can be digitally manipulated.

IN-CAMERA EFFECTS

In optical effects multiple elements must be separately filmed and assembled on the optical printer into one seamless shot. In-camera effects also composite multiple elements but do so wholly through the eye of the camera lens on negative film, thus retaining first-generation film quality.

INPUT SCANNER

A device that converts film images into digital information.

INTERPOSITIVE

Background elements are typically created as a "positive image," a print made from an original negative that becomes an element used in optical compositing (also called "Interpositive" or "IP").

LATENT IMAGE

Different elements, such as live action and a matte painting, are composited in-camera using this technique. When the live action is shot, the portion of the lens in which the painting will be composited is blacked out. After the live action is exposed, the film is rewound and the previously blacked-out portion of the frame exposed with the matte painted image.

LOCKED-OFF CAMERA

A camera that doesn't move during a shot is said to be "locked off." Early composite-effects photography, even in-camera effects shots, usually required a locked-off camera.

LOW-RESOLUTION IMAGE

Digital image processing and computer-generated animation are produced at this resolution, which requires less memory and thus is quicker for a computer to process, before a final can be scanned out to film at high resolution.

MAINFRAME

The central computer apparatus

that links numerous computers and terminals.

MAKE STICKY

ILM software, developed for *Terminator 2*, that allows digital artists to project the 2-D forms of a digitized live-action plate onto 3-D computer models.

MATADOR

A digital rotoscoping software system utilized for *Jurassic Park*. Instead of traditional, hand-drawn roto matte work, Matador (a trademark) allows rotoscopers to generate curves and lines for key frames digitally. The computer is able to complete the in-between frames.

MATCHED MOVE

A shot is "matched" if a camera move on one element is matched frame-by-frame to another, such as the flame element that was matched to the torch of the lumbering Statue of Liberty in *Ghostbusters II*.

MATTE

Mattes are opaque images that prevent exposure in a particular area of film, allowing the blacked-out space to be filled in with another image.

MATTE LINES

The scourge of optical compositing, matte lines are literally the visible edges of an element that has not been seamlessly matted into a shot.

MATTE PAINTINGS

Matte paintings, which can be used to provide expansive establishing shots and extend soundstage and back-lot sets, have been a key effects technique since the earliest days of filmmaking. Traditional matte painting is rendered with brush and oils on glass, a surface that will not buckle or warp and thus betray the two-dimensional nature of the medium.

MM2

An in-house match-move software used to add virtual camera movement to "match" the camera movements on the live-action plate photography. First developed and tested on *Hook* (1991) and *Memoirs of an Invisible Man* (1992), the software was extensively used on 1992's *Death Becomes Her*.

MORPHING

An image-processing technique that allows different digitized images to transmute progressively one to the other. Its first feature-film use was in the transformation sequence for the 1988 Lucasfilm production *Willow*.

MOTION CONTROL

The computerized system pioneered by ILM that allows cameras, props, and models to be programmed to move in specific and repeatable ways. This system, with its ability to synchronize many different separately photographed elements into one composite shot, became the foundation of modern visual effects.

MULTIPLANE EFFECTS

A production technique that allows separate pieces of two-dimensional artwork to be positioned relative to each other beneath a vertically moving camera, allowing for an illusion of depth of field when photographed. The multiplane concept dates back to the animation innovations on Walt Disney Studio's Oscar-winning *The Old Mill* (1937) and the "Ave Maria" sequence in *Fantasia* (1940). In 1980 ILM created the multiplane Automatte camera,

a horizontal-motion control setup that utilized a fifty-foot-long camera track.

MULTIPLE EXPOSURES (OR "PASSES")

The process of making different exposures on the same strip of film.

NEGATIVE FILM

A piece of film with which a scene is first photographed.

OPTICAL COMPOSITING

The traditional photochemical method of combining two or more separately filmed elements onto a fresh piece of negative film stock with the aid of an optical printer.

OPTICAL PRINTER

Printers are basically constructed with one or more projectors and lamphouses that can project film elements into the lens of a taking camera loaded with fresh (or "negative") film stock. The process allows numerous previously exposed elements to be rephotographed and combined on the same strip of film. ILM optical printers through the years have been christened with such nicknames as the "Quad," the "Work Horse," the "L.S.," and the "Anderson" (the last two named after their designers, John Ellis and Howard Anderson).

OUTPUT DEVICE

Hardware, such as a laser printer, that scans digital images out to film.

PAINT SYSTEM

Computer graphics software that can simulate, with the aid of digitizing tablets or pens, the effect of paintbrushes and ink pens.

PAN

A panoramic shot in which the

camera moves horizontally across a scene.

PARTICLE-GENERATING SYSTEM

A software effect designed to generate organic particles capable of random movement. It was first used extensively by ILM to create the deep-sea debris, submarine wakes, and torpedo trails for *The Hunt for Red October* (1990).

PATCHES

Curved, four-sided shapes that help model a 3-D image.

PERSISTENCE OF VISION

This phenomenon allows the mind to retain an image a moment after it has been viewed, allowing increments of action to be perceived as seamless movement. At the movies, where still-frame images are individually projected at twenty-four times a second, we can perceive the illusion of realistic movement thanks to this natural phenomenon.

PHOTOSHOP

A draw-and-paint software system specifically designed for use on Macintosh computers that was created by ILMer John Knoll and his brother Thomas. Although a key tool in film effects work, the software is mainly used in the print industry to prepare color images. Photoshop is a trademark.

PICTURE ELEMENT

A computer image at high resolution is composed of hundreds of thousands of microscopic picture element points, or "pixels." One of the advantages of digital compositing over traditional opticals is that while the latter is limited by photochemically produced photographic elements, digitized data

can be manipulated and finessed down to the individual pixel.

PINBLOCK

The pinblock technique, developed for the photochemical opticals process, involves rephotographing composite elements under an animation stand, by utilizing an automated shuttle to position and register the film.

POLYGONS

The interconnecting planar surfaces that are the building blocks of a three-dimensional image.

PRELIMINARY COMPOSITE

A rough composite using the main elements of a shot. It is used as a reference for the production of additional shots (also called the "precomp").

PYLON

Pylons can be used to both mount and move models and props during blue-screen photography and are usually connected to the motion-control system. Pylons are generally formed from custom-made metal structural supports, over which is placed neon tubing with holes for rods to rotate the model. The whole is covered with vacuformed Plexiglas, which is painted blue to be in balance with the blue screen.

PYROTECHNICS

The creation of explosives, smoke, and fire effects (also known as "pyro").

REAR PROJECTION

An in-camera process by which a camera can photograph both a foreground subject and a translucent screen onto which a background image is projected from behind. Many matte painting effects can be created with live-

action photography rear-projected into the clear areas of a glass painting.

REGISTRATION PINS

In a camera or projector movement these pins position and hold each frame of film during exposure or projection.

RENDERMAN

A trademarked Pixar software program used to create 3-D computer-generated images.

ROTOSCOPE

An old animation technique by which individual film frames can be projected onto a surface, allowing the outline of a particular image to be traced by hand. Rotoscoping can be used to create traveling mattes or to produce animation effects (such as the lightsabers in *Star Wars*).

SABRE SYSTEM

A nonscript-based digital compositing and editing tool that emulates in the features world the interactive freedom of a Harry and other such digital video tools. The Sabre (not an acronym, but a title evocative of the mythic power of the lightsaber of *Star Wars* mythology) was designed as an "open architecture" system that could accept both off-the-shelf and proprietary software to work on an SGI hardware system. It is also "resolution-independent," meaning that the system can be used for high-resolution features, large-format mediums such as the 65mm Imax format, and low-resolution TV work.

SLIT-SCAN

A form of photography in which a streaking distortion effect is achieved by photographing artwork through a slit placed in front of the camera. Douglas Trumbull used the technique to produce the spectacular "Stargate Corridor" sequence for *2001*. In that film, Trumbull built what was basically a horizontal animation stand, with the camera mechanically interlocked to move with five-and-a-half feet high, twelve-feet-wide glass pane easels, the lens filming the artwork through a slit-scan partition.

SOFTIMAGE

A commercial animation software system first tested by ILM on *Death Becomes Her*. SoftImage is a trademark.

SOFTWARE

The actual programs and data that provide the functions to be undertaken by the computer (to the best of its memory and processing capacity).

SOLITAIRE

An output device that scans digital images out to film.

STOP-MOTION ANIMATION

The three-dimensional animation technique of manipulating inanimate puppets or props and shooting film for each incremental positioning, resulting in the illusion of motion when filmed out. The most realistic stop-motion animation is achieved with an animation/exposure ratio of twenty-four frames per second.

STORYBOARDS

A series of drawings that illustrate the action and composition of a shot. In effects work, storyboards also usually include technical notes for camerawork and the appropriate effect.

STREAK PHOTOGRAPHY

A technique in which camera moves and long exposure times can provide a streaking effect to an image. The effect has been used on everything from flying TV advertising logos to the streaking stars in the jump to hyperspace in *Star Wars*.

SUITE

The editing room, or facility, equipped with the tools necessary for postproduction work.

TAKING CAMERA

The camera that films a scene or, in the case of optical printing, rephotographs projected film elements.

TEXTURE MAPPING

A computer graphics technique by which surface textures from one image can be applied to another. An example is the "Neverland Flyover" scene in *Hook*, in which a matte painting of Neverland island was digitized and applied to the surface of a 3-D, computer-generated, wire-frame model of the island.

THREE-DIMENSIONAL (3-D)

Computer-generated images that are detailed in the dimensional realities of height, width, and depth. Such CG objects can be fully rotated and moved in computer space.

THROUGH-PUT

The process by which a digital image is processed and scanned out.

TRACK CAMERA

Motion-control track cameras are traditionally used to film pylon-mounted models or miniature sets. The system consists of a steel track on which rides a boom unit that has a remote camera equipped for pan, tilt, and roll movements.

TRACKING

Shots in which a camera, generally placed on a dolly cart, follows and moves with a subject.

TRAVELING MATTE

A matte that perfectly forms the black photographic silhouette of a subject and "travels" from frame to frame and into which the specific image can be optically composited.

TWO-DIMENSIONAL (2-D)

A flat, digital image that is defined only by height and width, not depth. When film and artwork are scanned in, the 2-D nature of the images limits the dimensional manipulations that would be possible with a 3-D image.

VIEWPAINT

A key ILM software on *Jurassic Park* and a breakthrough in creating CG surface-texture maps, allowing artists to paint on surface textures to a dimensional, not flat, surface.

VIRTUAL (OR SYNTHETIC) CHARACTERS AND SETS

Three-dimensional characters and sets that have a photorealistic quality yet are created in the digital realm.

VISTAFLEX CAMERA

A live-action camera capable of synching sound and filming in the preferred effects film format of Vista-Vision, created specifically for the live action/cel animation composites of *Who Framed Roger Rabbit?* The design featured a special blimp (a device to deaden a camera's sound) and a special three-pin movement for producing the steady image vital for combining with other elements in the opticals phase.

Vista Glide Motion-Control System

A breakthrough live-action motion-control system, featuring a computer-controlled dolly, specially designed to create complex split-screen shots in *Back to the Future, Part II*. The system allowed director Robert Zemeckis to shoot normal live action with a precision repeatability formerly restricted to a motion-control stage. The system could also be rigged to ILM's VistaFlex cameras, allowing synchronized sound shooting as well.

VistaVision

The eight-perf film format that yields twice the image area of a stan-dard four-perf 35mm film frame. Unlike four-perf film, which runs vertically through standard camera and projection systems, VistaVision runs horizontally, creating a larger film format. VistaVision was developed by Paramount in the fifties in response to Twentieth Century-Fox's Cinema-Scope.

Wipe

A transition from one scene to another, accomplished with one image replacing another with a sweeping motion across the frame.

Wire-frame model

Computer-generated models comprised of lines connected at key points to approximate a specific form.

Wire removal

The process of digitally removing wires, props, and other unwanted elements from a scene. Wire-removal software replaced the "garbage matte" process of traditional opticals.

Workstation

The setup for input, processing, and retrieval of data with a computer. A workstation is comprised of such hardware as the monitor, keyboard, and mouse or digitizing tablet.

Zoom

The effect of going from a long shot to a close-up, or vice versa, in one continuous camera move accomplished with a special zoom lens that allows for the change in focal length.

ILM: THE CAST
1986-1996

ABRAMS, LAUREN J.
ABRAMS, RONALD
ACCURSO, MICHAEL
ACKEL, CRISTINE
ADAMS, STEVEN
ADLER, BRIAN
ADLER, MARK
AFFONSO, BARBARA
AFFONSO, KEVIN
AGHA, ALIA ALMEIDA
AIDALA, MARCO
AIKEN, JAMES
ALBERTS, DANETTE
ALBO, DOMINIC
ALBRECHT, PETER HARRIS
ALDANA, JUAN FRANCISCO
ALDRICH, KIPP
ALEXANDER, JENNIFER
ALEXANDER, JON
ALEXY, PHILIP E.
ALGER, ROBERT M.
ALLELUIA, DOMINIC
ALLEN, DAVID WILLIAM
ALLEN, JAMES
ALLEN, PETER THATCHER
ALTER, JOSEPH S.
ALTROCCHI, ALEXANDRA
ALVARE, CHARLES
AMADOR, DEBRA
AMBRICO, WILLIAM
AMIDANO, KIRK ROBERT
AMINI, ARIANA
AMIOT-BURNS, COLLEEN
AMORELLI, MICHAEL
AMRON, MICHAEL
ANDERSEN, WILLIAM
ANDERSON, COLIN
ANDERSON, DANNY
ANDERSON, GLENN
ANDERSON, KEVIN
ANDERSON, MARK
ANDERSON, RICK
ANDERSON, SCOTT E.
ANDERSON, STEVEN EDWARD
ANDRADE, BERNAL
ANDREWS, DAVID L.
ANDREWS, LINE-MICHELE
ANDRIANOS, AGAMEMNON
ANGLAND, CARRIE A.
ANGST, SUSAN M.
ANSEL, KAREN V.
ANTHON III, EDMUND H.
ANTON, LEAH R.
ARAMENDIA, EMILIO
ARAVENA, ARTHUR
ARGUE, KRISTIN
ARMANINO, RODNEY
ARMANINO, VINCENT PAUL
ARMAS, JOSEPH T.
ARMES, PATRICIA
ARMOUR, BARRY S.
ARMSTRONG, CHRISTOPHER
ARMSTRONG, ERIC L.

ARMSTRONG, JOHN A.
ARNOLD, KEVIN
ARNOLD, LORI E.
ARON, JOEL D.
ARVEDON, SHERI
ARVIO, LESLIE
ASHBY, JEWELL
ASHDOWN, PAUL C.
ASHE, MATTHEW
ASKEW, R.S.
ASSMUS, CARL F.
ATAMAN, OKAN
ATHERTON, S. GRACE
ATTEBERRY, NATALIE
ATWELL, BARBARA JOAN
AUBERT, MICHEL
AUGUST, TIM
AUSTIN, KIRK N.
AUSTIN, MARK A.
AVERY, RAMSEY
AVERY, RAY
AYER, EDWARD
BACH, TRANG
BACH, VAN
BACH-Y-RITA, CAROL J.
BACKAUSKAS, MICHAEL
BACKO, STEPHEN
BAGANO, LAURA
BAILEY, ALAN C.
BAILEY, CHARLES E.
BAILEY, JUSTIN
BAILEY, SUZANNA
BAINUM, DEBRA C.
BAIRD, KATHARINE C.
BAKER, DONNA KIRSTEN
BAKER, FORREST MICHAEL
BAKER, GORDON
BAKER, MARY J.
BAKER, TERRY LAWRENCE
BAKKILA, JOHN T.
BALCEREK, SCOTT
BALDA, KYLE S.
BALDWIN, JAMES F.
BALIEL, TERRELL L.
BALLARD, JEFF
BALLIET, STEPHEN
BANFIELD, CAROL
BANOWICZ, JEAN-PIERRE
BARBEE, STEWART
BARNARD, DAVID
BARNARD, ROBERT
BARNES, ROBERT E.
BARNETT, JONATHAN Q.
BARNHILL, KEVIN E.
BARR, CHERYL
BARR, WILLIAM
BARRICK, SUSAN
BARRON, CRAIG
BART, GRETA ROSE
BARTLE, JOHN
BARWICK, THOMAS
BASSETTI, JEFF
BATLIN, ALEX

BATTLE, RICHARD W.
BAUER, JOSEPH
BAUER, MICHAEL P.
BAUER, ROBERT W.
BAUMAN, CAROL E.
BAUMANN, GREGORY J.
BEACH, DUGAN
BAYLO, RACHELLE A.
BEACH, DUGAN
BEAN, RANDALL K.
BEAR, RYAN
BEARD, DONNA A.
BEASLEY, JENNIFER
BEASLEY, STEPHEN
BEATTY, TINA YVETTE
BEAUMONTE, GREG R.
BEAUMONTE, JAMES S.
BEAUREGARD, JON PAUL
BECK, STEVEN M.
BECK, WILLIAM
BECKER, ANNA
BECKER, DENNIS D.
BECKER, EILEEN R.
BECKER, GWENDOLYN
BEELER, KATHLEEN F.
BEESLEY, MAURICE
BEL, LINDA M.
BELL, JOHN
BELL, MARJORIE
BELL, PHAEDRA D.
BELLEN, ALEX
BELLEN, STEVE
BENDER, DRAKE
BENEDICT, JEFFREY
BENNES, ADAM
BENNES, MARIA T.M.
BENNETT, BILL
BENNICI, ANDREA
BENSON, DANNY
BENSON, DAVID J.
BERESFORD, AMY
BERG, JON
BERGIN, JIL-SHEREE
BERGLUND, TIMOTHY
BERKELEY, CRAIG
BERNARD, MICHAEL
BERNHARDT, ERIKA
BERNSTEIN, ANDREW
BERRY, DAVID
BERTINO, THOMAS G.
BERTON, JOHN
BERTSCH, STEVE
BETTENDORFF, PETER
BEUTTLER, JOHN F.
BEVER, SCOTT J.
BEYER, EARL W.
BEYER, KENNETH E.
BIAGIO, J. CHUCK
BIBER, MICHAEL
BIEDNY, DAVID
BIES, DONALD
BIGGINS, JESSICA
BIGGINS, JOSEPH P.

BIGGS, ADRIENNE
BIKLIAN, ANDREA
BING, CHRIS
BIOCINI, PEGGY
BISHOP, AMY
BITTLE, KIMBERLY
BLACK, JOHN
BLACK, MARQUE' C.
BLACKMAN, CORY
BLAIR, CHRISTOPHER LEE
BLAIR, PAUL CURTIS
BLAIR, RONNIE DEE
BLAKE, BRUCE
BLANCHARD, MICHAEL J.
BLAU, PATRICIA
BLAUSEY, JOHN C.
BLAUVELT, ALAN
BLAUVELT, CHRISTOPHER
BLICHER, LEIGH
BLOMQUIST, KANDI LEE
BLOOMFIELD, JOANNE L.
BLUE JR., JAMES
BLUFORD, DAVID
BLUM, ERIC M.
BLUMENFELD, JASON
BOATWRIGHT, CHRIS
BOATWRIGHT, JOHN P.
BOES, BILL
BOGART, RODNEY
BOGLE, NICHOLAS A.
BOLLES, MICHAEL
BOLTE, JEAN
BOLZ, GISELA M.
BONN, WENDY A.
BONNEAU, PATRICK
BONNENFANT, SCOTT A.
BOOTH, NESDEN
BORELIS, MICHAEL STEVEN
BOSTROM, DENISE
BOSWELL, STEVE
BOTT, JOHN
BOVILL, ROBERT M.
BOWEN, PHILLIP BOYCE
BOWLES, BRUCE V.
BOWMAN, CARTER
BOWMAN, PETE
BOYCE, MITCHELL
BOYKO, TRACY
BRACISCO, NICK
BRACKETT, JASON A.
BRACKETT, LANCE
BRACKETT, TRAVIS O.
BRADFORD, J. CARLTON
BRADLEY, KAREN
BRAGGS, STEPHEN M.
BRATRUD, JAMES A.
BRAUNER, URSULA
BRAY, TODD MCCUNE
BREEN, DENNIS J.
BRENNAN, BARBARA
BRENNEIS, MARTIN R.
BRESHEARS, VINCENT L.
BREVICK, NOEL

BREVIG, ERIC M.
BREWER, ELAINE
BREWER, JEFF M.
BREWER, TERRIA
BRITTEN, CONSTANCE
BRODSKY, RICHARD A.
BROMLEY, KIM
BRONSTEIN, RONNA L.
BRONZO, ANDREA M.
BROOKS, JILL K.
BROPHY, ROBERT
BROWDER, WILLIAM J.
BROWN, DAVID BYERS
BROWN, ELIZABETH A.
BROWN, KARRIN
BROWN, MARIE
BROWN, RICHARD E.
BROWN, ROBERT K.
BROWN, RONALD HARRY
BROWNING, CHANCE
BRU, DAVID
BRUBAKER, DEBORAH A.
BRUCE, ROBERT J.
BRUNETTE, DEAN F.
BRYAN, CLYDE E.
BRYANT, REGINALD
BRYANT, ROBERT
BRYCE, IAN WILLIAM
BRYDON, BRINK
BUCKLEY, BRUCE D.
BUFF, CONRAD
BUNCH, MICHAEL
BUNDSCHU, ELIZABETH ANN
BURBANK, STEVEN BRADLEY
BURCKSEN, EDGAR
BURG, ROBERT G.
BURKE, JAMES
BURKE, WILLIAM F.
BURR, DIANE
BURROWS, ENDLA M.
BURTON, ROBERT T.
BUSALACCHI, RYAN
BUTECH, JOHN
BUTLER, DAVID L.
BUTLER, DONALD S.
BUTLER, GREGORY S.
BUTTS, ERLING
BYRD, TYREE
CABALLERO, PAT
CALAMANDRE, CAMILLA
CALANCHINI, ANNE L.
CALDWELL, ANNA L.
CALDWELL, DAVID
CALIVA, DIANE M.
CAMPANA, JAMES THOMAS
CAMPBELL, COLIN J.
CAMPBELL, D.L. CHARLEY
CAMPBELL, GEOFFREY K.
CAMPBELL, HOWARD C.
CAMPBELL, SUSAN J.
CANEJO, CINDY M.
CANFIELD, CHARLES D.
CANNON, CATHERINE S.

CANNON-REESE, POPPY
CAPELLA, ROCKY
CARDELLINI, STEVE
CARLSON, MEGAN I.
CARLSON, PETER W.
CARLSON, VICTORIA
CARMICHAEL, LUCINDA
CARROLL, NICOLAS JOHN
CARSON, DAVID
CARSON, JO
CARTER, ANDREA
CASEY, SEAN
CASH, JULIAN L.
CASSEDY, SHANNON L.
CATALANO, JOSEPH F.
CATTANEO, DOUGLAS
CAUDLE, JAMES C.
CAVALLERO, NICOLE Y.
CECCHINI IV, FRANK J.
CEFALU, JOHN R.
CELLUCCI, CAMILLE
CERF, DAVID
CERMAK, LANNY RICHARD
CESARZ, THOMAS A.
CHADWICK, JOHN E.
CHADWICK, MICHAEL
CHAMBERS, BOB
CHAN, ELAINE K. P.
CHANDLER, JAMES
CHAPLIN, CHRISTOPHER T.
CHAPOT, JOHN F.
CHAPPUIS, LOUIS A.
CHATTAN, ALONSO D.
CHAUVIN, ERIC D.
CHENEY, PATREA T.
CHENOWETH, AMELIA E.
CHERENE, JIM
CHERNOW, SHERRIE E.
CHESLOFF, PETER
CHESLOFF, PETER
CHEUNG, SIMON
CHEW, JAY R.
CHEY, DOUG
CHIANG, DOUG S.
CHIANG, ELIZABETH
CHILDERS, CATHERINE F.
CHILDERS, DAVE
CHILDERS, GREGORY M.
CHILDRESS, WADE
CHING, JERRY YU
CHOSTNER, TERRY L.
CHRIST, JOHN
CHRISTENSEN, ERIC
CHRISTENSEN, PER H.
CHRISTIANSEN, DANA
CHRISTIE, BILL
CHRONIS, ELENA
CHU, ERIC DALE
CHU, MARC
CHUMLEY, DANIEL W.
CHUNG, KYENG-IM
CHUNG, PAUL
CHURCH, EDWARD R.
CIUFFO, ART
CLARK, CRAIG
CLARK, DONALD
CLARK, GORDON PATERSON
CLARK, KEVIN BLAIR
CLAVADETSCHER, CHARLES
CLEAVER, CRAIG A.
CLINARD, JENNIFER
CLINGAN, KIMBROUGH E.
CLOSSIN, MICHAEL
CLOT, RICHARD W.
CLOT, ROBERT PETER
CLOUTIER, THOMAS
CLUCAS, PATRICIA
COATES, MILO MERRILL
COCHRANE, MICHAEL WOOD
COCKCROFT, JAMES GREGORY
COFFEY, KEVIN P.
COHEN, CRAIG M.
COHEN, NANCY E.

COHEN, RICHARD L.
COHEN, SETH A.
COHEN, STEVEN
COHN, DARCY
COLE, TOM
COLE, VICTOR
COLEMAN, DEBRA
COLEMAN, ROBERT
COLLETTA, SUSAN ADELE
COLLINS, PHILLIP E.
COLLIS, GREGORY
COLLUM, DOUGLAS
COLLURA, DEBRA
COMBS, DAVID
COMMINGS, AL
CONNOR, JOHN
CONRAD, MICHAEL ALBERT
CONROY, RICHARD
CONSAGRA, GEORGE
CONSTANTINOU, SOPHIA
CONTE, MICHAEL J.
CONTENT, CAITLIN
CONTI, WALTER
COOK, ROBERT
COOPER, ANDREA L.
COOPER, LAURIE
COOPER, MARC A.
COOPER, MICHAEL
COOPER, ROBERT
COPPOLA, CHRISTOPHER A.
CORCORAN, MIKE
CORDOVA, DAVID C.
CORNELIUS, DIANE
CORNFORTH, E. JANELL
CORRAO, THERESA R.
CORRELL, STEVEN
CORSO, ROBERT A.
CORVINO, KENNETH H.
COSTA, DAVID J.
COSTALUPES, KIM PETER
COSTELLO, TOM JR.
COTTON, JAY
COULTER, ALLEN D.
COURTNEY, KELLY
COUVILLION, ELISE
COX, ELIZABETH A.
CRAIG, CATHERINE
CREEL, MELINDA BETH
CREIGHTON, JULIE
CREWS, KEVIN C.
CRIMLEY, CAROLYN
CRISWELL, DENNIS
CROPLEY, JOHN
CROPLEY, STUART
CROSMAN, PETER
CROSS, CHARLES S.
CROSS, PAMELA
CROSSLEY, SUSAN A.
CROVER, LORI S.
CROW, DONALD B.
CROWE, JONATHAN
CROWELL, AUBIN
CROWLEY, FRANCIS
CROWLEY, JOSEPH G.
CROZIER, DIANA L.
CUCINOTTA, RICHARD
CUCINOTTA, RICHARD P.
CUETO, WILLIAM
CUFFEL, DALE
CULLEN, SEAN
CUMMINS, MICHAEL
CUNHA, FRANK
CUNNINGHAM, JEAN M.
CUNNINGHAM, NILS M.
CURL, PAUL
CURRERI, LYNN MARIE
CURREY, GAIL C.
CURTIS, MERRILL
CURTIS, CHRISTINE
CURTIS, MICHAEL T.
CUTLER, DAVID W.
D'ANGELO, RICHARD
DAHL, BRUCE J.
DAMERON, PHOEBE

DAMON, WILLIAM E.
DANAHER, KATE
DANIEL, BRETT J.
DANIEL, JOHN W.
DANNENBERGER, GAIL A.
DARANYI, JENNIFER
DAULTON, PETER K.
DAVALLE, NATHAN A.
DAVID, LAURA
DAVID, VIRGINIA
DAVIDSSON, LENNERT
DAVIES, CRAIG
DAVIS, DONALD
DAVIS, ELIZABETH A.
DAVIS, JAY KOLB
DAVIS, JONATHAN MICHAEL
DAWSON, GEORGE
DAY, MATTHEW B.
DECANTUR, TRENT
DECHANT, STEFAN P.
DECHELLIS, R. MICHAEL
DEFARIA, WILLIAM
DELBAR, MICHELLE M.
DELGADO, DAN
DELLAROSA, LOU R.
DELOREFICE, ANNA M.
DELOSSANTOS, CAROLYN
DELUCCI, CHRISTOPHER P.
DEMOLSKI, RICHARD B.
DEMOLSKI, RICHARD W.
DENISE, DEBORAH A.
DEOUDES, MITCHELL P.
DEROBERTIS, MARK
DESMOND, CHRISTOPHER
DEUBER, DAVID P.
DEUTSCH, DAVID
DEVAUD, NATASHA
DEVLIN, LISA MARIE
DEWE, BRYAN J.
DI STEFANO, JAMES
DIAZ, CATHY
DIAZ, MARC
DIERDORFF, CHRISTOFER
DIGGORY, RONALD E.
DILLAHUNTY, ROGER L.
DINTENFASS, ANDY
DIPPÉ, MARK
DIXON, GEOFF
DIXON, MARTHA A.
DODD, ROGER W.
DOELING, GARY
DOHERTY, JAMES D.
DOHERTY, JAMES E.
DOHERTY, ROBERT M.
DOLAN, ERIN J.
DOLETO, SCOTT
DOMABYL, RICHARD
DONAHUE, ELY
DONOVAN, GIOVANNI
DORAN, JEFFREY L.
DOUGHERTY, BRIAN T.
DOUGHERTY, BRUCE
DOUGHTY, MIKE R.
DOUGHTY, PATRICIA K.
DOUGLAS, SEAN
DOVA, DICK
DOW, DONALD
DOWLING, GARY E.
DOYLE, LORING
DOZORETZ, DAVID P.
DRANITZKE, DAVID S.
DREISCHMEIER, LORI L.
DRESSLER, DAVID
DREYFUS, WILLIAM R.
DRISCOLL, SUSI
DRUCKER, PAMELA J.
DUBE, KAREN
DUDDY, CHRISTOPHER
DUGAN, CHRISTINE
DUGGAL, SHEENA
DUGGAN, DANIEL
DUGGAN, ROBERT
DUIGNAN, PATRICIA R.

DUIGNAN, SHEILA
DUNCAN, JOHN J.
DUNKLEY, EDWIN G.
DUNN, ANDRA
DUPUIS, STEPHAN
DUROSSETTE, RICHARD A.
DURST, JOHN D.
DUTRA, RANDAL M.
DYAS, GUY O. H.
EAGLE, DAVID P.
EAMES, MICHAEL E.
EARL, RUSSELL W.
EASON, CHARLES
EAST, GERTRUDE
EATON, TIMOTHY ANDREW
ECKLUND, GREGORY L.
EDDY III, SELWYN
EDWARDS, BETH ANN
EDWARDS, CATHLEEN LISBET
EDWARDS, ROBERT
EFRON, PAUL
EHLINE, THOMAS P.
EISENBERG, CRAIG
EISING, ROSMARI
EISLER, LARRY
ELDREDGE, JAMES
ELEFTHERIOU, LISA
ELIAS, PATRICIA
ELIE, PHILLIP A.
ELIZONDO, HUGO
ELLINGSON, TYRUBEN
ELLIOTT, DOUGLAS R.
ELLIOTT, MARY JO
ELLIS, JOHN C.
ELLIS, MICHAEL
ELSEN, KATHERINE D.
EMANUELE, JOSEPH G.
EMBERLY, JENNIFER A.
EMMERICHS, DAVID
ENDERTON, ERIC B.
ENGEL, VICKI L.
ENGLAND, CHRISSIE
ENGLEBRECHT, MARIETTA
ENKE, RORY
ENRIGHT, MARGUERITE K.
EPSTEIN, AMIR H.
ERBACH, ROBERT H.
ERNST, BOB
ESHELMAN, CARLTON A.
ESHOM, JAMES R.
ESPOSTO, NICHOLAS J.
ESSIG, RAUL C.
EVANOCHICK, JACQUELINE
EVANS, CHRISTOPHER
EVJE, MICHAEL
EWALD, RICK
EWING, BRADLEY C.
EWOALD, RICHARD
EYLER, CHARLES SPARKS
EYRICH, JANN
FALK, RACHEL A.
FALOONA, ALISA
FANGMEIER, STEFEN
FANTE, JOHN V.
FARMER, CHRISTOPHER J.
FARRAR, SCOTT D.
FAULDS, DERMOT
FEASTER, TOD
FEDORCHUK, DENISE
FEIL, JUDY
FEJES, THOMAS
FELIX, THERESA
FERDINANDSEN, GUNNAR
FERGUSON, AARON P.
FERGUSON, JANE
FERGUSON, MATTHEW
FERINI, STEPHEN
FERNANDEZ, MANNY
FERNLEY, ROBERT MARTIN
FERREIRA, CHARMA
FERRY, WILLIAM SCOTT
FIGUEROA, PATRICK
FINEGAN, SANDRA

FINK, TRINA L.
FINKS, JEANNE H.
FINLEY III, ROBERT
FINLEY JR., ROBERT G.
FINLEY, CAROL
FINLEY, MICHAEL SCOTT
FISCHER, JIM
FISHWICK, DENNIS
FITZSIMMONS, PATRICK H.
FLANIGAN, REBECCA N.
FLEMING, STANLEY B.
FLETCHER, JODI
FLETCHER, WILLIAM J.
FLORA, BRIAN A.
FLOUTZ, THOMAS W.
FLYNN, JAMES C.
FODE, RONALD G.
FOERTSCH, BILL J.
FOKES, PAMELA QUINNE
FONG, NORRIS J.
FORD, ROCKY
FORD, THOMAS
FOREMAN, JON
FOREMAN, NANCY HILL
FORST, JON E.
FORTE, CHRISTIAN
FORUTANPOUR, BIJAN
FOUGHT, DEBORAH L.
FOWLER, BRUCE
FRANK, PHILIP
FRANKEL, PAULA
FRANKEL, SCOTT M.
FRANKLIN, SHAN
FRANKLIN, WARREN
FRANKLIN, WENDY L.
FRANKS, JACK
FRANZ, MIKE
FRASER, JOSEPH J.
FRASER, MARK
FRAY, RICHARD
FRAZEE, CHRIS
FRAZEE, MERRILL
FREDERICK, CARL
FREEMAN, ANDREA J. C.
FREGULETTI, ROBERT
FRENCH, ED
FRENCH, JONATHAN D.
FRENCH, MARTIN
FRERICHS, KAREN
FRIEDMAN, DANA
FRIEDMAN, TAMARA
FRISBIE, ANGELA
FROST, KARENNE T.
FRUCHTMAN, LISA
FUERTES, MIGUEL A.
FULLE, JEANETTE E.
FULLER, DANA
FULLERTON, CLAUDE
FULMER, JOSEPH S.
FULMER, MICHAEL
FULMER, NATHAN P.
FULTON, PHILL
FUNGHI, AMELIA M.
FURIE, ERIC A.
GABRIEL, WHITNEY R.
GAGAN, DOUGLAS
GAGNON, GILBERT
GAINSFORTH, SANDRA
GALLAGHER, JOHN
GALLEN, FREDERIQUE C.
GAMBETTA, GEORGE
GAMBLIN, JIM
GAMMON, WILLIAM
GANZ, ELISE
GARCIA, RUDOLPH
GARDNER, MICHAEL J.
GARDNER, STEVE J.
GARLAND, CLARK K.
GARY, NORM
GAWLEY, STEPHEN
GAYNER, WENDY
GAZDIK, JOHN STEVEN
GEARY, PEGGY

GEESEYO-GUIMOND, RENIE
GEHRINGER, DENNIS M.
GEIDEMAN, TIMOTHY
GENNE, MICHAEL
GEORGE, LAURIE A.
GEORGE, STEPHEN R.
GEORGE, WILLIAM T.
GERNAND, BRIAN
GERRARD, WARREN
GERSH, HOWARD P.
GHIDINI, SHEILA PEREZ
GIACOPPO, PAUL A.
GIANAKOS, PAUL H.
GIBSON, TOM
GIERING, SAUNDRA
GIKAS, PETER
GIL, RICHARDO L.
GILBERTI, RAY
GILL, GARY
GILLETT, TIM
GILLIAM, JEFFREY E.
GILMORE, DANIEL
GILPIN, BETH
GIOFFRE, ROCCO A.
GIOIA, GERMAINE
GIOIELLA, DAVID H.
GIOMI, BOB
GIOVANNETTI, BART P.
GLEASON, MICHAEL
GLEICH, DANIEL
GLUSKIN, LISA L.
GMAHLING, GARY W.
GODCHAUX, ZION B.
GOEHE, CHRISTOPHER
GOETZ, GRETCHEN
GOFF, RICHARD BRENT
GOLDBERG, MICHAEL
GOLDBERG, REUBEN
GOLDMAN, CLINT P.
GOLDMAN, DANIEL R.
GOLDSMITH, SUSAN K.
GONG, REGINA
GONZALES II, JESSE
GONZALES, RICHARD
GONZALEZ, JUNE PATRICIA
GOODMAN, BRIDGET MARIA
GOODMAN, CLIFFORD S.
GOODMAN, JAMES M.
GOODNO, DAVID C.
GOODSON JR., JOHN
GORAK, CHRIS
GORDON, RALPH
GORMAN, EDMUND NASH
GORSISKI, DIANA
GORSISKI, GREGORY A.
GRAHAM JR., JAMES A.
GRAHAM, KELLY
GRAVATT, FRANK
GRAVEN, CHRISTIAN Z.
GRAVES, ALEXANDER J.
GRAVES, JOHN C.
GREELEY, JEFFREY
GREEN, CAROLEEN
GREEN, CHRISTOPHER
GREEN, HOLLY E.
GREEN, JEREMY
GREENBERG, RYAN F.
GREENFIELD, DANNY M.
GREENFIELD, LYDIA
GREENLEE, KAREN
GREENWOOD, TIMOTHY A.
GREIG, KEITH MALCOLM
GRIFFIN, PAUL J.
GRIFFIN, ROBERT
GRIFFITH, RAE ANN
GRIMM, THOMAS M.
GRIMSHAW, PAUL W.
GRINDER, WILLIAM H.
GRINDLE, NICOLE P.
GRISWOLD, CAROL L.
GRODNER, SCOTT H.
GRONKE, EDWARD P.
GROSS, ALLEN S.

GROVE, RICHARD
GRUHLER, KURT
GRUNBERG, LAWRENCE J.
GUAGLIANONE, SANDRA
GUARDINO, GREG
GUAY, JOHN
GUENIN, GRANT T.
GUERRIERI, INDIRA
GUIDRY, CYNTHIA
GUSTAFSON, D. C.
GUSTAFSON, LYNN
GUTERRES, JONATHAN
GUTHRIE, KIM
GUTSCHMIDT, GERALD
GUTTERUD, MARK
GUYER, BROOKS
GUYER, TIMOTHY W.
GUYETT, ROGER J.
HABOUSH, TAMMY K.
HAFNER, JOANNE
HAGEDORN, JAMES RICHARD
HAGER, JAY
HAGGERTY, MARY BETH
HAGOPIAN, CHANDRA
HALDEMAN, ANDREW D.
HALE, MARGARET
HALE, MARGOT LOUISE
HALL, ANTHONY
HALL, MINDY
HALL, NELSON KIRBY
HALLBERG, CARL
HALLINGER, DAVID
HALSTED, MICHAEL J.
HALVORSON, RICHARD L.
HAMMOND, CHRIS
HAMPTON, BILLY
HANDLEY JR., HUGH H.
HANKS, DAVID
HANKS, JEFFREY
HANNAH, RACHEL
HANRAHAN, DENNIS
HANSON, SHARI
HANWRIGHT, JOF
HARDBERGER, DAVID R.
HARE, ZOE A.
HARKIN, JOHN R.
HARO, MARIA
HARRIGAN, KELLY M.
HARRINGTON, TIMOTHY P.
HARRIS, HEATHER
HARRIS, HILDA M.
HARRIS, MICHAEL T.
HARRIS, PAUL GARDNER
HARRISON, ANDREW
HARRISON, LORI
HARROLD, JEANNE ELEANOR
HARTRICH, JOSEPH
HARTZELL, KATHARINE M.
HATCH, AMY Y.
HATCH, DAVID BREWIS
HATCH, DAVID R.
HAUGO, DALE
HAVENER, KEVIN B.
HAYDEN, BEN
HAYDEN, CAROL C.
HAYE, AARON
HAYE, JACK
HAYNES, BRYAN D.
HAYS, JOHN
HAZLETT, THOMAS H.
HEALY, JANET
HEATH, MARIANNE
HECHT, JAMES
HEDGES, RYAN S.
HEIBERT, IAN JAMES
HEID, JOSEPH
HEIDER, GARY C.
HEIMERDINGER, EDWARD
HEINDEL, ANTHONY
HEINDEL, TODD
HELBIG, FRANK
HELBIG, MIKE W.
HELLER, DEBORAH

HELMS, MICHAEL T.
HENDERSHOT, MATTHEW R.
HENDERSON, DON L.
HENDERSON-SHEA, JANE
HENDRICKSON, ANDREW
HENDRICKSON, WENDY S.
HENNEMAN-ADAN, CAMILLA
HENNES, PAUL
HERON, DAVID
HERON, GEOFFREY
HERON, MATTHEW K.
HERON, PHILIP E.
HERRERA, MIMI
HERY, CHRISTOPHE
HERZIG, MARK B.
HERZINGER, NEIL A.
HESKES, REBECCA A. P.
HETTLER, PAUL
HICKS, KELA
HICKS, WILLIAM R.
HIGGINS, CLARK W.
HIGGINS, SCOTT
HIGHT, CAROL
HILL, PAUL
HILL, RICHARD J.
HILL, ROBERT
HILLMAN, LOREN H.
HINES, R. SUE
HINTON, MICHAEL R.
HIRSH, EDWARD T.
HIRSH, MARGARET E.
HO, PHILLIP
HOFFMAN, LORI
HOGAN, MICHAEL J.
HOGUE, CHRISTIAN P.
HOLDEN, JAMES A.
HOLLAND, DIANE K.
HOLLOWAY, TOM
HOLMAN, LARRY
HOLMES, MARK E.
HOLMES, STACEY
HOOBYAR, PETER S.
HOON, SAMIR
HOPKINS, BEATA
HOPKINS, STEPHEN
HORN, JOHN
HORNBECK, LAWRENCE
HORNISH, STEPHANIE A.
HORSLEY, DAVID F.
HORTON, JONATHAN
HORTON, KATHERINE L.
HOSFORD, STEPHEN WESLEY
HOSODA, CRAIG EDWARD
HOSSNER, ERIC
HOTH, LISA M.
HOUGHTON, SCOTT
HOURIHAN, JIM
HOUSE, CLYDE
HOUSTON, SANDY
HOVERSON, RUSS
HOWARD, DANIEL R.
HOWELL, SANDRA A.
HOWIE, WADE
HRASTAR, PEGGY
HU, LINCOLN
HUBBARD, TIMOTHY
HUDSON, ANTHONY D.
HUDSON, BONNIE M.
HUDSON, GUY A.
HUDSON, PETER D.
HUGHSTON, LANCE
HUGUET, MERLYN
HULCE, SHAWNEE A.
HULL, GEORGE J.
HUNT, DOUGLAS W.
HUNT, PAUL M.
HUNT, PETER J.
HUNTER, JOHN M.
HUNTER, LARRY W.
HUNTER, LLOYD
HUNTER, MARGARET
HUNTER, MARLO
HUNTER, STEVEN CLAY

HUNTINGTON, JULIE B.
HURLEY, CHRISTIAN
HUSSEINI, MOHAMMED M.
HUSTON, PAUL
HUTCHINSON, ELIZABETH
HUTCHINSON, THOMAS L.
HYMAN, GREG J.
ING, POLLY
INGWERSEN, SHANE D.
IRVIN, TIMOTHY B.
IRWIN, TOBY A.
ISAAC, JAMES ALLEN
IVANOWSKI, RICHARD
JACKNOWITZ, JIRI ALEXI
JACKSON, JAGE
JACOBS, JOHN P.
JACOBS, MARK
JACOBS, PAMELA D.
JAEGER, ALEXANDER
JAFFEE, STEPHANIE S.
JAMES, DAVID P. I.
JAMES, STEVEN H.
JANG, MARYROSE O.
JANUSCH, ROD M.
JAQUA, DENISE A.
JARVIS, JON P.
JAY, LAURIE
JEAN, PAULA
JEANNETTE, DANIEL J. M.
JENICHEN, BARBARA H.
JENICHEN, BARRY
JENKINS, ANNIE
JENKINS, CHERYLL
JENKINS, KENNETH W.
JENNINGS, ELIZABETH ANN
JENSEN, E. ERIK
JERRELL, BRAD L.
JESSUP, HARLEY WILLIAM
JEW, BENTON
JIMENEZ, VICTOR
JOBE, MICHAEL R.
JOBLOVE, GEORGE
JOEL, BOBBY
JOHNSON, BROOK C.
JOHNSON, DAVID KENT
JOHNSON, EDEN L.
JOHNSON, KEITH L.
JOHNSON, PAUL A.
JOHNSON, RANDOLPH W.
JOHNSON, ROBERT A.
JOHNSTON, JOSEPH
JOHNSTON, PETER JOSEPH
JONES JR., W. DOUGLAS
JONES, EDWARD L.
JONES, JODIE
JONES, JULIE
JONES, MEGAN L.
JONSSON, RANDY
JORDAN, CHRIS
JORGENSEN, KIMBERLY A.
JOSLIN, VALERIE
JOVEL, RUTH M.
JOYCE, JOANNE
JOYCE, SEAN FREDERICK
JURKOWITZ, JILL L.
JUSTIN-GOLD, JULIE
KACIC-ALESIC, ZORAN
KAID, JOSEPH
KAINZ, FLORIAN
KAISER, GRANT
KALIONZES, KIT
KANE, MICHAEL
KANE, PATRICK
KAPLAN, CARISA
KAPUT, JOHN CARL
KARPMAN, DAVID P.
KARPMAN, SANDRA FORD
KARSH, PAULA S.
KASSAL, BARBARA
KATZ, LINDA BONNIE
KAUFMAN, KURT M.
KAUL, DAVID
KAY, DOUGLAS S.

KAY, JEFF
KAYE, PAMELA J.
KAZMIEROWSKI, PATRICIA
KEELER, IRA
KEITH, ELIZABETH
KELLER, PAMELA
KELLY, CHRISTOPHER
KELLY, JACK
KELLY, LARRY
KELLY, SIOBHAN
KELLY, SUSAN M. C.
KENDELL, DEBRA
KENLY, PAT
KENNEDY, ANDREW
KENNEDY, DOUGLAS
KENNEDY, JAMES M.
KENNEDY, SUELLA
KENNEDY, TOM
KENNEDY, WAYNE
KENNETT, MATT
KENNEY, ROBERTA L.
KEOUGH, PATRICK
KEPPEL, PETER
KERN, JANET C.
KERNS, DONALD E.
KERWIN, MICHAEL D.
KESSLER, MARK E.
KEY, FOREST
KHOURY, MICHAEL
KIBBEE, PAMELA E.
KIEVMAN, CHRISTOPHER T.
KILLMASTER, GREG S.
KIMBALL, JOHN D.
KIMBERLIN, BILL
KIMBRELL, KERIE E.
KINAVEY, JENNIFER
KINDLON, DAVID M.
KING, ANITA
KING, JEANMARIE
KING, STEPHEN
KING, TODD A.
KINGDON, HENRY C.
KINGERY, MARIE LOUISE
KINSELLA, DONNA
KINZEY, SCOTT
KIRBY, KEVIN THOMAS
KIRKLAND, KENNETH E.
KIRKWOOD, JOHN
KIRWIN, DAVID C.
KITCHENS, MIKE
KIYONO, DWIGHT M.
KLAUSNER, DREW
KLEINHESSELINK, JAY
KLEMM, ROBERT L.
KLICK, LAUREL E.
KNEEDLER, CHRISTIAN
KNEP, BRIAN
KNOLL, JENNIFER ANN
KNOLL, JOHN ANDREW
KNOWLAND, WILLIAM F.
KNUTSON, KURT
KOBLENZER, KEN A.
KOENIG, ERIC
KONARSKI, SCOTT
KOONCE, RUSSELL I.
KOSTELNIK, JACK M.
KOTCHER, JAY
KOUVONEN, HARRI
KOZACHIK, PETER A.
KRAEMER, JEFFREY
KRAJEWSKI, JOHN
KRAMER, EDWARD A.
KRASSER, MARSHALL R.
KRAUS, PAUL B.
KREDO, TED
KRUG, MATTHAIS M.
KRZANOWSKI, TADEUSZ
KUBSCH, CHRISTIAN
KUEHN, BRADLEY
KUNITAKE, TANI
KURTZMAN, WOOF
KUTCHAVER, KEVIN
KUTCHINS, BEN

KWAN, AMY H.
KWONG, PETER
KWONG, TSANO
KYLE JR., STEPHEN C.
LABOUNTA, BARBARA
LABOUNTA, HENRY L.
LACER, NANCY
LACKEY, TOM
LACY, SHAWN
LAGIOS, DEMETRE
LAKE, GEOFFREY TODD
LAKE, GREGORY K.
LAKNER, GREGOR
LAMB, RICK
LAMERDIN, LISA A.
LANE, CYNTHIA M. F.
LANE, ERIC
LANGER, JEAN-CLAUDE
LANGHAM, GREG
LANGHAM, JERRY
LANSBERRY, KAREN M.
LAPIDES, BETH
LARGE, DANIEL F.
LARISKY, MIRCHAEL
LARLARB, KITISAK
LARSEN, KIP
LARSEN, KLAUS
LATAILLE, BRIAN
LATHAM, CEDRIC
LAUDATI, ANTHONY ANGELO
LAUMANN, BRETT
LAWRENCE, DANIEL
LAWRENCE, TIMOTHY LEE
LAZZARINI, DAN
LEAPER, ANGELA T.
LEARIE, JULIJA E.
LEBERECHT, SCOTT C.
LECKMAN, TAD
LECLEAR, LEONARD E.
LEE, DAVID
LEE, JENNIFER H.
LEE, ROBIN JON
LEE, THOMAS
LENCI, JULIAN JOHN
LEONARD, MARYELLEN
LEPENIOTIS, PETER
LEPERI, MICHAEL
LEPKOWSKY, KELLY H.
LESH, STEPHANI D.
LESSA, MICHAEL
LETOURNEAU, FRED
LETTERI, JOSEPH B.
LEVIN, KEN
LEVIN, PEGI
LEVINE, ROBERT
LEVITT, LEN
LEVY, THOMAS
LEW, STEWART
LEWIN, JANET T.
LEWIS, ANNE B.
LEWIS, EMMETT R.
LEWIS, JEFF
LEWIS, JOHN S.
LEWIS, MARK A.
LEWIS, PAUL
LEWIS, VICTORIA B.
LICHTEN, LAUREL
LICHTWARDT, ELLEN
LICTHMAN, SUSAN
LIGHT, JEFF
LIGHTHILL, JOCELYN
LILES, SARAH
LIM, JAMES C.
LIMM, CRISTI A.
LIN, FRED
LIND, DON L.
LINDEMUTH, MARK
LINDSAY, KENNETH A.
LINN, BETTY
LIPNER-DROSTOVA, LISA
LISTER, JOHN HAROLD
LITWAK, JAMIE
LIVINGSTON, PETE

LLOYD, JEFFERY DAVID
LLOYD, WALT
LOBELL II, JAMES V.
LOGAN, CRAIG
LONDON, JOHNNY JR.
LONDON, KEITH A.
LONG, MICHAEL
LONG, RAE
LOOKINLAND, TODD
LOPEZ, JACQUELYN
LORENTE, ROSS QUENTIN
LOSCH, ANDREA B.
LOUNGWAY, PATRICK
LOVALLO, TOBIAS
LOVE, CRAIG
LOVE, ZACHARY Z.
LOVELESS, DAN
LOVERRO, LEO M.
LOVETT, PETER
LOWDEN, DOUGLAS SCOTT
LOWERY, DAVID FRANK
LUCAS, GEORGE W.
LUCAS, JANIE
LUCAS, LINDY
LUCAS, PAUL F.
LUCAS, PETER
LUCCHESI, PAULA
LUCKOFF, NANCY J.
LUDLAM, MICHAEL D.
LUHN, MATTHEW R.
LUI, KEYA
LUJAN, STEVE
LUKASZEWSKY, AGGIE
LUNDBERG, DAWN
LUNDIN, GAIL
LUSKIN, JONATHAN PETER
LUTZ, DANIEL D.
LYNCH, ARTHUR
LYNCH, JAMES
LYNCH, MARGARET B.
LYNCH, MICHAEL
LYNCH, MOLLY
MACDONALD, EUAN K.
MACINNIS, RONALD G.
MACK, ROBERT G.
MACKENZIE, MICHAEL
MACKLIN, CHARLES
MACMILLAN, DOUG
MACSWAIN, LUCY
MACUAGA, MARIA-EMIKO
MADISON, JOHN
MAGANA, GUILLERMO
MAGLIOCHETTI, ALBERT J.
MAGRUDER, ELIZABETH
MAGUIRE, RICHARD
MAHONEY, MAY A.
MAIER, JODIE L.
MAIRANDRES, GERD
MAJOR, LESLIE T.
MAKRIS, PATRICIA J.
MALAKIE, SUSAN
MALCOMB, MARYANN
MALERBA, RICHARD
MALEY, JILL
MALEY, MICHAEL
MALEY, WILLIAM E.
MALIONE, MICHAEL M.
MALIVERT, CLAUDE
MALONEY, GREGORY G.
MALOOLY, MARCIE
MALVINO, JOHN
MALYN, SHARI E.
MANDYAM, HARISH D.
MANGAN, KEVIN
MANN, JEFFREY
MANN, JULES
MANNIE, LORI
MARBURY, PAUL
MARG, TAMIA
MARGLIN, JOSEPH S.
MARINIC, ROBERT M.
MARISPINI, MARK
MARKOWITZ, BARRY

MARKS, KIM
MARSALIS, NANCIE
MARSHALL, TIA L.
MARTIN, ANTHONY J.
MARTIN, DAWN E.
MARTIN, NED
MARTIN, RUSSELL
MARTINEK, THOMAS
MARTINEZ, BRADLEY T.
MARTINEZ, JOSEPH V.
MARTLING, ELIZABETH M.
MARTONE, DEBORAH
MARUYAMA, KEN T.
MASCHWITZ, STUART T.
MASSIMINO, FRANCES
MASSON, TERRENCE D.
MATHER, WILLIAM K.
MATHERLY, PAUL DAVID
MATHESON, DAWN D.
MATHIS, STEVEN
MATTSON, ERIK A.
MAY, JAMES M.
MAYBERRY, WILLIAM
MAYO, HENRY A.
MAYS, ALAN W.
MCADAMS, LORI
MCALILEY, IRA
MCALISTER, MICHEAL
MCARDLE, PATRICK
MCBEATH, DALE W.
MCCABE, MICHAEL
MCCAIG, IAIN R.
MCCANN, ROBERT J.
MCCARTHY, MICHAEL J.
MCCARTNEY, DICK
MCCLENDON, GARY
MCCOMBE, BETH
MCCORMICK, SEAN A.
MCCRACKEN, KATHI
MCCUE JR, ERROL D.
MCCULLOCH, MARY B.
MCDIFFETT, BRUCE
MCDONALD, EDWARD
MCDONALD, SPENCER
MCENERY, THOMAS
MCEVOY, MELANIE K.
MCFARLANE, ROBERT C.
MCGAUGH, MICHAEL
MCGEE, MARTIN
MCGORRIAN, SHAWN
MCGOVERN, MICHAEL JOSEPH
MCGOVERN, SCOTT
MCGOWAN, KATHLEEN E.
MCGRATH, ROBERTO
MCGREGOR, BRUCE
MCGUIGAN, MAUREEN
MCINROY, KIRK
MCKAY, RICH
MCKINLEY, RONI L.
MCLAUGHLIN, CHRIS
MCLAUGHLIN, EVERETT
MCLAUGHLIN, SUZANNE C.
MCLAUGHLIN, TIMOTHY D.
MCLAUGHLIN-LUSHER, MEGAN
MCLEMORE, MATTHEW T.
MCLEOD, JOHN
MCMAHON, MARGHE
MCMILLAN, DONALD A.
MCNAMARA, DANIEL J.
MCNAMARA, LEE TONY
MCNAMARA, SCOTT THOMAS
MCNAMEE, SANDRA JEAN
MCNEILL, MICHAEL E.
MEASOM, PAUL
MEIDL, HELENE
MEIER, MICHAEL
MEISEL, MELODY
MELICK, WILLIAM L.
MELTZER, KATHRYN
MENDEZ, ROBERT L.
MENY, DAVID W.
MERKERT, GEORGE L.
MERRIM, ANDREA

MERRITT, KEVIN
MEYER, GARY A.
MEYERS, FRED J.
MEYERS, MARK
MICHALSKE, DANIEL J.
MIKOLAS, STEVEN
MILELLA, MICHAEL
MILES, BRADLEY S.
MILLER III, RALPH W.
MILLER, ADAM
MILLER, CARL
MILLER, MARK S.
MILLER, RANDY
MILLER, RICHARD
MILLER, ROBERT
MILLER, SUSANNA IRENE
MILLER, THOMAS
MILNE, LES
MIN, AUNG
MIN, MICHAEL
MIRAMONTEZ, MARTY L.
MIRMAN, KENNY
MITCHELL, JAMES D.
MITCHELL, RUSSELL M.
MITCHELL, SUSAN
MIYASHIRO, CURT I.
MOBLEY, DOUGLAS
MOBLEY-DAVIS, TAWNY
MOEHNKE, THEODORE
MOHAGEN, CRAIG
MOIDEL, MARK
MOLATORE, TERRY A.
MOLEN, STEVEN
MOLIN, STEVEN J.
MOLLER, MARK
MOLLICONE, ANTHONY
MONDOUX, RAYMOND E.
MONGOVAN, JOHN
MONROY, BERT
MONTANTE, CAREN ANNE
MONTEROSSA, MELISSA
MONTGOMERY, AMANDA
MONTGOMERY, LAWRENCE
MONTIJO, DAVID CHARLES
MOODY, DONALD R.
MOODY, JUNIKO
MOONEY, ROBERT J.
MOORE, AMY E.
MOORE, GEORGE A.
MOORE, MARK
MOORE, MICHAEL S.
MOORE, STEVE R.
MOORE, WILLIAM BRADLEY
MORALES, RENE
MORELAND, RON
MORENO, THOMAS R.
MORENSTEIN, JOSHUA
MORGAN, DEBORAH M.
MORGAN, RODNEY
MORGAN, TIMOTHY J.
MORIARTY, PATRICK
MORITA, NANCY
MORMAN, NEAL
MOROCCO, JACK
MORRIS, DAVID M.
MORRIS, JAMES W.
MORRIS, KATIE K.
MORRIS, MARY GAIL
MORRIS, SEAN
MORRISON, CANDACE
MORTON, DAVID R.
MORTON, WENDY L.
MOTISHER, LEWIS
MOTT, JEFF
MOUNTAIN, ALBERT
MUELLER, ELLEN RAE
MUGGENTHALER, JODI JEAN
MULLALY, CLAUDIA
MULLEN, CHARLES A.
MULLEN, DESMOND
MULLEN, MARK M.
MULLENS, CRAIG
MULLIN, MELISSA E.

MULLINS, CRAIG
MUNN, LEE ANITA
MUNOZ, ROBERT
MURATA, CHERYL
MURDAY, SUSAN K.
MUREN, DENNIS
MURPHY, DAVID M.
MURPHY, GEORGE J.
MUTTERSBACH, LORI A.
MYERS, CHARLES
MYERS, LISA
MYERS, PATRICK T.
MYLES, ROSALYN
MYRICK, J. THOMAS
NAHEM, GREGORY A.
NAPOLITAN, ANTHONY
NARITA, HIRO
NATIVIDAD, EDWIN L.
NATKIN, MICHAEL J.
NAUGHTON, MOLLY E.
NAZZARI, IAN
NEACE, DONALD
NEAL, AMANDA FORD
NEAL, CANDACE E.
NEARY, JULIE ADRIANSON
NEARY, PATRICK B.
NEDDERMEYER, ANDREW
NEFT, DEBORAH B.
NEIDIG, JERROLD R.
NELDNER, ERIK
NELLIS, BARBARA L.
NELSON, ANDREW
NELSON, DAN MARK
NELSON, JOHN
NELSON, KIMBERLY K.
NELSON, LAWRENCE C.
NELSON, LORI J.
NELSON, PETER
NELSON, WILLIAM
NESS, KJELL
NEUHAUS, REBECCA A.
NEWCOMB, LESLEE
NEWELL, SCOTT R.
NICHOLS, PAMELA
NICHOLS, STEVEN B.
NICHOLSON, BRUCE
NICOLAI, PETER
NIEDERHOLZER, KRISTEN
NIEDZWETSKI, HARRY W.
NIELSEN, KENNETH J.
NIEUWENHUIS, ESTHER
NIGHTINGALE, PAUL
NILES, DAVID F.
NIMITZ, ANDREW A.
NISHIMINE, KENDALL
NOBLE, CAMERON J.
NOLL, LAURIE
NORDQUIST, KERRY
NORDQUIST, RENEE M.
NORMAN, MONTE R.
NORWOOD, PHILLIP
NOVAK, ALLAN FRANCIS
NOWELL, DAVID B.
O'BRIEN, WINIFRED M.
O'BRIEN, TERRY
O'BYRNE, LUKE C.
O'DONNELL, JOHN M.
O'DONNELL, MICHAEL
O'HARE, HARRY J.
O'MALLEY, GERRY
O'NEILL, KATE A.
O'REAR, RALPH
O'REILLY, STEVEN G.
OATES, JENNIFER
ODERMATT, KYLE D.
OHM, MERLIN
OHTA, MICHAEL
OHYOUNG, WADE
OLAFSSON, GUDJON
OLAGUE, MICHAEL R.
OLDHAM, GEORGE L.
OLDHAM, ROBERT
OLIVA, LAURIE PETRIE

OLIVER, BARBARA E.
OLSEN, JAMES KEITH
OLSEN, JOHN DAVID
OLSON, JEFFREY E.
OLSON, KEN
OLSON, RAYMOND PAUL
OLSSON, GREGG
OLTMAN, DAWN
OLWEN, SHAWNA
OMAHEN, JOHN C.
OMOROGIEVA, MICHAEL
ONGPIN, MIGUEL R.
ONO, HIROMI
OPFAR, TROY
ORDAZ, FRANK
ORFALI, KHATSHO
ORNELAS, JOHN
ORONA, ORLANDO J.
ORTENBERG, JASON
OSSORGUINE, ANDREW
OSTER, JOHN
OSTERMAN, SELENA
OTOSHI, KATHRYN
OTTENBERG, RANDY
OUTTEN, TODD
OVERBEY, LINDA M.
OWEN, DAVID J.
OWEN, LAWSON W.
OWENS, CHERYL
OWENS, CHRISTINE METCALF
OWENS, MICHAEL L.
OWYEUNG, EASE
PACHECO, NATE
PADDEN, CHARLES SCOTT
PAIGE, JENNIFER
PALM, CARIS D.
PALYKA, DUANE M.
PAMPEL, ERIK
PAMPEL, UDO
PANGRAZIO, MICHAEL
PAPANICKOLAS, GEORGE
PARDTO, TOM
PARKER, BRICE R.
PARRA, ROLAND
PARRISH, DAVID
PARSONS JR., LINDSLEY
PARSONS, JOE CARL
PARSONS, LEON P.
PARSONS, MARK S.
PASQUALE, JOE
PASQUARELLO, EDWARD M.
PASTERNACK, ELLEN R.
PATCHETT, WILLIAM J.
PATERNO, MARY F.
PATSEL, KENNETH WAYNE
PATTERSON, CRAIG ALLEN
PATTERSON, JAY
PATTERSON, ROBERT M.
PATTON, MICHAEL
PAULSEN, KIM
PAYNTER, A. W.
PEACOCK, RICHARD E. C.
PEARSON, HASSAN AL FALAK
PECK, DAVE
PECK, TERRY E.
PEDEN, ROBERT L.
PEHRSON, KRIST-ANN
PELKEY, BILL
PELL, MARTIN L.
PENNA, EDWARD C.
PEREZ, ANTHONY
PERKINS, MILES D. V.
PERKINS, PHILIP
PERTUIS, MARGERY
PETERSON, ALAN H.
PETERSON, LORNE E.
PHELPS, KEN
PHILIPS, CARY B.
PHILLIPS, G. ANTHONY
PHILLIPS, KATHLEEN A.
PHILLIPS, ROBERT
PHILLIPS, ROBERT ALLEN
PHILLIPS, WES

PIEPGRAS, COLIN
PIERCE, MARCUS
PIKE, MARTIN J.
PIKE, RICHARD
PINES, JOSHUA
PINO, JASPER
PINSKER, ANNIE
PIPER, VANCE R.
PITTMAN, CATHERINE
PIZIO, DAVID
PLACE, JEFFREY
PLETT, TONY B.
PLOTH, WILLIAM M.
POCHAPIN, LEE
POHL, JAMES
POLLAND, ANNE
POLLEK, GUS
POON, KWOK YUE ELLEN
POPE, DENNIS A.
POPE, THADDEUS J.
PORTER, MADRONE
PORTUGES, KAMELA BETHENE
POTTHAST, CYNTHIA
POWELL, ROBERT E.
POWERS, JOHN
POYNTER, JAMES
POZZI, DAVID
PRESTON, HENRY
PRICE, JAMES E.
PRICE, MICHAEL
PRICE, RONALD
PRICE, STEPHEN L.
PROBERT, JACQUELINE
PUTZ, RICHARD J.
QUALE, STEVE
RADER, RICK
RAFFERTY, KEVIN P.
RALSTON, KENNETH
RAMIREZ, MARK A.
RAMOS, MEDEL
RAMOS, RICARDO
RANSHAN, TIMOTHY
RAO, RAMAN
RAPERE, THOMAS JOSEPH
RATCLIFF, MARY CURTIS
RATLIFF, KENNY
RAVEN, STACY
RAY, CHARLES H.
RAYMOND, EDWARD L.
REAM, DENISE E.
RECLITE, DAVID J.
RECORD, ANDREA
REDING, STEVEN J.
REDLIN, RICHARD
REDMOND, MARK
REED III, JOHN A.
REED, CHRISTOPHER A.
REED, MELISSA
REED, RONALD
REED, SANDY
REID, BRIAN
REID, CYNTHIA K.
REID, DEWEY
REID, RANDALL A.
REINHARDT, GEORGE
RENARD, ANDY
RENDU, CAROLYN ENSLE
RENFRO, JAMES
REPOLA, PATRICK
RESPINI, ENRICO
REUTER, KEVIN
REYER, BRET J.
REYNOLDS, CHRISTOPHER
REYNOLDS, GLENDA
REYNOLDS, RICHARD
RICE, DRAKE
RICHARD, PRESTON J.
RICHARDSON, EDWARD
RICHARDSON, JUDY
RICHARDSON, KEVIN ANDREW
RIDDLE III, ARCH J.
RIEBLI, ARNOLD
RIGAUDIAS, MAGALI

RILEY, PAT
RILEY, PATRICK
RILEY, WESLEY E.
RING, CRAIG M.
RITTENBURG, JILLIAN
RITTS, SANDY
RIVAMONTE, JOAQUIN
RIVERA, LOUIS
ROBBINS, ALEX
ROBBINS, MATTHEW
ROBBINS, SONYA
ROBERT, NICKI
ROBERTS, MARSHA R.
ROBERTSON, STUART
ROBINSON, ANTHONY C.
ROBINSON, DANA
ROBINSON, ELISABETH
ROBINSON, MICHELLE
ROBINSON, PHILIP I.
ROBINSON, SCOTT
ROBLES, RAUL
RODDIE, CHALLENGE
RODMELL, JOSEPH
RODOLEWICZ, EVERETT
RODRIGUEZ, ELSA M.
ROGENSTEIN, DANIEL
ROHRMEIER, MARK A.
ROKICKI, THEODORE R.
ROLOFF, GARY E.
ROMANO, PETE
RONAI, AMANDA
RONSEN, DAVID A.
ROOD, KELLY RAE
ROSEN, ALICE
ROSEN, COREY E.
ROSEN, SARI M.
ROSENBAUM, STEPHEN
ROSENBERG, MARTIN ELLIOT
ROSENFELD, ALAN
ROSENTHAL, DAVID
ROSS, ALEX
ROSS, DANIEL A.
ROSS, KRISTEN RENEE
ROSS, MICHELLE
ROSS, SCOTT A.
ROSS, SUSAN
ROSSEN, GREGG D.
ROSSENBERG, KIMBERLEY
ROSSETER, THOMAS
ROSSI, TIM
ROTHBART, JONATHAN
ROTHSTEIN, BRIAN D.
ROTTIERS, JULIE
ROUET, CHRISTIAN J.
ROUGH, KATHERINE L.
ROWLINGS, GARRICK
RUBEN, MICHAEL
RUERTIN, RICHARD
RUNGE, PENNY
RUNNER, FRED
RYAN, CHRIS
RYAN, JENNIFER
RYAN, PATRICK E.
SAENZ, PATRICE D.
SAGER, KAREN
SALISBURY, ALICE C.
SANCHEZ, PAUL
SANDERS, CHRIS
SANGER, JEFFREY S.
SANMIGUEL, DARIO
SANTY, G. MICHAEL
SARLES, BOB
SASSEEN, ELIZABETH
SATKOWSKI, DEAN
SAVIGNY, PETER
SCARINGI, T. D.
SCHAFER, DAVID
SCHAFER, ERIC
SCHENCK, CHRISTOPHER
SCHER, EMILY R.
SCHIFRIN, LAURA J.
SCHLAG, JOHN
SCHLAIN, TIFFANY

SCHMAKER, DAN
SCHMIDT, ANDREW H.
SCHMIDT, HEIDI
SCHMIECHEN, BRUCE D.
SCHMITT, PETER
SCHNEIDER, DAVE
SCHOENFELD, JOHN
SCHOENING, JOHN
SCHOENING, PAUL
SCHOON, BENJAMIN D.
SCHOR, LESLIE
SCHORLEMER, MARK
SCHOWALTER, FRED H.
SCHRIMPF, PIXIE
SCHROEDER, ERIC
SCHROEDER, THOMAS R.
SCHULDT, RICK H.
SCHULER, RICHARD
SCHULTZE, JAN
SCHULZE, RICHARD P.
SCHUMACHER, CARL
SCHUMAN, CHARLES A.
SCHUR, SEAN
SCHUTZ, PATRICIA A.
SCOTT, CANDANCE
SCOTT, SANDRA L.
SEARS, RICHARD
SEEDS, WESLEY
SEERVELD, LUKE L.
SEIDEN, ALEX D.
SEKOWSKI, MAREK
SELHORN, MARLA I.
SELINGER, MATTHEW C.
SERAFINI, GERARD
SERAFINI, MARY EGAN
SERRA, ANNABELLA
SERVIN, NANCY HART
SETRAKIAN, MARK SOX
SEVERSON, DIANNE
SEY, JENNIFER
SHANKEL, MARK
SHANNON, MICHAEL
SHAYS, TIMATHEA M.
SHEFIK, JAMES
SHELDREW, JAMES G.
SHELLENBERGER, CHRIS
SHEPARD, AMY
SHERRITT, NIKKI
SHERWOOD, KEVIN
SHINDLER, MARTIN B.
SHING, RICHARD
SHINN, ERIC D.
SHORE, MICHAEL
SHOWERS, LINDA
SHULTZ, ALAN
SHUSTER, JAY
SIDJAKOV, KATHLEEN
SIEGEL, LINDA JOY
SIEGEL, MARK
SILBERMANN, PETER J.
SILER, JOHN W.
SILVERMAN, LOUIS J.
SILVERTHORNE, IAN
SIMMONS, KRISTI
SIMON, ALAN
SIMON, DANIEL R.
SIMON, SARA
SIMON, STEPHEN
SIMONSEN, JERALD A.
SIMONSON, LISA
SINDICICH, THOMAS F.
SINGLETON, TRACY
SIPERSTEIN, LINDA J.
SKOTCHDOPOLE, JOHN
SLADE, JUDY S.
SLATER, CONRAD
SLEAP, STEVEN FREDERICK
SLOAN, JOSEPH A.
SLY, KENNETH LEE
SMALL, JOHN
SMALL, SIDNEY
SMARZ, MAGDALENA
SMITH, TANA EMMOLO

SMITH, ANDREA
SMITH, DANIEL L.
SMITH, DOUG J.
SMITH, DOUGLAS E.
SMITH, E. LEE
SMITH, HEATHER A.
SMITH, JAIME L.
SMITH, JEFF
SMITH, KELSEY
SMITH, KENNETH
SMITH, KIM
SMITH, LEE E.
SMITH, MARK T.
SMITH, MICHAEL
SMITH, SANDRA LISA
SMITH, THOMAS JOSEPH
SMITHSON, MIKE
SMYTHE, DOUGLAS
SNEGOFF, TONY
SNOW, BEN R.
SOFRANKO-BANKS, VALERIE
SOIL, JAMES
SOLOMON, AMY
SOMAN, LOREN D.
SOMMERS, TONY
SORBO, BRIAN
SORRENTI, CHRISTOPHER
SORUM, KAREN L.
SOULIERO, MICHAEL
SOUZA, MICHELLE L.
SPAH, RICHARD
SPEAKMAN, MICHAEL
SPEHAR, MICHAEL
SPELMAN, DANE JOHN
SPENCER, IAN
SPERLING, ALAN M.
SPIEGELMAN, ANNIE
SPIVEY, BRETT
SPRAGUE, MICHAEL
SQUIRES, SCOTT WM.
ST. AMAND, THOMAS B.
ST. JOHN, NANCY
STACCHI, ANTHONY F.
STALKER, PAMELA S.
STAMATIN, ANDREW
STAMPER, THOMAS MARK
STANDISH, CHUCK
STANFORD, NANCY
STARKEY, STEVE
STARNES, DON
STAROBIN, MIKE D.
STARR, CHRISTA
STARR, MICHAEL
STAUROPOLLOS, KEN
STEARN, HEIDI
STECK, JIM
STEEL, DAMIAN R.
STEFFE, MICHAEL
STEIN, HOWARD
STEINER, SHAUNA
STEPHENS, FRANCES E.
STEPHENSON, BRETT
STERLING, TODD
STERN, NICHOLAS D.
STEVENS, KITT ERIN
STEVENS, SHELLY PAGE
STEVENSON, FRANKLIN
STEVENSON, TIM
STEWART, HUGH
STEWART, SCOTT C.
STICKEL, SUSETTE C.
STILLMAN, JOHN
STOLL, NELSON
STOLZ, PETER R.
STOYE, JAMES T.
STRAUB, DON
STRAUS, JAMES S.
STRINGFELLOW, SHERRI
STRITZEL, GAIRD
STROHMEYER, CHRIS
STROMQUIST, EBEN
STRUNK, HEINZ
STRZALKOWSKI, FRANK

STURGILL, JEFFREY R.
STURZ, LISA A.
SULLIVAN, MARK
SULLIVAN, TERRY
SURGES, CARL J.
SUSSMAN, STUART
SUTHERLAND, DUNCAN J.
SUTHERLAND, RICHARD
SUZUKI, LISA A.
SWAIN, KATHY
SWEENEY, MICHAEL KEVIN
SWEENEY, PATRICK
SWEET, JAMES
SWENDSEN, PAUL
SWENSON, ERIC
SWINDERSKI, DAWN
SYLLA, THOMAS
SYLTEBO, L. K.
TAGER, SETH
TAGUE, GEORGE
TAIT, GORDON
TAKAHASHI, WES FORD
TAKEMOTO, STEVEN ERIC
TAKEUCHI, LISA
TAKEUCHI, PETER
TAN, LAWRENCE
TANAKA, DAVID H.
TARANTINO, FRANK WILLIAM
TASK, PAT
TATE, CATHERINE
TATE, STEPHEN A.
TAUPIER, ANNE
TAVERNA, CHERYL C.
TAYLOR, CHAD M.
TAYLOR, CRAIG J.
TAYLOR, DANNY G.
TAYLOR, DAVID
TAYLOR, MELISSA
TAYLOR, RICHARD F.
TAYLOR, RODNEY
TAYLOR, TIMOTHY
TE'O, BENJAMIN U.
TENNLER, EDWARD
TERRILL-SCOTT, DIANA
TEXEIRA, EUGENE M.
THEISEN, VIRGINIA A.
THEREN, PAUL
THOELE, GWEN
THOMPSON, DEREK
THOMPSON, KEVIN
THOMPSON, KIM E.
THOMSEN, ROY L.
THOMSON, BRENT
THORPE, MARC
THUREOCKES, KYLAN
THURLOW, CAROLE H.
THURMAN, ANDREW
THURRELL, PETER G.
TIEMENS, ERIK
TILKER, VINCENT
TIMMER, WILLIAM
TIMMERS, AILEEN
TIPPETT, PHILIP
TODD, JAMES E.
TODD, LISA
TOLMIE, J. SCOTT
TOMPKINS, ALICE H.
TOMSKY JR, BILL
TONAI, ANN
TOOLEY, JAMES R.
TOOLEY, SUZANNE V.
TOPALLI, BLERIME
TORRES, ALLISON J.
TORRIJOS, JOHN
TOSIC, KENNETH
TOWNSEND, CHRISTOPHER
TOWNSEND, KEVIN M.
TOWNSEND, RICHARD
TRAFELET, THOMAS
TRAINOR, PAMELA
TRAMMELL, SHELLEY D.
TRATTNER, KRISTEN DEE
TREMBLAY, MARJOLAINE

TREWEEK, LAURENCE W.
TRIMPE, JOAN
TRUNK, JOHN
TRUONG, TIEN
TUCKER, ROBERT
TULLIS, ELIZABETH A.
TURKO, JENNIE-KING
TURNER, DENNIS S.
TURNER, JACQUELINE
TURNER, PATRICK ALAN
TUTTON, GREGORY
TYO, CINDY
UESUGI, YUSEI
UHRY, AMANDA
URBAN, KEITH S.
URBAN, ROBERT J.
URFER, TIMOTHY S.
URRETABIZKAIA, OSKAR
VAGTS, RICHARD D.
VALENTIN, DAVID
VAN CLEEF, LISA
VAN COTT, LISA A.
VAN DUYN, MAREN
VAN EPS, MICHAEL D.
VAN LINT, LARRY C.
VAN PERRE JR., I. J.
VAN THILLO, WILLEM
VAN TO, LAM
VAN'T HUL, BRIAN A.
VANDE MOORTEL, CRAIG R.
VANDER WENDE, RICHARD S.
VANEVERY, AMY
VANN, CHRISTOPHER
VANSTONE, PETER
VANVLIERBERGEN, MARY
VARON, BRETT D.
VARVARO, MARIA PAOLA
VAUGHN, LAMAIA
VAUGHN, LISA
VECCHITTO, BRUCE
VERMONT, LAURIE
VETO, RONALD
VINE, JEFFREY
VIRANI, RAJEEV
VIVIAN, MARY
VOGEL, DOUGLAS
VOGT, LAUREN M.
VOLOSHIN, LARISSA
VOLPE, JOHN
VON NAGEL, SEBASTIAN C.
VONKOSS, DOUGLAS
VUKOVICH, PETER M.
WACHEL, BRENDA
WADDY, TIMOTHY J.
WADE, TERRENCE E.
WADLEIGH, THAD
WAGNER, DANIEL J.
WAINIO, LORI
WALAS, MARK J.
WALD, WILLIAM
WALKER, JOHN
WALL, ROBERT SCOTT
WALLACE, BRUCE A.
WALLACE, KEVIN C.
WALLACE, LARRY
WALLACE, WENDY
WALLER, DONALD R.
WALLIN, MATTHEW
WALTER, COREY
WALTER, MARY E.
WALTERS, BRUCE ALLEN
WALTERS, GREG
WALTON, HARRY V.
WALTON, PAMELA
WALTON, STEVEN J.
WALTON-SCHOEN, MARTI
WANG, ANDY
WANGBERG, ERIKA K.
WARD, KEVIN
WARD, STEVEN
WARREN, LUIGI A.
WASHBURN, DAVID E.
WASHBURN, SHANE L.

WASILCHIN, TIMOTHY
WASSERMAN, STEFANIE
WATSON, DAVID
WATSON, DON
WAX, MARTHA
WEAKLEY, CHRISTOPHER A.
WEAVER, JOHN
WEAVER, JUDITH A.
WEAVER, ROBERT B.
WEBER, SHAWN
WEDSELTOFT, JORGEN
WEED, HAROLD
WEEKS, SUSAN
WEGNER, DON
WEHNER, RICK
WEICHEL, DAWNA
WEINERT, LOUIS C.
WEINKAUF, DIANE M.
WELISCH, CRISTINE
WELKER, PETER
WELLS, MARY
WELLS, SIMON F.
WELLS, WILLIAM B.
WESSLING, TIMOTHY F.
WEST, PETER
WESLEY, KEN
WEYAND, HEATHER
WHISNANT, JOHN DAVID
WHITE, CHRIS
WHITE, COLIN R.
WHITE, JENNIFER
WHITE, MATTHEW
WHITE, NELSON ANDREW
WHITE, SUE
WHITEHURST, MICHAEL
WHITLATCH, TERRYL A.
WHITMORE, ARLEEN
WHITSON, CAROL ANN
WICK, MICHAEL J.
WIENBAR, CHARLES
WIESER, BETH
WIEZER, DAVID M.
WILCOX, JEFFREY SCOTT
WILDBERRY, ANICE
WILEY, CELIA
WILEY, CHARLES H.
WILEY, TOMIANNE
WILHELM, JAMES J.
WILKINS, JEFFREY A.
WILLEY, ALLEN
WILLEY, FREDERICK
WILLIAMS, ARTHUR S.
WILLIAMS, DOUGLAS E.
WILLIAMS, DWIGHT
WILLIAMS, JAMES R.
WILLIAMS, SANDRA J.
WILLIAMS, STEPHEN
WILLIAMS, TERESA NIELSEN
WILLIAMS, THOMAS A.
WILLIAMSON, ROBERT A.
WILLMERING, KEVIN D.
WILSON, JAISON D.
WILSON, LORI RAY
WILSON, MARK BRYAN
WILSON, RYAN
WILSON, SHANNON
WILSON, TIMOTHY M.
WISKES, ANDY
WITTE, KATHRYN ANNE
WITTER, JOSEPH R.
WITTING, MATTHEW C.
WOHL, LAUREN
WOLFERSPERGER, KARL
WOLFF, DEBRA L.
WOLKOVITCH, LINDA
WONG, ARNOLD G.
WOOD, DARRYL S.
WOOD, LINDA
WOODBYRNE, CYNTHIA
WOODS, EVAN
WOODS, LAUREL E.
WORKER, JOE JR.
WRIGHT, JAMES D.

WRIGHT, SEAN J.
WRIGHT, WILLIAM
YAMAMOTO, NAGISA
YAP, LOPE JR.
YARYAN, LUKE
YAU, VINCENT
YEE, VINCENT
YETTER, DEIDRE
YOSHIKANE, FRANKLIN
YOST, JEFFERY B.
YOUNG, CYNTHIA L.
YOUNG, JONATHAN
YOUNG, KENNETH W.
YOUTT, JONATHAN
YRIGOYEN, PENNY
YU, REBECCA S.
YU, THEODORE
YURKOV, DREW
YUSEM, LAURIE N.
YUTECH, JOHN
ZABIT, HEIDI J.
ZAJONC, ROBERT MICHAEL
ZARCHY, WILLIAM C.
ZARGARPOUR, HABIB
ZELLNER, DAVID J.
ZIGA, JAMES
ZIMMERMAN, JOEL
ZIMMERMAN, KEVIN
ZIMMERMAN, RITA E.
ZIMNINSKY, GEORGE
ZITCER, ANDRE
ZURKAN, VICTORIA

INDEX

PHOTO CREDITS

THE ABYSS Copyright © 1989 by 20th Century-Fox Film Corporation. All rights reserved. Photos appear on pages 159, 194–99.

AKIRA KUROSAWA'S DREAMS Copyright © 1990 by Warner Bros., Inc. Photos appear on pages 174, 175.

ALIVE Copyright © 1995 by Paramount Pictures. All Rights Reserved. Photos appear on pages 156, 157.

ALWAYS Copyright © by Universal City Studios, Inc. Courtesy of MCA Publishing Rights, a Division of MCA Inc. Photos appear on pages 39–47.

BACK TO THE FUTURE II Copyright © by Universal City Studios, Inc. Courtesy of MCA Publishing Rights, a Division of MCA Inc. Photos appear on pages 31, 33, 34, 112, 115.

BACK TO THE FUTURE III Copyright © by Universal City Studios, Inc. Courtesy of MCA Publishing Rights, a Division of MCA Inc. Photos appear on page 13.

BACKDRAFT Copyright © by Universal City Studios, Inc. Courtesy of MCA Publishing Rights, a Division of MCA Inc. Photos appear on pages 184, 185, 186.

BATTERIES NOT INCLUDED Copyright © by Universal City Studios, Inc. Courtesy of MCA Publishing Rights, a Division of MCA Inc. Photos appear on page 52.

CASPER Copyright © by Universal City Studios, Inc. Courtesy of MCA Publishing Rights, a Division of MCA Inc. Photos appear on pages 267–72.

COCOON Copyright © 1985 by 20th Century-Fox Film Corporation. All rights reserved. Photos appear on pages 35, 36.

CONGO Copyright © 1995 by Paramount Pictures. All Rights Reserved. Photos appear on pages 255, 256.

DEATH BECOMES HER Copyright © by Universal City Studios, Inc. Courtesy of MCA Publishing Rights, a Division of MCA Inc. Photos appear on pages 211–13.

DIE HARD 2 Copyright © 1990 by 20th Century-Fox Film Corporation. All rights reserved. Photos appear on pages 140–43, 147–55, 183.

Disneyland ® Park attraction CAPTAIN EO Copyright © by Disney/Lucasfilm Ltd. Used by permission from The Walt Disney Company. Photos appear on pages 77, 78.

DRAGONHEART Copyright © 1996 by Universal City Studios, Inc. Courtesy of MCA Publishing Rights, a Division of MCA Inc. All rights reserved. Photos appear on pages 274, 275.

THE DOORS Stills appear courtesy of Carolco Pictures Inc. Motion Picture. Copyright © 1991 Carolco Pictures Inc. (U.S. & Canada); Carolco International Inc. (All other countries.) All Rights Reserved. Photos appear on pages 93, 176.

EMPIRE OF THE SUN Copyright © 1987 by Warner Bros., Inc. Photos appear on page 146.

THE EMPIRE STRIKES BACK Copyright © by Lucasfilm Ltd. Photos appear on pages 10, 11, 12, 37, 38.

FIRE IN THE SKY Copyright © 1995 by Paramount Pictures. All Rights Reserved. Photos appear on pages 74, 240.

THE FLINTSTONES Copyright © by Universal City Studios, Inc. Courtesy of MCA Publishing Rights, a Division of MCA Inc. Photos appear on pages 99, 241, 276.

FORREST GUMP Copyright © 1995 by Paramount Pictures. All Rights Reserved. Photos appear on pages 239, 247–54.

GHOST Copyright © 1995 by Paramount Pictures. All Rights Reserved. Photos appear on pages 170, 171.

GHOSTBUSTERS II Copyright © 1989 Columbia Pictures Industries, Inc. All Rights Reserved. Courtesy of Columbia Pictures. Photos appear on pages 22, 23, 26–28, 34, 68–73, 95, 96, 122.

THE GOLDEN CHILD Copyright © 1995 by Paramount Pictures. All Rights Reserved. Photos appear on pages 62, 63, 91, 92, 121.

HOOK Copyright © by TriStar Pictures, Inc. Courtesy of TriStar Pictures, Inc. Photos appear on pages 99, 102–5, 166–68, 238.

HOWARD THE DUCK Copyright © by Lucasfilm Ltd. Photos appear on page 100.

THE HUNT FOR RED OCTOBER Copyright © 1995 by Paramount Pictures. All Rights Reserved. Photos appear on pages 48–51, 53–55, 122.

INDIANA JONES AND THE LAST CRUSADE Copyright © by Lucasfilm Ltd. Photos appear on pages 11, 24, 97, 135–37, 177–82, 192.

INNERSPACE Copyright © 1987 by Warner Bros., Inc. Photos appear on pages 84–86.

JUMANJI Copyright © by TriStar Pictures, Inc. Courtesy of TriStar Pictures, Inc. Photos appear on 273.

JURASSIC PARK Copyright © by Universal City Studios, Inc. Courtesy of MCA Publishing Rights, a Division of MCA Inc. Photos appear on pages 76, 214–18, 220–27, 229–31, 281, 282.

THE MASK Copyright © 1994 by New Line Productions, Inc. All rights reserved. Photos appear courtesy of New Line Productions, Inc. Photos appear on pages 260–66, 276.

MEMOIRS OF AN INVISIBLE MAN Copyright © 1992 by Warner Bros., Inc. Regency Enterprises V.O.F. Le Studio Canal+ Photos appear on pages 22, 172, 173.

RADIOLAND MURDERS Copyright © 1994 by Universal City Studios, Inc. Photos appear on page 258.

RAIDERS OF THE LOST ARK Copyright © by Lucasfilm Ltd. Photos appear on pages 4, 5, 280.

RETURN OF THE JEDI Copyright © by Lucasfilm Ltd. Photo appears on page 108.

Walt Disney Pictures' feature film THE ROCKETEER used by permission from The Walt Disney Company. Photos appear on pages 17, 18, 94, 187–91.

STAR TREK II: THE WRATH OF KAHN Copyright © 1995 by Paramount Pictures. All Rights Reserved. Photos appear on page 107.

STAR TREK IV: THE VOYAGE HOME Copyright © 1995 by Paramount Pictures. All Rights Reserved. Photos appear on pages 57, 113.

STAR TREK VI: THE UNDISCOVERED COUNTRY Copyright © 1995 by Paramount Pictures. All Rights Reserved. Photos appear on pages 58, 59, 114, 118.

STAR TREK GENERATIONS Copyright © 1995 by Paramount Pictures. All Rights Reserved. Photos appear on pages 32, 60.

STAR TOURS is a trademark of Lucasfilm Ltd. and The Walt Disney Company. Associated stills are copyright © 1985 Lucasfilm Ltd. All rights reserved. Photos appear on pages 78–80.

STAR WARS Copyright © by Lucasfilm Ltd. Photos appear on pages 2, 3, 5, 7, 8, 9, 35, 285, 286, 289–93, 295.

THE TEN COMMANDMENTS Copyright © 1995 by Paramount Pictures. All Rights Reserved. A poster appears on page 9.

TERMINATOR 2: JUDGMENT DAY Stills appear courtesy of Carolco Pictures Inc. Motion Picture Copyright © 1991 Carolco Pictures Inc. Still photo courtesy of Carolco Pictures Inc. Arnold Schwarzenegger's likeness courtesy of Oak Productions, Inc. All Rights Reserved. Photos appear on pages 119, 201–9.

TUCKER Copyright © by Lucasfilm Ltd. Photo appears on page 34.

Touchstone Pictures and Amblin Entertainment's feature film WHO FRAMED ROGER RABBIT? Copyright © by Touchstone Pictures & Amblin Entertainment, Inc. Used by permission from The Walt Disney Company. Photos appear on pages 123, 124, 125, 126, 127–29.

WILLOW Copyright © by Lucasfilm Ltd. Photos appear on pages 20, 25, 28, 29, 33, 67, 87–90, 98, 101, 130–34, 144, 161–65.

THE WITCHES OF EASTWICK Copyright © 1987 by Warner Bros., Inc. Photos appear on pages 64–66, 169.

Wonders of Life Pavilion attraction BODY WARS used by permission from The Walt Disney Company. Photos appear on pages 81–83.

YOUNG INDIANA JONES Copyright © by Lucasfilm Ltd. Photos appear on pages 160, 243, 245.

YOUNG SHERLOCK HOLMES Copyright © 1995 by Paramount Pictures. All Rights Reserved. Photos appear on pages 108–10.

Acura commercial copyright © American Honda Motor Corp. Grateful acknowledgment to American Honda Motor Corp. Photo appears on page 235.

BP Oil commercial copyright © 1990 by BP America Inc. Permission of BP America Inc. gratefully acknowledged. Photos appear on pages 117, 235.

Dodge commercial copyright © 1991 by Chrysler Corporation. Thanks to the Dodge Division of Chrysler Corporation. Photo appears on page 233.

Energizer Bunny/Darth Vader commercial copyright © by Eveready Battery Co. Grateful acknowledgment to Eveready Battery Co. Photo appears on page 236.

Ants commercial copyright © 1995 by H. J. Heinz Company. Special thanks to Heinz USA for granting us permission to use their photograph. Photos appear on pages 116, 234.

Perrier commercial copyright © by Nestlé Sources International. Grateful acknowledgment to Nestlé Sources International. Photo appears on page 234.

"Seasons Greetings" Old Spice commercial copyright © by Procter & Gamble Productions, Inc. Grateful acknowledgment to Procter & Gamble Productions, Inc. Photo appears on page 233.

"GODZILLA vs. Barkley" Nike commercial copyright © 1996 Toho Co., Ltd. GODZILLA and KING OF THE MONSTERS are trademarks of Toho Co., Ltd. Special thanks to Toho Co., Ltd. for granting us permission to use their photographs. Photos appear on pages 61, 75, 235.

Toyota commercial. Grateful acknowledgment to Tohokushinsha Film Corporation. Photo appears on 116.

Off the Ground photos copyright © 1993 by MPL Communications, Inc. Grateful acknowledgment to MPL Communications, Inc. Photos appear on page 236.

WILLOW drawings copyright © by Lucasfilm Ltd. Grateful acknowledgment to Starwatcher Graphics. Photos appear on pages 30, 31.

PHOTOGRAPHERS' CREDITS

Photos from Akira Kurosawa production art/Warner Bros., courtesy of ILM, appear on pages 174 (right), 175 (top).

Photos from Lucasfilm Ltd., appear on pages 2–4, 5 (left), 7, 10 (above right), 11 (below), 24 (right), 25, 28 (top left and right), 29, 30, 31 (left), 33 (left), 34 (top right), 35 (bottom), 67 (top, far left, and bottom left), 78 (near right), 79, 80, 87, 88, 89 (above), 90 (directly above and top left), 97, 100, 101, 108 (above), 130, 131 (below left and below right), 132, 135, 136 (below), 161, 163, 164, 165 (left and far left), 179 (above), 180 (right), 181, 182, 192, 243, 258, 289–93, 295.

Photo from Mike McAlister, ILM, appears on page 149.

Photos from Roberto McGrath appear on pages 57 (bottom), 62 (below left), 63 (bottom left), 92 (top and middle right).

Photos from Ralph McQuarrie, ILM, appear on pages 35 (top), 36–38.

Photos from Ralph Nelson, Jr., Lucasfilm Ltd., appear on page 8.

Photos from New Line Cinema, courtesy of ILM, appear on pages 260, 261, 262 (bottom), 263 (bottom), 264–66.

Photos from Kerry Nordquist, ILM, appear on pages 12 (above), 44–55, 57 (top), 63 (top left), 64–66, 68 (below), 69 (far left), 70 (below left and far right), 72 (below far right and right), 91 (left), 92 (middle left), 96 (top), 109 (bottom left and below), 113 (top left and top right), 121, 126 (top right), 131 (left), 138 (below right and opposite), 140, 147 (left), 151 (top right), 156, 157, 159, 166 (right), 168 (right), 169 (left), 170 (right), 188 (below), 190 (top right and below), 196 (below), 236 (middle and bottom).

Photos from Kerry Nordquist, Lucasfilm Ltd., appear on pages 67 (far left), 78 (far right and below), 86, 89 (below), 90 (top right), 133, 134, 137 (left), 162, 165 (top left and top right), 177, 178 (right and below right), 179 (left), 180 (below).

Photos from David Owen, ILM, appear on pages 17 (left), 74, 148, 150 (below), 151 (bottom and top left), 152 (middle), 153, 171 (above), 190 (near right), 240, 284.

Paramount photos, courtesy of ILM, appear on pages 58, 59, 62 (right), 91 (below), 92 (below), 107, 110 (above and right bottom), 113 (middle), 114, 170 (far right top and far right bottom), 171 (left), 239, 247 (top left and bottom right), 248, 249 (top and bottom), 250 (bottom), 252 (left bottom), 253 (bottom), 254.

Photos from Howard Stein, copyright Black Falcon, Ltd., appear on pages 12 (below left and below right), 14 (above).

Photos from Touchstone Pictures, courtesy of ILM, appear on pages 124, 126 (below), 127–29.

Photos from TriStar Pictures, courtesy of ILM, appear on pages 93, 176.

Photos from Universal Studios, courtesy of ILM, appear on pages 13 (left), 99, 112, 115, 212 (top), 217, 222–25, 226 (far right top to bottom), 227, 228, 230, 241 (middle right), 267–72.

Photos from Warner Bros., courtesy of ILM, appear on pages 22 (right), 84 (above), 85 (left), 146 (below), 169 (top right and bottom right), 173 (bottom), 174 (below), 175 (bottom).

Image courtesy of Western Images, courtesy of ILM, appears on page 235 (top left).

Photos from 20th Century-Fox, courtesy of ILM, appear on pages 141, 154 (below), 183 (left), 194, 195, 198, 199.

MARK COTTA VAZ

Vaz is a senior writer for *Cinefex*, "the journal of cinematic illusions." His published books are *Spirit in the Land: Beyond Time and Space with America's Channelers*, an investigation of both new and ancient mystical practices in the United States (Signet/NAL, New York, 1988); *Tales of the Dark Knight: Batman's First Fifty Years* (Ballantine Books, New York, 1989); *From Star Wars to Indiana Jones: The Best of the Lucasfilm Archives* (Chronicle Books, San Francisco, 1995, with Shinji Hata); and *Star Wars: The Secrets of Shadows of the Empire* (Ballantine Books, New York, 1996), a behind-the-scenes look at a special, multi-media *Star Wars* adventure. His interest in popular culture includes a tenure on the board of directors of the Cartoon Art Museum in San Francisco, for which he curated several exhibits, notably the 1992 show "Visions of the Floating World," one of the most comprehensive exhibits ever of original Japanese comic art. Vaz was born in the San Francisco Bay Area, where he still makes his home.

PATRICIA ROSE DUIGNAN

For two decades Patricia Rose Duignan served in production and senior management positions at ILM including production supervisor, operations manager, and director of marketing. Rose is executive producer of ABC's stop-motion animated series, *Bump in the Night*, as well as a visual effects consultant to the feature-film and interactive multimedia industries.

EDITORS

At Lucasfilm: Allan Kausch
At Ballantine/Del Rey: Elizabeth Zack

DIRECTOR OF PRODUCTION

Frederic L. Dodnick

MANAGING EDITOR

Nora Reichard

INTERIOR AND JACKET DESIGN

Michaelis/Carpelis Design Associates, New York, NY

TEXT COMPOSITION

Creative Graphics, Allentown, PA

COLOR SEPARATIONS, PRINTING, AND BINDING

Jacket separations: Stevenson Photo Color, Cincinnati, OH
Jacket foil stamping/embossing dies: Creative Label, Chicago, IL
Text separations, printing, and binding: Dai Nippon Printing Co., Hong Kong